DOGS

from
to

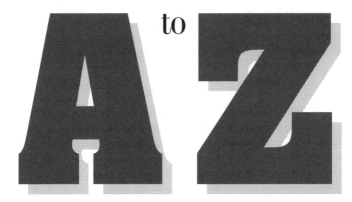

A Dictionary of Canine Terms

Dan Rice, D.V.M.
Illustrations by Michele Earle-Bridges

BARRON'S

Acknowledgments

I gratefully acknowledge the input of my editor, Mary Falcon, without whose help this volume would never have been possible. Many thanks go to my illustrator, Michele Earle-Bridges, who rendered accurately and beautifully the hundreds of postage-stamp-size illustrations shown throughout this book and the detailed anatomical illustrations in the front of the book. A special thank you to Grace Freedson, Managing Editor at Barron's, who had faith in my ability to compile this book.

Most of all, I wish to thank my lovely wife Marilyn, whose understanding and support over the past months has been an inspiration.

Photo Credits

Ashbey Photography: pages 15 bot., 16 bot., 34 bot.; Barbara Augello: pages 17 bot., 22 bot., 25 top, 35 bot., 39 bot.; Paulette Braun: 17 top, 31 top, 34 top, 35 top, 38 top, 39 top, 43 middle; Donna Coss: pages 20 top, 44 top; Kent Dannen: pages 13 top, 15 top, 18 bot., 25 bot., 26 top, 28 bot., 30 bot., 38 bot., 43 bot.; Hal and Jodi Engel: page 16 top; Dee Ross: page 29 top; Pam Ross: page 44 bot. left; Bob Schwartz: pages 22 top, 26 bot., 32 bot., 41 top, 44 middle; Judith Strom: pages 40 top, 44 bot. right; Toni Tucker: page 37 top; Wim van Vugt: page 27 top; Missy Yuhl: page 36 top; all other photos by Paola Visintini.

All inquiries should be addressed to:
Barron's Educational Series, Inc.
250 Wireless Boulevard
Hauppauge, New York 11788
http://www.barronseduc.com

International Standard Book No. 0-7641-0158-7

Library of Congress Catalog Card No. 97-22432

Library of Congress Cataloging-in-Publication Data

Rice, Dan, 1933–
    Dogs from A to Z : a dictionary of canine terms / Dan Rice.
       p.   cm.
    Includes bibliographical references (p.   ).
    ISBN 0-7641-0158-7
    1. Dogs — Dictionaries. I. Title.
  SF422.R535   1998
  636.7'003—DC21   97-22432
                                                  CIP

Printed in Hong Kong/China

987654321

Contents

Preface

The purpose of this book is to collect in one place all the words and phrases related to the canine species and its long-standing partnership with humans. This broad scope of coverage includes a number of categories: the breed names given to the hundreds of domesticated forms of the species; the paraphernalia associated with the myriad activities that have been devised for dogs; the terminology used in caring for dogs, for example, veterinary terms; and those dog-related words and phrases that have slipped, often unnoticed, into everyday language (e.g., hot dog, doggone, three-dog night).

Alphabetization: All entries are alphabetized by letter rather than by word, so that multiple-word terms are treated as single words. For example, the term *brace mate* follows *bracelet* rather than preceding it as would be the case if *brace* were treated as a separate word. Abbreviations and acronyms that appear as entries are treated as if they were words. For example, *AAFCO,* which stands for *American Association of Feed Control Officials,* precedes rather than follows *Abakaru* (the name of Egyptian Pharaoh Cheops' favorite dog).

Capitalization: In the style set by the AKC (American Kennel Club) and followed by most of the print media written by or for the American community of dog fanciers, the names of dog breeds are fully capitalized (e.g., German Shepherd Dog, Yorkshire Terrier, Miniature Pinscher).

Multiple Definitions: Because this is a dictionary of canine terms, only canine-related definitions of terms are included. The word *apricot,* for example, is defined simply as a coat color—the fact that it is a fruit is not mentioned. Even when defined only in terms of dogs, some words have distinctly different meanings, depending upon the context in which they are used. The various meanings of a term are listed numerically.

This type of book isn't written; it is compiled. When I started, I had no perception of the thousands of terms and phrases that have been coined and used to name, describe, care for, work with, and otherwise enjoy our canine friends. I'm sure that I have yet to uncover all of the references and terms available. Accuracy has been my goal, but I am certain that there have been some slipups that will have to be addressed in the second edition. Please feel free to contact me, in care of Barron's Educational Series, Inc., about any mistakes or omissions.

Canine Anatomy

The Body and Parts

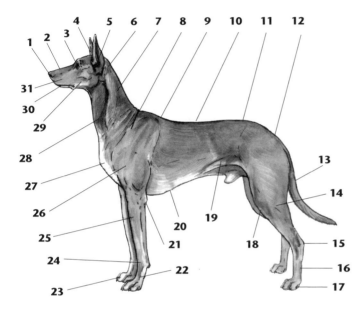

1. Nose rubber
2. Bridge of the nose
3. Stop
4. Occiput
5. Ear
6. Crest
7. Neck
8. Shoulder
9. Withers
10. Back
11. Loin
12. Croup (rump)
13. Tail
14. Thigh
15. Hock
16. Pastern (rear)
17. Hind foot
18. Stifle
19. Flank
20. Ribcage
21. Elbow
22. Front pastern
23. Forepaw
24. Carpus or wrist
25. Forearm
26. Upper arm
27. Brisket
28. Throat
29. Cheek
30. Flews
31. Muzzle

The Head and Parts

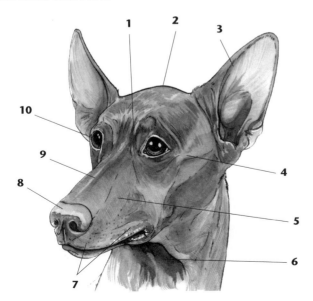

1. Stop
2. Crest
3. Ear
4. Zygomatic arch
5. Muzzle
6. Throat and dewlaps
7. Flews
8. Nose rubber
9. Bridge of nose
10. Eye

1

Types of Ears

1. Bat
2. Bear
3. Blunt
4. Button
5. Tulip
6. Erect
7. Down
8. Drop
9. Cropped
10. Pendulous
11. V-shaped
12. Prick
13. Trowel
14. Rose
15. Semiprick

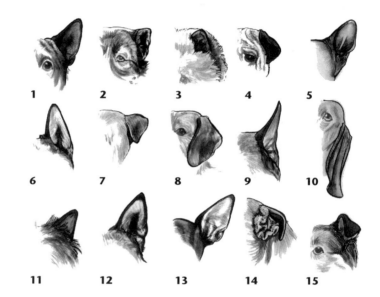

Types of Eyes

1. Triangular
2. Oriental
3. Round
4. Bug-eyed
5. Oval
6. Almond

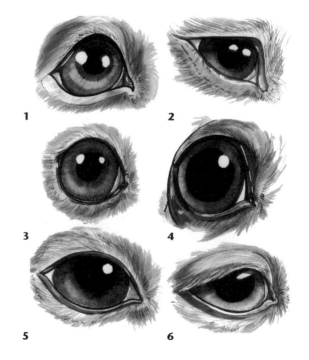

Types of Tails

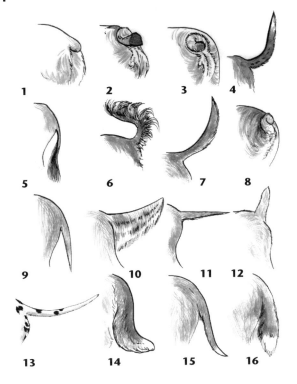

1. Bobbed or docked
2. Kink
3. Coin
4. Pipestopper
5. Plume
6. Pot hook
7. Scimitar
8. Screw
9. Bee sting
10. Flag
11. Carrot
12. Gay
13. Whip
14. Saber
15. Sword
16. Brush

Front Foot Faults

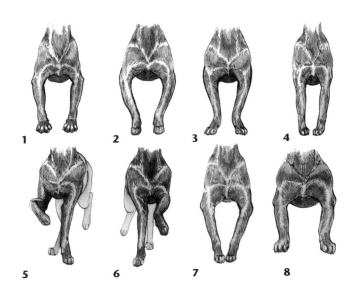

1. Elbows out, splayed feet
2. Bowed legs, knuckled over
3. Chippendale
4. Pidgeon toed
5. Weaving
6. Paddling
7. Queen Anne front
8. Bench leg

Hind Foot Faults

1. Wide hocks
2. Cow hocks
3. Toes in
4. Narrow hocks
5. Barrel hocks
6. Moving close
7. Sickle hocks

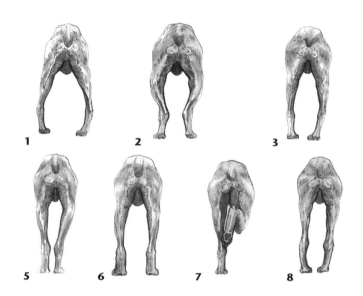

Feet

Front

1. Metacarpus (front)
2. Thumb or dewclaw pad
3. Dewclaw
4. Carpal pad
5. Digital pad
6. Web
7. Nail or claw

Hind

1. Plantar pad
2. Toe (phalanx)
3. Digital pad
4. Nail or claw

Front

Hind

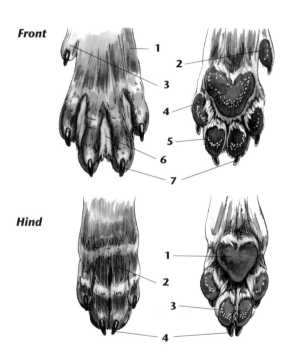

Angulation of the Legs

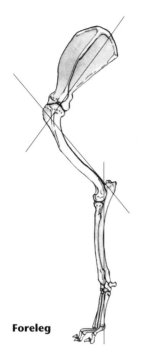 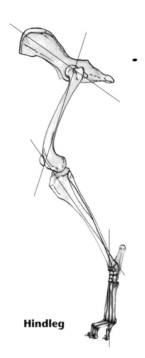

Foreleg **Hindleg**

Head Types

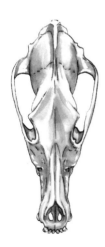 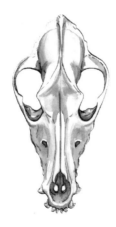 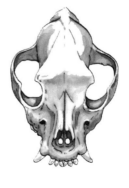

Dolichocephalic **Mesaticephalic** **Bracheocephalic**

Skeletal System

Skeleton—side
1. Nasal bone
2. Frontal bone
3. Auditory bulla
4. Atlas
5. Axis
6. Scapula
7. Thoracic vertebrae
8. Lumbar vertebrae
9. Ilium
10. Sacrum
11. Acetabulum pelvic socket
12. Pubis
13. Ischium
14. Coccygeal vertebrae
15. Tarsus
16. Metatarsus
17. Phalanges
18. Fibula
19. Tibia
20. Stifle joint
21. Patella (knee cap)
22. Femur
23. Os penis
24. Rib cage
25. Ole canon of the Ulna
26. Ulna
27. Metacarpus
28. Carpus
29. Radius
30. Humerus
31. Sternum
32. Mandible

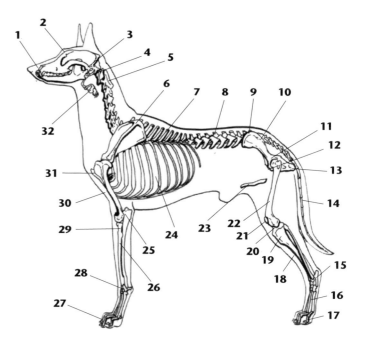

Skeleton—front
1. Skull
2. Zygomatic arch
3. Cervical vertebra
4. Scapula
5. Shoulder joint
6. Humerus
7. Sternum
8. Elbow joint
9. Radius
10. Ulna
11. Carpus
12. Metacarpus
13. Phalanges

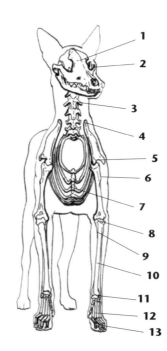

Types of Bites

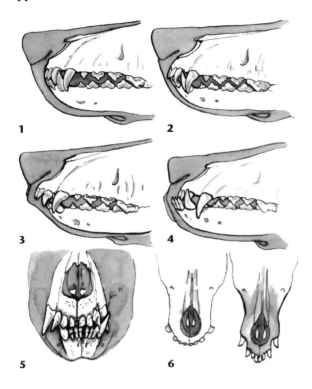

1. Level smooth
2. Scissors
3. Overbite
4. Underbite
5. Wrymouth
6. (a) Normal
   (b) Parrot mouth

Skull

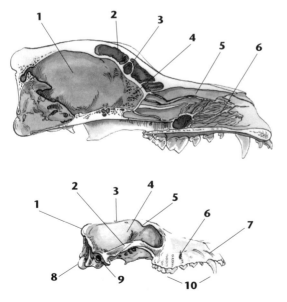

Skull—cross section
1. Cranial cavity
2. Lateral part of frontal sinus
3. Medial part of frontal sinus
4. Cribriform plate
5. Dorsal nasal concha
6. Ventral nasal concha

Skull
1. Exterior occipital protuberance
2. Zygomatic arch
3. Sagittal crest
4. Temporal fossa
5. Zygomatic process
6. Infraorbital foramen
7. Nasal cavity
8. Occipital condyle
9. Exterior acoustic meatus
10. Teeth

Muscles

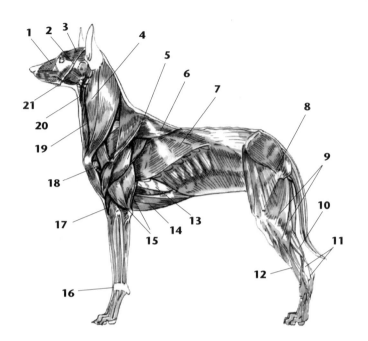

Muscles—side
1. Maxillaris
2. Zygomaticus
3. Scutularis
4. Mastoideus
5. Deltoid
6. Trapezius
7. Latissimus
8. Gluteus maximus
9. Biceps
10. Gastrocnemius
11. Achilles tendon
12. Greater
    saphenous vein
13. Intercostals
14. Pectoralis major
15. Triceps
16. Carpal sheath or
    annular ligament
17. Brachialis
18. Acromion
    deltoid
19. Jugular vein
20. Sterno hyoideus
21. Masseter

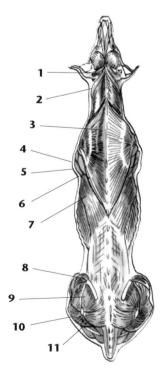

Muscles—top
1. Temporalis
2. Mastoideus
3. Trapezius
4. Deltoid
5. Triceps
6. Triceps
7. Latissimus dorsi
8. Sartorius
9. Gluteus medius
10. Biceps
11. Gluteus
    maximus

Internal Organs

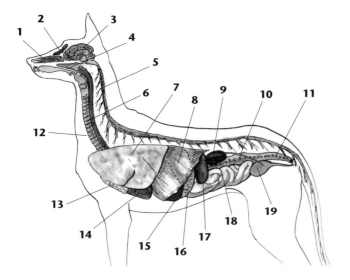

1. Nasal cavity
2. Sinus cavities
3. Brain
4. Palate (soft)
5. Spinal cord
6. Esophagus
7. Lungs
8. Diaphragm
9. Kidney
10. Ureter
11. Descending colon
12. Trachea
13. Thymus
14. Heart
15. Liver
16. Stomach
17. Spleen
18. Small intestine
19. Urinary bladder

Digestive System

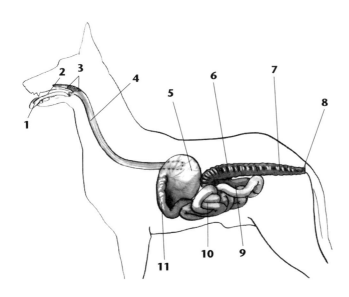

1. Mouth and tongue
2. Palate
3. Pharynx
4. Esophagus
5. Stomach
6. Transverse colon to descending colon
7. Rectum
8. Anus
9. Ileum
10. Jejunum
11. Duodenum

Respiratory System

1. Mouth
2. Larynx
3. Trachea
4. Bronchi
5. Bronchioles
6. Lungs
7. Alveoli

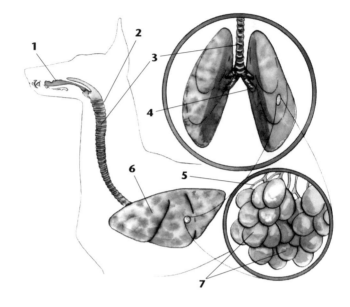

Sinus (Olfactory) System

1. Sinus cavities
2. Nose rubber
3. Nasal bone
4. Labyrinth
5. Canine tooth
6. Nostril

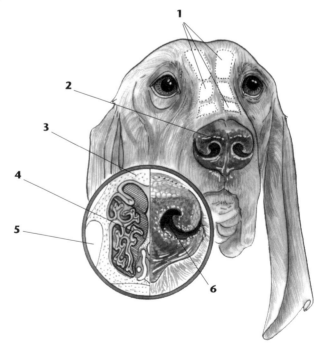

The Ear—Inner and Outer

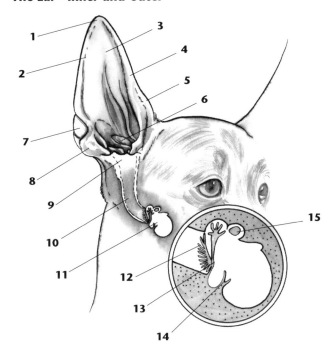

1. Apex
2. Lateral border of helix
3. Scapha
4. Medial border of helix
5. Spine of helix
6. Anthelix or vertical canal
7. Cutaneous marginal pouch
8. Antitragus
9. Tragus
10. External ear canal
11. Middle ear
12. Tympanum or ear drum
13. Malleus
14. Incus
15. Stapes

The Eye

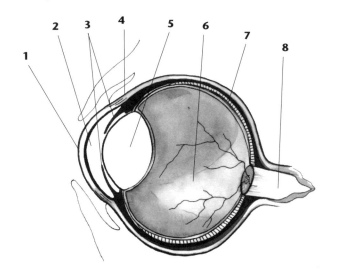

1. Cornea
2. Aqueous humor
3. Iris
4. Sclera
5. Lens
6. Vitreous humor
7. Retina
8. Optic nerve

Reproductive Organs

Female
1. Clitoris
2. Vagina
3. Cervix
4. Uterine horns
5. Mesosalpinx
6. Ovary

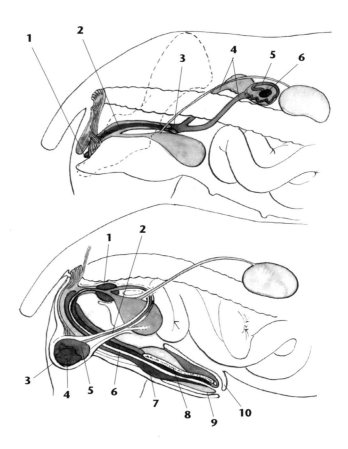

Male
1. Prostrate gland
2. Spermatic cord containing vas deferens
3. Scrotum
4. Testicle
5. Epididymis
6. Ureter
7. Bulbus glandis
8. Os penis
9. Glans penis
10. Sheath

Photo Gallery of Popular Breeds

Popular Breeds in the AKC Sporting Group

Golden Retriever

Cocker Spaniel

German Shorthaired Pointer

English Springer Spaniel

14

Chesapeake Bay Retriever

Labrador Retriever

Brittany

Weimaraner

Popular Breeds in the AKC Hound Group

Dachshund

Rhodesian Ridgeback

Beagle

Bloodhound

Whippet

Greyhound

Basset Hound

Basenji

Popular Breeds in the AKC Working Group

Rottweiler

Boxer

Siberian Husky

Doberman Pinscher

Great Dane

Saint Bernard

Great Pyrenees

Newfoundland

Samoyed

Akita

Mastiff

Alaskan Malamute

Popular Breeds in the AKC Terrier Group

Miniature Schnauzer

West Highland White Terrier

Scottish Terrier

Cairn Terrier

Airedale Terrier

Soft Coated Wheaten Terrier

Wire Fox Terrier

American Staffordshire Terrier

Popular Breeds in the AKC Toy Group

Shih Tzu

Yorkshire Terrier

Chihuahua

Pomeranian

Miniature Pinscher

Maltese

Pug

Pekingese

Popular Breeds in the AKC Non-Sporting Group

Poodle

Dalmatian

Bichon Frise

Boston Terrier

Chinese Shar-Pei

Lhasa Apso

Chow Chow

Bulldog

Popular Breeds in the AKC Herding Group

Border Collie

Shetland Sheepdog

German Shepherd Dog

Collie

Welsh Corgi, Pembroke

Australian Shepherd

Australian Cattle Dog

Old English Sheepdog

Popular Breeds in the AKC Miscellaneous Class

Havanese

Lowchen

Anatolian Shepherd Dog

Jack Russell Terrier

Spinone Italiano

Some Other Popular Breeds

Toy Fox Terrier

Nova Scotia Duck Tolling Retriever

A

AAD abbreviation for Advanced Agility Dog.

AAFCO abbreviation for American Association of Feed Control Officials, a national association of state officials who design testing trials and set voluntary standards for dog food manufacturers.

Abakaru Egyptian Pharaoh Cheops' favorite dog. It was entombed with him in the Great Pyramid.

abasia inability to walk.

abate to reduce in intensity; to improve an illness or diseased state.

abaxial situated out of, or away from, the body's central axis.

abdomen 1. trunk of the body; external anatomical region located between the thorax and pelvis; belly. **2.** body cavity that contains the chief viscera.

abdominal 1. related to the anatomical region of the belly. **2.** related to the body cavity that contains the stomach, intestines, liver, kidneys, urinary bladder, and other organs.

abductor muscle muscle that pulls a limb away from the body's central axis.

Aberdeen Terrier *see* Scottish Terrier.

aberrant deviating from the normal; abnormal in placement or makeup.

ablactation process of weaning puppies from their dam, or removing puppies from their source of milk.

ablation surgical removal of an organ such as an eye.

ablepsia loss of sight; blindness.

ablution act of washing, as in the cleansing of a wound.

aboral away from the mouth; in another direction from the mouth.

aborigine native to an area; first of a species known to inhabit a region.

abort 1. to end a pregnancy before full term, or to deliver a dead fetus before term. **2.** to check or stop the usual course of a disease.

abortifacient agent that causes abortion.

abortus species name of *Brucella abortus* bacteria, a contagious bacterial pathogen of dogs that causes systemic illness, infertility, and sterility.

abrasion raw spot on the skin or mucous membrane where the integrity of the skin or membrane covering has been interrupted.

Abruzzi Sheepdog *see* Maremma Sheepdog.

abscess localized pus-filled sac or cavity surrounded by inflamed tissue.

abscission excision; cutting tissue away.

Abso Seng Kye Chinese breed that was an ancestor of the Lhasa Apso. The literal translation of the breed name is "bark sentinel lion dog."

absorption taking up of liquid substances by the skin, mucous membrane, or other surfaces within the body such as the gastrointestinal tract.

Abyssinian Dog, African Hairless Dog, or African Sand Dog breed of hairless dog that is thought to be an ancestor of the Mexican Hairless.

Abyssinian Kaberu little-known wild dog of medium size, found in the Ethiopian forests.

acampsia loss of flexibility; stiffness of a joint.

acanthosis nigricans skin disorder that appears primarily in the axillary or groin areas and is characterized by tissue thickening and dark pigmentation; seen most frequently in Dachshunds.

acaracide chemical or drug that destroys ticks and canine mange mites.

acardia congenital absence of a heart.

acariasis infestation with skin mites, ear mites, or ticks.

acaudate animal born without a tail; animal having no caudal vertebrae.

acclimation physiological adjustment to an environmental change. Example: a dog that produces a heavier coat when moved to a colder climate.

accounted for foxhunting term that indicates that a fox has been killed or run to earth by the pack.

acetabulum cup-shaped socket of the pelvis that holds the femoral head; one half of the hip articulation.

Achill Island Dog small, wild doglike wolf found off the west coast of Ireland.

Achilles tendon tendon of the gastrocnemius muscle complex that inserts on the hock bone.

achondrodysplasia imperfect ossification of the long bones of the body; also known as fetal rickets or dwarfism.

acid substance with a pH of less than 7.0; opposite of base.

acid milk mammary secretion that has a low pH or high acidity; often incriminated as the cause for puppy colic.

acidosis clinical condition indicating a low blood bicarbonate.

acne condition manifested by blackheads and pustules of hair follicles and sebaceous glands of the skin. In dogs it is commonly seen on the chin and lip regions between three months and a year of age, especially in Dobermans and German Shepherd Dogs.

acquired immunity resistance to infection that is the result of an actual exposure to the disease or a vaccination.

acral lick granuloma or acropruritic granuloma abrasion and scarring of an animal's extremities, accompanied by intense itching. It is usually caused by the self-trauma of licking, and its cause is often thought to be psychological.

ACTH abbreviation for the adrenocorticotropic hormone; secreted by the pituitary gland and has its greatest effect on the cortex of the adrenal gland.

actinomycosis chronic fungus infection of many animals including dogs, that is caused by *Actinomyces*.

action 1. in field trials the manner of movement of a hunting dog; **2.** function or movement of a dog.

acuity clearness of vision.

acupressure treatment regimen that employs digital pressure to certain points on the body to relieve pain.

acupuncture ancient traditional Chinese healing system in which thin metal needles are inserted at specific points to relieve pain or the signs of illness; used in canine medicine with some degree of success.

acupuncture

acute describing a disease that has a short, severe, sudden course.

AD abbreviation for Agility Dog.

adaptability propensity to accept changes in life, treatment, environment, or use.

adaxial located toward or near the central axis.

Addison's disease failure of the adrenal glands to secrete the normal quantity or quality of steroid hormones; also known as hypoadrenocorticism.

adductor muscle that pulls an appendage toward the body's central axis.

adenocarcinoma tumor in which the cells originate from glandular tissue or are arranged in the form of a gland; usually a malignancy.

adenoma benign tumor of a hormone-secreting endocrine gland.

adenopathy any disease of glands, particularly the lymph glands.

adenosarcoma cancer of a hormone-secreting gland that is usually malignant.

ADH abbreviation for the antidiuretic hormone. Secreted by the pituitary gland, it acts to increase blood pressure and decrease urine flow.

adipose tissue fat; body's fatty tissue deposits.

Adjutant black Labrador said to have had the longest life of any dog on record—27 years and three months. He died in 1963.

adrenal glands pair of endocrine organs located near the kidneys that secretes epinephrine, androgenic hormones, and other steroid hormones.

adult dog that has attained its full growth and maturity and has reached puberty. Dogs become adults at varying ages; generally the smaller the dog, the sooner adulthood is reached.

Advanced Agility Dog award earned for successful completion of agility competitions.

Aeolurostrongylus abstrusus lungworm that lives in a dog's pulmonary tissue and causes coughing and wheezing.

aerobics physical exercise such as running, walking, or swimming.

aerophagia propensity of an animal to swallow air, accompanied by the disagreeable passage of a mixture of gasses and air from the bowel; seen especially in Bulldogs and other brachycephalic breeds.

Affenpinscher AKC group: toy; of German origin: It stands about 10 inches (25 cm) tall, has black, silver, or gray coloring, and is a sturdy, wiry-coated dog with erect ears, large round eyes, and a bristly face. It is sometimes called Monkey Dog or Monkey Pinscher.

Affenpinscher

affinity inherent attraction, interest, or kinship for another; a positive relationship. Example: My Brittany has a particular affinity for upland bird hunting, but doesn't like the water.

Afghan Hound AKC group: hound; one of the oldest breeds in the world, originated in the Sinai Peninsula. A long-coated sighthound of any color, it stands about 27 inches (69 cm) tall and weighs about 60 pounds (27 kg).

Afghan Hound

A-frame in agility trials, 3-foot (90-cm)-wide obstacle that is constructed of two 9-foot (270-cm)-long boards that are joined together with a hinge. The peak of the obstacle is set at 6 feet 3 inches (187 cm) from the ground, and makes a 90 degree angle where the boards meet at the top. Horizontal slats are placed about 12 inches (30 cm) apart on each side of the frame. The dog must run up one side and down the other, and finish in a straight line.

African Hyena Dog Cape or South African hunting dog that slightly resembles a hyena.

African Lion Hound *see* Rhodesian Ridgeback.

Aftcharka sheepdog found in Russia that is similar to the Komondor in appearance and size.

A-frame

afterbirth individual placental membranes that supply embryonic and fetal support; in dogs, it is shed at the time of whelping after each puppy is born.

after-pain short-lived pain that follows whelping and is caused by continued uterine contractions.

agalactia lack of milk production in a postparturient animal.

agastric congenital absence of a stomach, a rare deformity of dogs.

age duration of an individual's existence measured by units of time. The historical standard is that one dog year is equal to seven human years, but that comparison doesn't always hold true. Some small breeds commonly live to 15 years old, and often giant breeds are very old at eight or nine years.

agent substance that acts upon an animal that produces an effect, whether curative or not.

Agility Dog title awarded upon successful completion of certain exercises in American agility trials.

Agility Dog Association of Canada R.R. 3, North Grower, Ontario K0A 2T0.

agility races or **trials** AKC-organized and -judged competitive timed events for dogs and their handlers in which dogs are trained to master different obstacles: bridges, tunnels, various types of high jumps, broad jumps, jumps through windows, and tires. The course also includes inclined planes, elevated planks to walk, A-frames to climb, and others. Various agility titles are awarded to dogs that successfully complete the courses in which they are entered.

agonad animal born without apparent sex glands.

agouti alleles genes that affect sable and merle coat coloration.

agreeable easy to get along with, amicable; indicating a favorable personality.

Aguarachay *see* Azara's Dog.

Aguara-Guaza South American wild dog found in Brazil, Argentina, and Paraguay; also called red wolf and maned wolf, but it has no mane and doesn't resemble wolves. A nocturnal, solitary hunter, about 30 inches (76 cm) tall, it weighs about 65 pounds (29 kg), has long legs and erect ears, and is colored red with black markings.

Aguara-Guaza

Aguti descendant of the Aztec tepetzcuintli; small dog-like rodent that lives in Mexico and is mistakenly thought by some to be the ancestor of the Chihuahua.

AI abbreviation for artificial insemination.

Aidi or **Chien de l'Atlas** breed native to Morocco where it is used as a shepherd guard dog and tracker. A powerful dog that stands about 24 inches (61 cm) tall and weighs about 55 pounds (25 kg), with a thick coat, seen in a variety of colors, it is usually has a docked tail and cropped ears.

Ailbe twelfth-century Irish Wolfhound that according to Irish legend was so swift, he could run through Leinster county in a single day.

Ainu or Hokkaido-ken breed that may be extinct; originally bred on the island of Hokkaido, Japan. This breed is small and stocky. Its dense coat, pricked ears, and curled tail indicates its relationship to the spitz breeds.

Airedale Terrier AKC group: terrier; originated in the Aire River valley in Yorkshire, England. It stands about 23 inches (58 cm) tall, is black and tan in color, with a dense, wiry, hard coat. It was once used for hunting otters, rats, and small game. (See photo, page 29).

Airedale Terrier

airway passage along which air travels to reach the lungs; includes the pharynx, trachea (windpipe), and bronchi.

aka term meaning "red" in Japanese that is applied to native breeds ranging from light tan to Tosa brown.

aka-goma Japanese term that means "red sesame" and refers to the black peppering on a red ground color seen in certain Japanese breeds.

aka-tora Japanese term for "red tiger" that refers to a black-striped brindle pattern on a red ground color.

Akbash Dog Turkish breed that is used for guarding livestock. It stands about 34 inches (86 cm) tall and is a white, long-legged, powerful dog with a short double coat.

AKC abbreviation for the American Kennel Club.

AKC Gazette periodical published by the AKC that carries dog show news, schedules, and dates: 51 Madison Avenue, New York, New York 10038.

akinesia inability to walk; a weakness of movement.

Akita AKC group: working; large northern Japanese working dog. It stands about 27 inches (68 cm) tall and weighs about 110 pounds (50 kg). It has a plush, heavy coat and a curled tail; and is seen in a wide variety of colors and patterns. It has been used for fighting, herding, and hunting. (See photo, page 25).

Akita

Alan *see* Mastiff.

Alangu shorthaired Mastiff-type dog from India that stands about 20 inches (56 cm) tall and weighs about 116 pounds (53 kg).

Alano now extinct; dog of the Great Dane or Mastiff type that was used by Spanish bullfighters to pin the bulls by grasping the bull's lower lip and applying intense pressure.

alarm dog dog trained to assist handicapped persons by barking or physically alerting them to possible dangers.

Alaskan Malamute AKC group: working; large, powerful, northern sled dog breed with wolflike markings. It stands about 25 inches (63 cm) tall, weighs about 85 pounds (39 kg), has a heavy, double coat, a plumey tail, and ranges in color from gray to black. It is often used for hauling freight. A 93-pound (42 kg) Malamute broke the world's weight-pulling record by moving a load of 2,103 pounds (954 kg). These dogs assisted the Byrd Antarctic expeditions, parachuted with sled and driver into Arctic country, and brought downed fliers to safety for the Air Force. (See photo, page 26).

Alaskan Malamute

Alaunt ancestor of the Staffordshire Terrier and Bulldog; a Mastiff-type dog that was bred for bullbaiting, bearbaiting, and dogfighting.

albino dog with a rare recessive trait that inhibits melanin (the pigment that is normally found in skin and coat) formation and causes the dog to have a white or ivory-white coat color, and white, pink, or pale blue eyes.

albumin simple, heat-coagulable, water-soluble protein; normally found in many body tissues.

albuminuria abnormal presence of albumin in the urine.

Alco, Fat Alco, or *Canis Americanus* breed that is probably extinct today. Found in Peru, it is said to be a lapdog that escaped and became feral. It was a fat, small-headed dog with a broad girth, pendulous ears, and an arched back. It was covered with yellow hair.

Alentejo longhaired Portuguese herding breed that stands about 26 inches (66 cm) tall and weighs about 80 pounds (36 kg).

alert in racing, describing a Greyhound that gets away quickly from the starting box.

aleukemia abnormal absence of white cells in circulating blood.

alible nutritive and usable as food; a substance that is absorbed by, and supplies nutrition to, the body.

alimentary canal digestive tract, including the mouth, esophagus, stomach, small and large intestine, that ends at the anus.

alimentation act of eating or providing nutrition.

alkalosis increased blood bicarbonate; opposite of acidosis.

all-age class in showing, a class in which dogs of any age are permitted to compete.

all-breed club dog fancy organization with members that represent many different AKC-recognized breeds.

all-breed show dog competition that exhibits all of the recognized breeds for which entries have been made.

allele gene that determines opposite inheritance character, such as smooth or rough coats, short or tall stature.

allergen substance capable of producing an allergy.

allergenic having the properties of an allergen; acting as an allergen.

allergin term that was formerly used to describe the antibody responsible for anaphylaxis.

allergy hypersensitive state acquired through exposure to a specific allergen.

all-meat diet dermatosis recognized deficiency syndrome that includes thinning hair and flaky skin, as well as skin and hair color changes; seen in dogs when they are fed a diet that is made up exclusively of animal tissues, and is thought to be caused by the low iodine content of such tissues.

all-rounder in showing, judge with the experience and training to judge several breeds.

almond eye small, elliptical-shaped eye; Oriental eye.

aloe juice of the aloe plant of the lily family. It is often used in canine skin ointments and other medications.

alopecia absence of hair, either in a localized area or generally over the entire body.

Alopex lagopus Arctic fox of Europe, Asia, and North America.

Alpendog name that was proposed for the Saint Bernard.

alpha dog dominant dog; leader of a pack.

alpha-tocopherol another name for vitamin E.

Alpine Mastiff *see* Saint Bernard.

Alpine Spaniel thought to be one of the ancestors of the Clumber Spaniel, possibly crossed with Bassets.

Alsatian historical name used interchangeably with German Shepherd Dog.

ALT abbreviation for alanine aminotransferase, an enzyme produced by the liver.

alter lay term for castrate, sometimes used as a noun to designate a castrated dog.

alum usually an aluminum sulfate compound having styptic or astringent properties; used as a topical coagulant for minor hemorrhages, such as on a nail that was cut too short.

Alunk terrier from India. It is about 12 inches (30 cm) tall and weighs about 13 pounds (6 kg).

alveolus 1. terminal microscopic air sac of the lungs. **2.** tooth socket.

Amateur Field Trial Clubs of America organization that holds bird dog field trials.

amaurosis blindness in which there are no apparent eye lesions.

ambient temperature surrounding environmental temperature of a room.

amble easy, leisurely gait.

amblyopia dimness of vision, without apparent eye lesions.

ambulance dogs K9 Corps dogs that were sent to the field of battle to search for wounded soldiers in a combat zone. They were instinctively able to recognize the faintest presence of life in seriously wounded men who were lying comatose among the dead. These dogs were responsible for saving thousands of lives in World War II.

ambulatory capable of walking about and moving from place to place.

Ambulance dog

Ambylomma genus of ticks that may infest dogs; includes the Lone Star tick.

amebic dysentery diarrhea condition of dogs that is caused by amoeba of various species.

ameliorate to improve, make better, or recover good health.

amentia gross mental deficiency; a congenital lack of mental ability; hereditary inability to be trained.

American Beagle Club P.O. Box 121, Essex, Vermont 05451.

American Boarding Kennel Association organization that publishes lists of approved boarding kennels. The address is 5475 Galley Rd., Suite 400-A, Colorado Springs, Colorado 80915.

American-bred AKC show class that is limited to dogs that were bred and whelped in the United States. Male and female classes are separated.

American Bulldog native to northern Georgia. It ranges from 90 to 130 pounds (41–59 kg), but its height is not standardized. It is bred for hunting bears, wild hogs, squirrels, and other game.

American Bull Terrier name formerly used for the colored variety of bull terriers.

American Coonhunter's Association, The Wickliffe, Kentucky 42087.

American Dog Owners' Association 1628 Columbia Turnpike, Castleton, New York 12033.

American Duck Retriever *see* Chesapeake Bay Retriever.

American Eskimo Dog AKC group: non-sporting; Nordic-type dog that is shown in three sizes. The Toy stands 9 to 12 inches (23 cm to 30 cm); the Miniature stands more than 12 inches to 15 inches (30 cm to 38 cm); and the Standard ranges from more than 15 inches to 19 inches (38 to 49 cm). All size divisions conform to the same standard. It is an erect-eared dog with a heavy, double coat, and a full tail. Its color ranges from pure white, which is preferred, to biscuit cream. The skin of all members of the breed is pink. Blue eyes are a disqualifying fault.

American Eskimo Dog

American Eskimo Dog Club of America Route 3, Box 211B, Stroud, Oklahoma 74079.

American Field, The periodical of pointer and setters: 222 West Adams Street, Chicago, Illinois 60606.

American Foxhound AKC group: hounds; American breed of foxhound that is smaller than the English version, with longer ears. It stands about 24 inches (61 cm) tall, and has a high set tail with a modest brush and a short glossy coat that is usually black, tan, and white in color. It is bred to hunt in packs, or as trail or drag hounds, for hunting foxes with a gun, or for field trials.

American Foxhound

American Hairless Terrier originated in Louisiana; has only a few hairs on its eyebrows, and the normal tactile whiskers on its muzzle. It is less than 10 pounds (4.5 kg) in weight, has erect ears, and some have naturally bobbed tails. It was developed from a mutation that occurred in a "rat terrier" cross and was linebred to produce a dog without hair.

American Hound *see* American Foxhound.

American Humane Association since 1877 the AHA has been a nationwide organization devoted to the prevention of cruelty and abuse of animals, notably dogs: P.O. Box 1266, Denver, Colorado 80201.

American Kennel Club, The organization that acts as a registry of 137 recognized dog breeds, the AKC. It provides pedigree information and breed standards, promotes and publishes rules for dog shows and other canine competitions and exhibitions, and trains and provides judges for those activities. Its address is 51 Madison Avenue, New York, New York 10010.

American Pit Bull Terrier former name of American Staffordshire Terrier.

American Pit Bull Terrier Rescue Program RR 2, Box 1427, Hinesburg, Vermont 05461.

American Rottweiler Club P.O. Box 23741, Pleasant Hill, California 94523.

American Society for the Prevention of Cruelty to Animals 441 E. 92nd Street, New York, New York 10128.

American Staffordshire Terrier

American Staffordshire Terrier AKC group: terrier; short-coated, muscular breed with cropped or uncropped ears, and wide-set eyes. It stands about 18 inches (46 cm) tall and is seen in any color—solid or parti-color. It was formerly known as the Pit Bull Terrier and was used for pit fighting. *See* Half-and-Half Dog. (See photo, page 30).

American Veterinary Medical Association national organization of veterinarians that publishes professional journals and gathers, stores, and makes available various data and facts related to animals, their care, and treatment. Its address is 930 North Meacham Road, Schaumburg, Illinois 60173.

American Water Spaniel

American Water Spaniel AKC group: sporting; American-origin water retriever. It stands about 18 inches (46 cm) tall, weighs about 40 pounds (18 kg), and has a thick, curly, liver-colored or brown coat.

American Working Collie Association c/o Mrs. Linda Rorem, 1548 Victoria Way, Pacifica, California 94044.

Amertoy or **American Toy Terrier** *see* Toy Fox Terrier.

ametria congenital lack of a uterus.

amino acid nitrogen-containing compound that combines to form proteins. Some amino acids are essential in a dog's diet.

amnion outer membrane of the placenta that produces fluid to cushions fetuses before birth.

Amoeba genus of protozoans, some of which are pathologic and may cause diseases in the dog.

amoxicillin antibiotic that is an analog of penicillin; commonly used for treatment of various canine diseases.

amphetamine drug that is legitimately used to treat respiratory congestion; occasionally misused as a performance stimulus in racing dogs.

ampule small sealed-glass vial that usually contains a hypodermic solution.

amputation surgical removal of a limb or part thereof.

amputee animal that has had one or more limbs amputated.

amyloid waxy, white protein deposit that is found in organs in various abnormal conditions.

Amytal® proprietary brand of amobarbital, an ultrashort intravenous anesthetic agent; formerly used extensively in dogs, but not in common use today.

anabasis progression of a disease that is becoming more intense or increasing in severity.

anabolism constructive or building phase of metabolism in which simple compounds are converted by living cells into more complex substances.

anadipsia intense thirst; craving for water.

anaerobe bacterial organism that is capable of living in the absence of air.

anal greeting instinctive sniffing of a dog's anus by another dog to establish recognition and acceptance.

anal sac impaction painful condition caused by obstruction of the opening of the anal sacs; usually results in a dog scooting on its bottom, or intense licking of the anal area; may form abscesses if not opened and drained promptly.

anal sacs pair of scent reservoirs that are located on either side of the anus of a dog and open immediately inside the anal opening; lined with glands that secrete an oily substance with a vile odor; homologous to the skunk's scent sacs.

Anal sacs

anal sphincter circular muscular structure located in the anus; effects opening and closing of the anus.

analgesia insensibility to pain without losing consciousness.

analinction licking the anus.

anamnesis remembering or recalling; memory function of the body's systems, organs, or cells.

anaphrodisia lack of a sexual urge; disinterest in mating.

anaphylactic shock severe, sometimes fatal systemic reaction upon exposure to a specific antigen after previous sensitization.

anaphylaxis exaggerated response to an antigen that may be a foreign protein or other compound.

Anaplasma a genus of sporozoan that invades and infects dogs' red blood cells; transmitted by ticks.

anasarca usually fatal accumulation of serum, or generalized edema; seen in neonatal puppies, most commonly in Bulldogs.

anastomose to surgically join two segments of hollow viscera such as the intestine or blood vessels.

Anatolian Karabash

Anatolian Karabash old breed developed in Turkey; shares common ancestry with the other mastiffs. Pale brown in color, often with black markings on the face, it has a thick coat of medium length. Used mostly as a herding dog, it is also a watchdog.

Anatolian Shepherd Dog ancient Turkish breed that is shown in the AKC miscellaneous class. It stands no less than 29 inches (73 cm) tall, weighs up to 150 pounds (69 kg) and is a fiercely loyal working guard dog that isn't considered a glamour breed. Its short thick, double coat may be seen in any color or combination of colors. (See photo, page 43).

anatomy structure of the physical body and the relationship of its parts.

anchor bound describes a Beagle that marks a check when hunting rabbits. *See* check.

anconitis inflammation of the elbow joint.

Ancylostoma caninum genus and species of the hookworm of the dog.

androgens hormones with masculinizing properties that originate from the male dog's testicles and adrenal glands.

**Anatolian
Shepherd Dog**

anemia deficiency of red blood cells, either in total number of cells or in a reduced hemoglobin quantity or quality of the cells. The principal early sign of anemia in the dog is the lack of normal pink color, or paleness of its mucous membranes.

anencephalia congenital absence of a brain.

anesthetic agent that is used to produce a loss of sensibility, feeling, and sensation; may be general, regional, or local.

anestrum or anestrus estrous phase that follows diestrus during which there is virtually no reproductive activity in the female.

aneurysm disease of a blood vessel wall causing dilation, thinning, and ballooning of the wall.

Anglo-Francais de Petite Vénerie a new hound breed being developed in France from French hounds and the Beagle; it stands about 22 inches (56 cm) tall, weighs about 44 pounds (20 kg), and has the same markings as English Foxhounds.

Angmagssalik Husky working sled dog of East Greenland that stands about 24 inches (61 cm) tall, weighs about 65 pounds (29 kg), and is colored red, red and white, or white with a red muzzle, ears, and saddle.

angulation relationship between adjacent bones, especially in the shoulder joint, hip joint, and stifle joint.

Anhui Dog Mastiff-Greyhound crossbred dog that is native to the Anhui district of China.

Animal Welfare Act legislation pertaining to shipping of dogs enforced by the U.S. Department of Agriculture. It prohibits shipping of puppies less than eight weeks of age that have not been weaned at least five days. It also specifies that the shipper must deliver shipped animals within four hours of departure time, notify the consignee no later than six hours after arrival, provide ventilation, temperature control, food, and water during the trip.

animation fullness of life and activity; liveliness, wakefulness, excitement, or spirit shown by a dog.

ankle 1. joint between the metatarsus and the tibia and fibula; hock joint or tarsus. **2.** joint between the metacarpus and radius and ulna; wrist joint or carpus.

ankylosis immobility of a joint due to the fusion of the bones involved.

annual special showing term referring to prizes that are offered by a specialty club for dogs' accomplishments in all competitions in AKC shows throughout the year.

anorchid animal with neither testicle in his scrotum. Both testicles are retained in the abdomen or inguinal canal.

anorectic 1. animal without a normal appetite that exhibits no evidence of hunger. **2.** drug or agent that causes anorexia.

anorexia failure to have a normal appetite or a will to eat.

anoscope speculum or fiber-optic instrument used for visual examination of the anus.

anosmatic animal with no sense of smell.

anotia congenital absence of ears.

anoxia lack of or serious deficiency of oxygen.

antacid compound that neutralizes stomach acid when given orally.

antagonist muscle that, by contracting, limits the action of another muscle that is paired with it.

antebrachium lower foreleg of an animal that extends between the elbow and the wrist; anatomical region of the radius and ulna.

antenatal prior to birth; describing fetal life.

anterior situated in front or toward the front.

anterior nares front part of the nasal cavity.

anthelmintic referring to an agent that is used to destroy or expel intestinal parasites from the body.

anthropomorphism assignment of human character or human qualities to dogs and other pets; interpreting animal actions in human terms.

antibiotic agent derived from microorganisms, such as certain fungi, which inhibits the growth of or kills other microorganisms. Example: The antibiotic called penicillin is obtained from the mold *Penicillium notatum*.

antibody serum protein manufactured within an animal that will react with and neutralize a specific antigen.

anticipation performance of a function by a dog before the appropriate command is given by its handler.

anticoagulant agent that prevents coagulation or clotting of blood, either *in vivo* (in a living animal) or *in vitro* (in an artificial medium such as a test tube).

antidiarrheal referring to medication that prevents or stops diarrhea.

antidote specific treatment or remedy for a poison.

antifreeze poisoning toxic reaction brought about by ingestion of ethylene glycol, an alcohol that causes kidney destruction. Antifreeze is deadly poison for which there is no antidote.

antifungal killing or inhibiting the growth of a pathogenic fungus.

antigen protein particle that causes the formation of a specific antibody when introduced into the body.

antiinfective counteracting infections.

antiinflammatory counteracting or relieving inflammation of the tissues.

antimicrobial killing or suppressing the growth of microbes.

antioxidant substance that inhibits oxidation or the metabolic reactions that are promoted by oxygen.

antiparasitic destroying or ridding the body of parasites.

antiprotozoal destroying or inhibiting the growth of protozoans.

antipyretic reduces fever in a living organism.

antiseptic chemical agent used to prevent putrefaction; one that will inhibit the growth of microorganisms without necessarily killing them.

antiserum blood serum harvested from animals that have been exposed to a specific antigen; by definition, it has a high level of antibodies for that particular antigen.

antisocial behavior of an animal that has not been in regular close contact with humans, and consequently shows fear or aggressiveness toward human beings.

antitoxin antibody that is able to neutralize the specific toxin produced by a microorganism, usually a bacterium.

antivaccinationist person opposed to the use of vaccinations.

antivenom or **antivenin** antitoxin for venomous snake or insect bites.

antiviral agent used to kill viruses or to inhibit their growth.

antivitamin substance that inactivates vitamins.

ANTU powerful rat poison; causes hemorrhage and congestion of the lungs, kidney, and liver. A dog that has eaten ANTU displays oral mucous membranes that are cherry red, and has difficulty breathing.

Anubis ancient Egyptian god of the dead that was depicted as a dog or jackal. According to legend, he helped Isis search for the body of her husband, Osiris.

Anubis

anuria lack of urinary production.

anury absence of caudal vertebrae; lacking a tail; having a naturally bobbed tail.

anus posterior opening of the alimentary canal.

anvil another name for the incus, one of the three ossicles or bones of the middle ear that are responsible for transmitting vibrations from the eardrum to the auditory nerve of the inner ear.

anxiety apprehension, uneasiness, or abnormal tension; a common problem of inexperienced show dogs, field trial dogs, and other exhibition or performance dogs.

Any Variety in showing, a class open to all breeds.

Any Variety not Separately Classified in showing, a class for breeds not provided with their own breed class.

aorta main arterial trunk of the circulatory system that arises from the left ventricle of the heart and branches to supply oxygenated blood to the body.

aperture opening or open space.

apex highest point. Example: The occiput is the apex of a dog's head.

aphagia lack of, or loss of, the ability to swallow.

aphakic congenital absence of a lens in the eye.

APHIS dog dog that belongs to the U.S. Department of Agriculture, Animal and Plant Health Inspection Services; one that is trained to nose out or scent illegal fruits and vegetables in luggage.

aphonia loss of ability to vocalize; absence of voice.

apis having monkeylike features, as in the Affenpinscher.

aplasia congenital atrophy; incomplete development of a tissue or organ.

apnea temporary cessation of respiratory function.

apocrine type of glandular, cellular secretion, such as milk from the mammary gland.

apomorphine crystalline alkaloid derived from morphine; when injected, it acts as an emetic to cause vomiting.

apoplexy *see* stroke.

aposia absence of thirst.

apothecary specially trained and licensed person who compounds and dispenses prescription drugs.

appendage dependent part; part that is attached to the main structure, such as a leg.

Appenzeller Sennenhund

Appenzeller Sennenhund, Apensell Mountain Dog, or **Appenzeller Mountain Dog** the third largest of the four types of Swiss Mountain Dogs; short-haired, curly-tailed dog that is black with white and rust colored markings. It stands about 23 inches (58 cm), weighs about 55 pounds (25 kg), and has been used as a guard dog, a shepherd, and as a draft dog. The German word *sennenhund* literally means cheese dog, because the dog was sometimes used to pull a cheese cart.

appetite natural desire to eat food or to perform any of the other functions that support life.

applehead a round skull without notable indentations; a high-domed head that is a common characteristic of the Chihuahua.

applehead

apricot off-white coat color that often has an orangish tint; seen in Poodles and other breeds.

apron heavy coat on the chest and under the neck of some dogs.

Apso previous name of the Lhasa Apso; from the Tibetan word *rapso* meaning goatlike or shaggy.

aptitude capacity to learn, or natural ability to perform.

aqueous humor watery contents of the forward compartment of the eye that is located in front of the lens and behind the cornea.

apron

aquiline nose when referring to a dog, the upward curving of the dorsum of the muzzle, forming a convex line from the stop to the nostril; eagle-beak appearance.

Arabian coursing dogs Greyhound-type dogs that were used to hunt antelope or hares in Arabia, Persia, and Egypt.

Arachnida taxonomic class of Arthropods that includes ticks and mites.

arched loin describing a slight elevation in a dog's topline over the lumbar region.

arched neck describing an upward curve of a dog's topline from the occiput to the withers.

arched toes dog's knuckles that are gathered together and slightly elevated.

arched loin

Arctic fox *see Vulpes leucopus.*

Arctic Husky *see* Siberian Husky.

Ardennes Cattle Dog *see* Bouviers des Ardennes.

arecolene hydrobromide chemical used in the past as a canine vermifuge, anthelmintic, and cathartic; extraction of the betel nut rarely used today because of the abdominal pain that accompanies its use.

arched neck

Arecuna Hunting Dog used by the Arecuna branch of the Carib Indians; a wild race of dogs that is frequently tamed and crossed with domestic breeds.

arf bark associated with Sandy, Little Orphan Annie's dog; a wimpy bark.

Argentine Dogo crossbred dog that includes the blood of 10 different breeds in varying amounts. *See Dogo Argentino.*

arched toes

Argentinian Mastiff or **Dogue d'Argentine** breed that resembles a white Boxer although larger in size; it stands about 26 inches (66 cm) tall, weighs about 100 pounds (46 kg), has cropped ears and loose folds of skin around the neck, typical of fighting dogs. A hunting dog, used to hunt large game such as pumas, it has been banned in Great Britain due to concerns about its temperament.

arginine crystalline amino acid, derived from guanidine.

Argos or **Argus** Ulysses' dog in Greek mythology.

Argus genus of ticks that parasitize dogs.

Ariégeois French hound with a good sense of smell, a strong voice, and uncommon liveliness. It stands about 23 inches (58 cm) tall and has a fine, shiny coat of black and white, with red markings on the cheeks and above the eyes.

Ariégeois

Ariège Pointer smooth-coated French gundog that stands about 25 inches (63 cm) tall and weighs about 63 pounds (29 km).

Arkansas Traveler Foxhound early strain of American Foxhound.

Arkwright Pointer named for William Arkwright who kept a kennel of all-black Pointers. The dogs were dish-faced and hare-footed but were excellent field dogs.

arm or **arm bone** humerus or bone that extends from the shoulder to the elbow; anatomical region of the upper forelimb.

Armant breed of Egyptian sheepdogs, used also as watch-dogs; originated from the Armant village in northern Egypt.

armored dogs mastiff-type dogs fitted with protective leather and metal armor and used in warfare by Romans, Gauls, and others.

army dogs trained dogs that performed specific duties in World War I and World War II. They were used for sentry duty, packing, patrol duty, mine detection, and messenger service. Many were decorated. *See* K9 Corps.

armored dogs

aromatic having a spicy, fragrant, or distinctive odor; describing a compound often used in the formulation of topical medicines.

arrest to cease or stop. **1.** discontinued function, as in cardiac arrest. **2.** stopping the course of a disease, as in cancer arrest.

arrhythmia intermittent or permanent change in the normal rhythm of heartbeats.

arsenic poisoning toxemia caused by the ingestion of arsenical compounds. The signs in a dog include vomiting, diarrhea, whining, and abdominal pain, with circulatory collapse and death a few hours later.

arterial pertaining to an artery or the function of arteries.

arteriole tiny, microscopic branch of an artery that connects with a capillary.

arteriosclerosis thickening and hardening of artery walls; loss of elasticity of arteries.

arteritis inflammation of an artery.

artery blood vessel that carries blood away from the heart into the system, furnishing oxygen and nutrients to the tissues of the body.

Artésian Normand

Artésian Normand or **Basset Artésian Normand** developed in Flanders. It has short, crooked legs, a body that is more than twice as long as it is tall, and resembles the Basset Hound. A French hunting dog, it stands about 13 inches (30 cm) tall and weighs about 33 pounds (15 kg). Its ears are long and pendulant and it is tricolored or white with dark markings.

arthritis inflammation of the cartilage, bones, and capsule of a joint.

arthropathy joint disease or joint injury of any kind.

Arthropoda taxonomic phyla or division of the animal kingdom, comprised of insects, mites, ticks, spiders, crustaceans, and the like.

arthroscopy visually examining the interior of a joint by means of a small incision and the introduction of a fiber-optic arthroscope.

articulation the state of being united by a joint; involves bones that are connected to one another by ligaments, surrounded by a joint capsule, and working together as a joint.

artificial insemination in dog breeding, human intervention that involves collecting semen from a male dog and introducing it into a bitch to effect pregnancy.

artificial selection in dog breeding, human intervention to bring about the dominance of certain characteristics that are displayed by individual dogs.

artificial vagina in dog breeding, receptacle used to collect semen from a male dog for examination or for artificial insemination.

Artois Dog *see* Basset Hound or Artesian Basset.

ascarid roundworm of the dog that includes *Toxocara canis, Toxascaris leonina*, and others.

ascites abnormal fluid accumulation in the peritoneal (abdominal) cavity; also known as dropsy.

ASCOB a showing term that refers to any solid color other than black; Cocker Spaniel color designation.

aseptic necrosis of the femoral head *see* Legg-Calvé-Perthes disease.

aseptic necrosis death of a tissue; dissolution of a structure, without infection.

asexual lacking sexual organs; without sex; having no sexuality; referring to spayed bitch or castrated male dog.

ashen light gray coat color.

Asian Molosser or ***Canis molossus*** gigantic dog that was brought to Switzerland by the Roman armies during the first two centuries A.D.; a probable ancestor of the Saint Bernard.

ASPCA *see* American Society for Prevention of Cruelty to Animals.

Aspergillus genus of fungi that includes certain pathogenic molds.

aspermatogenic not producing sperm; referring to sterile stud dog.

asphyxia suffocation; loss of oxygen to the tissues.

aspirate to draw or suck in; to inhale; to pull the fluids from a cavity.

aspirin acetylsalicylic acid; antipyretic and mild antiinflammatory agent often used in dogs.

assimilation transformation of food by living tissues to produce growth, energy, and body function.

assistance dogs canines that have been trained to help disabled people. *See* hearing dogs, guide dogs, alarm dogs.

assisted breeding hand-breeding dogs or physically helping them in the act of copulation.

associative learning method of teaching a dog by linking an act to a reward; application of Pavlov's theory. *See also* conditioned reflex.

assortive mating breeding different phenotypes of animals to each other.

asthma allergic respiratory condition manifested by labored breathing and wheezing. *See* reverse sneeze.

astragalus bone that articulates with the tibia and fibula; anklebone or the talus.

astringent substance that causes a contraction or drawing together of tissues.

asymptomatic having no symptoms or signs of disease.

at a walk in showing, judge's direction to take a dog around the ring at a slow pace.

atavistic reaction instinctive desire of a sick or injured animal to get away from humans and other animals; an animal's propensity to seek a cold, damp, dark place in which to recover or die.

ataxia inability to walk; staggering and falling when walking is attempted, due to lack of muscular coordination.

atelectasis collapsed lung, or a lung that did not normally fill with air at birth.

Atelocynus microtis small-eared Zorro Dog of South America.

at fault in tracking, referring to a dog that has lost the scent in a tracking trial.

atherosclerosis pathological closing of arteries and the resultant restriction of blood flow due to plaques of cholesterol and other lipids that have been deposited on the inner walls of the arteries; not a major problem in dogs.

atlantoaxial joint first intervertebral joint of the neck. The articulation of the atlas (first vertebra) with the axis (second vertebra).

atlantooccipital joint first joint of the neck, or the articulation of the atlas (first vertebra) with the skull.

atlas first cervical vertebra below the skull.

Atlas Sheepdog smooth-coated herding dog from Morocco that stands about 14 inches (36 cm) tall and weighs about 48 pounds (22 kg).

atomizer device that breaks a liquid into a fine spray; used for treating certain respiratory diseases.

atonic lack of normal muscle tone.

atopic displaced; something that is away from its normal place or out of place.

atopy an allergic reaction to inhaled allergens that usually appears as a skin problem.

atoxic nontoxic; nonpoisonous.

atresia ani congenital absence of an anal opening.

atrium either of the paired upper chambers of the heart that receive blood and, by means of valves, transfer the blood to the ventricles.

atrophy shrinking or wasting away of a part due to lack of nutrition, insufficient exercise, or lack of use.

atropine drug that dries up bodily secretions by its stimulation of the sympathetic nervous system; an antispasmodic.

attack dog dog that has been trained to attack people. *See* schutzhund.

attenuate to weaken, lessen, or eliminate virulence.

attitude 1. posture of a dog's body. **2.** presentation of fetuses at the time of delivery. **3.** mental disposition or character of a dog.

attitude run in sledding, a short sprint, usually downhill, to train young dogs and improve their pulling desire.

attrition wearing away of a part by friction.

atypical not conforming to type; referring to dogs, differing in conformation from others of the same breed.

auditory related to hearing; experienced by hearing.

augment to increase the effectiveness of a product.

Aujeszky's disease viral infection of pigs that renders uncooked pork dangerous to dogs; not generally of consequence in United States because of federal meat inspection.

aural pertaining to or having to do with the ear or hearing.

auricle 1. pinna, leather, or flap of the ear. **2.** ear-shaped appendage that is a part of the atrium of the heart.

auricular hematoma swelling within the leather of an ear caused by broken vessels between the cartilage and skin layers, with the resulting formation of a pocket of blood.

auricular hematoma

auscultate to listen to sounds that emanate from within the body as an aid in diagnosis.

Aussie fond name for the Australian Shepherd.

Australian Cattle Dog AKC group: herding; previously known as the Australian Heeler, Queensland Heeler, or Queensland Blue Heeler. It stands about 19 inches (48 cm) tall, weighs about 35 pounds (16 kg), is short-coated, and seen in two colors: blue speckle or red speckle. A quiet, natural heeler, it is reported to be a breed derived from crossing the Collie, Dalmatian, and Australian Kelpie with the dingo. (See photo, page 42).

**Australian
Cattle Dog**

Australian Greyhound well-muscled dog that is stocky and slightly smaller than the English Greyhound. It was bred to catch game that eluded the traditional breeds of dogs in the rough terrain of Australia.

Australian Kelpie also known as Barb, Australian Sheepdog, or Kelpie, this dog was for a while shown in the AKC Miscellaneous class. It is a Border Collie-type herding dog from Australia that stands about 20 inches (50 cm) tall, weighs about 30 pounds (14 kg) and is seen in colors of

Australian Kelpie

black, black and tan, red, red and tan, fawn, chocolate or smoke blue. It has a short coat, erect ears, and a long tail.

Australian National Kennel Council Australia's national kennel club, functioning much the same as the AKC: Royal Show Grounds, Ascot Vale, Victoria, Australia.

Australian native dog *see* dingo or *Canis dingo*.

Australian Sheepdog *see* Australian Kelpie.

Australian Shepherd

Australian Shepherd AKC group: herding; common dog on farms and ranches of the western and southwestern United States; said by some to be a dingo cross, by others to be a Kelpie or Australian Cattle Dog cross, and by still others to be a Border Collie cross. It is a herding breed that was developed mainly in the United States. There is evidence that points toward a Basque origin on the Spanish-French border. It is usually seen in blue or red merle colors, has a long, flat coat, bobbed tail and often has one or two blue eyes. It stands about 20 inches (2.5 cm) tall and weighs about 50 pounds (23 kg). (See photo, page 41).

Australian Terrier AKC group: terrier; medium-sized dog that stands about 10 inches (25 cm) tall. Blue, tan, sandy, or red in color, with shadings of various complementary hues; it has a coat that is harsh and straight over a soft undercoat. It is a working terrier that is kept mostly as a companion, but it is also capable of going to ground after game.

Australian Terrier

Australian wild dog *see* dingo.

Austrian Hound breed that is smooth-coated with black and tan markings, and white on the lower parts. Its ears are relatively long and the body is medium-sized.

Austrian Kennel Club Osterreischischer Kynologen Verband, 3 Karl schweighofer Gasse, Vienna.

Austrian Pinscher or **Oesterreichisher Kurzhaariger Pinscher** virtually unknown outside of Austria. Small, short-haired breed, similar to other pinschers in appearance. It stands about 15 inches (38 cm) tall and weighs about 30 pounds (14 kg). It has down ears, its tail may be natural or docked, and its coat is yellow to fawn, or red with white markings. Its tail is short and it curls if left undocked.

Austrian Pinscher

Austrian Terrier smooth-coated medium-sized dog that stands about 16 inches (41 cm) tall and weighs about 33 pounds (15 kg).

autoantibody antibody that acts upon the cells of the body in which it is developed.

autoimmune disease condition in which autoantibodies or white blood cells destroy cells or tissues of the organism that produced them.

autoimmune hemolytic anemia specific autoimmune condition in which the red blood cells of the organism are destroyed by self-produced antibodies.

autonomic self-controlled, such as the sympathetic and parasympathetic nervous systems of the dog.

autosome any ordinary paired chromosome, other than a sex chromosome.

Auvergne Pointer, or **Braque d'Auvergne** developed in the Auvergne region of France, a heavy dog that stands about 22 inches (58 cm) tall, weighs about 60 pounds (27 kg), and is black and white, with a reputation for working well. This breed is quiet, intelligent, and easily trained.

Auvergne Pointer

avalanche dogs canines of any breed, especially German Shepherd Dogs, that are trained to locate human bodies that have been buried under avalanches or snow slides; also known as ski dogs.

avascular without blood vessels; lacking a blood supply.

avidin protein of a raw egg that reacts with biotin in the body, rendering both the protein and the vitamin unavailable nutritionally.

avitaminosis lack of some specific vitamin or vitamins in the body.

avulsion pulling or tearing away of a part.

awards trophies or ribbons that designate placements achieved in dog shows or other exhibitions.

away here in herding, a handler's command that sends the herd dog to the right.

AX in agility training, abbreviation for the Agility Excellent title.

axial skeleton that part of the skeleton that consists of the spinal column and skull.

axilla anatomical space between the upper humeral region and the lateral chest; armpit.

axion central nervous system, or the brain and spinal cord.

axis 1. second cervical vertebra. **2.** central plane about which a body normally turns.

Azara's Dog, Azara's Fox or *Canis acarae* wild dog of Brazil, Chile, Argentina, Paraguay, and Patagonia that is easily tamed; feeds mainly on poultry and reptiles. It is smaller than the crab-eating dog, with legs that are reddish on a ground color of gray. It has erect ears, and the tail is black and white mottled, with a black tip.

Azawakh breed that bears the name of the valley of northeastern Mali where it was first discovered. It is a gazehound that is used on hares and other small game, as well as gazelle or antelope. It stands about 28 inches (70 cm) tall and weighs about 50 pounds (23 kg).

azotemia toxemia manifested by the presence of a urinary component (urea) in the bloodstream.

Aztec sacred dog dog worshipped by the Aztecs. It was a puglike ancestor of the Chihuahua, and was seen in brindle, fawn, or cream colors.

B

Baal Phoenician god often represented by a dog's head.

babbler foxhunting term for a dog that gives voice, tongue, or talks when not on the scent trail or the track of a quarry.

babesiasis or **babesiosis** infection with *Babesia canis*, a protozoan parasite found in the red blood cells of dogs and transmitted by ticks; causes cellular destruction and subsequent anemia.

babiche in sledding, long strips of a special rawhide that are used to secure the joints of a sled, giving strength and flexibility to the parts.

Bacillus genus of spore-forming, rod-shaped, gram-positive bacteria that are pathogenic for dogs.

Bacitracin® antibiotic that is produced by *Bacillus licheniformis*.

back dorsum, from the neck to the pelvis.

backbone in a dog, the spinal column or the sum of the vertebrae from the skull to the tail.

back-cast 1. in field trials, to search for game to the rear, or behind the handler. **2.** in scenting, to cause dogs to retrace their paths to rediscover the scent.

backcross system of inbreeding in which a dog is mated to one of its parents.

backers 1. field trial term referring to members of the gallery, or a collection of individuals who support a particular dog. **2.** financial supporters of a dog show or exhibition.

backing field trial term referring to one dog that supports and confirms another dog's point; dog that stops hunting to point birds already found and being pointed by a brace-mate; honoring another dog's point.

backline 1. in sledding, another term for the tugline. **2.** dog's topline from the withers to the pelvis; sometimes includes the top of the neck as well.

backpacking hiking with a dog that has been trained to wear a special pack that may be loaded with its food, medical supplies, or other items.

backraking extraction of feces from the rectum.

backskull posterior part of the skull, behind the occiput.

backtrack in scenting and beagling, to follow the line of scent in a reverse direction; considered a major fault in competition.

backup dog in herding, second dog used to help quiet or settle livestock; the backup dog is removed when the trial begins.

backyard breeders hobby breeders or people engaged in breeding animals for fun or profit, but who are not necessarily interested in improving the breed.

backyard champion dog that performs perfectly at home, but fails to do well in a dog show or exhibition.

bacteria plural of bacterium; microscopic single-cell plants that can invade tissues and cause a disease by their presence or their toxins. Not all bacteria are harmful.

bacterial pertaining to bacteria.

bactericide agent that destroys bacteria.

bacteriotoxemia disease state caused by the presence of toxins produced by bacteria in the bloodstream.

bacterium singular form of bacteria.

baculum os penis, or bone that normally occurs in the penis.

bad doer inefficient user of nutrition; poor keeper.

badger common quarry for hunting dogs; member of the weasel family, named for its white facial stripe, the "badge."

badger color coat color of grizzly appearance, consisting of black, brown, gray, and white hairs.

badgerbaiting sport of pitting badgers against dogs.

badger-digging or **badger-drawing** sending terriers to ground to dig out a badger or pull it from its tunnel or den.

badger dog another name for the Dachshund. "Dach" translates to "badger" in German.

bad mouth crooked teeth, overbite, undershot or wry jaw.

bad shower show term for a dog that does not do well in the show ring because it does not enjoy it.

bag 1. hunting term that refers to the product of one day's shooting, or the birds that are carried in a bag or hunting vest by the shooter. **2.** in Beagle trials, the product of one day's shooting, or the game carried in a bag.

Baganda Hunting Dog breed used by several Uganda tribes for hunting; resembles the Lurcher, and is colored tan, yellow, and black, with a short coat.

bagged hunting term that denotes the number of birds shot in a day.

Bagust dogs Australian progeny of a cross between Hall's Heelers and Dalmatians. They were fine speckled dogs with a love of horses, but with less sheep-working ability than desired. *See* Blue Heeler and Hall's Heeler.

bait **1.** show term for the use of tidbits to keep the dog's attention in the show ring. **2.** liver-flavored snacks used to bait a show dog.

baiting harassment of other animals by dogs as seen in the sports of bearbaiting, bullbaiting, and badgerbaiting.

balance **1.** dog show term for the bilateral symmetry of a dog, as judged in the show ring. **2.** in herding, the point at which a dog has the most influence on the livestock to control their behavior.

balance and feel relating to the distance between a herd dog and its sheep.

balanced diet in a dog, the ration that provides nutritional adequacy or perfection; ration that contains all the necessary nutritional requirements for the age and status of the dog, such as youth, old age, health, breeding, growth, or lactation.

balanitis inflammation of the dog's glans penis.

balanoposthitis inflammation of the glans penis and prepuce.

balanus glans penis of a dog.

bald mask white mask on a dog's face, extending behind the ears.

Balearic Hound *see* Eivissenc.

Balkan Hound or **Balkanski Gonic** reddish-colored dog with black markings above the eyes and a black saddle on the body; used as a tracker and hunter. It stands about 20 inches (51 cm) tall and weighs about 44 pounds (20 kg).

Balkh Greyhound *see* Afghan Hound.

ball large pill or bolus that is used in large-animal veterinary medicine, and sometimes is broken in pieces to treat dogs; most often so used in worm medications. This practice is discouraged because of the possibility of administering an incorrect dosage.

bald mask

ballooning forcing quantities of air into a dog's abdominal cavity prior to performing abdominal laparoscopy.

ballottement palpation technique used to diagnose a floating object or organ within body cavities.

balm healing lotion, usually aromatic, which is applied topically.

Balto Eskimo Dog that led the first Iditerod, a 650-mile (982 km) sled dog run that carried diphtheria serum from Nenana to Nome, Alaska, in 1925.

Baluchi Hound *see* Afghan Hound.

banded hair that is a different color at the tip than at the skin.

bandog dog that is tied up with a collar and chain and used for guarding purposes; historical description of the Mastiff or Bullmastiff.

Bandogge or **Mastive** *see* Mastiff. Once described by Abraham Fleming as: "(a dog) vast, huge, stubborn, eager, of a heavy and burdensome body, and therefore but of little swiftness, it took fast hold with its teeth and held on beyond all credit."

bandy-legged having short, bowed forelegs.

bangled ears pendulous, droopy ears, as in the Basset.

Banjara Hound smooth-coated gazehound from India that stands about 27 inches (69 cm) tall and weighs about 57 pounds (26 kg).

Banjara Mastiff longhaired medium-sized mastiff-type dog from India that stands about 23 inches (58 cm) and weighs about 80 pounds (36 kg).

Banjara or **Banjara Greyhound** native to India, a Greyhound-type dog that is not a purebred. Slightly smaller than the Rampur Hound, it is sandy, wheaten, fawn, gray, or brindle-colored.

bank storehouse of transplant parts or blood that are used therapeutically, such as: blood bank, bone bank, or corneal bank.

BAOS abbreviation for brachycephalic airway obstruction syndrome; collection of physical anomalies that include an elongated soft palate and uvula, nostril obstruction, and tonsil enlargement. The syndrome results in difficult respiration, and is commonly found in Bulldogs.

bar jumps in agility training, obstacles that are basically the same as pole jumps or high jumps.

Barb *See* Australian Kelpie.

Barbanter or **Brabanter** extinct breed believed to be an ancestor of the Boxer.

Barbet believed to be one of the oldest French breeds; ancestor of Poodles, Bichons, and various sheepdogs. It stands about 22 inches (56 cm) tall and weighs about 55 pounds (25 kg). A popular dog with the wildfowlers, it is a good water retriever and may be related to the English Water Dog.

barbiturate salt of barbituric acid; used medicinally as a sedative.

bare pastern refers to short hair on the pasterns of an Afghan Hound.

Barfy canine companion of the kids in Bil Keane's comic strip *The Family Circus*.

Barge Dog *see* Schipperke or Belgian Barge Dog.

barium metallic powder that is radiopaque and is used in radiology to make contrast X-rays.

barium series set of tests used to determine gastrointestinal function. It makes use of a suspension of barium that is swallowed or administered into the lower intestinal tract, followed by X-rays.

bark or **speak** verbal command that is given to a dog to cause it to give voice.

barker dog that barks a lot; a nuisance dog.

Barking Bird Dog *see* Finnish Spitz.

barkless dog Basenji.

barrel ribcage.

barrel chest wide thoracic expanse; exaggerated rib-spring.

barrel hocks bowed hind legs with the feet toed inward.

barrel kennel weatherproof kennel that can be constructed from a 55-gallon (21 L) oil drum.

barren sterile; incapable of producing offspring.

barrier 1. partial or complete obstruction or obstacle used in training dogs. **2.** racing term for the box from which a Greyhound race is started; starting gate.

Barry Saint Bernard that rescued 40 people who had lost their way in the snows on Saint Bernard pass, Switzerland, circa 1800. Since that time, there has always been a Barry in the hospice there.

barrel kennel

Barryhund name that was proposed for the Saint Bernard, after the famous hospice dog Barry.

Barukhzy Hound *see* Afghan Hound.

basal situated near the base.

basal cell one of the innermost cells of the deep epidermis layer of the skin.

Basenji

Basenji AKC group: hound; Egyptian or African barkless dog. It stands about 17 inches (43 cm) tall, and weighs about 24 pounds (11 kg); is short-coated, with erect ears and a tightly curled tail. It is seen in colors of chestnut and white, black and white, or black, tan, and white. (See photo, page 20.)

basewide refers to a wide-tracking dog that paddles and rocks from side to side when gaited.

basic having the chemical property of a substance that neutralizes acids.

basket part of a dogsled that carries the load.

basket sled conventional snow vehicle that is pulled along the snow or ice on runners. It has an elevated basket set up on stanchions, as opposed to a toboggan; the same as a stanchion sled.

basket sled

basophil white blood cell that has basic staining properties.

basset word derived from the French word *bas*, meaning "low." Pioneer Basset breeding was undertaken by the friars at Saint Hubert's Abbey in France.

Basset Artésian Normand *see* Artésian Normand.

Basset Bleu de Gascogne

Basset Bleu de Gascogne descended from the French Bleu de Gascogne, this dog is only about 14 inches (36 cm) tall and weighs about 40 pounds (18 kg). It has an outstanding nose, a short, thick coat, large head, and wide, floppy ears. Its colors are white with large black patches and small red markings. It is used to hunt both feathered and furred game.

Basset d'Artois dog with a relatively long and powerful body that may be related to the Basset Hound of Great Britain. Rarely seen outside France, the dog is normally tricolored.

Basset Fauve de Bretagne native to the Brittany province of France, this breed has a short, flat, hard, coarse coat that differs from other Bassets. It is hunting dog that stands about 14 inches (36 cm) tall and weighs about 40 pounds (18 kg). It is related to the Grand Griffon Fauve and the

Basset Griffon Vendéen. It is a solid red or tawny color, and is occasionally called the Tawny Brittany Basset.

Basset Griffon Vendéen French breed produced by crossing a white Saint Hubert Hound with an Italian Bloodhound. It stands about 16 inches (41 cm) tall, and has a rough coat and whiskers. Its colors vary from fawn or grayish white to black and white, gray and white, or tricolored.

Basset Griffon Vendéen

Basset Hound AKC group: hound; originated in France from an outcross of Bloodhounds; short-legged, bulky-bodied dog, is black, tan, and white in color, and has very long ears and crooked forelegs. It stands about 15 inches (38 cm) tall and weighs up to 60 pounds (27 kg). (See photo, page 20.)

bat-eared having large, forward-facing, rounded ears.

Basset Hound

Bavarian Mountain Hound, or Bavarian Schweisshund, or Bayrischer Gebirgs-Schweisshund gundog originated in the Bavarian region of southern Germany that was developed by crossing a Bavarian Hound with a Tirolean Hound. It is used as a trail hound, bird dog, and deer-hunting dog. It has a short coat of yellowish-red or shades of bronze or gray, stands about 20 inches (51 cm) tall, weighs 70 pounds (35 kg), and has long, pendulant ears and a long tail.

bawl 1. scenting term for the sounds of hounds' voices when not on a scent trail of their quarry. **2.** bag, or game obtained in a day's hunting.

bawler hound that tends to bawl excessively.

Bavarian Mountain Hound

bawl-mouthed hunting term for a dog that displays a long, drawn-out voice while on the trail.

bay mournful howl of trailing hounds on scent.

beady describing small, deep-set eyes.

Beagle AKC group: hound; shown in two classes: 13 inches to 15 inches (33–38 cm) tall, and 13 inches (33 cm) and under. It is a packhound that is black, tan, and white in color with a close, hard coat and a tail that is carried straight up. It is bred for both showing and hunting trials.(See photo, page 18.)

Beagle Harrier dog that in France is kept almost exclusively for hunting hares; cross between the Beagle and the Harrier. It stands about 17 inches (43 cm) tall, with a short, tricolored coat.

Beagle

beaglers those individuals who exhibit Beagles in field trials, and hunt with them.

beagling rabbit hunting with Beagles; engaging in Beagle field trials.

bearbaiting blood sport in which several dogs were pitted against a bear. Mastiffs, Staffordshire Terriers, Bulldogs, and their outcrosses were used in this endeavor.

beard prominent, long hair on or under the chin that is seen in griffons; different from the whiskers of terriers.

Bearded Collie AKC group: herding; originally a British breed. It stands about 21 inches (53 cm) tall, weighs about 60 pounds (27 kg), and is, black, blue, brown, or fawn-colored, often with white markings on the face. It has a soft undercoat and a flat, harsh, shaggy outer coat.

Bearded Collie

bear dog large, heavy, long tailed animal with a massive skull. An ancestor of the dog known as *Daphaenus*. It lived in the Miocene period and was about the size of a coyote.

bear ear small, erect ear.

bear pit enclosure used for bearbaiting.

beat 1. pulsation or throb of an artery or the heart. **2.** creation of noise and commotion to cause game to leave their hiding places.

beater person used to flush game during a shoot.

Beauce ancient herding dog of the midlands of Italy.

Beauceron French sheepdog of ancient origin; first bred in the region of Brie, not Beauce. It stands about 28 inches (71 cm) tall, weighs about 65 pounds (29 kg), and is colored dark liver with fiery red patches on the feet and thighs, or black and tan. It has similar conformation to the Briard, and resembles a German Shepherd Dog-Doberman Pinscher cross.

Beauceron

beauty spot in a dog, distinct spot of colored hair on the top of the skull between the ears.

beaver coat color somewhat deeper than fawn.

Bedlington Terrier AKC group: terrier; quick, lightly built English dog with a slightly arched back. It stands about 15 inches (38 cm) tall, weighs about 24 pounds (11 kg), has a thick, white, linty coat and a long, narrow head, and is often said to resemble a lamb.

beauty spot

bee sting tail thin, pointed tail.

beefy coarse, muscular, fleshy.

behavior in a dog, its attitude, manners, or manner of conducting itself; its response to stimulus.

behavioral period "imprint" season of a dog's life when it is most easily bonded with its owner and quickly forms its lasting habits. The most important period is from three weeks to three months of age.

behavioral therapy modifying an animal's behavior by specific techniques such as substitution, prevention, diversion, positive reinforcement, and redirection.

behaviorist person who studies behavior and specializes in modifying that behavior.

Belgian Barge Dog *see* Schipperke.

Belgian Cattle Dog *see* Bouviers des Flandres.

Belgian Congo Dog *see* Basenji.

Belgian Griffon rarely seen Belgian dog that can be black or reddish brown or a combination thereof, and has a stiff, wiry coat. One of three types of Brussels Griffon seen in Europe, similar in height and weight to that breed.

Belgian Kennel Club Union Cynologique Saint-Hubert, 25 Avenue de l'Armée, Bruxelles IV.

Belgian Malinois AKC group: herding; closely related to the Belgian Sheepdog, except that it is fawn- to mahogany-colored, with black tips on the hair. It stands about 24 inches (61 cm) tall.

Belgian Malinois

Belgian Pointer or **Braque Belge** one of a number of gundogs with a restricted distribution. It is a slate-gray color with brown markings and is bred predominantly for working rather than exhibition.

Belgian Sheepdog AKC group: herding; large, black, sheepherding breed developed in Belgium. It has a long, abundant coat and stands about 24 inches (61 cm) tall.

Belgian Tervuren AKC group: herding; medium size, standing about 23 inches (58 cm) tall, and weighing about 62 pounds (28 kg). The color of its long, flat coat is fawn to mahogany, with a black overlay.

Belgian Sheepdog

belladonna atropine, a medicine commonly used for pre-anesthesia; plant derivative of *Atropa belladonna*, nightshade, or deadly nightshade.

bell ear pinna or leather of the ear that is shaped like a bell.

belly abdomen or the ventral region of the body from the xiphoid cartilage of the sternum to the brim of the pelvis.

belton term named for a village in Northumberland that is used to describe the roan pattern of intermingled color with white hairs that is commonly seen on English Setters. It typically has two colored hairs intermittently appearing in a coat. Blue belton results from black and white hairs intermingled, orange belton from red and white hairs, lemon belton from yellow and white.

Benadryl® proprietary name for the antihistamine diphenhydramine hydrochloride.

bench 1. dog showing term for an elevated platform or table on which dogs are kept when not being shown. **2.** table on which small dogs are placed for judging.

bench and field champion dog that has both a working Championship and conformation Championship; dual champion.

bench legs forelegs wide at the elbows with the toes turning out, giving a squatty appearance; bowed forelegs.

bench show organized conformation exhibition in which purebred dogs are judged by professional judges, comparing individual dogs to the published breed conformation standard. Bench shows are held under the rules of a dog fancier organization such as the AKC.

benched show show in which all dogs that are entered must be present in a designated cubicle for the entire day of the show.

beneficial nematodes living organisms that attack and consume immature life forms of fleas; applied to a yard, to help rid the yard of flea eggs and larvae.

benign term used to describe tumors that are unlikely to become malignant.

benzoin astringent resin from a species of the Styrax plant; often applied in its tincture form to a dog's pads to toughen them.

Bergamaschi or **Bergamasko Herder** Italian sheepdog that is an outcross of the Kuvasz; named for Bergamo, in the Lombardy region of Italy. Its color is all white or gray, it has a profuse, undulating, and matted coat, its muzzle is often bearded, and its tail is long. It stands about 24 inches (60 cm) tall and weighs about 80 pounds (38 kg).

Berger de Languedoc five distinct breeds that are named after the area in which they were developed in Languedoc, France. Working sheepdogs, they are about 20 inches

(51 cm) tall, with brown or black coats. They are known as: Grau, Farou, Larzac, Carrigues, and Carmargue.

Berger Picard kept as a working sheepdog since the ninth century, this is a large breed, standing about 26 inches (66 cm) tall.

Berger Polonais de Vallée possibly developed by the Huns in the eighth century in the area that is now Poland; a tough and hardy sheepdog somewhat similar to the English Sheepdog.

Berner Laufhund descendent of the Nile Dog. It stands about 16 inches (41 cm) tall and weighs about 35 pounds (16 kg). A short-coated dog that is tricolored with white predominating, it has long, folded ears and short legs and is seen in both rough and smooth coat varieties. One of the numerous Swiss hounds; it has a great sense of smell and is a trail hound of great ability.

Berner Laufhund

Bernese Mountain Dog AKC group: working; the second largest of four types of Swiss Mountain Dogs that are black with tan and white markings. It stands about 26 inches (66 cm) tall, weighs about 90 pounds (44 kg) and has a soft, silky coat, and short, pendulant ears. Used in Switzerland for draft work, herding, and guarding, it is also known as Berner Sennnhund, which translates literally to Bernese Cheesehound.

Bernese Mountain Dog

Bernese Mountain Dog Club of America 812 Warren Landing, Fort Collins, Colorado 80525.

Bertillon system in racing, system or method of identification of racing Greyhounds; certification of a dog's breeding, age, sex, and physical features; named for French criminologist Alfonse Bertillon, who measured and described criminals for future identification.

Best in Group winner of the contest among entire group's Best of Breed winners.

Best in Show winner of the contest among all the Best in Group dogs.

Best of Breed winner of the contest among the Winners Bitch and Winners Dog together with all of the champions of the breed being shown.

best of losers slang for Reserve winners award.

Best of Opposite Sex best dog of the opposite sex of the Best of Breed.

Best of Winners winner of the competition between Winners Dog and Winners Bitch; award is presented to the male or female that is chosen by a judge to be the best example of a breed's open class.

beta blocker category of drugs that slow the heart rate and reduce the blood pressure, prevent anxiety or panic, control irregular heartbeats, and sometimes control tremors. Some are used to reduce elevated blood pressure in the eye from glaucoma; others are used to treat thyroid disorders. Examples: propanolol, metoprolol, atenolol, pindolol. In general, these drugs act to relax the blood vessels by blocking certain nerve impulses.

Betadine® organic or "tamed" iodine product that has many of the same properties of iodine, with fewer detrimental side effects; available as an ointment or solution.

bevy flock of birds.

bibulous substance or tissue that absorbs moisture.

bicaudal genetic phenomenon; having two tails.

biceps brachii muscle with two heads that is located in the upper foreleg.

biceps femoris muscle with two heads that is located in the upper hind leg.

bichon group of Belgian breeds that are, or have been known as, bichon; include the Maltese, Havanese, Havana Spaniel, and Teneriffe Dog.

Bichon Bolognaise Italian lapdog, or companion dog, similar to the Bichon Frise.

Bichon Frise AKC group: non-sporting; descendant of the Bichon Teneriffe; formerly used by Italian organ grinders due to its clownish antics. It is an all-white, curly-coated, small breed about 10 inches (25 cm) tall, weighing about 10 pounds (4.5 kg), known for its outgoing, playful personality and happy attitude. (See photo, page 36.)

Bichon Frise

Bichon Frise Club of America 186 Ash Street North, Twin Falls, Idaho 83301.

Bichon Havanese similar to the other bichons, but smaller in stature; developed in Cuba.

Bichon Maltaise thought by some to be an ancestor of the Maltese.

Bichon Petit Chien-Lion rare variety of bichon that derives its name from the usual lionlike style of clipping the dog. It stands about 14 inches (36 cm) and, although white is the preferred color, it is seen in all self colors.

Bichon Teneriffe supposed ancestor of the Bichon Frise.

bicolor having two dominant colors in the coat.

bicornuate having two horns, such as a uterus that is divided into a body and two distinct hollow projections or horns.

bicuspid structure having two points, such as a tooth or heart valve.

b.i.d. Latin abbreviation for *bis in die* that sometimes is seen on a prescription and means to administer twice daily.

biddable refers to a dog that is cooperative and willing to do the owner's or handler's bidding.

bifurcate to fork or split into two parts, divisions, or branches.

bilateral cryptorchid redundant term that is sometimes used to describe a male that has neither testicle descended into scrotum; animal that displays cryptorchidism.

bilateral symmetry refers to coat colors, or skin and coat lesions, which occur equally, in essentially the same pattern, on two sides.

bile fluid secreted by the liver into the gallbladder, then to the intestine; bile acts to split fat into tiny globules for digestion.

bile duct hollow channel or tube through which bile is transferred from the gallbladder into the intestine.

biliary pertaining to bile secretion, the gallbladder, or bile ducts.

bilirubin red bile pigment sometimes found in urine and blood; formed by the breakdown of the hemoglobin of red blood cells.

biliuria presence of bile salts in the urine.

biliverdin green pigment formed by the oxidation of bilirubin.

billet feces of a fox.

Billy quarrelsome French hunting dog, distinguished by its excellent scenting ability; developed by Hublot du Rivault in Poitou, France, around 1800. It is a large hound, standing about 26 inches (66 cm) tall and weighing about 60 pounds (30 kg), that is often hunted in packs for boars and wolves. The breed has a short, hard coat and colors of white, café au lait, white with orange patches, or white with lemon patches.

binaural pertaining to both ears.

Bingley Terrier early name for the Airedale Terrier; also known as Waterside or Working Terriers.

binocular microscope type of magnifying instrument that is used with both eyes.

binocular vision pertaining to the field of vision, or the amount of overlapping vision from each eye to produce a singular image. The binocular vision of humans is about 140 degrees; a dog's is less than 100 degrees; thus a human's vision is more three-dimensional and has a more acute depth perception than that of a dog. *See* visual field.

biochemical screening imperfect tests used to predict the transmission of hereditary traits.

biocidal having the ability to destroy living organisms.

biokinetics study of the movement of animals.

biological vector living organism that provides the means of transmitting a disease from one dog to another. Example: the mosquito in heartworm disease, or a tick in Lyme disease.

biologicals agents made from living organisms and their products, including vaccines, bacterins, and antitoxins.

biologist scientist who studies life's phenomena.

biometry mathematical analysis of biological data.

biopsy diagnostic section of an organ or tissue taken from a living organism by surgical means.

Biosorb® proprietary name of a starch-derivative dusting powder that is commonly used as an aid in surgical gloving; also used to whiten a dog's dirty or stained white coats.

biotin one of the essential B complex vitamins; found in every living organism.

biotype of the same genotype.

bird dog any of several dogs used for hunting fowl, including pointers, setters, spaniels, and retrievers.

Bird Dog Field Trials organized, judged competition of bird dogs in the field, in simulated hunting conditions; tests of dogs' performance of the function for which they were bred.

bird work finding, pointing, flushing, and retrieving game birds.

birds in hunting, the legal game or quarry being hunted.

birdy in hunting, propensity of a gundog to work its ground closely and intently.

birth defects congenital maladies that are not necessarily hereditary but are present at birth.

birth order sequence of births in a litter.

birthing whelping; giving birth, or assisting in whelping.

BIS abbreviation for Best In Show.

biscuit 1. creamlike, light fawn color. **2.** hard, baked, cereal product used as a dog food or treat.

biscuit eater in hunting, dog that performs only for food, and has no heart or interest in the sport of hunting.

bisexual hermaphrodite; having both male and female sexual organs.

Bisten long-coated herding dog from India that stands about 27 inches (69 cm) tall and weighs about 70 pounds (32 kg).

bistoury long, narrow surgical knife used for opening abscesses.

bitch female dog.

bite 1. grip of a dog with its teeth. **2.** position of a dog's teeth when closed. *See* separate bites, level bite, underbite, overbite, and scissors bite.

Bitter Apple® proprietary, terrible tasting, but harmless, product used to stop dogs from chewing objects.

bivvy sack sledding term for the cover that fits over a sleeping bag and protects it while on the trail.

black and tan, black and fawn, or **black and fallow** color combination occurring on certain dogs such as Bloodhounds, Coonhounds, Beagles, Bassets, and certain terriers.

Black and Tan Coonhound AKC group: hounds; one of its ancestors was probably the Bloodhound. It stands about 25 inches (63 cm) tall, weighs about 70 pounds (30 kg), and has long ears and a clean head. Its coat is short, dense, and jet black, with tan markings. It is used to hunt raccoon, bear, deer, bobcat, mountain lion, and other game.

Black and Tan Coonhound

Black and Tan Miniature Terrier *see* Toy Manchester Terrier.

Black and Tan Setter *see* Gordon Setter.

Black and Tan Terrier *see* Manchester Terrier.

Black and Tan Wirehaired Terrier *see* Welsh Terrier.

Black Elkhound possibly extinct breed of Norway that is lighter and smaller than its gray relative. It has pricked ears, curled tail, and a thick coat. Kept primarily for hunting, they also made good guard dogs.

Black Kelpie *see* Australian Kelpie.

black mange *see* demodectic mange.

black mask term used to describe a lower face and muzzle of black.

black mouth old wives' tale that assigned great intelligence to dogs with black-pigmented oral mucous membranes.

black muzzle term used to describe a black muzzle, on a self-colored face.

Black Pointer *see* Arkwright Pointer.

Black Russian Terrier

Black Russian Terrier large, very strong hunting breed courageous enough to go after bear; originated from the Giant Schnauzer, the Airedale terrier, and the Rottweiler. It stands about 28 inches (71 cm) tall, weighs about 80 pounds (36 kg), and is a sturdy dog with a profuse coat that grows to 10 inches (25 cm) long. Its color is black or salt and pepper.

black tongue *see* pellagra.

bladder reservoir for fluids, such as the urinary bladder and gallbladder.

bladder stones urinary calculi or concretions that form from minerals in the urinary bladder.

blade bone scapula; shoulder blade.

blain inflammatory swelling or boil on the surface of the skin.

bland 1. having mild or soothing properties. **2.** describing food that is easy to digest and often without seasoning or taste.

blank 1. describing a region or section of the country in which no foxes are found. **2.** describing any day when the hounds don't start a fox.

blanket 1. in racing, solid-colored, numbered cloth worn by each hound during competition. **2.** in coursing, colored, numbered cloth worn by each dog in the event. **3.** color of the coat on the back and sides from the withers to the base of the tail.

blanket finish racing term for a closely bunched field at the finish of a race, or a photo finish; finish in which all the racing hounds could be covered with a blanket.

blastoma tumor exhibiting independent localized growth.

blastomycosis chronic infection of the skin, lungs, bones, liver, or kidneys that is caused by *Blastomyces* species.

blaze showy white area on a dog's face, located between the eyes.

bleb blister, or skin vesicle that is filled with fluid.

bleeder hemophiliac; animal with a poor clotting time.

Blenheim coat color with a pearly white ground color and patches of chestnut-red that are well distributed; seen in the Japanese Chin and King Charles Spaniel.

blepharism spasm of the eyelids.

blepharitis inflammation of the eyelids.

blind 1. having no sight. **2.** in retrieving, man-made place from which to shoot water fowl, such as a boat or covering where dogs and hunters are hidden from the duck's view.

blind retrieve retrieve that is made when the dog has not seen the bird fall; quarry that is found and retrieved based on the hunter's hand signals and the bird's scent.

blind search or **blind track** tracking and searching for quarry based on scent alone, when neither hunter nor dog has seen where the bird fell.

blind shooting shooting water fowl from an artificial structure used to hide the dogs and hunters from the quarry.

blinker 1. in field trials, bird dog that can't make up its mind where the birds are; one that avoids a definite point. **2.** in hunting, gundog that deliberately avoids game. **3.** in racing, leather shield that is attached to the racing muzzle to obstruct view from both sides (now obsolete in the United States).

blister localized collection of fluid between the layers of skin; vesicle.

bloat disease that is common in large breeds of dogs. *See* gastric torsion, dilatation, and volvulus.

block to administer a local or regional anesthesia to block the sensory nerve stimulus from the skin; used in minor skin suturing procedures or small skin tumor excision.

blockage obstruction of the intestine, bowel, or other channel.

blocky square in body conformation; solid appearance.

blocky head cubelike head construction.

blood fluid that circulates in the heart, arteries, capillaries, and veins of an animal to carry nourishment and oxygen to, and bring away waste products from, all tissues of the body.

blooded 1. describing a dog of good breeding. **2.** referring to hounds that have killed their quarry. **3.** referring to a novice hound that is anointed with the blood of its first kill.

Bloodhound AKC group: hounds; large scent dog about 25 inches (63 cm) tall weighing over 110 pounds (50 kg). It has deeply sunken eyes, long thin ears, and a copious amount of wrinkled skin on the face; its colors are black and tan, red and tan, and tawny. The Bloodhound is known for its keen sense of smell. (See photo, page 18.)

Bloodhound

blooding in foxhunting, rubbing the blood of a killed quarry on the faces of dogs that were not in on the kill.

bloodline 1. group of related dogs, usually developed over several generations by a breeder; a strain or a family of related dogs. **2.** sequence of direct ancestors in a pedigree.

Bloodlines UKC magazine, 332 West Cedar Street, Kalamazoo, Michigan 49007.

blood plasma fluid portion of the blood containing fibrinogen, but no cells; extraction of whole blood to which an anticoagulant has been added.

blood serum clear, nearly colorless fluid that remains when blood clots and the cells are extracted from whole blood.

blood sports those endeavors that employ dogs and involve killing animals.

blood urea nitrogen abbreviated BUN; laboratory test for kidney function.

bloom shine or glossiness of a coat; sign of good nutrition and conditioning.

blotch localized spot on coat or skin, related to an active or former skin infection.

blousy coat coat that is woolly and soft, as opposed to hard and tight.

blown coat referring to a coat loss that is due to pregnancy and lactation, seasonal shedding, or other natural occurrence.

blue inherited dilution of a black coat color caused by a recessive gene; a legitimate color of Doberman Pinschers and other breeds.

blue belton intricate mixture of black hairs and white hairs; blue roan.

blue Doberman syndrome hereditary condition of Doberman Pinschers in which the dog has a thin, short, gray-blue coat that is often patchy and scaly; color dilution alopecia.

blue dog dog's coat color having black hairs and white hairs blended together uniformly or in patches, resulting in a blue appearance.

blue eye 1. opacity of the cornea that results from an infection with CAV-l virus (hepatitis), or as a reaction to a hepatitis vaccination. **2.** lack of pigmentation in the iris of blue merle dogs that results in a blue-colored eye.

Blue Heeler dog that was the result of the original cross between the Bagust Dog and the Black and Tan Kelpie. This cross was to eventually become the Australian Cattle Dog.

blue merle coat color that has a light or dark blue-gray ground color, with shades of black throughout the coat; mottled or marbled color with black shadings and white markings and an overall blue hue.

blue mottle or **blue speckle** blue ticking on a white coat; seen in Blue Tick Hounds.

Blue Paul or **Blue Poll** Scottish dog that was bred for fighting.

blue slip AKC puppy registration document that is sent to the dam's owner, and is made available with each puppy of a registered litter.

Blue Tick Hound hound descended from English foxhounds. Smaller than the Black and Tan Coonhound; it stands about 27 inches (69 cm) and weighs about 80 pounds (36 kg), with black spots on a generalized blue ticked background. It is used in raccoon hunting, and specializes in treeing the quarry.

Blue Tick Hound

Bluey *see* Australian Cattle Dog.

bluie dog with a smoky appearance to its eyelids, lips, and nose pad; condition is usually associated with extremely light blue eyes, and is a manifestation of dilute pigmentation.

blunt 1. describing a muzzle that is short and blocky. **2.** describing ears that are too short and rounded at the tips.

B-lymphocytes or **ß-cells** white blood cells that originate in the bone marrow and comprise the antibody-producing plasma cells when mature.

board to house dogs for a fee.

Boarhound *see* Great Dane.

Boatswain Newfoundland that rescued Lord Byron and is eulogized on his headstone.

BOB in showing, abbreviation for Best of Breed.

bob to dock or cut off a tail; to perform a caudectomy.

bobtail or bobbed 1. animal that was born with short tail. **2.** docked tail.

bodied up describing a strong, well-muscled dog in good condition.

body the thorax and abdomen; trunk, or all of an animal except the legs, head and neck, and tail.

body climber dog that has the bad habit of jumping or climbing up on humans when greeting them.

body language physical attitude of a dog that lets its handler know what the dog is preparing to do, or what it is considering.

body length 1. distance from front of sternum to the rear of the pelvis. **2.** distance from the withers to base of the tail.

body loosely strung referring to a dog that lacks good muscular tone and conditioning.

body temperature normal adult dog's temperature is 101°F to 102.5°F (38°C–39.2°C).

bold referring to a dog that exhibits a courageous, aggressive look.

Bolognese member of the bichon family also known as the Bolognese Toy Dog. It is an Italian dog that is pure white in color with a long, silky coat, and has semierect, feathered ears, and a gay, plumed tail. It stands about 12 inches (31 cm) tall and weighs about 9 pounds (4 kg).

Bolognese

bolt in sledding, refers to the action of a team that is overcome by excitement and runs uncontrollably into a crowd or off the trail.

bolter dog that is given to sudden breaking away from its handler's control.

bolting eye prominent, protruding eye.

bolus mass of food or other material being swallowed; large pill.

bond invisible attachment between an animal and its master and family that includes love, loyalty, and obedience.

bonding time time required for an animal to form an attachment to its owner. The most important time of a puppy's life for bonding is from three weeks to three months of age.

bone material that makes up the skeleton of vertebrates.

bone burying act of hiding bones. Dogs bury their bones for one of two reasons: they aren't particularly hungry at the present and wish to save them for future gnawing, or they want to hide them from other dogs.

boned or **well-boned** possessing limbs that give the appearance of strength without coarseness.

bone marrow soft, fatty, highly vascular tissue that occupies the central cavity of bones.

bone-marrow aspiration removal of a small amount of bone marrow for microscopic evaluation.

bone plating any of several surgical techniques of fracture repair in which a fixation device is used to fasten the broken ends of bones together to promote healing; usually the plate is applied with special bone-screws. *See* compression plating.

Bones Bret Harte's mongrel dog in his amusing story *A Yellow Dog.*

bones of the dog total number of bones in a dog's skeleton: 310 in the female, 311 in the male. *See* os penis.

booster vaccinations additional vaccinations given periodically after the initial vaccination is administered; designed to increase the level of immunity.

borborygmus growling noise made by the propulsion of flatus through the intestine.

Bordeaux Mastiff originally bred to hunt wild boars and bears as well as to fight in pits. It stands about 26 inches (66 cm) tall, weighs over 100 pounds (45 kg), and its color is red with white markings. Although somewhat aggressive, it has a loyal nature.

Border Collie

Border Terrier

Border Collie AKC group: herding; working stock dog that originated in Scotland. It stands about 21 inches (54 cm) tall, weighs about 40 pounds (19 kg), and has a soft, dense, double coat or a rough, wavy coat. The most common color is black with white markings, but it may occur in any color except white. This highly intelligent dog is frequently seen in herding tests and trials and is a superb sheep dog. (See photo, page 39.

Border Terrier AKC group: terrier. It is a working dog that weighs about 15 pounds (7 kg), has a harsh, dense coat that is colored red, wheaten, grizzle and tan, or blue and tan, and is used to hunt otter and fox in England.

Bordetella bronchiseptica genus and species of one of the bacterial organisms that is included in the highly contagious kennel cough complex, sometimes called bordetellosis. The disease usually occurs as a part of tracheobronchitis, or bronchopneumonia.

bore out racing term for an interference accomplished by carrying or forcing another contestant wide.

borelliosis *see* Lyme disease.

boric acid soothing solution that is prepared for either ophthalmic use or for skin application; obtainable without a prescription from pharmacies; does not kill germs but retards their growth.

Borzoi

Borzoi AKC group: hound; name means "the swift one." This breed was formerly known as the Russian Wolfhound, and was originally kept for coursing wolves. It is a powerful gazehound, that stands about 29 inches (74 cm), and weighs 100 pounds (45 kg). It has muscular, tucked-up loins, a deep chest, and its long silky coat is predominately white but may be marked with tan, brindle gray, or black.

BOS abbreviation for Best of Opposite Sex.

bossy heavy musculature over the shoulders.

Boston Bull Terrier *see* Boston Terrier.

Boston Terrier

Boston Terrier AKC group: non-sporting; originally bred as a pit fighter. It is shown in three classes: under 15 pounds (38 kg), 15 to 20 pounds (38–51 kg), and 20 to 25 pounds (51–63 kg). It is a lively, smooth-coated, compactly built, short-headed terrier with erect ears, and a short, crooked tail. It is usually seen with a white apron and neck, and a white blaze on its face. (See photo, page 36.)

Bothia long-haired herding dog from India that stands about 22 inches (56 cm) tall and weighs about 73 pounds (33 kg).

botulism food poisoning produced by the toxin of the bacteria *Clostridium botulinum.*

bouillon broth prepared from animal flesh, frequently used to flavor dog food for finicky eaters.

Bouledogue Français *see* French Bulldog.

Bouncer Pomeranian in a Charles Dickens story.

Bourbonnais Pointer or **Braque de Bourbounais** French hunting breed primarily used on upland game birds, such as partridge, pheasant, and grouse. It has a keen nose and is particularly adept at scenting out cripples; its coat, not its instincts, limit its water retrieving in cold weather. It stands about 22 inches (56 cm) tall, weighs about 50 pounds (25 kg), and many are born without tails. The coat is short and fine, and is seen in shades of faded lilac and wine colors. Its maroon-colored spots blend together into a streaked appearance.

Bourbonnais Pointer

bouvier literally translated as "cow herd," or "ox driver"; any of a number of breeds of dogs developed in Belgium for herding work.

Bouvier Briarde extinct Belgian breed that appears in the ancestry of the Bouvier des Flandres.

Bouvier des Ardennes Belgian droving dog from the Ardennes mountain area. Its color is any shade of gray, all black, and gray and white, and its coat is medium, thick, and shaggy.

Bouvier des Flandres AKC group: herding; large, powerful Belgian breed with a rough, harsh, double coat. It stands about 26 inches (66 cm) tall, and weighs about 88 pounds (40 kg). Its tail is docked, its ears are usually trimmed, and its coat ranges from fawn to black in color.

Bouvier des Flandres

Bouvier Pikhaar *see* Moerman.

BOW abbreviation for Best of Winners.

bowel intestine, especially the large intestine.

bow hocks barrel hocks; wide at hocks with toes pointing inward.

bowleg outward curvature of the forelegs.

box racing term for the enclosed starting gate used in a Greyhound race.

Boxer

Boykin Spaniel

bracelets

box broken racing term for a dog that is trained to start from an enclosed starting box.

box buster Greyhound that starts quickly.

Boxer AKC group: working; German breed originally used for bullbaiting, now a family companion dog. It stands about 23 inches (58 cm) tall and weighs over 65 pounds (29 kg). The breed is characterized by clean lines, cropped or uncropped ears, and a docked tail. It has a short coat, and is seen in colors from fawn to dark red, including brindle, with white markings, and a dark mask. (See photo, page 21.)

boxer tumor heart-base tumor seen often in Boxers.

Boykin Spaniel South Carolina breed developed from a dog owned by Whit Boykin; probably of Cocker Spaniel heritage; developed specifically to hunt turkey. The dog stands about 16 inches (41 cm) tall, is mahogany or liver in color, and is an excellent water retriever.

Brabançon dog similar to the Brussels Griffon except that its coat is short. It is seen in reddish brown or black with reddish brown markings.

braccoid dog of the brachycephalic facial type.

brace pair of dogs working together as a team in a contest.

bracelet tuft of hair surrounding a Poodle's lower legs when it is in a show clip.

brace mate each of the dogs in a working pair or brace.

brace work two dogs performing together or competing as a pair, as in herding trials or field trials.

brachial pertaining to the arm above the elbow; anatomical region of the humerus.

brachycephalic skull type manifested by the Bulldog; short, broad muzzle, rounded skull, well-defined stop, and undershot jaw.

brachygnathia shortened mandible, accompanied by an undershot jaw.

Braco Navarro breed first developed in southwestern Spain. It has a short white coat with brown markings. It is used as a gundog.

brady- prefix indicating slow.

bradycardia slowed heart beat.

bradytocia slow birth or parturition that progresses without difficulty.

brain mass of nerve tissue within the cranium that governs conscious and unconscious activity.

brain room indicating a skull of normal proportions, one that is not pinched and narrow. Some breeds of dogs are said to have more brain room because of the shape of their heads.

brake that appendage of a sled used to slow the sled's progress; also known as a drag brake.

bran portion of the outer shell of grain kernels that is often used to furnish the fiber portion of dog foods.

branding imprinting a permanent identification of ownership plainly on an animal, by means of liquid nitrogen or a hot iron.

braques hunting breeds developed as pointers in France. Some have naturally bobbed tails, and were crossed with other breeds to produce this characteristic.

Braque Ariégeois French pointer that stands about 28 inches (71 cm) tall, and is white with orange or chestnut patches and a pink or light brown nose pad.

Braque Bleu d'Auvergne French hunting dog that stands about 24 inches (61 cm) tall, has a dark brown, short coat with blue highlights, and chestnut-colored eyes.

Braque Saint Germain or **German Pointer** French breed descended from pointers and braques. It has a short, fine coat and is white with orange or lemon shadings. It stands about 24 inches (61 cm) tall and weighs about 57 pounds (26 kg).

**Braque
Saint Germain**

Bravo first dog born on the South Pole during Operation Deep Freeze in Antarctica in 1957. Bravo was a Husky-Malamute mix.

Brazilian Dog *see* Azara's Dog.

Brazilian fox *see* Carrisissi.

Brazilian Tracker smooth-coated scenthound from Brazil. It stands about 25 inches (63.5 cm) tall and weighs about 65 pounds (29 kg).

break 1. term for the action of a dog that acts before the handler's command to do so. **2.** normal start of a Greyhound race. **3.** in herding, movement of the dog before the command is given by the handler. **4.** a fold in the ear, as in the Collie. **5.** to train, such as: housebreak a puppy, gunbreak a hunting dog, or harnessbreak a sled dog.

break cover in foxhunting, the sudden leaving of a fox or other quarry from its hiding place.

breaker professional dog trainer.

breaking teaching a gundog to obey its handler's commands.

break out in sledding, to start a frozen-down sled by jiggling it from side to side or slightly moving it.

break up in foxhunting, referring to the action of hounds that eat their quarry.

breastbone sternum, breast plate, or keel bone; ventral bone to which the ribs attach.

breast high describing a scent that hangs above the ground allowing dogs to follow the trail with their heads up and their noses high.

breast plate wide piece of harness that fits over the sternum of a sled dog, and extends between its front legs.

breast plate

breath air taken in and expired with contractions of the chest; respiration.

Bred by Exhibitor Class AKC class in which a dog is shown only by the owner (or member of the owner's family) of the dog's dam when the puppy was whelped. The male and female classes are separated.

bred in purple or **blue** referring to the fact that the dam and sire are of Championship quality and all ancestors in the pedigree are successful show dogs.

breech pertaining to the buttocks of a dog.

breech birth

breech birth whelping presentation in which only the puppy's tail and buttocks are showing.

breeches long hair growth on the upper hind legs.

breeching 1. tan-colored markings on some breeds. **2.** furnishing of long hair on the thighs of the dog.

breeching strap part of a carting harness that runs behind the rump, under the anus of dog. It allows the dog to hold a cart back or slow its progress when traveling down hills.

breeching strap

breed 1. domestic race of dogs of similar appearance and genetic composition that, when bred together, produce offspring closely resembling themselves. **2.** mate dogs, raise, and sell their offspring.

breed club specialty club formed to promote and standardize an individual recognized breed.

breeder 1. one who breeds purebred animals. **2.** owner of a bitch at the time she is bred.

breeders' code of ethics "code" established by some individual breed clubs that includes a list of malformations and degeneracies that should not be permitted to survive.

breeders' terms moneyless transaction by which a purebred bitch is loaned to another party for the purpose of breeding. Various terms are agreed to regarding stud fees, selection of sire, and litter division.

breeding mating of selected parents.

breeding program entire series of events and influencing factors that must be considered when mating dogs.

breeding quality referring to a dog that has sufficient worth and merit to be used in a purebred breeding program; describing a dog that compares favorably with the standard for the breed, in terms of conformation, temperament, showiness, and style.

breeding records documents that relate how a brood bitch or stud has performed previously; may include breeding dates, number of times bred, dates of whelping, number of puppies whelped, survival rate, and their show records.

breeding stock males and females used for breeding.

breeds groups of dogs. There are over 400 known dog breeds in the world. They range in size from over 200 pounds (91 kg) (Saint Bernard), to less than 2 pounds (.91 kg) (Chihuahua), and from over 37 inches (94 cm) tall (Great Dane, and Irish Wolfhound) to less than 8 inches (20 cm) (Toy Poodle).

breed standard detailed description of the breed that is written by breed clubs and published by the AKC; is used in judging the dogs.

Breton Spaniel *see* Brittany.

Brevipilis *see* Pug (Bastard).

Briard AKC group: herding; French dog named for the region of Brie, France, much used as war dog in World War II. It stands about 25 inches (63.5 cm), weighs about 75 pounds (34 kg) and is seen in all solid colors except white, its ears are held high, and its coat is stiff and wavy. It is presently a herding dog and companion.

Briard

brick head describing a skull and muzzle of similar width.

bridge top of the muzzle from the nostrils to the stop.

bridle ropes or lines that run from the dogsled to the gangline ring.

Brie ancient herding dog of the Italian midlands.

brindle or brindling obscure dark streaks on a lighter background, such as black or dark brown streaks on a tawny color.

bring command of the handler to the dog to fetch or retrieve an object.

bring to bag hunting term for shooting the game after a dog has located it.

bring to bay in foxhunting, to catch the quarry.

Briquet Griffon Vendéen wire-haired scenthound from France that stands about 21 inches (53 cm) tall and weighs about 55 pounds (25 kg).

brisk or briskly obedience term for acting keenly alive, alert, or energetic.

brisket breast or lower chest of a dog; anatomical region of the ventral neck line to the sternum.

bristle stiff, short, harsh coat.

British Agility Club c/o John Gilbert, Keba Cottage, 100 Bedford Road, Barton-le-Clay, Befordshire, England, MK454LR.

British Kennel Club 1 Clarges Street, Piccadilly, London, England W1Y8AB.

Brittany

Brittany (formerly Brittany Spaniel) AKC group: sporting; pointing dog that stands about 20 inches (81 cm) tall, and weighs about 35 pounds (16 kg), has a dense flat or wavy coat and few furnishings or feathers. It is frequently born without a tail and its colors are dark orange and white or liver and white. (See photo, page 16.)

Brittany Hound *see* Chien Fauve de Bretagne.

Broadbridge Michael Kent, England Irish Wolfhound; tallest dog ever recorded, at 39½ inches (100 cm).

broad jump

broad jump in agility training, obstacle that is constructed of boards laid on edge, comprising a barrier over which the dog must jump.

brock another name for a badger.

broke down racing term that refers to the action of a dog that pulls up suddenly, as if injured.

broken describing a dog that has been trained.

broken coat rough hair cover that is neither smooth, wire, short, or long. Example: A Scottie has a broken coat.

broken color mixed colors; describing a self-colored dog with the main color broken by white.

broken ear ear that has been damaged and deformed; one that is not standing or being held in a normal attitude; cauliflower ear.

broken pasterns condition of the forefeet in which the ventral ligaments of the carpus are weak, and the toes turn upward; often a sign of poor nutrition and conditioning.

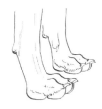

broken pasterns

broken-up face describing a receding nose, deep stop, wrinkled and undershot jaw.

bromelain enzyme supplement derived from the pineapple plant that combats nonspecific inflammation in the dog.

bronchiole fine, tiny, or even microscopic division of the bronchi or airpassages.

bronchitis inflammation of the bronchi that usually causes a cough.

bronchopneumonia inflammation and often an infection of the lungs and terminal bronchi; also called bronchopneumonitis.

bronchoscope fiber-optic instrument used to visually examine the lining of the trachea and bronchi.

bronchus paired, hollow, tubular, air flow channels leading from the trachea to the lungs. The primary bronchus divides to form the secondary, and so forth. The plural of bronchus is bronchi.

bronzing tan coloring that is undesirably mixed with black, resulting in a diluted appearance.

brood bitch female dog kept for breeding and raising puppies.

brood stock sires and bitches used to produce broods or litters of puppies.

broth soup prepared by boiling meat or vegetables, often mixed with dog food to enhance palatability.

brought to their noses foxhunting term that hounds that are made to scent their quarry when it is out of sight.

brow region of a dog's face above its eyes, or the ridge of the frontal bone.

brown dog tick *Rhipicephalus sanguineus*, a one-host tick that infests a dog in each of the three phases of its life cycle.

brown nose faded nares, from natural or dietary cause.

Brown Water Spaniel *see* American Water Spaniel.

Brucella canis rod-shaped bacteria that are highly contagious; usually spread during breeding. They cause brucellosis, a generalized infection that leads to reproductive problems and sterility in dogs.

Brucella titer blood test used to determine the presence of *Brucella abortus* in the bloodstream.

bruise contusion or injury resulting in discoloration due to a hemorrhage within the tissues, caused by blunt trauma without breaking the skin.

bruit abnormal sound heard on auscultation of the heart.

brush 1. coursing term referring to hurdles that are topped with broom straw. **2.** grooming tool made up of multiple bristles or wire pins and attached to a handle. **3.** dog's tail that is heavy with hair, similar to that of a fox.

brushbow the curved front of Arctic sleds. *See* bushbow.

brush hook another name for the snow hook.

brushing action of a dog's pasterns that pass so close that the hair of the legs touch when passing.

Brussels Griffon AKC group: toy; sturdy, reddish brown dog with cropped ears and wiry coat. The smaller variety does not exceed 7 pounds (3.2 kg); the larger size limit is 11 pounds (5 kg). The breed has a short muzzle, and an undershot jaw.

Buansu of Nepal or Buansuah one of the wild dogs of India; close relative of the Dhole. It has a short to medium coat of red, rust, gray, and light brindle colors, and feeds on domestic sheep and goats.

bubo inflammation, swelling, and tenderness of a lymph gland.

buccal pertaining to the inside surface of the cheek that is covered with mucous membrane.

buck 1. stuffed canvas dummy used to train dogs to retrieve. **2.** male deer or stag, a common quarry of early hunting dogs. **3.** in herding, male sheep or ram.

Brussels Griffon

buck

Buck Saint Bernard-Scotch Sheep Dog crossbred hero of Jack London's classic story *Call of the Wild.*

Buddy first Seeing Eye dog to arrive in America from his training kennel in Switzerland. He belonged to Morris S. Frank, in 1928 and was trained by Mrs. Dorothy Eustis who bred dogs for intelligence duties and border patrol work.

buffer agent used to reduce the acidity or alkalinity of a medication.

Bugeilgi *see* Welsh Sheepdog.

bugs *see* ectoparasites, fleas, ticks, lice, and mites.

bulbus glandis vascular structure along the shaft of the penis that engorges, enlarges, and ties the male dog to the female during copulation.

bulimia abnormal increase in hunger.

bulkage inert material that is added to a diet to increase its volume and aid peristalsis in the intestine.

bulla large blister or cutaneous vesicle filled with serous fluid.

Bulldog

Bull and Terrier *see* Staffordshire Bull Terrier or American Pit Bull Terrier.

bullbaiting sport of putting dogs into a ring to attack bulls.

Bulldog AKC group: non-sporting; English breed originally bred for bullbaiting. Standing about 14 inches (36 cm) tall and weighing about 60 pounds (27 kg), it has evolved into a heavy-chested, brachycephalic breed with a short, wrinkled face and an undershot jaw, a smooth coat, thick-set, low-slung body and bowed forelegs. It is seen in red, brindle, solid white, fawn, or piebald colors. (See photo, page 38.)

Bulldog Terrier *see* Staffordshire Bull Terrier and American Pit Bull Terrier.

Bullet Roy Rogers' famous German Shepherd Dog and movie companion.

Bull Mastiff

Bull Mastiff AKC group: working; English breed obtained by crossing the Bulldog and the Mastiff. It stands about 26 inches (66 cm) tall, weighs about 115 pounds (52 kg), has a smooth coat, a large square head, with a flat forehead, pendulant ears, and a long, tapering tail. It is seen in any shade of fawn or brindle.

bull neck 1. heavy, well-muscled neck. **2.** excessive neck musculature.

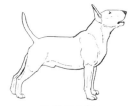
Bull Terrier

bullring enclosure in which bulls were baited.

Bull Terrier AKC group: terrier. There are two types: the all-white and the colored variety. It stands about 22 inches (56 cm) tall, weighs about 40 pounds (18 kg), and was produced originally to fight, catch rats, badgers, and bait bulls. Said to be the strongest of all dogs pound for pound; it has small, close-set eyes, a muzzle without a stop, erect or cropped ears, and a whip tail.

bully heavy, thick, and bulky.

bumping 1. in hunting, flushing a bird before the command to do so is given. **2.** in racing, interfering with another dog during competition.

bunny-hopping gait in which the hind legs are moved in unison.

Burgos Pointer *see* Spanish Pointer.

Burmese Wild Dog wild canine found in Upper Burma. It resembles the wild dogs of Malay, except it is heavier and stronger.

burning scent freshly made scent trail.

burr irregular projection or cartilage formation within the normal ear.

burrow underground lair of a rabbit, badger, or other small animal.

bursa naturally occurring sac containing heavy fluid, usually situated where friction develops, under a tendon, or over a bony prominence.

bursitis inflammation of a bursa.

burst in foxhunting, a particularly fast start of a pack of hounds, or the sudden speed exhibited when a fox is sighted.

burst him foxhunting term to describe when the fox is caught and killed in a burst of speed.

bury rabbit's burrow.

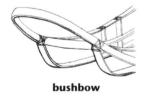
bushbow

bushbow or brushbow prow of a sled; curved structure that is attached to the front of the sled to protect it from trees, brush, and other obstacles.

Bush Dog of Brazil short-legged, short-faced, short-tailed, primitive-appearing wild dog found in small numbers in Brazil.

Butcher Dog or **Cantonese Butcher Dog** *see* Chow Chow.

Butcher's Dogge *see* Bulldog.

Butcher's Dog of Rottweil Rottweiler dog that drove a butcher's herd to market and guarded the butcher's purse that was appropriately tied around the dog's neck. The dog was also harnessed to the butcher's cart to deliver meat.

butterfly nose partially unpigmented nose pad with pink splotches on the nostrils.

Butterfly Spaniel *see* Papillon.

buttock gluteus maximus muscle mass, or in a dog, the derriere.

button ear unusually short ear, folded down in front and close to the head, as seen in the Fox Terrier.

by or **sired by** describing the male parent of the dog. Example: Pal is out of Missie, by Toby.

bye in field, herding, and beagling trials, the odd dog remaining after all other dogs have been paired by a drawing.

by-product substance produced secondarily to the primary product; meat by-products such as cheek meat, diaphragm, tail muscle, and others are used in the production of dog foods.

Bytheuad *see* Welsh Hound.

C

cachexia generalized and profound malnutrition and malaise; wasting away.

cadaver body of a dead animal.

Caesar terrier that belonged to King Edward VII of Great Britain. The dog marched ahead of kings and princes in his master's funeral in 1910.

café au lait coat color that is about the color of coffee with cream.

caffeine bitter white powder that is derived from coffee or tea and used as stimulant.

Cairn Terrier AKC group: terrier; Scottish breed closely related to Scottish Terriers and West Highland White Terriers. It stands about 10 inches (25 cm) tall, weighs about 14 pounds (6 kg), has erect ears and a harsh and profuse outer coat. It is seen in any color except white. (See photo, page 28.)

Cairn Terrier

calamine lotion soothing cream or ointment compounded of zinc oxide and ferric oxide; sometimes used to treat dogs' noninfectious skin conditions.

calcaneus hock, or posterior tarsal bone.

calcification hardened calcium deposits in the internal organs of the body.

calcinosis small deposits of calcium in nodules under the skin.

calculus stone formed of mineral salts within an organ or cavity of the body.

calf bone tibia, one of two bones extending from the stifle to the hock. The other bone is the fibula.

calf knee sloping pastern.

caligo reduced or impaired vision.

call name name by which a dog is known to its family; usually a shortened version of its registered name.

call off agility training term to describe a dog being "called off" by its handler when an inappropriate obstacle is placed in its path.

callous being hardened and thickened or having calluses.

callus 1. thickening of an area of skin over a bony prominence in response to friction, often caused by kenneling on concrete or wooden floors. **2.** mass of exudate and connective tissue that forms around a break in a bone and is converted into bone during the healing of the break.

calmative medicinal preparation that has a sedative or tranquilizing effect.

calorie unit of heat; a small calorie is the amount of heat required to raise the temperature of 1 gram of distilled water 1°C.

calorie requirements for maintenance, a 20-pound (10 kg) dog requires about 740 calories per day; more is required when the dog is being bred, in training, competition, or under the stress of illness or injury.

calvaria cranium or cranial vault; brain case.

calyx cup-shaped cavity such as the pelvic recess in the kidney.

camel coat color that is about the same shade of fawn or tan as a dromedary.

camel back dog's topline that is elevated like a hump, behind the withers.

camel back

Camp beloved dog of Sir Walter Scott (the breed was not identified).

camphor aromatic granular or crystalline compound that is sometimes used in topical medicines and liniments.

Canaan Dog AKC group: herding; breed that looks like a smooth Collie with a curly tail. It stands about 24 inches (60 cm) tall and weighs about 55 pounds (25 kg). It is either solid colored with or without white trim, or predominantly white with a mask of a darker color. The solid color ranges from black to brown, red, or liver. Self-ticking may be present. Descended from the Pariah Dogs of the Middle East, it has thus become linked with Israel.

Canaan Dog

Canadian Kennel Club 111 Eglington Avenue, Toronto 12, Ontario.

canal narrow passage or channel. "The bitch's birth canal was reduced in size due to a previous pelvic fracture."

Canary Dog or **Perro de Presa Canario** powerful mastiff-type dog developed originally for pit fighting; it stands about 25 inches (65 cm) tall, weighs about 106 pounds (48 kg), and its short, coarse coat is usually fawn or brindle with white markings. Introduced to the Canary Islands from Great Britain in the 1800s, it was nearly extinct by the 1960s when dogfighting was banned.

cancellous describing a spongy, latticelike bony structure.

cancericidal capable of destroying cancer cells.

Candida genus of yeastlike fungi that may be pathogenic for dogs.

cane Italian word for "dog."

Cane Corso or **Cane da Macellaio** *see* Sicilian Branchiero.

Cane da Pastor Bergamasco *see* Bergamaschi.

Cane da Pastor Maremmano *see* Maremma Sheepdog.

caniche poodle's generic name, derived from the term meaning "duck-canard"; presently used to designate a Poodle of a size that falls between the Miniature and Standard.

canid member of the family *Canidae*, including wolves, jackals, foxes, coyotes, and domestic dogs.

Canidae the canine family that contains the genera *Canis, Vulpes, Dusicyon* and others, including the African Wild Dog *(Lycaon pictus)*, Bat-eared Fox *(Alpex lagopus)*, Dhole *(Cuon alpinus)*, Maned Wolf *(Chrysocyon brachyurus)*, Raccoon Dog *(Nyctereutes procyonoides)*, Small-Eared Dog *(Atelocynus microtis)*, and the Crab-Eating Fox *(Cerdocyon thous)*.

canine of the Canidae family; pertaining to dogs.

canine adenovirus type 1. infectious canine hepatitis virus.

canine adenovirus type 2. any of several viruses implicated in the kennel cough syndrome.

canine cognitive dysfunction syndrome loss of memory associated with old age; loss of house training; senile forgetfulness.

canine coronavirus pathogenic virus that causes fever, anorexia, diarrhea, and vomiting. It has a high mortality rate in untreated puppies.

canine cough complex tracheobronchitis, or kennel cough; syndrome that includes various contagious viral and bacterial respiratory diseases of the dog.

canine distemper debilitating and often fatal viral disease of puppies and older dogs. In its early phases, it may mimic canine kennel cough, but it often culminates in convulsive seizures.

canine endometrial hyperplasia complex thickening of the lining of the uterus that is seen in bitches that have received repeated doses of female hormones. It is usually accompanied by various other hormonal problems that may include prolonged estrus, sterility, ovarian cysts, uterine infections, and others.

canine erlichiosis tick-borne, often fatal dog disease that is transmitted by the brown dog tick and caused by a rickettsial organism that invades and destroys the dog's red blood cells.

Canine Eye Registration Foundation organization that certifies eye normalcy: South Campus Court, Building C, West Lafayette, Indiana 47907.

Canine Good Citizen Certificate certificate awarded to a dog by the AKC acknowledging that the dog has passed 10 different activities that a Good Citizen Dog is expected to perform, including obedience and good manners.

canine herpes virus contagious causative organism of a specific dog genital infection or venereal disease.

canine hypertrophic osteodystrophy disease seen in rapidly growing puppies; causes lameness and swollen joints.

canine infectious tracheobronchitis kennel cough syndrome.

canine parainfluenza upper respiratory virus of dogs that is involved with the kennel cough syndrome.

canine parvovirus virus causing "parvo," a debilitating and often fatal disease of dogs that is accompanied by vomiting and diarrhea.

canine piroplasmosis infection with a canine red blood cell parasite. *See* babesiosis.

canine tooth first premolar; long grasping tooth or a dog's fang.

canine venereal granuloma transmissible disease manifested by soft tumors in the dog's genital regions; spread by breeding or licking; seen in both males and females.

canine viral rhinotracheitis highly contagious upper respiratory disease of dogs; part of the kennel cough complex.

caninophile lover of dogs; one who appreciates dogs.

Canis genus of the family Canidae.

Canis adustus side-striped jackal of Africa.

Canis alpinus dhole of Malaysia and Indonesia; wild dog that is larger than the jackal, and is a cousin of the domestic dog. It has a tight red coat, and tall, erect ears.

Canis aureus golden wolf or golden jackal; African, southern European, and Asiatic jackal that is smaller than a wolf but larger than a fox; cousin of the dog.

Canis cancrivorus South American wild dog, native to Brazil, Dutch and French Guianas, and Central Argentina. It eats crabs and other shellfish, deer, and agoutis. It is red or brindle with black markings, with a ruff or frill. It looks something like a jackal with the croup higher than the shoulder. This wild dog crosses with domestic dogs.

Canis dingo

Canis dingo near-domesticated Australian dog that is smaller than the wolf, slighter of build, and not nearly as strong. Its legs are long; it stands about 24 inches (61 cm) tall. It is a long-coated bushy-tailed animal of varying colors from yellowish white to black. It frequently has a white tip on its horizontally held tail, white feet, and a black muzzle. It is timid, and not difficult to tame until sexual maturity. There is a controversy over whether it is truly a wild dog or a domesticated dog that has turned feral.

Canis duckhunensis wild dog of Deccan. It has a compressed and elongated head, oblique eyes, and looks something like a Persian Greyhound.

Canis familiaris worldwide domestic dog; garden-variety dog; a purebred or a mutt.

Canis latrans prairie wolf or common coyote of North America.

Canis lupus

Canis lupus or **gray wolf** most common wolf of the United States, Mexico, Canada, and Europe.

Canis magellanicus *see* Colpeo.

Canis mesomelas black-backed jackal of Africa.

Canis microtis *see* Sclater's Dog.

Canis niger red wolf of North America.

Canis nubilus timber wolf; easily crosses with *Canis familiaris*.

Canis palustri genus and species name given to a prehistoric canid that is often referred to as the "peat dog."

Canis nubilus

Canis pellipes pale-footed wolf of India; rare cousin of the dog.

Canis primaevus *see* Buansu of Nepal, a wild dog that hunts by scent and overwhelms its quarry by force.

Canis simensis Abyssinian Kaberu; packing animal closely related to the dog; may be a dog, a wolf, or a fox, depending on the reference one reads.

canish common misspelling of caniche. *See* Poodle.

canker ulceration or infection of the mouth, lips, or ear.

canned food type of dog food that is packaged in cans; has a long shelf life, but is generally more expensive to feed than dry food.

canned meat diet canned dog food that is composed of all meat.

cannibalism propensity of a bitch to eat her newborn puppies; usually the result of crowding.

cannonball racing term for the action of a dog in a desperate drive through the pack, near the finish of the race.

cannon bones metatarsal bones or the bones that extend from the hock to the foot in the hind leg.

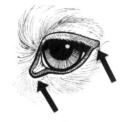

canthus

canter intermediate gait between a trot and a gallop. Sometimes called a short lope; it is an easy gait for the dog and can be maintained for hours.

canthus angle formed by the meeting of the upper and lower eyelids; medial canthus is near the nose; lateral canthus near the ear.

Cantonese butcher dog *see* Chow Chow.

Cão d'Agua *see* Portuguese Water Dog.

Cão de Castro Laboreiro *see* Portuguese Cattle Dog.

Cão Serra da Estréla *see* Portugese Sheepdog.

cap 1. referring to darkly shaded colors appearing on the heads of some breeds. **2.** in scenting, to direct hounds with hand signals.

cape shoulder growth of harsh or long hair.

Cape Hunting Dog or *Lyacon pictus* hyena dog, or South African Hunting Dog; long-legged, Greyhound-sized dog that is colored and marked randomly with splotches of white, fringed with black. It is a packing wild dog that lives in underground burrows.

capelet swelling on the point of the hock or point of the elbow.

Capillaria acrophila lungworm that lives in the bronchial tubes of dogs, causing them to cough.

capillary microscopic blood vessel that connects arterioles to venules.

capped hock bursitis and swelling of the hock area.

capsule 1. soft, digestible container filled with a dose of medicine. **2.** fibrous tissue envelope that surrounds a body structure or an organ. *See* joint capsule, lens capsule, kidney capsule.

capsulectomy excision of a capsule.

Carasissi *see Carius cancrivorus.*

carbohydrates part of a commercial dog food diet that includes starches, sugars, gums, and cellulose.

carbon tetrachloride old, outdated capsule-enclosed vermicide. If the capsule is bitten and the fumes are released, those fumes can be fatal.

carbuncle infection of the skin and subcutaneous tissue by *Staphylococcus* species.

carcinogen substance or agent that can produce or cause cancerous neoplasia.

carcinoma malignant tumor that originates in the epithelial tissues of the body.

cardiac pertaining to the heart.

cardiac output measure of the efficiency of the heart and its ability to circulate the blood.

Cardigan Welsh Corgi *see* Welsh Corgi, Cardigan.

cardiomegaly enlargement of the heart.

cardiomyopathy 1. diseased heart muscle. **2.** inherited heart condition of the Great Dane; sometimes seen in other giant breeds.

cardiopulmonary resuscitation (CPR) technique that is used to restore heart and lung function by manual manipulation; technique in which intermittent pressure is applied on the chest over the heart together with artificial respiration.

cardiovascular pertaining to the heart and blood vessels.

carditis inflammation of the heart.

care command to a dog in hunting to "watch carefully."

cargo bag another name for the sled bag.

Carlin *see* Pug.

carnasial abscess swelling or lesion seen outwardly on a dog's cheek, just under its eye. It sometimes drains through the facial skin, and is caused by an infected, abscessed upper premolar.

carnasial tooth second premolar; shearing tooth.

carnivore animal that normally subsists primarily on the flesh of other animals.

carnophobia abnormal aversion to dietary meat.

Carolina Dog pariah dog similar in appearance to the Dingo. It stands about 22 inches (56 cm) tall, weighs about 40 pounds (18 kg), and is semiwild. It has a dense yellow or fawn coat, and may be related to the dogs of North American Natives. If captured as a puppy, the dog can be trained to herd or hunt.

carotene orange or red pigment found in carrots and other vegetables, a precursor to vitamin A.

carotid paired principle artery of the neck that supplies blood to the brain.

carp back roached or arched back.

carpal joint wrist, or fore pastern; complex joint between the distal ends of the radius and ulna and the metacarpal bones.

carpal pad soft, horny structure similar to the toe pads located on the posterior aspect of the carpus.

Carpathian Sheepdog *see* Rumanian Sheepdog.

carpitis inflammation of the wrist joint.

Carré disease *see* canine distemper.

carpal pad

carriage dog 1. guard dog of the mastiff variety; used in the Middle Ages when travel was dangerous. Many of the dogs were trained to precede the carriage on the road to ward off and give warning of bandits. **2.** *see* Dalmatian.

carrier 1. animate or inanimate object that is able to transmit a disease-causing organism from one animal to another. *See* vector. **2.** portable dog crate.

carrisissi *see Canis cancrivorus.*

carrot tail thick, short, tapering tail.

carry a good head foxhunting term to describe hounds that keep abreast when running the scent line.

carry a line in foxhunting, ability to stay on the line of scent.

carsickness motion illness; nausea or vomiting as a result of the motion of an automobile.

cart in sledding, summer training vehicle with wheels that is used to keep dogs in condition and to train puppies to pull together.

cartilage shiny, elastic material that covers the articular surfaces of joints.

carting using a dog to pull a cart by means of a special harness.

cast **1.** in field trials, search a field dog makes in one general direction without an abrupt turn; **2.** foxhunting term meaning to spread out in search of the scent. **3.** in retriever trials, to send a retriever in search of downed gamebirds. **4.** in hunting, to release a gundog in the field to find birds.

cast back in scenting, to cause hounds to return to the line of scent.

casting the womb *see* uterine prolapse.

cast off in scenting, to release leashed hounds to the hunt.

castor oil quick-acting cathartic; usually causes defecation within two hours. It is highly irritating, and the dosage is critical.

cast out in herding, to send a sheepdog to other side of the flock.

castrate to surgically remove the reproductive organs (testicles) of a male; to perform an orchiectomy.

casts elements in the urine that are created when proteinaceous material is compressed into the tiny tubules of the kidney to form a mold of the interior of that tubule. Some types are found in normal dogs; others are diagnostic of certain diseases.

catabolism negative side of metabolism that involves the breakdown of complex substances into simple substances.

Catahoula Leopard Dog

Catahoula Leopard Dog, Catahoula Hog Dog, or **Leopard dog** the state dog of Louisiana although not a purebred by AKC standards; bred in Southern United States for over a hundred years and used for cattle herding and hunting wild pigs. It stands about 25 inches (66 cm) tall, weighs about 50 pounds (23 kg), and its short coat is a mottled blue color with brown markings.

Catalan Sheepdog

Catalan Sheepdog variety of the Gos d'Atura that originated in the Catalonia region of Spain; long-haired dog that resembles a Bearded Collie. A herding dog that stands about 20 inches (51 cm) tall, and weighs about 40 pounds (18 kg), it resembles the rare Gos d'Atura Cerda, except for its wavy coat that is colored various shades of brown, red, and mahogany.

catalase enzyme found in all body cells that catalyzes the decomposition of hydrogen peroxide.

catalogue list of events and participants in dog show.

catalyst substance that enhances or changes the speed of a biochemical reaction but takes no part in the reaction.

cataract opacity of the lens capsule of the eye. A result of age in nearly all dogs, and a hereditary disease in some breeds.

catarrh discharge and inflammation of the mucous membranes of the throat.

catch command that may be used to alert a dog to an object such as a ball that is being tossed to it.

catechu plant derivative that acts as an astringent; formerly used to treat canine diarrhea and a sore throat.

cat foot small, compact foot with bunched toes.

catlike feet bunched toes with no evidence of spreading. *See* knuckled up.

cattle dog herding dog used principally for working cattle. *See* Australian Cattle Dog.

Caucasian Sheepdog Russian dog bred for its working ability, not its appearance. It stands about 22 inches (56 cm) tall, and weighs about 55 pounds (25 kg), is dark gray, brindle, or brindle and white in color, and has a smooth coat and curled tail.

Caucasian Sheepdog

cauda tail.

caudad toward the tail.

caudal vertebrae bones of the tail-spine.

caudate possessing a tail.

caudectomy amputation or docking of the tail.

cauliflower ear permanently swollen and disfigured ear flap; in dogs, usually the result of encounters with foxes, badgers, and other quarry; a badge of honor in working breeds that is theoretically overlooked in dog shows.

Cavalier King Charles Spaniel AKC group: toy; has a similar background to the English Toy Spaniel, but is a separate breed. It stands about 13 inches (33 cm) tall, weighs about 15 pounds (6 kg), and has a silky coat of moderate length that is shown without trimming. Its colors are either Blenheim, which is white with chestnut markings, ruby which is solid red, or black and tan.

Cavalier King Charles Spaniel

CAV-I current designation for Infectious Canine Hepatitis virus or the disease caused by that virus.

cavity hollow space within the body: abdominal cavity, chest cavity.

CBC abbreviation for complete blood count.

CCDS abbreviation for the canine cognitive dysfunction syndrome; canine senility.

CD 1. abbreviation for canine distemper. **2.** abbreviation for Companion Dog.

CDX in obedience, abbreviation for Companion Dog Excellent.

CEA abbreviation for collie eye anomaly.

cecocolic 1. referring to the physical junction of the cecum and colon. **2.** affecting both the cecum and colon.

cecum blind intestinal sac that is located at the junction of the colon and the ileum. The dog doesn't have an appendix, but the appendix of the human is an outgrowth of the cecum.

CEHC abbreviation for canine endometrial hyperplasia complex.

Centralized Tattoo Registry tattoo-based dog registry; 15870 Allen Road, Taylor, Michigan 48180.

cephalic pertaining to the head.

cephalic index ratio that compares the length of the head to its width.

cephalocadal from head to tail.

cephalopelvic dystocia typical dystocia that is encountered in brachycephalic breeds. The dam's pelvis is very small, and the fetus' head is large, which often prevents normal passage of the puppy through the birth canal.

Cerberus terrible three-headed dog that guarded the underworld in Greek mythology.

cerclage binding together; a bone repair using wire bands. Example: The spiral, oblique fracture was repaired using a set of cerclage bands.

Cerdocyon thous crab-eating South American fox.

Cerberus

cereal edible grain and grain parts that are used in formulating and producing dog food.

cerebellum hind brain; that part of the brain concerned with ordinary living, such as breathing, eating, sleeping, urinating, biting, growling, and coordination of movement.

cerebrospinal pertaining to the brain and spinal cord.

cerebrum largest part of the brain; that portion of the brain that controls positive, willing, conscious actions.

cerumen or **cera** wax or waxy material that is secreted by the glands of the external ear canal; ear wax.

cervical spondylopathy canine wobbler syndrome that is sometimes inherited in Great Danes.

cervical vertebra bones of the spine.

cervix 1. back of the neck. **2.** narrowed aperture of the uterus that communicates with the vagina.

cesarean section delivery of puppies by a surgical operation.

Cesky Terrier or **Bohemian Terrier** medium-sized breed that was developed in Czechoslovakia for hunting. It was used to go to ground for foxes and badgers, and was originally bred from Scottish and Sealyham terriers but is larger than either. It stands about 14 inches (36 cm) tall and weighs about 18 pounds (8 kg).

cestodiasis intestinal parasitic infestation with *Cestoda,* a dog tapeworm.

Ceylon wild dog jackal-like animal that breeds freely with the pariah dogs of the area.

CGC abbreviation for Canine Good Citizen.

Ch in showing, abbreviation for Champion of Record.

chalazion tumor or swelling of a gland of the eyelid; stye.

challenge in foxhunting, the first hound's opening upon finding the scent of the quarry.

chamber enclosed space or cavity, such as the chambers of the eye, or chambers of the heart.

Chambray French breed of hound that is tall and powerful. It is seen in lemon and white colors.

chamois ear soft, thin ear leather.

Champion of Record AKC title awarded to a dog that has won at least 15 points, under three different judges. It must include two or more "major" wins of three or more points each, awarded by different judges.

championship points points awarded for each win; may range from one point to a maximum of five points, depending upon the number of dogs being shown in a class.

chan means "the dog." In ancient Persia, Chan was the symbolic appellation of the spirit of gentleness and wisdom.

change in foxhunting, when the dogs leave one scent trail for another.

chap droopy jowl; one with deep flews.

character individual nature, temperament, or personality; the manner in which stresses are handled by a dog.

characteristic 1. said of a physical or personality trait that is typical of an individual dog. **2.** said of predictable traits of a breed collectively. Example: The colors and pattern of my Dalmatian are characteristic of the breed.

charcoal 1. pulverized carbon used as a universal antidote for poisons. **2.** color of Poodles and other breeds that are dark gray, nearly black.

Charlie Chaplin feet feet that turn away from each other.

Charlie's Hope Terrier *see* Dandie Dinmont Terrier.

Charnéque *see* Evissenc.

chase reflex innate, instinctive reflex of puppies to pursue moving objects.

Chase, The periodical pertaining to hounds; 152 Walnut Street, Lexington, Kentucky 40507.

chasing in field trials, running after flushed birds (a serious fault).

Chastek paralysis thiamin deficiency caused by feeding a dog raw fish in relatively large quantities (raw fish contains a vitamin B_1 inactivator).

check 1. in foxhunting, the dogs' temporary loss of the scent trail. **2.** to stop a dog's progress with a quick jerk of leash.

check collar choke collar or chain collar.

check cord or **check line** in field trials, a long cord that is fastened to a dog and used to check, or stop, the dog.

checked in racing, describes a dog that slows or hesitates during the race.

checkpoints periodic stops along a sled race course where the dogs are examined, supplies are picked up, and injured or ill dogs are left.

cheek walls of the oral cavity.

cheeky having thick, well-developed masseter or chewing muscles.

cheer in foxhunting, a cry that is given to encourage the hounds.

cheilitis inflammation of the lips.

Cherami favorite Greyhound of King Louis XI.

cherry eye inversion of the third eyelid or nictitating membrane that exposes the gland of the third eyelid (Harderian gland).

cherry nose unpigmented nose pad.

Chesapeake Bay Retriever AKC group: sporting; water retriever that originated in the United States. It stands about 23 inches (58 cm) tall and weighs about 80 pounds (36 kg) and is a powerful breed with great strength and stamina. It is a solid-colored dog that ranges from reddish brown to dead grass with a wedge-shaped head and a short, thick, double coat that is water-resistant. (See photo, page 15.)

chest 1. external anatomical region of the thorax or ribs. **2.** cavity that contains the thymus, lungs, heart, and related structures.

chestnut rich reddish brown color.

Cheviot Terrier original name for the Dandie Dinmont Terrier that was renamed for a character in Sir Walter Scott's novel *Guy Mannering*.

chewer dog that has developed the bad habit of chewing or biting objects other than its toys; destructive and expensive pet.

chews nearly indestructible nylon or plastic products that are made for dogs to chew.

chew sticks treats for dogs made of rawhide strips that are twisted and dried.

Cheyletiella yasguri large parasitic mite that is often seen on puppies, and causes itching, dandruff, and a scaly skin.

chick embryo vaccine viral product grown in hens' eggs to attenuate or reduce the virulence of the virus.

chien French word for "dog."

Chien Canne *see* Poodle.

Chien Courant de Bosnie à Poil Dur descendant of the old Celtic Hound; remains mainly in the area formerly known as Yugoslavia. It was used to hunt wild boar and lesser game. It varies in color from white or fawn to gray.

Chien Courant de la Vallée de la Save Yugoslavian-bred hound of yellow or red color with white markings. It has a loud, bell-like bay and is used to hunt small game.

Chien d'Artois descendant of the Saint Hubert Hound; resembles the Foxhound. It is believed to be the ancestor of many other French breeds. It is tricolored with a saddle of gray or fawn.

cherry eye

Chesapeake Bay Retriever

Chien de Berger Belge Malinois *see* Malinois.

Chien de Berger des Pyrénées *see* Pyrenean Sheepdog.

Chien de Malet *see* Maltese.

Chien de Montagne des Pyrénées *see* Great Pyrenees.

Chien de Saint Hubert smooth-coated scenthound that stands about 26 inches (66 cm) tall and weighs about 100 pounds (45 kg). *See* Saint Hubert Hound.

Chien de Vacher *see* cowherd's dog.

Chien Écuriel *see* Papillon.

Chien Fauve de Bretagne originated in Wales and was introduced to Brittany where it was used for wolf and boar hunting; probably extinct today. It stood about 34 inches (86 cm) tall, had a medium coat, and was fawn, wheaten, red, or gray colored.

Chien Français Blanc et Noir

Chien Français Blanc et Noir large French breed. It stands about 26 inches (66 cm) tall and is seen in colors of white and black, white and orange, and tricolored. It is used to hunt boars and deer.

Chien Français Tricolore

Chien Français Tricolore French hound kept originally for deer hunting. It was mixed with English Foxhound blood to increase its speed in hunting. The breed is consistently tricolored, with long, folded ears, like the Celtic Hound.

chigger larva of the harvest mite that is a temporary, opportunist parasite of dogs.

Ch'ih Hu or **Red Tiger** Persian dog that was given the rank and privileges of a duke by the Emperor of China in 565 A.D.

Chihuahua AKC group: toy; smallest dog shown, sometimes standing only 8 inches (20 cm) tall and less than 6 pounds (2.7 kg). It has an apple-domed head and full eyes and is shown in smooth-coated and long-coated varieties. (See photo, page 32.)

Chihuahua

Chihuahua Club of America, Inc. 5019 Village Trail, San Antonio, Texas 78218.

Chika smooth-coated gazehound from China that is seen in two sizes: 20 inches (51 cm) and 24 inches (61 cm) tall.

Chile fox *see* Colpeo.

chills *see* shivering.

chin jaw, mandibular, or mentum region of the head.

china eye iris that is usually a clear blue color, but sometimes is flecked or spotted light blue or white, as is found occasionally in blue merle Collies or Australian Shepherds; synonymous with watch eye.

Chin Chin *see* Japanese Chin.

Chinese Coolie Dog spitz-type dog; possibly a cross between the Akita and the Chow Chow. Its height is about 20 inches (51 cm), its weight is about 45 pounds (20 kg), it is white with lemon markings, has a coat that is close and coarse, pendulant ears, and a sickle tail.

Chinese Crested Dog AKC group: toy; probably related to the hairless dogs of Mexico and Africa. Its body is totally hairless except for a tuft on top of the head. Its skin colors are pink with red or blue flecks or spots, slate-blue, blue-mottled, pied, or all white. There is also a second variety of the breed that is called the "powder puff" and is totally haired. Both varieties stand about 12 inches (30 cm) tall, and have erect ears. The powder puff is seen in any combination of colors.

Chinese Crested Dog

Chinese Fighting Dog longhaired northern-type dog from China that stands about 17 inches (43 cm) and weighs about 40 pounds (18 kg).

Chinese Greyhound native to the Kansu and Shensi districts of China, and used for coursing. It is bred in two sizes: larger is slightly smaller than the English Greyhound; smaller is between the Italian Greyhound and the Whippet. The colors seen are yellow to chestnut, with a white front, and it has a short coat and large, semierect ears.

Chinese Greyhound

Chinese Hairless Dog *see* Chinese Crested Dog.

Chinese Hound native to Kashmir; is similar to the Greyhound, but considerably heavier. The breed is scarce and may possibly be extinct. It was bred to hunt in packs and used principally on wild boar.

Chinese Pug *see* Happa Dog.

Chinese Shar-Pei AKC group: non-sporting; Oriental breed that stands about 19 inches (48 cm) tall and weighs about 50 pounds (23 kg), has bluish black or lavender-colored oral mucous membranes, a harsh coat, and is seen in any solid colors. The most outstanding characteristic of the breed is a profusely wrinkled, loose skin over much of the body. (See photo, page 37.)

Chinese Shar-Pei

Chinook freighting sled dog of great stamina; not a pure-bred. The type is found over much of the North where

Huskies are bred for their ability rather than their looks. One of the rarest of breeds according to the *Guinness Book of Records*, it was used on the Byrd expeditions to Antarctica. It stands about 26 inches (66 cm) tall, weighs about 90 pounds (41 kg), and is tawny in color.

Chippendale front chair-legged; bowed elbows with toes turned outward; bench-legged.

Chippipari Hound smooth-coated sighthound from India that stands about 29 inches (74 cm) tall, and weighs about 65 pounds (29 kg).

chiseled head describing clean definite facial lines.

chlorinated hydrocarbon poisoning condition caused by contact with a household insecticide; may be absorbed through the skin, especially in puppies, or may be inadvertently consumed. The signs in the dog: hyperexcitability, exaggerated responses to stimuli, and twitching of muscles, followed by tonic-clonic convulsions similar to those seen with strychnine poisoning.

chloroform colorless volatile liquid with strong anesthetic properties.

chlorophyll tablets pills that contain the green photosynthetic pigment found in plants; produced as a deodorant and used to moderate the odor of a bitch in heat. They do not prevent pregnancy.

chocolate coat color that ranges from dark fawn to rich brown.

chocolate poisoning reaction to theobromine, a chemical derivative of the kernels of the cacao plant that is a stimulant and is present in chocolate. In large quantities, chocolate is toxic to dogs.

choke 1. foreign body or lump of undissolved dog food or other substance that has become lodged in the dog's esophagus before reaching stomach. **2.** a respiratory interruption caused by an obstruction or compression of the trachea.

chokeboard nose referring to a dog with exceptionally keen scenting powers.

choke collar chain collar used for training that, when properly applied, does not choke the dog; a check collar.

Choken *see* Shishi.

cholecystitis inflammation of the gallbladder.

choleric describing an evil-tempered, irascible dog.

cholesterol lipid that is found in all animal fats but is absent in all vegetable fats.

choline vitamin found in many vegetable and animal-origin foods; important constituent of dog foods.

cholinesterase enzyme found in all normal body tissues. A cholinesterase-inhibitor is present in many insecticides and plays a dynamic role in dog poisonings with those insecticides.

chondritis inflammation of the cartilage of joint surfaces.

chondrodysplasia abnormal growth of the cartilage of long bones.

chops pendulous upper lips or flews that are seen in the Bulldog and some hounds.

chordectomy removal of a dog's vocal folds; surgical debarking.

chorea convulsive disorder; jerky, involuntary movements of a dog's body that are related to canine distemper.

chorion covering of a zygote or embryo in the formation of the placenta.

chorioptic mite parasitic skin mite of the dog; *Chorioptes*.

choroid brown-colored vascular part of the eye that is located between the sclera (white) and retina. It contains the vessels that carry nutrition to the retina and lens.

Chortay purebred Russian coursing dog that is heavier than the Greyhound and stands about 25 inches (63.5 cm) and weighs about 55 pounds (25 kg).

chortle subdued sound produced by the barkless Basenji.

Chow Chow AKC group: non-sporting; Chinese-origin dog that stands about 18 inches (46 cm) tall, weighs about 70 pounds (32 kg), and is square and well-proportioned. Seen in smooth or rough coats, and is solid-colored red, black, blue, cinnamon, or cream. The mucous membranes of the mouth and tongue are pigmented black or dark blue. It was originally used to pull carts, as a guard dog, and its flesh was often consumed by humans. (See photo, page 38.)

Chow Chow

chronic interstitial nephritis inflammation of the tissue within the kidney; a common disease of old dogs.

chronic obstructive pulmonary disease emphysema; a breakdown of lung tissue that is debilitating and virtually incurable.

Chrysanthemum Dog *see* Tibetan Terrier.

chrysanthemum tail Pekingese deformity in which the tail is held to form a full circle or "wheel" on one side.

Chrysocyon brachyurus *see* Aguara-Guaza.

Chrysocyon jubatus South American maned wolf; its puppies resemble foxes. The adults have extremely long legs.

Chukchi Dog spitz-type dog found in the Arctic coastal region of Siberia; nearly extinct ancestor of the Siberian Husky.

chunky head short, thick head.

chute

chute 1. in sledding, the fenced area at the beginning of a race that starts the teams onto the correct trail. **2.** the fabric extension of a tunnel that makes up one of the obstacles in an agility trial. *See* closed tunnel.

chyle lymph and emulsified fat from intestinal digestion that is transported into the venous system.

chylothorax abnormal presence of lymph within the chest cavity.

chyme digested food; creamy, semifluid material found in the intestines.

Ci Sawdl *see* Welsh Corgi, Pembroke.

cicatrix scar tissue that is formed in wound healing; a drawn, constricted scar.

Cicero's dogs dogs written about by the famous philosopher Cicero some 2,000 years ago. He wrote of the affection, keen hunting ability, and protective qualities of dogs.

ciliary pertaining to eyelashes or other fine hair or hairlike appendages.

ciliated having a fringe of hairs or hairlike appendages.

circuit referring to dog shows that are held in relatively close proximity to one another.

circuit champion in showing, a dog that earns its AKC Championship points in a minimum number of shows in a single circuit.

circuit shows multiple dog shows in the same place or nearby places within a minimum time period; shows organized to facilitate the winning of Championship title (with a good dog) in a minimum period of time with a minimum of driving.

circumanal gland series of small oil-secreting glands that surround the anus, immediately below skin of a dog; not the same as the anal sacs.

Cirneco dell'Etna Sicilian hound built somewhat like a Greyhound that originated in the volcanic region of Mount Etna. It stands about 19 inches (48 cm) tall, has a short coat of light tan or sand color, and enormous erect ears.

Cirneco dell'Etna

cistern lymph reservoir. *See* lymphatic system.

clap on in scenting, to put hounds on the quarry's scent.

class 1. competitive group of dogs, similar in experience, that are entered in a show, exhibition, or obedience trial. **2.** in field trials, a dog's bird sense, speed, range, style, and stamina; attribute of a dog that takes advantage of the wind, responds to the handler's commands, locates its quarry accurately, and is staunch and steady. **3.** taxonomic category between phyla and order.

class dogs in showing, dogs entered in the Puppy, Novice, Open, Bred by Exhibitor, and American-Bred classes of either sex.

claudication limping, or lameness.

clavicle collarbone. It extends from the shoulder to the sternum in the human and avian skeleton; a vestigial structure in the dog.

clean cheeks describing a lack of droopiness of the masseter muscles; minimal jowls.

clean eye tight, well-fitting eyelids without sagging; absence of ectropion, entropion, or wrinkles.

clean head no flews or excess lip tissue.

clean shoulders free of sag and excess skin in the upper forearm.

cleavage first cell division of a zygote to form an embryo.

cleft lip unjoined upper lip; central fissure of the upper lips that occurs congenitally in some newborn puppies.

cleft palate appearance of a central longitudinal split; lack of normal union of the palate in some newborn puppies.

clinic 1. animal hospital or veterinarian's outpatient office. **2.** discussion of a particular phase or discipline of dog training or care by a professional for the benefit of others; instructional class that is given by an expert.

clinical signs overt symptoms of a diseased animal that are visible or palpable.

clip type of trimming, pattern, or style, such as a "Dutch clip" on a Poodle.

clipped referring to ears that have been shortened by surgery. *See* ear clip.

clipped keel short sternum, or breastbone.

clitoris small erectile, highly vascular structure in the forepart of the vulva.

cloddy lacking elegance; built low and cumbersome.

clone replica or nonsexual reproduction of an individual; progeny of a single cell rather than two gametes.

clonus spasm of rigidity, followed by relaxation, in rapid succession; a sign of epilepsy in the dog.

close describing legs that brush the opposite legs when moving; legs that pass so near as to brush one another.

close-coupled short in the loin or back.

closed tunnel in agility trials, an obstacle with a rigid opening about 20 inches (51 cm) in diameter, with a long cylindrical chute of fabric about 12 feet (30 cm) long. The dog must enter the rigid opening, then burrow through the tunnel.

close hound dog that will stay on scent and never waver.

closely set ears ears that have pinna or leathers that lie tight to the head.

Clostridium genus of spore-forming, rod-shaped, pathogenic bacteria.

clot coagulation of blood or lymph; accumulation of blood cells, platelets, and fibrin.

clown face having different colors on opposite sides of the face.

Clumber Spaniel AKC group: sporting; heavy, powerful spaniel that stands about 20 inches (51 cm) tall and weighs about 75 pounds (34 kg). It has a massive head and square jaws, its coat is dense, and it is colored white with lemon or orange markings.

Clumber Spaniel

Clydesdale Terrier small terrier from Scotland that is thought to be an ancestor of the Yorkshire Terrier.

CNS abbreviation for the central nervous system, which consists of the brain and spinal cord.

coach dog *see* Dalmatian or carriage dog.

coarse describing a dog with heavy features that is ungainly and lacks quality or refinement.

Coast Guard dog one of the German Shepherd Dogs adopted by the U.S. Coast Guard and the U.S. Navy during World War II as their "official dogs," and that served on many of their ships.

coat hair covering over a dog's body; type of hair covering or quality of the hair.

cobby short body; compact; well-muscled and having well-sprung ribs; stocky, blocky conformation.

coccidioidomycosis fungal disease of the lungs, liver and kidneys, caused by *Coccidioides*; also known as valley fever or San Joaquin valley fever.

coccidiosis microscopic protozoan infection of the intestinal tract that often causes diarrhea. *See* isospora.

coccus spherical bacterial cell, such as steptococcus or staphylococcus.

coccygeal pertaining to the coccyx, the terminal vertebrae of the spinal column; pertaining to the tail.

coccygectomy surgical tail amputation or docking; caudectomy.

cochlea spiral-shaped bony labyrinth of the inner ear that is the seat of hearing.

cocked ears **1.** prick ears. **2.** body language of pendulant-eared dogs that indicates increased alertness.

cocked tail tail that is carried gaily.

cock his leg male dog's physical attitude for urination and urinary marking, a learned characteristic that is sometimes seen in female dogs and occasionally in cats.

Cocker Spaniel AKC group: sporting; shown in three color varieties: ASCOB (any solid color other than black), parti-color, and black. It has a short body, is about 15 inches (38 cm) tall, weighs about 28 pounds (13 kg), with well-laid-back shoulders, a long neck, and a heavy, silky, wavy, or flat coat. It is shown trimmed. (See photo, page 13.)

Cocker Spaniel

Cocking Spaniel early name for the Cocker Spaniel.

cod liver oil frequently used dietary supplement for dogs that is derived from fish liver; usually contraindicated due to the possibility of providing a vitamin D excess.

coin tail tightly curled tail.

coitus mating act; copulation.

cold-blooded dog dog that appears to be purebred but has no pedigree or proof of registration or lineage.

cold line in foxhunting and scenting, a faint scent trail that has deteriorated due to age.

cold nose old wives' tale that supposes a cold nose to be a sign of good health. Unfortunately, cold noses are sometimes seen in dogs with high fevers, and warm noses are found in normal dogs. *See* Noah's dog.

cold scent in foxhunting and scenting, the ability of a dog to follow a cold line.

colic any acute abdominal pain; abdominal pain of unknown cause.

coliform having the general form and character of *Escheria coli* bacteria.

colitis inflammation of the colon.

collagen supportive protein substance contained in skin, tendon, bone, and cartilage.

collapsing trachea birth defect seen in small dogs that causes coughing and labored breathing.

collar 1. band of leather, nylon, or metal that encircles the neck and is used for identification or restraint of a dog. **2.** in obedience training, a chain, nylon, or leather slip collar that is used in exhibition. **3.** contrasting color of the neck coat in some breeds, such as the Collie or Boxer.

collar harness in sledding, padded leather harness that resembles a draft horse collar that is used on some sled dogs, mainly freighters.

collateral ligaments strong, fibrous bands located on either side of a joint that function to stabilize the joint and hold the bones of the joint in normal apposition to one another.

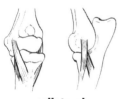

collateral ligaments

colley breed of Scottish black-faced sheep; probable origin of the word "collie," which designates sheep-herding dogs.

Collie AKC group: herding; shown as rough or smooth-coated dogs. It stands about 26 inches (66 cm) tall and weigh about 70 pounds (32 kg), and is shown in colors of sable and white, tricolor, blue merle, and white. The rough coat is abundant, with a heavy mane and frill. Collies have a flat skull, a long, narrow muzzle, no stop, and ears that break forward in a semierect position. (See photo, page 40.)

Collie

Collie Club of America 1119 South Fleming Road, Woodstock, Illinois 60098.

Collie Club of America Foundation Inc. 47 Wicks End Lane, Wilton, Connecticut 06897.

collie eye anomaly inherited deformity of the Collie's eye that is present at birth; includes retinal ectasia, a degenerative condition of the retina.

collie nose scabby, irritated lesion that sometimes occurs on the dorsal surface of the muzzle of Collies and Shetland Sheepdogs and is the result of a lack of pigment in the tissues. It is thought to be an inherited sensitivity to the sun; also called solar dermatitis.

colon section of large intestine that extends from the cecum to the rectum.

colony group of rigidly controlled, experimental dogs that are kept for feeding trials or other investigative purposes.

color blindness inability to differentiate colors. Dogs are believed to be color blind, and only perceive black, white, and shades of gray.

color breeding mating dogs in an effort to produce puppies of some particular color or combination of colors.

color clearing age when a dog's coat coloration becomes defined. The Dalmatian is born nearly white, as are some of the blue merle dogs.

Colored Working Terrier *see* Lakeland Terrier.

colostrum milklike fluid secreted by a dog's mammary glands immediately after whelping. It is rich in protective antibodies and provides vital nutrition to puppies.

Colpeo or *Canis magellanicus* large wild dog that resembles a wolf; common wild dog of Bolivia, Ecuador, Chile, and Patagonia. It has a dense coat that is colored red, tipped with darker shades, and a long bushy tail with a black tip. Fearless of man, it possesses great speed and is a nocturnal hunter, feeding on small deer, rodents and poultry.

Colpeo

coma absence of normal responses in a living organism; profound unconsciousness.

come bye or **go bye** herding command to move the dog clockwise around the livestock, circling to the left.

comedo plug of sebum in a skin duct or pore of the face, that sometimes becomes infected. It often contains demodex mange mites.

come gee or **come haw** in sledding, driver's command to the lead dog to change the course of the sled and make a right-angle turn to the right (gee) or left (haw).

come-home dogs some dogs in Yorkshire, England, that are trained to always return to their masters, and are thus called come-home dogs. This was the original meaning of the title of the movie *Lassie Come Home*.

Comforter *see* English Toy Spaniel.

coming on showing an improvement in training.

command verbal order from a handler to a dog to perform a particular maneuver.

command leader in sledding, a lead dog that has been trained to follow voice commands from the driver.

commercially available obtainable from pet supply stores, pet shops, drug stores, or grocery stores; for sale over the counter, without a prescription.

comminuted fracture bone that has been fragmented into several pieces.

common describing a dog that appears coarse and lacks refinement.

communal pad large footpad situated behind the toe pads that carries most of the dog's weight.

communication bell single bell or a string of bells that are placed within reach of the dog, usually near a door. The dog is taught to ring the bell when it wishes to go outside.

compact describing a body that is joined together firmly and tightly.

compact coat one that lies close to body; opposite of a "fly-away" coat.

compact foot cat foot or an arched foot with the toes bunched.

companion animal contemporary designation used instead of "pet" when describing a dog or cat that is kept basically for human companionship.

companion dog man's best friend; any dog, whether purebred or not, that serves as a friend for a human.

Companion Dog in obedience, a title awarded to a dog for having completed the Novice class requirements successfully.

Companion Dog Excellent in obedience, highly coveted title awarded to a dog that has successfully completed the requirements of the Open class.

compensation counterbalance of the weight of the body in order to rest or minimize the use of an injured limb.

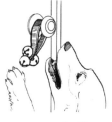

communication
bell

competitive spirit in field trials, a good dog's ace in the hole; a dog's ability to overcome its fear of an audience, concentrate on its work, and perform well in a field trial away from home.

compound commands more complex directions that are given to a trained dog, or commands that have two or more objects: *"Tinker, go to the door and bark."* Those commands may be used only after the dog has mastered each of the commands individually: *"Go to the door,"* and *"bark."*

compound fracture bone break in which the skin is torn and the bone fragments are exposed; fracture in which fragments of the bone have penetrated the skin.

compression fracture broken bone in which the broken ends of the bone are forced upon one another in an overriding fashion.

compression plating surgical technique of fracture repair that involves the use of bone plates that force the broken ends of the bone together.

computer chip identification proof of the ownership of a dog by means of a tiny computer chip that is implanted under the dog's skin with a special needle.

conception fertilization of an ovum by a sperm cell, and the resultant zygote formation; beginning of an embryo.

conditioned reflex involuntary response to a natural or learned stimuli.

conditioning getting into the finest state of health possible; includes proper nutrition, adequate exercise, regular grooming, and a good general attitude.

condyle rounded bony projection.

conformation form and structure of a dog as compared to the breed standard.

congenital diseases deformities present at birth, whether hereditary or not.

congestion accumulation of blood or fluid in the body's tissues.

Congo Bush Dog *see* Basenji.

Congo dogs or **wild dogs of the Congo** feral dogs that are not related to the Basenji. They hunt in large packs and are powerful animals with the fortitude to tackle lions and elephants.

Congo Hunting Terrier *see* Basenji.

conjunctiva mucous membranes that line the inner surfaces of the eyelids.

conjunctivitis inflammation of the conjunctiva.

constipation retention of feces in the colon; inability to defecate and evacuate the colon.

contagious describing a disease that can be transmitted from one animal to another.

continental clip style of poodle trim.

contusion bruise with damage to underlying tissue without breaking the skin.

convalesce to recover from an illness or injury; to attain good health and grow strong.

convex describing a rounded, elevated surface.

convolution rolled together; a tortuous folding of tissues.

convulsion series of violent, involuntary muscular contractions; uncontrolled fit of muscular activity.

cooling out racing term for the controlled exercise that follows a race.

Coomb's test specialized blood test used to assist in the diagnosis of autoimmune hemolytic anemia.

Coonhound *see* Black and Tan Coonhound.

co-ownership two or more persons being listed on a dog's AKC registration as the owners of a single dog.

COPD abbreviation for chronic obstructive pulmonary disease, more commonly known as emphysema.

copro- denotes anything to do with feces.

coprophagia eating or feeding upon feces, disgusting habit of some dogs that may be brought on by continuous confinement and boredom.

coprostasis plugged bowel; bowel obstruction; constipation.

copulating lock *see* tie breeding; action of a male and female dog that are naturally locked together during the act of coitus.

corded coat allowed to grow into long, uncombed dreadlocks, as seen in the Komondor.

corded Poodle any Poodle with a coat that is allowed to grow unhindered and form long, cylindrical, ropelike cords; sometimes known as a curly Poodle.

corgi Celtic word for "dog." *See* Welsh Corgi, Pembroke, or Welsh Corgi, Cardigan.

corded Poodle

corium true skin or the dermis.

corker eye-catching dog of lively demeanor.

corky 1. referring to a dog that is compactly built. **2.** lively, alert, bright dog.

cornea clear, transparent, foremost part of the eyeball that is surrounded by the sclera or white of the eye and joins with it at the limbus.

corneal dystrophy "spots" on the transparent cornea; nondebilitating acquired condition of the eye.

cornu- prefix meaning "horn-shaped projection." Example: The uterus of a bitch is a bicornuate organ.

corona virus causative organism of a serious, sometimes fatal, systemic disorder of dogs that also has gastrointestinal signs, such as diarrhea and vomiting.

corpus luteum literally means "a yellow body"; the scar that remains after an ovum (egg) is released from the ovary. The canine corpus luteum secretes progesterone.

coryza acute catarrhal condition of the mucous membranes of the nasal sinus that produce a copious discharge.

cosmetic surgery plastic surgical intervention to correct conditions in dogs such as ectropion, entropion, tail fold dermatitis, lip fold dermatitis, and others. Dogs that require such plastic surgery should not be shown or bred.

Cosmopolitan Canine Carriers professional pet travel agent; 5 Brook Street, Darien, Connecticut 06820.

Coton de Tulear breed that is primarily a housepet in its native city of Tulear in southern Madagascar. It stands only about 12 inches (30 cm) tall, and weighs less than 10 pounds (4.5 kg). Appearing something like the Maltese with not as much hair, its single coat is profuse and cottony white with yellowish markings on its head.

coucher dog used to drive game birds into a net.

couple 1. to copulate or breed. **2.** in foxhunting, paired dogs or a brace of dogs.

coupled in foxhunting, two dogs that are held together by collars while hunting.

coupler in foxhunting, two leather buckle-collars that are joined by a chainlink or two with a swivel in the center; used to fasten two hounds together.

couplings anatomical region of the torso or trunk, that is situated between the limb joints. Example: Dachshunds are long in the couplings.

couplers

course 1. in foxhunting, to chase or follow by sight rather than by scent. **2.** in herding, and agility trials, a designated pattern of obstacles through which a handler directs the dog. **3.** to hunt with sighthounds or gazehounds.

course delay delay caused by handlers who are not ready to start the course; delay caused by hounds that break away from and avoid their handlers.

courser racing term for a dog that runs from side to side on the track like a coursing dog that is trying to head off the hare.

coursing in lure field trials, a coursing race consists of one, two, or three gazehounds that pursue a lure that is either mechanical or electrical and, that is driven over a selected pattern.

coursing dogs sight dogs or gaze dogs that are used to hunt hare or antelope as well as wolves.

coursing field coursing term for a fenced area that is about 450 yards (411 m) long and 150 yards (137 m) wide. Penned hares are kept at one end, and at the other end, escapes are available for hares that are not caught.

cover hair guard coat; outer coat of a double-coated dog.

covert or cover in foxhunting, the woods where a fox is sheltered.

covey in hunting, a number of game birds hiding together.

cow-hocked having hocks that turn inward with the toes turned outward.

cowlick hair that grows in a whorl, and does not lie flat; the reverse pattern of hair on the head of a Rhodesian Ridgeback.

coxa pelvic side of the hip joint; the pelvic "socket" that holds the head of the femur.

coxofemoral joint hip joint, composed of the acetabulum (socket in the pelvis) and the ball, or head of the femur.

coydog hybrid cross between a coyote and a dog.

coyote or *Canis latrans* prairie wolf. The only true wild dog of North America that is found on most prairies and in the mountains of the country, it runs in small packs or families, feeds on poultry, small rodents, amphibians, and birds, and has been known to take newborn lambs and calves. It has a long, reddish brown, gray, or gray and fawn coat, and is smaller than the wolf.

coyote

CPRA central progressive retinal atrophy, an inherited eye disease that affects the pigment cells in the center of the retina. The mildly affected dog is unable see stationary objects, but perceives movement.

crabbing 1. walking sideways like a crab, moving with the body at an angle; tracking to one side, or side-winding. **2.** sledding term for a sidewise movement that is often taken to avoid interference; usually seen at a trot.

crab-eating dog *see Canis cancrivorus.*

craniad anterior; toward the cranium or head.

cranial cruciate ligament another name for anterior cruciate ligament of the stifle.

craniomandibular osteopathy abnormally large jaw and distorted temporal bones of the skull; "Scottie jaw."

cranium skull or brain vault.

crank sharp bend in the tail.

crank-stern screw tail; short, twisted tail.

crash in foxhunting, the pack of hounds giving tongue together upon finding a fox or the hot scent of a fox.

crating confining a dog to a carrier or other small pen or confinement.

cream light yellowish color.

creatinine nitrogen-containing end product of metabolism, the blood levels of which measures kidney function in the dog.

cremaster muscle fibers of the scrotum that draw the testes into the scrotum as a male grows.

crepitus abnormal crackling or grating sound heard or palpated when the ends of bones rub together.

crest arched neck topline.

crisis turning point in the course of a disease.

Croatian Sheepdog Yugoslavian herding breed that stands about 22 inches (56 cm) tall and weighs about 50 pounds (23 kg). It is black with white spots and has a typical long coat and sheepdog conformation.

crooked in obedience, describes a dog that is not straight in line with the direction the handler is facing.

crooked mouth abnormality of the facial bones in which the teeth don't match; a "tipped" mandible that holds the teeth at an angle; wry mouth.

crop to surgically remove a portion of a dog's ears. *See* ear cropping.

cropped referring to ears that have been surgically shortened or trimmed to make them stand erect.

cropper in foxhunting, a bad fall.

cross bite *see* wry mouth.

cross-eyes eyes that point toward the plane of the nose instead of straight ahead; convergent strabismus.

crossbred describing a dog with parents of dissimilar breeds.

crossing over having a gait in which the front feet pass over one another in a weaving pattern with elbows twisting and toes going outward; undesirable gait.

cross-over also known as the dog-cross or the cross-walk. In agility trials, an obstacle that is a 2-feet 8-inch (81-cm) square, 4-foot (122-cm) table with narrow ramps hinged to each side. The judge determines which direction the dog will enter and exit from the obstacle.

cross-over

cross-track scenting term for a more recent scent that passes over the trail being followed.

croup region of the body immediately anterior to the root of the tail, adjacent to the sacrum, and above the hind limbs.

crowding in obedience, a dog that moves so close to its handler as to interfere with the handler's freedom of motion.

crown 1. dorsum of head, or the topskull. **2.** part of a tooth that reaches above the gums.

cruciate ligaments two crossed ligaments within the stifle joint that allow a rocking action between the femur and tibia.

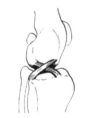
cruciate ligaments

Cruft's Dog Show largest dog show in the world, with entries of more than 10,000; held in February in London. It began in 1886.

cry, voice, or **tongue** in foxhunting, the sound that a hound makes when trailing or running a quarry.

cryogenic branding means of identifying dogs by freeze-branding an initial or symbol on their bodies; usually makes use of liquid nitrogen to cool the branding iron. *See* liquid nitrogen.

cryptococcosis systemic fungal disease of dogs' lungs that is caused by *Cryptococcus*, a genus of yeastlike organisms.

cryptorchid male animal that has neither testicle in his scrotum, both being retained in his abdomen.

Ctenocephalides canis genus and species name of the common dog flea.

Cuban Bloodhound large and ferocious cross between the Dogue de Bordeaux and the Bloodhound; possibly extinct breed that was previously used for hunting fugitives in Cuba.

cub hunting in foxhunting, hunting early in the season, when cubs, or young immature foxes, may be found.

cull 1. to weed out the weak or undesirable puppies of a litter. **2.** to reduce the numbers of breeding stock by eliminating the poor performers.

culotte feathery hair on the backs of the forelegs as seen on the Pomeranian.

Cumberland Sheepdog herding dog that is nearly extinct; was found in the Cumberland, Westmorland, and Peak districts of England. It stands about 22 inches (56 cm) tall, and weighs about 50 pounds (23 kg), and is black with a white blaze.

cunnilinction licking the vulva, a habit of the female dog in season.

Cuon alpinus dhole of Asia.

cur 1. Celtic word meaning "to watch over something," that was used originally to refer to watch dogs. **2.** dog of unknown parentage or one whose parents were of questionable lineage.

cure successful treatment of a disease.

curette scraper; process of scraping projections from wall of a cavity.

Curly-Coated Retriever AKC group: sporting; favorite hunting dog in New Zealand. It stands about 24 inches (61 cm) tall, weighs about 80 pounds (36 kg), and is black or liver colored with a tightly curled coat and a moderately short, tapered tail. It works well in water or on land, and excels in diving for wounded ducks.

Curly-Coated Retriever

curtain 1. fringe of hair hanging over the eyes in some breeds. **2.** escape hole at the end of the race into which the artificial hare darts.

Cushings syndrome *see* hyperadrenocortism.

cushion fullness or thickness of the upper lips; appearance of padding of the upper lips that is seen in the Mastiff and Bulldog.

curtain

Customs dogs canine detectives that sniff out contraband, explosives, and drugs at border stations.

cut in herding, the number of sheep used in a trial, and separated from the flock by the dog.

cut back in field trials, movement of a dog toward the handler after being cast.

cute in coursing, showing cleverness in coursing the hare.

cutis epidermis or outer layer of skin.

cutting back in field trials, casting toward the handler after a forward cast has been made.

cut up arched, elevated, or raised.

cyanosis blue coloration of the mucous membranes and skin due to a lack of oxygen in the tissues.

cynegenics science or study of the dog.

cynic means literally "like a dog." From the Greek word *kuon*, meaning "dog," "cynic" was coined to apply to a doglike sneering expression.

Cynodesmus one of two lower Miocene period "dog" evolutionary lines. The progeny of these dogs are supposed to be the American and European dogs, wolves, and foxes, through the genus known as *Tomarctus*. *See Miacidae.*

Cynodictis long-bodied, short-legged dog-like animal of Miocene period.

cynology study of the origin of dogs.

cynophobia morbid fear of dogs.

Cynopolis "City of Dogs," founded in ancient Egypt, and built in honor of the dog.

Cyon deccanensis *see* Indian Wild Dog.

Cyon primaevis *see* Buansuah.

Czechoslovakian Pointer gundog of considerable value; similar to the German Wirehair Pointer. It is brown and white.

Czesky Fousek hunting breed developed in Czechoslovakia. It stands about 26 inches (66 cm) tall, weighs about 75 pounds (34 kg) and has a rough-textured coat with a soft, thick undercoat. It was crossed with the German Shorthaired Pointer in the 1930s and resembles the German Wirehaired pointer in color.

D

Dachsbracke German bloodhound breed that exists in two varieties: one under 13 inches (33 cm), the other between 13 inches and 16 inches (41 cm) tall; common colors are black with red markings, brown with light streaks, and yellow-red. Somewhat resembling the Dachshund, it is used for hunting hares and foxes and has been known to take on a boar.

Dachsbracke

Dachshund AKC group: hound; German hunting breed developed to dig out badgers and pull them from their dens. This dog is short-legged, long-bodied, and is shown in three coat varieties: smooth, wirehaired, and longhaired. It is also shown in two sizes: miniature, 11 pounds (5 kg) and under, and standard, 16 to 32 pounds (8 to 15 kg). (See photo, page 17.)

Dachshund

Dachshund paralysis herniated disc syndrome; paresis (partial paralysis) or total paralysis of the hind legs that occurs spontaneously in the Dachshund breed. This disease may have a hereditary predisposition.

dactyl toe or digit.

Daiargi *see* Welsh Terrier.

Daisy movie star dog. Rennie Renfro, a professional dog trainer, bought the mongrel (named Spooks) for $2.00 at a pet show, and trained her for the *Blondie and Dagwood* movies. She is also the intelligent little mutt in the *Blondie* comic strip by Young and Drake.

Dalmatian AKC group: non-sporting. Its origin is unclear but it had an early association with Gypsies. It bears the name of Dalmatia, a region of Yugoslavia. Also known as the firehouse dog, coach dog, or carriage dog, it stands about 22 inches (56 cm) tall, weighs about 55 pounds (25 kg), and has a short coat with distinct markings of clearly defined black or brown spots on a pure white background. It is said to have a great memory and is used as a war dog, draft dog, shepherd, bird dog, circus dog, trail hound, retriever, and occasionally for stag hunting. In recent years, it has been made popular by Disney movies. (See photo, page 35.)

Dalmatian

dam mother or female parent of puppies.

dander small scales from the skin, sebaceous glands, and hair of dogs.

**Dandie Dinmont
Terrier**

Dandie Dinmont Terrier AKC group: terrier; from the British Isles. Its height is about 10 inches (25 kg), with the length of its body nearly twice its height. Its weight is about 20 pounds (9 kg), it is a sturdy dog with a silky coat and muscular body, and it appears in two colors, pepper and mustard.

dandruff abnormal scaling of the skin, often caused by *Cheyletiella* mites in puppies.

Danish dog *see* Great Dane. It was misnamed, since it sprung from Tibetan Mastiff origins and was developed in Germany.

Daphaenus doglike animal the size of a coyote with a massive skull and very long tail; said to have lived in the Miocene period and thought by many to be an ancestor of the domestic dog.

dapple inherited coat color that is determined by a single or multiple dominant gene or genes. The characteristic is expressed as a mottled or variegated pattern, with neither ground color or marking predominating; seen in the dachshund.

Darjeeling Terrier *see* Tibetan Terrier.

Dartmoor Whisht Hounds legendary hounds in a British folktale that were said to contain the spirits of unbaptized children, doomed to hunt forever.

Dash Charles Lamb's favorite dog that was of mixed heritage.

data collection of facts relating to a subject.

Davie President Woodrow Wilson's Airedale Terrier.

daylight distance from a dog's chest to the ground.

DD *see* Draft Dog.

DDD U.S.D.A. designation for dead, dying, and diseased, a term used to identify the origin of meat and meat by-products used in dog food. This category of meat must be cooked at high temperatures. Most DDD meat is used in inexpensive canned dog food.

dead in hunting, command to wait before retrieving birds.

dead dog elementary "trick" taught to dogs in which they lie down on their backs and remain very still for a few seconds.

dead game total commitment to the fight; term once used in pit dogs, now used to describe terriers of extreme courage.

deadgrass color of a Chesapeake Bay Retriever that is fawn, tan, or light brown.

deaf lacking the ability to hear; may be congenital in dogs; affects one out of ten Dalmatians and occasionally blue merle dogs.

deafness loss of hearing due to trauma, disease, or heredity. Genetic deafness occurs most often in Dalmatians and blue-eyed white dogs, and is common in old dogs of every breed.

dealer buyer and seller of dogs bred by others. Pet shops are dog dealers.

debark performance of a surgical operation that renders a dog incapable of barking. It involves removing all or a major part of the animal's vocal folds.

Deccan wild dog wolf-sized wild dog similar to the Buansu of Nepal. *See* Indian Wild Dog.

deciduous temporary. Example: A puppy's deciduous teeth are shed before maturity and replaced by permanent teeth.

decline **1.** to turn downward. **2.** to tend toward a weaker health condition.

decubital ulcer pressure sore occurring mainly over bony prominences in old or debilitated dogs that is caused by constant or frequent positional pressure.

deep brisket or **deep chest** chest that reaches below the level of the elbows.

deep-flewed having heavy folds of the upper lips. Early Beagles were separated into two classes: deep-flewed and shallow-flewed. The shallow-flewed were said to be the fastest but the deep-flewed were the surest and had more musical voices.

deep in the heart having a deep brisket or a large heart girth.

deer tick tiny, almost imperceptible tick that has wide distribution in the United States; biological vector for the transmission of Lyme disease.

defecate to empty the bowel; to pass feces from the bowel.

defect imperfection. A birth defect is a congenital imperfection.

defense reaction instinctive behavior related to self-protection from injury.

deferens referring to the vas deferens or ductus deferens; a tube that carries semen from the epididymus, located on the testicle, to the urethra.

deficiency abnormal absence of something usually found in an animal's makeup, its diet, or its environment.

degenerative pannus progressive vascularization and pigmentation of the cornea; inherited condition that is seen in German Shepherd Dogs and other breeds and leads to blindness if not treated; also known as pigmentary keratitis or keratitis pigmentosa.

degree 1. unit of temperature measurement. **2.** various titles, such as the obedience awards are referred to as degrees. Example: My dog has just earned his CDX degree.

dehydrate to remove water or natural fluids from the body.

delayed shot in field trials, when a handler flushes the bird being pointed, he then delays his or shot to gain more control over the dog.

delegate dog club's representative to the AKC.

deliver to whelp; to remove a fetus from the dam during parturition.

delousing removal of lice from the body; application of chemicals to a dog to destroy lice; use of an insecticide dip.

Delta Society, The dog organization; P.O. Box 1080, Renton, Washington 98057.

demasculinize to remove the male characteristics.

Demerol® proprietary name for meperidine hydrochloride, an analgesic and sedative commonly used on dogs.

demodectic mange skin disease caused by *Demodex canis* mites; also known as red mange or black mange.

Demodex canis genus and species name of an alligator-shaped microscopic skin mite that infests the hair follicles of dogs; often seen in young dogs that are under stress; causes hair loss, itching, scaling, scabbing, and localized skin inflammation.

demulcent soothing, oily ointment used to treat abrasions and burns.

demyelination destruction or removal of the myelin sheath of nerves; seen in certain hereditary conditions of dogs.

den in foxhunting, home of a fox or its burrow.

den bark in foxhunting, peculiar cry of hounds when a fox is run to earth.

dendrite branched projections of a neuron or nerve cell.

denning instinct propensity of a dog to look for and appreciate the seclusion of a den, such as an enclosed crate.

dental cavities caries; holes in the enamel of teeth, a condition rarely seen in dogs.

dentine inner material of teeth; layer immediately under the enamel.

dentition canine tooth development and eruption. In the dog, there are 12 deciduous incisors that erupt at four to five weeks of age, three on each side, six in the upper jaw and six in the lower. Behind them are four deciduous canine teeth, one on either side, in the upper and lower jaws that erupt at about the same time as the incisors. The 12 deciduous premolars erupt about a week later, and are positioned behind the canines, three on each side, in the upper and lower jaws. They complete the set of 28 deciduous or milk teeth. At about three months of age, the central incisors are replaced by permanent teeth. The four permanent canine teeth are often the last to appear, and typically are not visible until about six months of age. Permanent premolars begin to erupt at about four months of age. There are four on each side, on both the upper and lower jaws, and the rearmost is usually visible by six months of age. Those 16 permanent teeth take the place of the 12 deciduous premolars. The two upper molars on each side and three lower molars on each side also begin to appear at about four months, with the last of the ten erupting at about six months. Those 42 teeth make up the permanent set of adult teeth.

depth of chest measurement of the chest's expansion, judged at the plane of the elbow.

derby 1. in field trials, a bird dog not yet 30 months of age. **2.** field trial Beagle less than one year old. **3.** field trial class for Novice dogs.

derby stakes in field trials, competition for dogs not yet 30 months old.

derby year in field trials, the year of a potential field trial dog between 18 months and 30 months of age.

Dermacentor genus of ticks responsible for tick paralysis; serve as a vector for tularemia in dogs.

dermoid cyst abnormal hair-filled cavity in the skin that is lined with hair follicles that exhibit active hair growth.

determination in foxhunting, the will to try and try again; personality that is dominated by perseverance.

Deutsch Dogge *see* Great Dane.

Deutsche Jagdterrier German hunting terrier similar to the old-type Welsh Terrier, but black with red or yellow markings. It stands about 16 inches (41 cm) tall and weighs about 22 pounds (10 kg).

devil dog term applied to the Rottweiler as a result of its appearance in the film *Damien*.

devouring dog Egyptian mastiff-type dog that was the "soldier's dog." These dogs were set upon the fleeing enemies to harass, overtake, and kill them.

dewclaw inside toe on a dog's legs that corresponds to the human thumb; vestigial digit that doesn't touch the ground or bear weight.

dewlap loose skin hanging under the neck of a dog.

deworming destruction or removal of intestinal parasites.

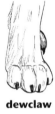

dewclaw

Dhangari Sheepdog smooth-coated herding dog from India that stands about 19 inches (48 cm) tall, and weighs about 26 pounds (12 kg).

Dhole wild dog of India, sometimes called *Canis scylax*; others have named it *Kolsun*, while others refer to it as the *Wah*; *see* Indian Wild Dog.

diabetes insipidus metabolic disorder manifested by a voracious appetite accompanied by a loss of strength; symptoms are thirst, hunger, and emaciation; caused by changes in the production of *vasopressin* hormone that is secreted by pituitary gland.

diabetes mellitus deficiency of insulin production by the pancreas; inability of body tissues to use insulin; results in an elevated blood sugar, sugar in the urine, thirst, hunger, and emaciation.

diabetic pertaining to diabetes; animal suffering from diabetes mellitus.

diagonals right front and left rear legs, or left front and right rear. Example: In the trot, a dog's diagonals move simultaneously.

diamond mark that is sometimes seen on a Pug's forehead.

diaphragm complex, flat, thin, expansive muscle that internally separates the thorax (chest) from the abdomen (belly).

diaphragmatic hernia tear or opening in the diaphragm that allows abdominal viscera to enter the thorax.

diarrhea frequent liquid or semiliquid passage of feces.

DIC abbreviation for disseminated intravascular coagulopathy, in which small blood clots form rapidly within vessels throughout the body. DIC often occurs in response to shock or an overwhelming systemic disease and is frequently fatal.

dicumarol product that is a natural anticoagulant originally obtained from spoiled, sweet clover hay. It is the principal component of some rodenticides and is often the cause or supposed cause of dog poisonings.

diehard another name for the Scottish Terrier.

diestrus third phase of the estrous cycle of a bitch during which pregnancy occurs; formerly called metestrus.

diet formula, quantity, and frequency of food that is provided; dog's ration.

dietary indiscretion consumption of foods or substances that are not normally fed to the dog.

dietary therapy to control or stabilize a diet as a tool to assist in treating diseases.

diethylcarbamazine one of several heartworm preventive medications.

diethylstilbestrol synthetic hormone that has potent estrogenic properties.

dig out to follow quarry into a hole and retrieve it.

digital pertaining to a toe or digit.

digits toes; terminal appendages of limbs.

diluent liquid that is added to a dry solid product to create a solution that can be injected. Example: Dog vaccine usually comes in two parts, one a freeze-dried solid, the other a diluent.

dimorphism property of having two forms or colors.

dingo *see Canis dingo.*

dip concentrated insecticide solution into which a dog is submerged to rid it of fleas, ticks, and other ectoparasites.

di-phenthane (Teniathane®) vermicide used in a treatment for tapeworms that digests and expels the worm.

diploid having the normal cellular number of chromosomes. *See* haploid.

dipped back topline that is concave between the croup and withers.

dipping snow in sledding, team dog taking an occasional mouthful of snow while moving to combat dehydration. Sprint racers are discouraged from dipping because it disrupts the team.

dipping snow

dipsesis intense thirst or a craving for water.

Dipylidium caninum most common tapeworm of dogs. It uses the flea as its intermediate host.

directly an obedience term for immediately; without deviation or hesitation.

dire wolf skeleton taken from La Brea tar pits in Los Angeles, assumed to be a prehistoric ancestor of the dog.

Dirofilaria immitis canine heartworm, transmitted by mosquitoes. The larvae reside in the dog's peripheral blood vessels and the adults live in the chambers of a dog's heart.

Dirofilaria immitis

dirty dog infidel; unclean human being.

discharge excretion of abnormal fluid.

dish-faced having a concavity of the face from the nares to the stop.

dishing dog's gait wherein the forefeet move outwardly in an arc.

disinfect to free from infection or contamination by use of a chemical or heat.

disinfectant agent that destroys pathogenic microorganisms.

disk or **disc** circular or rounded plate of cartilage that acts as a cushion, or shock absorber between two vertebrae. *See* intervertebral disk.

dislocation displacement of a bone from a joint.

display behavior body language used by a dog to show dominance or submission: raising its hackles, rolling over onto its back, showing its teeth, or smiling.

disqualify 1. in herding, a judge's decision to end the run because the competing dog has attacked a person. **2.** in showing, a judge's decision to deprive a dog of an award and change the placement of winners.

disqualifying fault fault considered so serious as to disqualify the dog from competition.

distal remote from a point of reference, the opposite of proximal. Example: The digits are distal to the elbow.

distemper highly contagious, usually fatal, canine viral infection that is especially devastating to young puppies. If not fatal, the infection may cause lifelong disorders.

distemper teeth teeth with mottled enamel, the result of canine distemper infection that occurred before the permanent teeth erupted.

distichia or distichiasis two rows of eyelashes, one or both of which are turned inward against the eye.

districhiasis two hairs growing from a single follicle.

divergent hocks barrel hocks; bowed hind legs.

divergent strabismus opposite of cross-eyed; eyes focusing away from the plane of the nose.

divided find in field trials, the situation in which two dogs point the same birds and the judges are unable to determine which dog had the first point. Each dog is credited with a divided find.

divided placement in field trials, division of the purse between two dogs that seemed to perform equally in third place.

divine dog Turkish dogs that in times past were considered sacred and roamed unmolested (and unfed) through the streets of Constantinople. The primitive peoples of that country substituted dogs for people in their religious sacrifices.

DMSO dimethylsulfoxide, a topical antiinflammatory agent used for treatment of soreness in many working dogs. It has the unique ability to assist the absorption of other products that are applied with it.

Doberman cardiomyopathy inherited Doberman Pinscher disease characterized by pulmonary and cardiac signs.

Doberman Pinscher AKC group: working; powerful Germanic breed named for the home province of Herr Karl Louis Dobermann. The dog stands about 27 inches (69 cm) tall, has a smooth, slick coat that is black, blue, red, or fawn (Isabella), with rusty brown markings, and its ears are usually cropped and the tail is docked. (See photo, page 22.)

Doberman Pinscher

dock to amputate the tail surgically to a length specified by the breed standard.

dog 1. *Canis familiaris* or any of the domesticated varieties of the Canidae family. **2.** male of the *Canis familiaris* species.

dog and pony show elaborate public relations exhibition.

dogbane tropical family of plants that are often poisonous.

Dogbert educated, tie-wearing, sarcastic, and cynical canine in Scott Adams' comic strip *Dilbert*.

dog biscuit hard, dry, cracker-type baked dog food.

dog box sledding term for a truck or trailer that is rigged with compartments for each dog and is used to haul the sled team from one competition to another.

dog box

dog bread poor-quality or old bread that is "fit only for dogs."

dog cage restraint used at dog shows to house entrants.

dogcart lightweight wheeled vehicle designed to be drawn by dogs.

dogcatcher official whose job it is to catch and incarcerate stray dogs.

dog cheap purchased or able to be bought for a very low price.

dog churn butter-making device that is turned by a dog walking on a treadmill or turnstile.

dogcart

dog collar 1. device placed around a dog's neck for restraint. **2.** clerical collar. **3.** snug fitting lady's necklace.

dog-cross agility term; *see* crossover.

dog days midsummer period from about July 3 to about August 11 when dogs were thought to be more susceptible to rabies (an old wives' tale).

dogdom world of dogs. Example: The greatest show in dogdom is the Westminster.

dog drop in sledding, point along the race course where injured or ill dogs may be left to be picked up by race officials.

dog-eared 1. describing the turned-down corner of a page of a book. **2.** appearing shabby and unkempt.

dog-eat-dog ruthless self-interest competition; no-holds-barred contest such as those seen in pit fights.

dogface soldier in World War II, especially an infantry-man.

dog fancier one who pursues an active interest in canine activities.

dog fancy appreciation of dogs and their attributes.

dog fennel weed that grows naturally along U.S. highways.

dogfight **1.** pit fight between two matched dogs. **2.** any conflict involving one-on-one combatants, fighting to the death; used to describe fighter planes' combat tactics.

dogfish bottom-feeding shark.

dog flea *see Ctenocephalides canis.*

dog flesh Kansas Indians believed that eating dog flesh before a battle gave them courage.

dogflower daisy.

dog fox male fox.

dog gauge oval ring, 7 by 5 inches (18 × 13 cm) in diameter, used to measure lapdogs to exempt them from knee cutting. *See* knee cut or toe cut.

dogged followed closely; hunted; stalked; tracked like a hound tracks its quarry.

doggedly stubbornly; behaving obstinately like an ill-mannered dog.

doggerel **1.** vaudevillian comedy that is loosely styled or irregular. **2.** trivial pursuit of an inferior nature. **3.** verse that makes no sense.

doggery cheap tavern or dive that is inhabited by people who have "gone to the dogs."

doggie stray calf; orphan calf in a range-cattle herd.

dogging hunting or shooting with retrievers, pointers, setters, or spaniels.

dogging it slacking or loafing in the workplace; always seeking shade, like a lazy dog.

doggish acting doglike; showy and stylish, as in a dog show; putting on the dog.

doggone common slang or euphemism for the blasphemous "God damn."

doggy **1.** dog fancier. **2.** resembling a dog. **3.** inferior product.

doggy bag container used for the extra portion served in a restaurant, presumably to be taken home to the family dog.

doggy door small opening or flap-covered entrance into a home by which the dog enters and leaves at will.

doggy panties elastic britches designed for a female dog to prevent carpet soiling, when she is in heat.

doghouse 1. kennel for housing dogs. **2.** any small house or building, whether built for dogs or not. **3.** expression for a person who is discovered in a state of disfavor with his wife or mother or employer: "in the dog house."

dog in the manger from the fable in which a dog lay on the oxen's hay and refused to allow the cattle to eat; guarding something one doesn't need or can't use.

dog it to fail to do one's best; to goldbrick, like a lazy dog.

dog killer man employed to kill stray dogs during summer to prevent rabies.

dogleg 1. abrupt angle, like a dog's hock joint. **2.** crook in the fairway of a golf course: dogleg to the left, dogleg to the right.

dog louse *Mallophaga spp.*

Dog Mart Day celebration of an event in Fredricksburg in 1698 when the Indian leader Powhatan declared a truce to trade Indian furs, gold, and handcrafts for the settler's hunting dogs; still celebrated annually with many canine activities.

dog match organized dog fight.

dogmatism positive, arrogant, assertion of an opinion.

dog measure showing term for a portable gauge used to measure certain dogs at a show to be sure that they are not too tall or short to meet the standard.

dog measure

dog meat flesh of animals, used in making dog food.

dog museum AKC museum in St. Louis Missouri that contains relics and artifacts relating to dogs.

dognap to steal a dog and keep it for a reward.

Dogo Argentino fighting breed that came from Europe to South America in the early 1900s. Standing about 27 inches (69 cm) tall and weighing about 100 pounds (45 kg), it is solid white in color with a few dark markings on the head and its coat is short, thick, and straight. It was developed for pit fighting but later became a hunting dog. It includes the blood of the Bulldog, Bull

Terrier, Mastiff, Great Dane, Pointer, Boxer, Dogge de Bordeaux, Irish Wolfhound, Great Pyrenees, and Spanish Mastiff. This dog is used to hunt large game and will face a 400-pound (181 kg) boar or a cougar.

Dog of Java also known as Dog of Sumatra and Golden Wolf; found on Malay Islands; ranging in color from tan-red to brilliant brown.

Dog of Procris dog that belonged to Diana, the goddess of hunting in ancient mythology. *See* Lelaps.

Dog of Sumatra *see* Golden Wolf or Dog of Java. When domesticated, these dogs have a great fondness for fruit.

Dog of Quirinal *see* Italian Volpino.

dog paddle human swimming stroke similar to a dog's swimming style, using all four limbs.

dog pit ring or pit in which dogs were placed to fight.

dog plague old, seldom-used term for canine distemper.

dog puncher sledding term for one of the Yukon freighters who drove dog teams during the Gold Rush.

dog run fenced enclosure used to confine dogs out of doors.

Dogs and Show Dogs periodical, 257 Park Avenue South, New York, New York 10010.

dog's chance slimmest possibility of success.

dog's death miserable, shameful demise.

Dogs for Defense forerunner to the famous K9 Corps that trained more than 10,000 dogs to serve with American troops in World War II.

dog show usually refers to a conformation show; any exhibition of controlled, judged dog events.

Dogs in Canada dog fancy periodical published by Apex Publishers, 89 Skyway Avenue, No. 200, Etobicoke, Ontario, Canada M9W6R4.

dogsled vehicle mounted on runners, pulled by a team of dogs in harness and used for transportation in snow country.

Dogs of Mahudes, The Cervantes' satire in which two dogs, Scipio and Berganza, spend the night chatting about crime and punishment.

dog soldier enlisted man in the infantry of the United States.

dog star Sirius, the star that appeared shortly before the annual overflowing of the Nile river.

Dogsteps AKC video on canine structure and movement.

Dogs USA canine periodical; P.O. Box 6040, Mission Viejo, California 92690.

dog tag 1. military serviceman's identification tag that is worn on a chain around the neck. **2.** small imprinted metal tag that attaches to a dog's collar, identifies the wearer as a legally licensed pet, and indicates that an annual fee has been paid. **3.** identification tag with dog owner's name, address, and telephone number. **4.** rabies tag, indicating that the dog is currently vaccinated for rabies.

dog tail superstition among early southern farmers claimed that if you cut off your dog's tail and buried it under your door stoop, the dog would never leave you.

dog that bites the hand that feeds it expression of contempt for a person who accepts favors from someone, then speaks ill of the benefactor.

dog tick *see* brown dog tick.

dog tired fatigued, worn out, exhausted, bushed, as a dog that has been hunted overlong.

dogtooth 1. fang, or canine tooth; long grasping tooth, or eyetooth. **2.** archictectural ornament.

dog track place in which Greyhound or Whippet races are held.

dog tribe in Chinese mythology, a race of Chuan-jung barbarians, whose chief was exceptionally formidable.

dogtrot easy human gait between a walk and run, similar to the natural gait of dogs moving with minimal effort.

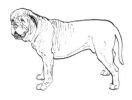

Dogue de Bordeaux

Dogue de Bordeaux mastiff-type dog bred in France for fighting; also pitted against bears, bulls, and wolves. It stands about 23 inches (58 cm) tall, weighs about 100 pounds (45 kg), and has a bulky head, with folds of skin across the muzzle, closely cropped ears, and a smooth coat of tawny, golden, or red fawn.

dog walk in agility trials, plank that is 12 inches (30 cm) wide, 12 feet (3.6 m) long, and elevated from the ground about 4 feet (10 cm). It has ramps at either end with longitudinal cleats at 12-inch (30 cm) intervals.

dog warden *see* dog catcher.

dog watch 1. night shift. **2.** two-hour evening watches on shipboard.

dog wolf adult male wolf.

dogwood North American hardwood tree.

Dog Works, Inc. manufacturer of dog carts and accessories; RR3, Box 317, Curvin Circle, Stewartstown, Pennsylvania 17363.

Dog World periodical; 10060 West Roosevelt Road, Westchester, Illinois 60153.

dog yard sledding term for the tie-out area or kennel area where sled dogs are kept when not working.

dolichocephalic skull type long, narrow, pinched skull.

domed or **domed head** convex, evenly rounded top skull as seen in the Cocker Spaniel.

domestication derived from the Latin word *domesticus* meaning "having to do with the home." There have been many books written speculating on how and when the first dogs were domesticated. Konrad Lorenz stated that people and wolves began hunting together, and found the association to be mutually advantageous. Wolf Herre proposed that wolves were kept caged as a source of food and gradually released from captivity when they showed a talent for guarding the camp. Erik Zimen suggests that young wolves were used to keep infants clean and warm; therefore they were treated with respect.

dominance assertive characteristics of a dog and its influence over other dogs.

dominant alpha dog of a pack that displays a behavior superiority or dominance over other dogs of the pack, and exerts a ruling influence.

domino reverse facial mask.

donor individual organism that supplies living tissue or material to be used in another body, such as a dog that furnishes blood for transfusion.

Don the Newfoundland dog in a Charles Dickens story, *My Father as I Recall Him.*

dormitory effect canine phenomenon in which a bitch in season causes other bitches in the kennel to also come into estrus.

dorsad toward the back.

dorsum back and upper part of the body; upper surface of an appendage

double bar jump

double teeth

down

double in foxhunting, when the fox turns back on its course.

double bar jump in agility training, an obstacle made of two parallel bars, situated one over the other, for the dog to jump.

double coat fine undercoat of some dogs that is combined with a harsher outer guard coat.

double-curled tail one that is tightly curled.

doubled up situation that occurs when the same ancestor appears on both the dam and the sire's side of the pedigree.

double handling 1. in herding, attempt to control the competing dog by a person other than the handler, from outside the exhibition ring (grounds for disqualification). **2.** in showing, attracting a show dog's attention from ringside.

double lead sledding team led by two dogs.

double marked retrieve in retriever trials, when two birds are downed at once and are retrieved on a single command.

double neckline in sledding, short line that extends between the collars of the double lead dogs.

double registration case of a dog that is registered in both UKC and AKC and can be shown in either registry's shows.

double teeth second row of teeth that occurs when the deciduous teeth don't loosen and fall out and the permanent teeth have erupted.

down command for the dog to lie down for three minutes in the Novice class with handlers across the ring, and for five minutes in the Open class with handlers out of sight.

down-charge in field trials, activity of a dog that interferes with another dog's birds in a field trial.

down-faced describing a dog's nose tip that is located well below the level of the stop due to a downward inclination of nasal bone.

down in pasterns having weak-appearing carpal-metacarpal joints or metatarsal-tarsal joints, usually a conditioning fault.

draft in foxhunting, to dispose of surplus hounds; to remove extra hounds from a pack.

draft dog dog used to carry or pull burdens.

Draft Dog abbreviated DD; title awarded to dogs competing successfully in single draft test competitions.

Draft Dog trial judged competition in a special course involving dogs that are trained to pull carts.

drag in foxhunting, **1.** an artificial line. **2.** a scent left by a fox returning to its den. **3.** in scenting, scent trail laid by a quarry.

draghounds in scenting, dogs that are trained to follow an artificial scent line.

drag hunting or **drag races** in scenting, starting young hounds to trail and to tree by laying a trail with a dragged hide or pelt on which a few drops of anise oil has been sprinkled.

Dragon Dog *see* Pekingese.

Drahtaar brown-colored, wiry-coated pointer from Germany. It stands about 25 inches (63.5 cm), weighs about 65 pounds (29 kg), and has bushy eyebrows and beard.

draught in sledding, large dogs that are used to haul freight or heavy passenger loads.

draught dog *see* draft dog.

draw **1.** in field trials, a command to a dog to move on the game cautiously. **2.** in field trials, a random selection to determine the sequence in which dogs in a field trial will compete. **3.** to search for a fox in a given cover. **4.** in coursing, random drawing to determine the order in which the hounds will run. **5.** to find birds by scent alone, without seeing where they fell.

drawer action abnormal sliding action of the stifle that occurs when the anterior cruciate ligament in a dog's stifle is torn or stretched.

drawing up coming close to a downed bird.

drawn-up loin concave or tucked abdomen; usually a sign of a lack of condition.

dreams experts tell us that dogs manifest fond dreams by making guttural noises and body motions as if running (the lucky dogs probably have no nightmares).

drench measured portion of liquid medicine poured into a dog's mouth.

Drentsche Partrijshsond ancient retriever breed, native to the Drentsche province of Holland. It stands about 24 inches (61 cm) tall, weighs about 50 pounds (23 kg), and is white with a cinnamon head and orange ticking.

Drentsche Partrijshsond

Drever

dress to groom a dog for a show or exhibition.

dressing bandage or wound covering.

Drever Swedish hunting dog that resembles a Dachshund; effective on hare, fox, and wild boar. It stands about 14 inches (36 cm) tall, weighs about 33 pounds (15 kg), and has a thick coat. All colors are acceptable providing that white is included.

drive 1. in hunting, propensity of a gundog or hound to perform at its best. **2.** power of a dog's hind legs.

drive bow in sledding, another name for the handlebow.

driving in herding, moving the livestock away from the handler, with the dog between the stock and the handler.

drooping hindquarters sloping croup.

drop 1. in hunting or field trials, a command to cause the dog to lie flat. **2.** command to release an object that is carried in the mouth.

drop completely *down* position that would be acceptable for a *long-down* exercise.

drop ear pendulant ear that hangs close to face, as seen in most hounds.

drop on recall in obedience training, exercise limited to Open classes. The dog sits at one end of the ring and handler goes to the other end, then calls the dog. On a signal from the judge, the handler, using a hand sign, causes the dog to drop to a *down* position. The handler then calls the dog as in a regular recall.

dropped back swayback or concave back.

dropped muscle in coursing, rupture of the loin or shoulder muscle.

dropper crossbred dog used for flushing game, usually of pointer-setter parents; not recognized by kennel clubs, but often bred purposefully by sportsmen.

dropping on point in field trials, action of some dogs that naturally drop to the ground when they have scented a bird, instead of striking the normal standing point; usually seen in over-cautious dogs that fear flushing birds before the shooter is ready.

dropsy accumulation of fluid in the tissues or in a body cavity such as the abdomen. *See* ascites and edema.

drover's dog name given to Standard Schnauzers that were used for pulling carts full of produce from farms to town, and guarding the carts. The dogs worked sheep, cattle, and hogs, and were generalized farm dogs.

drug enforcement dogs canines trained to detect by scent certain drugs that are in traveler's luggage, airport lockers, homes, autos, and other places.

drum tympanic membrane, or eardrum, that separates the middle ear from the inner ear.

dry 1. having no excess jowls or dewlap. **2.** describing a lack of drooling. **3.** describing a lean, muscular dog with a thin skin that is stretched tightly over its body, so that its muscles, tendons, and bones are clearly visible.

dry bib Newfoundlands or Saint Bernards that are selectively bred to salivate less, thus maintaining a dry coat under the chin.

dry dog food commercial dog ration that is prepared by mixing various ingredients together, then extruding the mixture, and baking it into a dry form that can be bagged and sold. *See* kibble and meal.

dry eye keratoconjunctivitis sicca, a pathological lack of normal tear secretion.

dry heat female dog's estrous in which no vaginal discharge or other outward signs appear; sometimes called a silent or quiet heat.

dry neck taut skin without wrinkles.

dry scab mange or ringworm lesions in which there is no suppuration or discharge.

dry shampoo any of the proprietary preparations used for cleaning dogs' coats without the use of water.

Dual Champion dog that has been awarded the title of Champion of Record in conformation shows and Field Champion in field trials.

dual-purpose dog in hunting and conformation showing, dog that is capable of performing well in both disciplines.

duckboat in retriever trials, flat-bottomed boat used as a blind to house both retrievers and their handlers.

duck feet large, splayed feet.

Ducking Dog early name for the Chesapeake Bay Retriever.

Dudley nose pink, or flesh-colored nostrils or nose pad.

duffleness undesirable coat, woolly, loose, and blousy.

dumbbell lightweight wooden object (shaped like a gymnasium weight) that can be picked up by the dog.

dumb rabies stupefying form of rabies that does not cause a dog to become viscious.

dummy stuffed canvas sack about the size of a pheasant, to which a game scent is sometimes applied; training tool for beginners in retrieving.

Dunker Norwegian breed developed by Wilhelm Dunker; scenting dog used on hares; rarely seen outside of Norway. It stands about 22 inces (56 cm) tall, weighs about 49 pounds (22 kg), and is black or blue on a white ground color, with markings of brown.

Dunker

duodenitis inflammation of the duodenum or first section of the small intestine.

duodenum the anterior portion of the small intestinal. It joins the stomach by way of the pyloric sphincter at its proximal end. It connects to the second small intestine section, the jejunum, at its distal end.

Dupuy Pointer or **Braque Dupuy** French pointer that is closely related to the English Pointer. It is bred exclusively for sportsmen, and is ignored for shows; thus it is seldom seen outside France. It is predominantly brown and white color, with some similarity to the Greyhound in conformation.

Dupuy Pointer

Dürbächler *see* Bernese Mountain Dog.

Dusicyon genus of the family Canidae.

Dusicyon culpaeolus South American wild canine with no common name.

Dusicyon culpaeus Colpeo Zorro of South America. *See* Colpeo.

Dusicyon culpaeus reissi *see* Ecuador Bush Dog.

Dusicyon fulvipes Chiloé Zorro of South America.

Dusicyon griseus Patagonian gray fox of South America.

Dusicyon gymnocercus Pampas gray fox of South America. *See* Azara's Dog.

Dusicyon inca Peruvian gray fox of South America.

Dusicyon sclateri *see* Sclater's Dog.

Dusicyon sechurae wild canine of South America with no common name.

Dusicyon silvestris *see* Arecuna Hunting Dog.

Dusicyon thous *see* Carrisissi.

Dusicyon vetulus Brazilian Zorro of South America.

dusting powder artificial whitener or cleaning agent that is applied to a dog's white coat at a show (sometimes forbidden).

Dutch Barge Dog *see* Keeshond; registered name of the Keeshond breed in England; also known as Fox Dog. It is related to the Samoyed, Norwegian Elkhound, Chow Chow, Finnish Spitz, and Pomeranian.

Dutch clip type of Poodle trim popular among pet Poodle fanciers.

Dutch Dog another name for the Pug, although the Pug originated in China.

Dutch Herder Dutch breed that resembles the Giant Schnauzer. Its height is about 24 inches (61 cm). The predominant variety is rough-coated, but it is seen in a smooth coat as well. Colored blue-gray, iron-gray, or steel-gray, its ears are small, pointed, and erect and its tail is natural.

Dutch clip

Dutch Partridge Dog or **Drentsche Partrijshsond** developed as a retriever of small game and used to hunt birds or hares in Holland; seen occasionally in the United States.

Dutch Schapendoes long-coated herding dog from the Netherlands that stands about 20 inches (51 cm) tall and weighs about 50 pounds (23 kg).

Dutch Herder

Dutch Sheepdog longhaired relative of the Belgian Sheepdog, about the same size. It is reddish brown or gray in color.

Dutch Smous *see* Smoushond.

Dutch Steenbrack smooth-coated scenthound from the Netherlands that stands about 15 inches (38 cm) tall and weighs about 18 pounds.

Dutch Water Spaniel curly coated flushing retriever of the Netherlands that stands about 21 inches tall and weighs about 50 pounds (8 kg).

dwarf abnormally undersized animal; displaying a genetically inherited characteristic that is seen in several large breeds in which puppies' leg bones fail to develop normally, and at adulthood, their legs are extremely short, with normal or near normal-sized bodies; also known as achondrodysplasia; seen in Malamutes and others.

Dwarf Spaniel toy dog of Spain and Italy that is said to be a forerunner to the Papillon.

dwell in field trials, hunting, and scenting, to linger on a scent and fail to make progress.

dwelling in foxhunting, spending unnecessary time lingering on a scent.

dys- prefix that signifies "difficult" or "painful."

dysbasia difficulty in walking; moving with pain; lame.

dyschondroplasia abnormal growth of cartilage on the ends of long bones, making movement very painful.

dyscrasia abnormal composition of blood.

dysdipsia difficulty drinking.

dysentery diarrhea, the result of intestinal inflammation.

dyspepsia impairment of normal digestion.

dysphagia difficulty swallowing.

dysplasia abnormality of development, especially of the hip or elbow, but it may refer to an organ of the body.

dyspnea labored or difficult breathing.

dystaxia difficult movement; pain or discomfort when walking.

dystocia abnormal, prolonged, delayed, or difficult parturition.

dystrophy defective nutrition that results in abnormal formation of bones or other tissues of the body.

dystropy abnormal behavior; behavior problems.

E

ear 1. organ of hearing: inner ear, middle ear, and external ear canal. **2.** pinna or earflap.

ear canal external duct leading from the tympanic membrane (eardrum) to the outside.

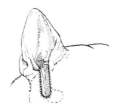

ear canal

ear canker external ear ulceration and infection.

ear carriage 1. describing the way the ears are held, indicating the dog's mood. **2.** position of the ear's attachment to the head.

ear clamps templates or patterns that are attached to an anesthetized dog's ears to outline where the surgical cropping cut is to be made.

ear clip act of cutting off and rounding the pendulant ears of hounds to give them a shortened, uniform appearance and to lessen the probability of tearing the ear leather in the field.

ear clip

ear cropping excising the outside portion of the ear leather to make the ear stand erect. Cropping is cosmetic surgery that is performed on the Doberman, Boxer, Great Dane, Schnauzer, and others. The practice is prohibited in England but is still common in other countries.

ear feather long hair on an earflap, typical of the Cocker Spaniel, Springer Spaniel, and many other breeds.

ear foreign bodies grass awns (seeds) and various other extraneous matter that finds its way into the external ear canals of dogs.

ear fringe long hair on the tip of the ear that is seen in Bedlington Terriers.

ear guide dog canine specially trained to aid deaf humans.

ear hematoma pocket of blood that occurs between the layers of the ear pinna cartilage and skin. It is often caused by shaking head and whipping the ears due to ear mites or foreign bodies in the external ear canals.

ear leather pinna or flap of the ear.

ear mange redness and crustiness of the ears that is usually caused by ear mites, *Otodectes cynotis.*

earmark

earmark tattoo that is impregnated in the ear leather as a means of permanent identification.

ear mite *Otodectes cynotis*, a tiny mite that parasitizes ear canals and causes intense itching and irritation.

ear notch in foxhunting, small notch, or notches, cut in the margin of the ear of the entire pack to immediately identify the dogs of that pack.

ear ossicles three bones of the middle ear: malleus, incus, and stapes. They transmit sound waves from the eardrum to the otic nerve.

ear set describing where on the head the ears are attached.

ears set high placement of ears high on the crown of the head.

ears set low placement of ears low on the sides of the head.

ears set wide placement of ears on the head at the maximum distance apart.

earth in foxhunting, the burrow or den appropriated by a fox. *See* ground.

earth dog terrier used to work below ground in a burrow.

earth trials hunting event sponsored by the American Working Terrier Club that is intended to preserve the natural instinct of working terriers.

ear tick *see* spinous ear tick.

ear trim *see* ear cropping.

earwax cerumen or cera, a yellow or brown, waxy substance normally secreted from the lining cells of the external ear canal.

East Greenland Husky *see* Angmagssalik Husky.

Eastern expression oblique almond eyes, as seen in the Afghan Hound.

East Siberian Laika long-coated sled dog from Russia that stands about 22 inches (56 cm) tall, and weighs about 50 pounds (23 kg).

east-west action throwing the forefeet out sideways or toeing out.

east-west front weak pasterns that cause the forefeet to toe out.

easy champions showing term applied to dogs that earn the title of Champion in three shows, winning five points at each, under different judges; also known as quick, circuit, or tour champions.

easy cover in retriever trials, field trials, and hunting, term describing quarry that has fallen on open ground or open water, is visible to the dog, or is located with a minimum of effort and few obstacles.

eccentric hunter in field trials, dog that seems to have a different technique each time it is in the field; one that has an erratic hunting or pointing style.

ecchymosis reddish discoloration of the skin or mucous membrane caused by the breakdown or bleeding of tiny capillaries into the tissues.

Echidnophaga gallinacea sticktight flea that is occasionally found in the ears of dogs.

echino- denotes a relationship to spines.

Echinococcus granulosus "hydatid" tapeworm of dogs that uses many mammals as secondary hosts. Hydatid cysts form in the abdominal cavity of sheep, cattle, and others, and serve as sources of infestation for the dog.

eclampsia convulsive disorder caused by a calcium imbalance shortly after (or occasionally prior to) whelping; also known as canine milk fever, parturient tetany, or purpural tetany.

ectasia dilation or outpocketing. Retinal ectasia in the Collie is an outpocketing of the retina and is a serious hereditary disease.

ectoparasite parasite living on the outside surface of its host. Examples: lice, fleas, ticks, or mites.

ectopia congenital displacement or malposition of an organ.

ectropion rotation outward or eversion of the lower eyelid, exposing the conjunctival membrane.

Ecuador Bush Dog wild dog first discovered in the Ecuadorian Andes and later found to be an Andean variety of Colpeo. *See* Colpeo.

eczema inflammation or redness of the skin, usually characterized by itching and oozing of serum, scaliness, and crustiness.

edema presence of fluid or serum in the intercellular spaces of the body, sometimes known as dropsy. "Pitting edema" occurs in the subcutaneous tissues of the body.

edible dog dog that at one time was commonly a menu item of human cuisine, such as the Chow Chow.

effeminate normal appearance of a bitch, or a light-boned, refined male that appears bitchlike.

Egyptian Hunting Dog *see* Tesem.

Egyptian Sheepdog old dog breed that is native to upper Egypt in the Armant region. It stands about 22 inches (56 cm) tall and weighs about 50 pounds (23 kg). The colors of its long shaggy coat are black, black and white, or grizzle and white. It has a ferocious disposition toward strangers but is an excellent herder.

Egyptian Sheepdog

Ehmer sling type of soft splint, usually fashioned of tape and applied to the hind leg of a dog to immobilize the lower leg.

Ehmer sling

ehrlichiosis rickettsial disease of dogs caused by *Ehrlichia canis*, which is transmitted by the tick *Rhipicephalus sanguineus*. The typical signs of infection are nose bleeds, ecchymotic hemorrhages in the skin of the abdomen, and petechial hemorrhages in the mucous membranes of the mouth; also known as tropical canine pancytopenia.

Eivissenc breed named for the island of Iviza in Spain; extremely fast Greyhound type, commonly seen in Spain. Its height is about 24 inches (61 cm), and it weighs about 50 pounds (23 kg), with a smooth, short coat of red and white, yellow and white, or red and yellow.

Eivissenc (wirehaired) Spanish dog, smaller than the smooth-coated variety. Its height is about 22 inches (56 cm), and its weight is about 40 pounds (18 kg). It has a short, wiry coat, that is colored red brindle, red and white, yellow and white, or red and yellow. It is used in packs to hunt rabbits.

ejaculate to suddenly expel semen from the penis during copulation; or semen expelled from the penis. A normal canine ejaculate is composed of sperm and fluids from the accessory sex glands.

elbow hinge joint that connects the humerus to the radius and ulna.

elbow dysplasia un-united anconeal process; a hereditary abnormality of the elbow that leads to arthritic lameness. It is relatively common in working dogs and other large breeds.

elbow subluxation hereditary or accidental partial dislocation of the elbow joint.

elephant action lumbering, shuffling walk.

Elinikos Ichnilatis smooth-coated Greek scenthound that stands about 20 inches (51 cm) tall, and weighs about 42 pounds (19 kg).

Elizabethan collar wide, flat collar that stands perpendicular to the dog's neck; funnel-shaped collar that is placed around a dog's neck and face. The objective of the collar is to prevent licking and chewing of lesions or bandages on the dog's body. It was named for the style of collar worn during Queen Elizabeth's reign.

Elizabethan collar

emaciation wasted condition of the body, indicating malnutrition or starvation.

emasculation castration; surgical removal of the testicles.

emetic agent given to cause vomiting. A safe canine emetic is the administration of hydrogen peroxide by mouth, at the dosage of one teaspoonful per 5 pounds (2.2 kg) of body weight. One teaspoonful of salt, placed on the back of the dog's tongue, is another safe emetic.

enamel hard, impervious, shiny, white covering of the teeth.

enarthrosis joint made up of a ball and socket such as the hip or shoulder joints.

encapsulated enclosed within a capsule.

encephalitis inflammation of the brain.

encephalo- prefix that indicates a relationship to the brain.

endemic prevalent in a particular region or area. Example: Lyme disease is endemic in the northeastern United States.

endocarditis inflammation of the lining membrane of the chambers of the heart.

endocrine pertaining to hormones; ductless glands or hormone producing organs.

endocrinology study of hormones, their relationships with each other and with the various organs of the body.

endometritis inflammation of the endometrium or lining of the uterus.

endometrium highly vascular, specialized mucous membrane lining of the uterus that enables embryos to be implanted therein.

endoparasites internal parasites of the dog such as roundworms, tapeworms, hookworms, or coccidia.

English Bob-tailed Sheepdog another name for the Old English Sheepdog.

English Bulldog former name for the Bulldog.

English Cocker Spaniel

English Cocker Spaniel AKC group: sporting; descended from Spanish types from which it obtained the spaniel name. It stands about 16 inches (41 cm) tall and weighs about 30 pounds (14 kg). A compactly built, short coupled dog, with black, liver, or red solid colors, or black, liver, or shades of red parti-colors, its coat is feathered, but not enough to interfere with field work.

English Coonhound smooth-coated scenthound that originated in the United States. Its colors are red, red and white, red tick, and, less often, black and white with blue ticking. It stands about 24 inches (61 cm) tall and weighs about 60 pounds (27 kg).

English Foxhound

English Foxhound AKC group: hound. Stouter and more solidly built than the American Foxhound, it has a chest girth of over 31 inches (79 cm) in a 24-inch-tall (61 cm) hound. A muscular dog with a straight tail and straight legs that is heavy-boned with catlike feet, its color is black, tan, and white, and its coat is short, dense, and hard.

English Pointer smooth-coated pointing and retrieving dog from Great Britain that stands about 25 inches (63.5 cm) tall and weighs about 70 pounds (32 kg).

English Setter

English Setter AKC group: sporting; apparently originated in Spain as a cross of the Spanish Pointer, Water Spaniel, and Springer Spaniel; modified in numerous American strains. Flat-coated with plentiful feathering, it stands about 25 inches (63.5 cm) tall and weighs about 65 pounds (29 kg). The breed's color is orange belton, blue belton, tricolor belton, lemon belton, and liver belton.

English Shepherd long-coated herding dog that originated in the United States. It stands about 20 inches (51 cm) tall and weighs about 50 pounds (23 kg).

English Springer Spaniel

English Springer Spaniel AKC group: sporting; medium-size dog, it stands about 20 inches (51 cm) and weighs about 50 pounds (23 kg) and the topline is equal to the height. Its colors are black and white, liver and white, or tricolor. It has a feathered, flat, wavy coat and a docked tail. (See photo, page 14.)

English Toy Spaniel AKC group: toy; origin of this dog is subject to debate, and may be either Spanish, Japanese, or Chinese; also known as the Blenheim variety of small Cocker Spaniels. Its present size ranges from 9 to 12 pounds (4–5.4 kg), the smaller the better. Its coat is well-feathered and ruby red and white in color. A thumb mark occurs on the top of the center of the skull.

English Toy Spaniel

English Treeing Walker raccoon specialist hound with a big voice; bred to tree a raccoon and announce the feat to the hunters.

English Water Spaniel extinct breed of hunting spaniel with a dense, curly coat, very much like the Welsh Springer Spaniel.

enter 1. in foxhunting, referring to young hounds that are first put in a pack and said to be "entered." **2.** to put a dog into competition in a show, trial, or test.

enteric-coated medicinal tablet that is covered with a substance that is not digested by stomach acids, so that the active ingredient is released and absorbed in the small intestine.

enteritis inflammation of the small intestine.

entire describing a male dog that has both testicles normally descended into the scrotum.

Entelbuch Mountain Dog or Entelbucher Sennenhund smallest of the four types of Swiss Mountain Dogs, named for the town of Entelbuch. Similar in color to the other Swiss Mountain Dogs, black with russet brown and white markings, it is a tailless dog that stands about 20 inches (50 cm) tall and weighs about 65 pounds (30 kg). Sometimes known as the Swiss Drover Dog, it is a gentle family pet.

Entelbuch Mountain Dog

entropion inversion; turning inward of the eyelids.

entry 1. in foxhunting, a new dog joining the hunting pack, either a terrier or foxhound. **2.** properly completed AKC document that allows a dog to be shown or exhibited.

enucleation removal of an organ intact, as a nut from a shell. An eye enucleation means the removal of the eye, including the lids.

enzootic disease that is commonly present in a region during a specific season of the year. *See* endemic.

eosin red stain used with hematoxylin to stain blood slides for examination and evaluation.

Epagneul Français

**Épagneul
Pont-Audemer**

eosinophil white blood cell that takes up eosin, and stains red; seen in abundance in the blood from a dog that is suffering from certain allergic reactions.

Epagneul Breton *see* Brittany Spaniel.

Epagneul Français breed that resembles the English Springer Spaniel in type and color. Classed originally as a setter, it is a versatile dog in the field and a valuable gundog.

Epagneul Nain drop-eared variety of Papillon.

Épagneul Pont-Audemer developed in Pont-Audemer, Normandy, from a combination of various French spaniels and other gundogs. It has a curly coat that is chestnut-colored or chestnut and gray with white markings; it stands about 23 inches (58 cm) tall, weighs about 50 pounds (24 kg) and resembles the English Springer Spaniel. The breed is a water retriever and is commonly used in duck hunting.

epaxial situated above, upon, or over the long axis of the body.

epidemic widely diffused, rapidly spreading, and usually highly virulent disease among the animals of a region.

epidermis outer layer of skin; cuticle.

epidural anesthetic regional anesthetic that is injected through superficial tissues and upon the dura of the spinal cord.

epilation removal of hairs, roots and all.

epilepsy convulsive disorder of varying intensities, the predisposition for which is hereditary. *See* seizure.

epileptic said of an animal that has exhibited convulsive seizures.

epinephrine powerful drug that increases blood pressure, stimulates heart muscle contractions, and accelerates the heart rate. *See* adrenalin.

epiphora excessive production of tears; overflow of tears. It is often caused by a clogged nasolacrimal duct, allergy, or facial conformation.

epiphyseal aseptic necrosis also known as Legg-Calvé-Perthes disease; hereditary, degenerative hip joint disease of dogs; also known as necrosis of the femoral head.

epiphysis cartilaginous growth plate near the end of the long bones from which the bones grow in length.

episiotomy surgical incision made in the vulva to ease parturition or assist delivery.

epizootic epidemic disease of animals. *See* epidemic.

epulus fibrous, benign, often multiple tumor that appears on the gums.

equipage all of the hunting accessories that are taken to a shoot.

Erdely Kopo originated as a cross between the Carpathian Sheepdog and the Polish Hound. It stands about 24 inches (61 cm) tall, weighs about 70 pounds (32 kg), has a short, blunt head, a long tail, a short flat coat, and is tricolor with very little white. It is used for hunts in the forests, mountains, and rivers for bear, deer, and large wild cats.

Erdely Kopo

erect ear prick ear; pinna of the ear that stands erect, either normally or assisted by ear cropping.

ergosterol compound occurring in animal tissue that becomes vitamin D when it is irradiated by ultraviolet sun rays.

Ermenti *see* Egyptian Sheepdog.

eruption 1. breaking out of a visible, circumscribed lesion of the skin. **2.** normal activity of the teeth as they break through the gums.

Erz Mountains Dachshbrake breed that originated in Bohemia; introduced into Austria where it was used to hunt hares and foxes; more recently concentrated in Corinthia. It is black and tan in color and is related to the Wesphalian Dachsbracke.

Esbilac® artificial bitch's milk formulated and sold by the Borden Company.

Escara-inu smooth-coated sled dog of Japan that stands about 23 inches (58 cm) and weighs about 75 pounds (34 kg).

Escherichia bacterial genus, including *E. coli*, which normally inhabits the bowel of animals.

Eskimo Dog a spitz-type dog with a plume tail carried over its back. It stands about 27 inches (69 cm) tall, weighs about 100 pounds (48 kg), and has small erect ears and a very heavy coat. Thought to be of Arctic wolf extraction, it is gentle with humans, but an incorrigible fighter with other dogs. It is able to pull great weights on a sled and was used by Admiral Peary on his trip to the North Pole. Also called Esquimaux and Husky.

esophageal achalasia failure to relax the muscles of the lower esophagus, resulting in dilation of the upper portion; also called megaesophagus, a congenital and possibly hereditary condition in some breeds.

esophageal dysfunction difficulty in swallowing.

esophageal worm endoparasite of a dog's esophagus; transmitted by dung beetles.

esophagus gullet, which is the hollow muscular tube that leads from the pharynx to the stomach; channel through which food is passed.

essential amino acids ten protein building blocks that must be present in a dog's diet to support life: arginine, histidine, isoleucine, leucine, lysine, methionine, phenylalanine, threonine, tryptophane, and valine.

essential fatty acids three unsaturated fat elements that are necessary for canine nutrition and life: linoleic, linolenic, and arachnidic acids.

Estonian Hound one of a number of old Russian scenthounds, displays some of the traits of its ancestor, the Saint Hubert Hound. It has long folded ears, and, although tricolored, the dog is predominately black. It is used in packs and is an eager hunter.

Estonian Hound

estradiol estrogenic steroid that has dynamic feminizing properties.

estriol estrogenic steroid; present in pregnant animal urine.

estrogen generic term for the estrus-producing compounds.

estrous entire reproductive cycle of the dog. It includes four phases: proestrus, estrus, diestrus, and anestrus.

estrus second phase of the canine estrous cycle; period of sexual receptivity.

Ethan Allen Setter bloodline of English setters that was begun in Connecticut.

etiology cause of a disease.

Eurasian wolf large gray or silver animal; thought by modern researchers to be the father of all domestic dogs.

Eurasier or Eurasian modern breed that was established in the 1950s. It is recognized by the German Kennel Club and its name reflects the link between Europe and Asia. It stands about 24 inches (60 cm) tall, weighs about 70 pounds (32 kg), and is a combination of the Chow

Eurasian wolf

Chow and Samoyed. It resembles the German Wolf Spitz, and has a profuse coat in solid colors of gray, red mahogany, and nearly black.

European-Russian Laika long-coated spitz-type dog from Russia that stands about 20 inches (51 cm) tall, and weighs about 40 pounds (18 kg).

euthanasia ending an animal's life in a humane manner by causing an easy or painless death.

evaporative cooling referring to the fact that dogs have few sweat glands; process by which dogs cool their bodies principally by means of evaporation of liquids from their tongues when panting.

even bite dog's bite in which its teeth are all in line, regularly set, neither scissor, undershot, or overshot, but meeting squarely.

every dog has its day old saying meaning "Don't give up; your turn will come."

evisceration disembowelment; a situation in which a loop of intestine has escaped though an abdominal incision.

ewe neck concave topline of the neck, like a sheep's neck.

exclusion diagnosis process of making a diagnosis by ruling out everything else that could cause the signs.

excrement fecal matter or body wastes.

ewe neck

excuse in herding, a judge's action that ends a run because the dog is attacking the livestock or gripping them abusively.

exercise to perform physical movement for the improvement of health.

exercise area area set aside at a show or obedience trial where all dogs may be walked.

exercise intolerance inability to participate in physical activity without becoming overly fatigued.

exercise pen indoor or outdoor portable confinement apparatus that allows a dog to move about yet stay confined to a room or small area.

exhibition only designation for dogs entered at a dog show without the privilege of competing in classes.

exhibitor handler or owner-handler of a dog in a competition.

exotic dogs foreign breeds of which little is known locally.

expression countenance or arrangement of the facial features. Example: The Pug exhibited a lively expression.

extended semen product that contains fresh sperm to which nutrients and stabilizers have been added to allow the semen to be safely chilled or frozen for storage or shipment.

extension movement of a joint to straighten it or to bring the limb toward a straight line.

extensor one of a group of muscles that extend a joint.

extensor brow long, bushy hair that acts as an eye covering.

extensor dominance response of a puppy that is over a week old. When it is picked up, it stretches and arches its back. *See* flexor dominance.

extremity terminal portion of the body, such as the limbs or tail.

extrovert dog that loves everyone and enjoys interaction with people.

exudate purulent discharge, emanating from a diseased part of the body, and usually containing pus.

eye in herding, the ability of a dog to stare at the sheep, almost hypnotizing them while creeping up on them, and moving them without causing alarm.

eye contact act of staring directly into the eyes. A human who achieves and holds eye contact with a dog is often perceived by the dog to be a threat and the action may precipitate aggressive behavior on the dog's part.

eye dog in herding, a dog that has developed or is born with the innate ability to hold (or freeze) sheep by staring straight at their eyes.

eye teeth upper canine teeth; upper first premolars; the fangs.

F

fabella sesamoid fibrocartilage that is found in the gasrocnemius muscle behind the knee or stifle joint.

face judging in showing or field trials, an unfortunate situation in which the handler's face means more to the judge than the dog he or she is exhibiting; also known as judging the wrong end of the leash, or, in the case of field trials, judging the wrong end of the shotgun.

face forepart of the head.

facial marking dog's instinct to use the oil glands on its cheeks to mark objects that "belong to" it, including its owners.

factor VII deficiency hereditary anemia.

factor VIII absence of blood. This clotting factor in the canine causes Von Willebrand's disease.

faculty normal power or function. Example: The dog looked normal, and had all its faculties.

faddist in showing, said of a judge who has strong feelings about the relative importance of some particular characteristic of the breed being judged.

fading litter or **fading puppy syndrome** gradual loss of puppies for no apparent reason. It is a lethal neonatal condition of unknown cause, but may be associated with herpes virus infection, vitamin C deficiency, or antibiotic therapy in the dam.

faking changing a dog's appearance by artificial means, such as cosmetic surgery, to qualify the dog for competition.

Fala President Franklin Delano Roosevelt's faithful Scottish Terrier that was his constant companion.

fall fringe of hair hanging over a dog's face.

fallaway posterior line of the croup.

fallow pale yellow or washed-out red color.

false fence in herding, two short lines of hurdles with a wide gap between them through which the dog must drive the sheep. *See* sheepdog trial.

false fence

false heat also known as a wolf heat; situation in which the external signs of a bitch's proestrus last only a few days. It is usually followed a short time later by a true heat.

false point in hunting, a pointing error, in which the dog strikes a point with no birds present.

false pregnancy fairly common situation in which a bitch displays many of the external signs of pregnancy without the production of puppies; also known as pseudocyesis.

familial relating to the family or bloodline; especially a genetic trait that recurs in related dogs of a certain bloodline.

familial selection selection of puppies based on the performance or appearance of their parents instead of the individual puppies' quality.

family group of individuals with a common ancestry.

fancier person who appreciates, studies, and enjoys dog activities; dog owner or breeder.

fancy appreciation, study, and exhibition of dogs; collective referral to the owners, trainers, breeders, and judges of purebred dogs.

fang canine tooth; first upper premolar or eye tooth; long tooth used for grasping.

fan hitch in sledding, method of hitching all dogs of the team directly to the sled on separate lines, allowing them to "fan out" without a leader.

fanning in herding, changing the course of a herding dog by a voice command from the handler.

fan hitch

farina meal or starchy flour of maze often used in dog food.

fatigue state of discomfort caused by prolonged exertion.

fatigue gait in sledding, a tired dog's pace; achieving an easy, ambling trot that allows the team to regain strength.

fault 1. in showing, characteristic of an individual dog that deviates from the breed standard. **2.** in scenting, referring to a hound that has lost the scent of the quarry.

fawn tan color of a newborn deer.

FCI *see* Fédération Cynologique Internationale, an international organization that governs dog shows in most of Europe and South America.

F coefficient amount of inbreeding in a dog's pedigree.

feathered well having profuse feathers.

feathering 1. in field trials, rapid wagging of a gundog's tail when it is following a newly discovered or questionable scent. **2.** in foxhunting, moving the tail from side to side with excitement, indicating the hound has found an interesting scent, but not sufficient to speak. **3.** digital stroking of the roof of a bitch's vagina to stimulate uterine contractions when she experiences a delay in parturition.

feathers long hair on the backs of a dog's legs, ears, and tail.

fecal incontinence loss of control of feces accompanied by an involuntary emptying of the bowel.

fecal marking territorial behavior in which the alpha dog deliberately deposits feces to signify its dominance or to claim a territory.

fecal specimen fresh sample of feces taken to a veterinary laboratory for microscopic examination to determine an internal parasite infestation by the presence of the parasite ova.

feces body's waste that is excreted through the bowel.

fecundate to impregnate or fertilize.

fecundity fruitfullness; ability to produce offspring.

Fédération Cyologique International Belgium's dog registry: Rue Leopold II, Thuin, Belgium.

feeder container that holds a supply of dry dog food and allows access to the food at all times.

feist rat terrier.

feisty spirited, scrappy, ambitious dog; one that is investigative and adventuresome; often used to describe terriers.

Fell Hound type of dog used to hunt foxes and other quarry in the fell counties of Great Britain.

Fell Terrier *see* Lakeland Terrier.

felted coat matted coat that has formed into dense wads or strands of hair.

female dog of the sex that bears the young; a canine bitch.

femoral head necrosis *see* epiphyseal aseptic necrosis or Legg-Calvé-Perthes disease.

femoral pulse throb or beat of the femoral artery that is perceived by placing a finger on a spot on the inside of the upper thigh.

femur thighbone; large bone that extends from the coxofemoral joint of the pelvis to the stifle or knee joint.

fence in hunting, a command to stay within the confines of the paddock or enclosure that is used for training.

fence jumper racing term for a dog that bolts and runs across the infield of the track in an effort to catch the lure.

Fennecus zerda Fennec fox of Asia and Africa.

feral 1. describing wild, savage, undomesticated dogs. **2.** describing domestic dogs that are living in a semi-wild state, having become wild due to the lack of human stewardship.

feral dog of Natolia extinct race or type of semidomesticated, feral shepherds or guard dogs with bushy tails that resembled wolves of the area but differed in habits.

fermentation decomposition of food, especially carbohydrates, which produces gas and alcohol.

ferrety conformation that exhibits long thin feet and is down in the pastern.

fertilization conception; uniting of a sperm and an ova to form a zygote.

fetal resorption dissimulation of a fetus in the uterus accompanied by absorption of the fetal tissues that occurs without illness or outward signs in the dam.

fetal rickets hereditary achondrodysplasia or dwarfism. Affected puppies develop with short legs and feet turned out.

fetch 1. in herding, to drive the sheep toward the shepherd, handler, or a pen. **2.** in retriever trials, command to retrieve an object or a bird.

fetcher herding term for a dog that will gather a small flock and bring it to the handler.

fettle dog's condition, including its mental state. Example: My dog is in fine fettle this morning.

fetus unborn offspring; usually the designation of the second stage of development that is an arbitrary designation beginning when differentiation of the unborn animal's tissues and organs become apparent. The undifferentiated first stage of development is called an embryo.

fever abnormally high body temperature; in dogs, body temperature of over 101.5 to 102.5°F (38–39.5°C).

fianis excrement or feces of a quarry, especially a fox or badger.

fibula smaller of the two bones of the lower hind leg that extend from the stifle to the hock. The paired bone is the tibia, or shinbone.

fiddle face long, concave foreface that is pinched in the middle.

fiddle front describing a leg conformation in which the front pasterns are turned in, the feet are turned out, and the elbows are turned out.

fiddle-headed having a long, wolflike head.

fiddle-shaped pinched in the middle.

fiddler in showing or field trials, judge who can't seem to make up his or her mind.

fiddling in showing, the action of a handler who uses unorthodox techniques in order to confuse the judge.

fido Latin word for "faithful"; common term for a companion dog.

field 1. area or open space where various outdoor dog activities are staged. **2.** spectators or gallery who attend and watch a field trial. **3.** in foxhunting, gallery or audience who follow the hounds, other than the master and hunt staff.

field immunity immunity gained from actual exposure to a disease.

Field Spaniel AKC group: sporting; sturdy hunter that stands about 18 inches (46 cm) tall, weighs about 50 pounds (23 kg), and is somewhat longer than tall. Its tail is docked, and its coat is moderately long, flat or wavy, dense, and water-repellent. Its color is black, liver, golden liver, or roan, with a small amount of white.

Field Spaniel

field sports in hunting, pursuing and/or shooting quarry in the field.

field trial organized test of canine training and skill in performing the work for which the dog is bred; contest between individual bird dogs to display their hunting quality in judged competition. The first field trial was held in Memphis, Tennessee on October 8, 1874. The winner was Knight, a black setter belonging to H. Clark Pritchett.

Field Ch. abbreviation for Field Champion, an AKC title awarded in field trials.

fighter 1. in coursing, a dog that interferes or impedes another dog in order to hold it back and gain an advantage. **2.** in racing, a dog that attempts to head off, intimidate, or attack other competitors.

fighting dogs canines that are used or were bred to fight one another in a pit, sometimes to the death. Among the breeds that were previously used as pit fighters are the Bulldog, Staffordshire Terrier, Bull Terrier, Boston Terrier, Bedlington Terrier, and Akita.

fighting pit arena in which dogs fight.

Fila Brasileiro mastiff-type dog that was developed in Central America and used as a guard dog and drover. It stands about 30 inches (76 cm) tall, weighs about 110 pounds (50 kg) and is extremely courageous when challenged. It guards live stock fiercely and is sometimes used to track escaped convicts.

Fila da Terceira found only on the island of Terceira, in the Azorean archipelago; rather like a Bull Mastiff, but with shorter legs. Its height is about 23 inches (58 cm), its weight about 120 pounds (54 kg). Colored yellow, fawn, orange, and white, with red or tan markings, it is smooth-coated, with the ears cropped, round, heavy chops, and a deep stop. It is heavy-boned.

Fila da Terceira

filariasis or dirofilariasis infestation of *Dirofilaria immitis*, the canine heartworm, or *Dipetalonema.*

filaricide agent that destroys the microfilaria of heartworms and is a treatment for heartworm.

filled or **filled-up face** having a head typical of the Bull Terrier, with no stop or indentations in its surface.

fill-in describing a strong zygomatic arch; face with heavy bone and musculature below the eye.

film 1. picture or image that has been produced by X-ray, ultrasound, or magnetic resonance. **2.** thin layer or covering.

find 1. in foxhunting, when hounds first smell the scent of the quarry and open on it, they are said to have made a find. **2.** in hunting, make an individual point on the quarry.

fine having slender, refined lines; being light-boned.

finish 1. describing the action of a dog that has acquired the necessary points to complete its championship. **2.** to complete the exercise, such as returning to the left side and sitting in an obedience trial. **3.** overall condition of the animal. Example: The winner was finished to perfection.

Finnish Barking Bird Dog or **Cock-Eared Dog** *see* Finnish Spitz.

Finnish Hound hunter of hare and foxes, with wide-set ears and an expressive head. It stands about 24 inches (61 cm) tall, weighs about 55 pounds (25 kg), and has a dense rough coat that is black with red markings.

Finnish Spitz AKC group: non-sporting; national dog of Finland. It stands about 18 inches (46 cm) tall, weighs about 35 pounds (16 kg), and is squarely built, double-coated, and ranges in colors from pale honey to deep auburn. It is a natural barking pointer that directs the hunter to the location of treed game with a yodel. Used in Finland to hunt turkeys, it has a bark that is said to mesmerize game. The hunting ability of this dog must be proven before conformation championship is awarded in its native Finland.

Finnish Spitz

fins heavy growth of hair on the feet.

fire dogs English war dogs of the fourteenth century that wore a leather covering and some metal armor and carried on their backs a bronze basin that was filled with fire. In battle they ran under the enemy's horses, burning the horses' bellies.

Firehouse Dog another name for the Dalmatian.

first dog show held in 1859, in Newcastle, England, where 50 pointers and setters were exhibited.

fire dog

fisheye round, light-colored eye that is usually a fault or undesirable characteristic. *See* walleye.

fissipeda carnivores animals of the Eocene period development that established the modern dog's ancestry. This classification is based on the development of shearing teeth, a characteristic of modern cats and dogs.

fissure cleft or groove that occurs naturally or is made surgically.

fistula abnormal or artificial deep sinus that often leads to a hollow organ.

fit 1. convulsive episode manifested by involuntary tonic and clonic spasms of the legs. *See* seizure. **2.** to groom and prepare a dog for a dog show or exhibition.

fix 1. to perform the cosmetic surgery that is sometimes needed to correct a conformation fault. **2.** to judge a class dishonestly for an under-the-table fee.

fixed describing a race that has been won before it has been run.

fixing setting or imprinting a specific genetic trait in a breed of dogs by consistent selection of breeding stock and careful control of the gene pool.

fixing type process of inbreeding to take advantage of favorable genetic characteristics. It sometimes backfires when unfavorable characteristics are also fixed.

flabbermouth new fancier, or self-appointed expert on breeds who disseminates rumors about purebred dogs.

flag fringe of feathers found on the posterior aspect of the tails of setters and some retrievers. A feathered tail is carried proudly as a flag.

flagging slow, deliberate, side-to-side movement of the tail of a gundog when on point.

flagpole tail long, stiff, straight tail that is carried vertically erect.

flagpost in herding, an obstacle around which the sheep are driven before they are driven through the false fence.

flag tail tail with abundant feathering, especially toward the tip.

flare

flanking in herding, circling the sheep from the right or left to keep them in a group or to change their direction.

flanks portion of the dog's body between the hind ribs and rear legs; lateral lumbar area.

flapper hunting 1. shooting young quail or pheasants before they are capable of flying well. **2.** poaching gamebirds out of season.

flare 1. head color that has a V-shaped white blaze on the face that is wider at the top than at the bottom. **2.** spreading erythematous flush of the skin; sudden appearance of a new skin lesion.

flashings

flared ears ears that are wider at the tips than at the skull; usually set wide on the dog's head.

flashings white trim or white markings, especially those on the dog's head; flashy white collar on a Boxer or Collie.

flat back describing a dog's topline that has no appearance of sag.

flat bone shoulder blade; scapula.

Flat-Coated
Retriever

Flat-Coated Retriever AKC group: sporting: versatile retriever with a flat coat of moderate length and high luster. This dog stands about 24 inches (61 cm) tall and should be lean and hard. Colors are either solid black or solid liver; all others are disqualified. It is often kept as a family dog and has an outgoing personality.

flat croup croup that has no downward slope.

flat feet splayed or toe-wide feet that tend to spread.

flat-sided having no spring to the ribs; describing a dog that is slab-sided and usually has a narrow chest.

flatulence having a great deal of intestinal gas; gas-filled bowel.

flea tiny, blood-consuming, biting parasite that causes a great deal of irritation to an infested dog, and acts as a secondary host for tapeworms; *Ctenocephalides canis.*

flea

flea-bite allergy phenomenon in which an animal becomes sensitized and allergic to the saliva of a flea and suffers an intense itching reaction when bitten by a flea.

flea-bitten derogatory term used to describe a poor-quality dog.

flea collar plastic dog collar that is impregnated with an insecticide chemical that either repels or kills fleas.

flea comb metal comb with teeth placed tightly together so as to trap fleas when the comb is drawn through the animal's fur.

flea powder dry preparation that contains an insecticide that is labeled for use on dogs to kill fleas.

flea comb

flea soap or flea shampoo soap or shampoo that contains insecticides that will kill a dog's fleas on contact.

flea spray liquid that is packaged as an aerosol or pump spray and contains an insecticide that will kill or repel fleas on contact.

flecked coat that is lightly ticked with other colors, as seen in the English Setter; neither roan nor spotted.

Flemish Draught Dog or **Vlaamsche Trekhond** dog that was developed for pulling carts. Typically gray with darker markings on the face, it is a very powerful breed that makes an excellent guard dog.

flesh 1. dog's condition. Example: The dog was in good flesh. **2.** muscle meat of an herbivorous animal that is used in the preparation of dog food.

fleshmark unpigmented patch on a dog's nose pad or nostril; Dudley nose.

fleshy cheek describing well-developed chewing muscles; describing heavy muscles of mastication.

181

fleshy ear thickened pinna or ear leather.

fleshy nose unpigmented nostrils; nose pad that is pink in color.

flews pendulous, fleshy upper lips; upper lips that hang in folds.

flex 1. to bend a joint to form a more acute angle. **2.** to contract a flexor muscle.

flexible 1. having the capacity to bend readily without breaking. **2.** describing an adaptable dog or one that is easily trained for more than one use. Example: My retriever is flexible; he hunts upland birds as well as waterfowls.

flexion state of a joint when bent.

flexor muscle that bends a joint.

flexor dominance tendency of neonatal puppies to curl up when handled; occurs during their first four or five days of life. *See* extensor dominance.

flight instinct period phase of a puppy's behavior, at about four months old, when it becomes more independent and responds to fright with flight.

flight zone in herding, invisible area around a group of stock into which the dog cannot pass without causing the stock to feel threatened and attempt to escape.

flighty foxhunting term describing an uncertain and changing scent.

floating rib thirteenth rib on either side of the rib cage that is not attached to the sternum by cartilage.

flock 1. collected group of livestock (usually sheep) that are used in a herding trial. **2.** farm birds or livestock that are gathered or herded together.

flocked having a soft, fine, blousy coat without curl.

flocking tendency of the livestock to instinctively cluster together in a compact group.

flop ear hound ear; drop ear; pendulant ear.

flora natural bacterial inhabitants of a dog's intestine.

flowered having two or more colors on a dog's coat or part of the coat.

fluctuation variation of color or character of a dog's coat.

fluffies coats of extreme length that contains copious feathers and furnishings.

fluffy describing a blousy, soft, woolly coat, or a flocked coat.

fluorescence characteristic of certain pathogenic dog fungi that causes them to glow when subjected to ultra-violet light rays in a dark room. *See Microsporum canis.*

flush to frighten birds out of their place of concealment on the ground and into flight.

Flush Elizabeth Barrett Browning's Cocker Spaniel to which several verses were written.

fluting median depression in a skull; furrow running longitudinally down the center of the muzzle.

flutter rapid vibration or pulsation of the heart.

fly-away coat loose, uncurled coat that doesn't lie close to the body.

fly-away ears ears that are held like wings, pointing away from the head; usually seen on drop-eared dogs.

flyball in agility trials, a competition that involves a course of jumps and ends with a treadle that the dog steps on to cause a ball to pop out of a box. The dog must catch the ball and return it to the handler.

flyball

flyblown infestated with fly larvae or maggots; occurs especially in old, debilitated dogs with fecal incontinence; also known as myiasis.

fly-catching pursuing imaginary objects in the air; jumping and snapping at nothing.

fly-eared describing a dog with ears that should stand erect but are tipped or falling over at tips.

flyer 1. young show dog of unusual promise. **2.** exceptionally fast coursing or racing dog; successful competitor in coursing or racing events.

Flying Fur Travel Service pet travel agent: 310 South Michigan Avenue, Chicago, Illinois 60604.

flying lips prominent flews.

flying off herding term for the action of a dog that yields to the sheep and doesn't face up to them.

flying trot *see* suspension trot.

foam cleaner commercially available waterless bath for dogs.

foiled in foxhunting, describing an area of the ground that is covered with the scent of farm animals and those scents interfere with the quarry's scent.

folic acid pterolyglutamic acid, a B complex vitamin that is sometimes used in the treatment of nutritional anemia.

follicle 1. small secretory gland. **2.** sac from which hair emerges. **3.** ovarian structure that produces an egg.

follicular mange *see* demodectic mange.

follower in foxhunting, a person who isn't involved with the hunt but follows along to watch and enjoy the sport.

follow-through in obedience training, the requirement that once a dog learns a command it must always obey it; handler's responsibility to always insist on the command being obeyed.

fontanel or **fontanelle** unossified top of the skull of newborns; "soft spot" in the cranium that persists for a few days after birth.

food allergy adverse reaction to some component of a dietary ration.

foot 1. speed, fleetness. **2.** terminal structures of each of the four limbs that consists of four toes and five pads.

foot follower handlers and competitors, together with the entourage, who follow foot hounds.

foot hound any hound that is followed on foot rather than on horseback; often Beagles or a Beagle pack.

footing in field trials, ability of a gundog to sort out a quarry's scent and follow it.

foot pack collection of foot hounds, hunted as a pack and followed on foot.

foot pad in sledding, a nonskid pad on the rear of the sled's runners where the driver can stand when the team is underway.

footpad principal weight-bearing pad of each foot as differentiated from toepads and the carpal pad.

footwarmer dogs small, furry dogs carried by early English church-going ladies. The dogs were trained to lie on the ladies' feet to keep them warm during the services.

force training system of retriever training that is used when the dog has proven to be refractory to standard methods of training or when natural retrieving isn't well established in the dog. Also known as dummy training.

fore- prefix meaning anterior, or front.

forearm lower foreleg, between the elbow and carpus; radius and ulna bones.

forechest sternum; front pair of ribs.

foreface muzzle.

forehead that portion of the face above the eyes.

foreleg either of the anterior limbs.

forelock abundant hair growth that is seen on the forehead, as in the Kerry Blue Terrier.

forepastern metacarpus; anatomical region between the carpus (wrist) and the toes.

forepaw front foot; paw of the anterior limb.

forequarters shoulders and anterior limbs.

forelock

form 1. in foxhunting, the seat or kennel of a rabbit. **2.** in racing, the probability of winning a race, based on the dog's recent outings.

formalin 40 percent solution of gaseous formaldehyde.

forty-nine-day theory popular belief that no puppy should leave its mother before it is 49 days old.

foster to transfer puppies from their dam to another nursing bitch to raise as her own.

foul color color that is not characteristic of the breed; poor coloring, atypical coloring, coloring that is not allowed in the breed standard.

foundation stock breeding animals that are used to begin a bloodline; ancestors.

founder principle ability of foundation stock to routinely pass a characteristic or feature to their inbred offspring.

four-eyed describing a dog with a spot over each eye.

four-toed dog *see* Colpeo.

Fousek Pointer wire-coated gun dog that originated in Czechoslovakia. It stands about 23 inches (58 cm) tall and weighs about 60 pounds (27 kg).

fox dog any hound or terrier used to pursue foxes.

fox-eared describing Greyhounds with ears that stand erect instead of folding.

foxhound scent hound of any breed or mixture of breeds that specializes in hunting foxes and running them to ground.

foxhunting sport composed of mounted huntsmen and dog handlers who take to the field with a pack of foxhounds and terriers in an organized and controlled pack with the intent of finding a fox and running it to ground.

fox-trot dog's easy gait between a walk and trot, that consumes minimal energy.

foxy having a pinched muzzle and erect ears, having the appearance or actions of a fox.

fracture broken bone. The types: see green stick, spiral, intercondylar, transverse, impacted, compound, comminuted.

Fred hero of the comic strip *Fred Basset,* drawn by A. Graham Ltd.

free choice feeding regimen that allows a dog to eat whenever it wants.

freedom vs. exercise theory that pet dogs that are given the opportunity or freedom to exercise often choose to lie about instead; that exercise must be stimulated or promoted by the owner.

free from change describing a hound that doesn't change scents and isn't easily confused by other scents.

free gait gait that is natural and unaffected.

free-opening hound in scenting, dog that gives tongue or voice early when on scent.

free return repeat breeding to the same stud dog at no cost, when conception and pregnancy does not occur on the first breeding.

free zone *see* no-man's-land.

freighting dogs sledding term usually reserved for the larger sled dogs of Alaska, Greenland, and Siberia. They are often of mixed lineage, many weighing 145 to 165 pounds (66–75 kg) each. Six or seven large, heavy dogs were harnessed single file in a "tandem hitch," wearing a padded leather collar, similar to a horse collar. Three miles (4.8 km) an hour was the usual loaded speed, but enormous weight, sometimes as much as 1,200 pounds (544 kg), was loaded on the sleds.

French Bulldog

French Bulldog AKC group: non-sporting; bat-eared dog of Bulldog ancestry. The dog stands about 12 inches (31 cm) tall and may not exceed 28 pounds (12.7 kg). Its head is large and square, and the forelegs are short, stout, and straight. It has a short, smooth coat, and its colors are brindle, fawn, and white, or brindle and white. It is a flat skull that curves upward above the eyes to give a domed appearance.

French front narrow forelegs with pasterns turned out, in a chairlike appearance; also called Chippendale front.

French Kennel Club Société Centrale Canine, 215 rue St. Denis., Paris 75002.

French Pointer also known as the Charles X Pointer; upland bird dog that refuses to retrieve from water. It stands about 25 inches (63.5 cm) tall and is seen in two sizes, the larger about 23 inches (58 cm) tall and the smaller about 20 inches (51 cm) tall. It has a fine, white coat with patches of chestnut.

French Pointer

French Spaniel or **French Epagneul** long-haired sporting dog from France that stands about 22 inches (56 cm) tall and weighs about 60 pounds (27 kg). It has a soft, wavy coat of white, with chestnut colored patches and speckles, and is a strong gundog popular with hunters all over France.

French Spaniel

frenulum small fold of mucous membrane that limits the movement of an organ. *See* persistent frenulum of the penis.

fresh fox in foxhunting, a new quarry, discovered while pursuing another fox in a hunt.

fresh, fresh line, or **fresh scent** in foxhunting, line of scent that is strong and recent.

Friends of Animals pet rescue agency: P.O. Box 1244, Norwalk, Connecticut 06856.

friendship symbiotic relationship between a human and a dog, in which the dog acquires room and board and the human acquires protection and companionship.

frill long feathering of soft hair found on Setters and Collies around the neck; often longer at the throat and chest than on the top.

fringes long, flowing coat at the rear of all four legs of a dog, along backs and bottoms of the ears and on the back of the tail.

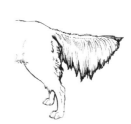

fringes

frogface Bulldog-like face with a nonreceding nose, as seen on a Boxer or Boston Terrier; a short muzzle and an undershot jaw.

froggy having upper lips that overhang an undershot jaw.

front forepart of the body that consists of the head, chest, forelegs, and brisket.

frontal relating to, or pertaining to, the forehead.

frontal bones skull bones of the face.

Frontier Guard dogs of certain Eastern Europe countries where national borders were sealed. Their keen sense of smell and hearing were used to detect movement close to the ground, out of radar range.

froufrou

frostbite irreversible necrosis (death) of tissue from long-term exposure to freezing cold.

frosting gray hairs occurring on the muzzle and face that are common to aging dogs.

froufrou abundant hair located on the tip of the tail.

frown wrinkled brow that is typical in the Bulldog, Shar Pei, and others.

FSH abbreviation for the Follicle Stimulating Hormone that originates in the pituitary gland and has its primary effect on the ovaries.

Full Cry coonhound periodical: Box 190, Sedalia, Missouri 65301.

full cry or **full tongue** in foxhunting, the chorus of voices from the pack on the scent of the quarry.

full mouth complete dentition; having all the normal teeth.

fumigant bomb aerosol spray that is set off in an empty house to kill fleas that are harbored in rugs, carpets, and upholstery.

fumigation exposure to smoke, vapor, or gas in order to disinfect the premises or destroy pests that are harbored therein.

function normal or proper action of a part or organ.

Fund for Animals, The pet-protection organization: 200 West 57th Street, New York, New York 10019.

fungal pertaining to a fungus; disease caused by fungus.

fungicide agent capable of killing a fungus.

fungus class of vegetable organisms of a low order of development that reproduce by spore formation. Under certain circumstances, they may parasitize dogs. *See* ringworm, microsporum.

funiculus umbilical cord; spermatic cord.

fur dog's coat, pelt, or hair covering.

fur and feather dog a sporting dog that may be used for both bird hunting and trailing furred game, such as rabbits or squirrels.

Furacin® proprietary brand of nitrofurazone, an antibacterial agent.

furious rabies form of the rabies infection that is manifested by viciousness, attacking, and blind aggression. *See* dumb rabies.

furnished describing a dog with a coat that is in excellent condition.

furrow median groove in the skull that begins at the stop and continues upward to the occipital bone.

furuncle painful, infected nodule of skin, encircled by inflammation.

fuscin brown pigment of retina.

fusion cohesion of adjacent parts or bodies; bonding together of parts that are normally separated.

futurity competition involving dogs that were nominated at or prior to their birth.

futurity stake in field trials, a class at trials for puppies that are entered at or before their birth and judged when the dogs are one year or 18 months old.

G

gag device for holding dog's mouth open while under anesthetic.

gagging persistent sign of kennel cough, choke, or foreign bodies in the mouth or throat.

gait particular manner or style of a dog's walking, trotting, or running.

galacturia milklike, thick urine; also called chyleuria.

Galapagos dogs varieties of dogs introduced by visiting ships to the Galapagos Islands that were left to fend for themselves. They have interbred and become feral, and have threatened the lives of native amphibians.

Galgo Espagnol or **Spanish Greyhound** smooth-coated gazehound that stands about 30 inches (76 cm) tall and weighs about 90 pounds (41 kg). Its colors are sable, brown, black, or mahogany with white markings.

gallbladder saclike structure that serves as a reservoir for bile and is located on the undersurface of the liver.

gallop dog's fastest pace except for a run; characterized by all four feet leaving the ground simultaneously.

gallstone mineral concretion that is formed in the gallbladder or a bile duct.

Galton whistle® "silent dog whistle" that emits sounds at a frequency that is audible to dogs but not heard by humans. *See* hearing.

Galton whistle®

game 1. hunted quarry such as upland birds, waterfowl, raccoons, opossum, squirrels, and other animals that are hunted with dogs. **2.** describing a dog that is willing to work or ready to accept a challenge, under all conditions. Example: A game Greyhound is ready to race, regardless of the weather.

game bird any of the feathered quarry normally hunted for sport and meat, including pheasants, quail, ducks, grouse, geese, white-winged doves, and wild turkeys.

game sense hunting term for a gundog's steady, working knowledge and inherent ability to locate game of any kind.

gang hitch in sledding, a team with a single leader. All other dogs are hitched two dogs abreast, in a tandem pattern.

gangline **1.** in sledding, another name for the towline to which all dog's harnesses are fastened. **2.** stakeout line to which the sled dogs are picketed temporarily while resting.

gangrene local death of soft tissues due to a lack of blood supply; decay or rotting tissue that occurs in a living animal.

gangline

garden digging action of dogs that are naturally attracted to freshly turned soil to investigate the possibility of a freshly buried bone. This instinctive behavior led to the training of landmine dogs in World War II. *See* K9 Corps.

Garm Rudyard Kipling's dog; "... one of the finest Bull Terriers... two parts bull and one part terrier... pure white with a fawn saddle and a fawn diamond at the root of his whippy tail."

Gascon-Saintongeois, Grand gascon-Saintongeois, or **Virelade** rare breed, nearing extinction; French hunting dog that was developed for pack hunting of wolves, roe deer, and smaller game. It stands about 28 inches (71 cm), weighs about 70 pounds (32 kg), and has a short black and white coat that is flecked with black ticking and spots and has characteristic dard markings above the elbows and hocks. It is rarely seen outside France. A smaller version of the breed is the Petit Gascon-Saintongeois that is identical except for its height.

Gascon-Saintongeois

gaskin hind leg muscle mass located between the stifle and the hock of a dog.

gastric dilitation and volvulus often fatal disease of large dogs. It is sometimes caused by feeding large quantities of food immediately before exercising. The syndrome includes stomach bloating and torsion, or twisting on its long axis, accompanied by intense pain, vomiting attempts, and shock.

gastric foreign body any indigestible material that has been swallowed and has become lodged in the stomach, commonly a bone, toy, or part of a toy.

gastric torsion twisting of the stomach on its long axis. *See* gastric dilitation and volvulus.

gastritis inflammation of the lining of the stomach.

gastro- prefix that denotes a relationship to the stomach.

gastroenteritis inflammation of the stomach and intestine.

gather in herding, when the dog collects the sheep from their scattered grazing positions into a compact group.

191

Gauchen Hound smooth-coated Spanish gazehound that stands about 20 inches (51 cm) tall.

gaunt bony, tucked up, poorly nourished, and thin.

gaunt head long, angular head without excess flesh, as seen in the Collie.

gauze open-meshed fabric that is used as a bandage or wound dressing.

gavage act of feeding by means of a stomach tube.

gawcie tail feathered tail that is carried over the back.

gay stern or **gay tail** tail that is curled up over the dog's back as in the Spitz, or erect as in some hounds.

gazehounds dogs that see and follow their quarry by sight instead of scent. They include the Greyhound, Saluki, Whippet, and others. *See* sighthounds.

Gazelle Hound *see* Saluki.

GDV abbreviation of gastric dilatation and volvulus, a specific bloating syndrome of large breeds of dogs.

gee in sledding, the driver's command to the lead dog to turn right.

gee-haw leader in sledding, another name for a command leader.

gee pole pole that extends forward from the right side of a sled. It is gripped by a driver on skis, on foot, or on a ouija board, to give better leverage for steering the sled.

gee pole

gelatin collagen that is derived from the bones and white connective tissue of slaughtered food animals.

geld to castrate.

gell colloidal suspension.

gene specific sequence of nucleotides (DNA or RNA) that is located in the germ plasm on a chromosome; functional unit of inheritance that controls the transmission and expression of traits; biologic unit of heredity.

genealogy study of the pedigrees, family trees, or the ancestry of a dog; bloodline of a dog.

gene pool sum total of animals of a particular pure breed that are available for breeding.

generic food dog food manufactured by a company that is not well-known to the public. Generic foods are often sold under various house brand names and are generally less expensive than popular brand names.

genetic defect inherited predisposition to a fault.

genetic expression way or frequency that certain inherited characteristics occur or are displayed in a breed.

genetic hybrid cross involving a single pair of traits in which both parents are of the same species.

genetic imprinting propensity of dogs to retain certain behaviors generation after generation, in spite of human intervention. Examples: turning around and around before lying down, as a wolf would do to pack the grass of its nest, a virgin bitch's knowledge about what to do during parturition.

genital pertaining to the generative or reproductive organs.

genitalia reproductive organs and tract. In a female: ovaries, fallopian tubes, uterus, cervix, vagina, and vulva. In a male: the testicles, epididymis, vas deferens, bulbus glandis, os penis, urethra, penis, and glans penis.

genitals visible reproductive organs: testicles and penis of a male, the vulva of a female.

genome genetic material possessed by an individual.

genotype all or part of the genetic constitution of an individual. *See* phenotype.

genotypic selection choosing canine breeding stock by their inherited characteristics.

gently in obedience training, with kindness; without harshness or roughness.

genus taxonomic term subordinate to a tribe and superior to a species. Example: The genus and species of the domestic dog is *Canis familiaris*.

germ 1. small mass of living tissue that is capable of becoming an organism or part of an organism. **2.** pathogenic, microscopic organism, such as a bacterium.

germ cell gamete; sperm cell or an egg.

German Army Dog School founded in 1848 to train dogs for warfare.

German Boarhound another name for the Great Dane.

German Bracke small, smooth-coated scenthound from Germany that stands about 15 inches (38 cm) tall and weighs about 18 pounds (8 kg).

German Bulldog former name for the Boxer.

German Drahthaar *see* German Wirehaired Pointer.

German Great Spitz or **Giant German Spitz** long-haired northern sled dog from Germany that stands about 15 inches (38 cm) tall and weighs about 39 pounds (18 kg). Seen in colors ranging from black to white, gray, and brown.

German Giffon wirehaired pointer from Germany that stands about 22 inches (56 cm) tall and weighs about 60 pounds (27 kg).

German Hound or **Deutscher Bracke** reportedly the only remaining purebred scenthound in Germany. It resembles the Harrier in size and is kept in packs for hunting. Also called the Olpe Hound, it is not exhibited.

German Hunting Terrier or **Deutscher Jagdterrier** stubborn little dog that was created from the Fox Terrier. It stands about 16 inches (41 cm) tall and weighs about 20 pounds (9 kg). It is either smooth or wirehaired, and is colored black and tan. A natural water retriever, it will go to ground for a fox, or attack wild boars. In its native land, it must undergo tests under working conditions before it may be judged a Champion.

German Kennel Club Verband für das Deutsche Hundewesen, 30 Schwanenstrasse, Dortmund.

German Longhaired Pointer or **Langhaar** breed that originated from the Water Spaniel and a number of French pointers and setters. It appears much the same as an Irish Setter, except for its liver-colored coat and white markings. It was first used in falconry, but is valuable as an independent gundog.

German Mastiff another name for the Great Dane.

German Pointer *see* Vorstenhund.

German Roughhaired Pointer or **Stichelhaar** wirehaired pointing gundog from Germany that stands about 24 inches (61 cm) tall and weighs about 60 pounds (27 kg).

German Sheepdog *see* Alsatian, or German Shepherd Dog.

German Sheep Pudel bred from barbets and water dogs and probably an ancestor of the Poodle. It is a rather large, predominantly white, shaggy dog that is a reliable guard dog and is kept for working sheep.

German Shepherd Dog AKC group: herding; versatile dog that was originally bred as a shepherd. It stands about 26 inches (66 cm) tall, weighs about 95 pounds (43 kg), and has a double coat of medium length. It

German Longhaired Pointer

German Sheep Pudel

German Shepherd Dog

varies in color, but saddle markings are common and white is not allowed. It has served as a companion, war dog, guard dog, police dog, and is in great demand as a Seeing Eye dog. (See photo, page 40.)

German Shorthaired Pointer or **Kurzhaar** AKC group: sporting; probably of Spanish pointer, English Foxhound, and German tracking dog lineage. It is a versatile, short-coated gundog, that stands about 24 inches (61 cm) tall and weighs about 65 pounds (29 kg). Its tail is cropped and is always held straight. Its color is liver, usually ticked with white and roan, but no other color is allowed. This dog has been used on upland game, ducks, rabbits, raccoon and opossum. (See photo, page 14.)

German Shorthaired Pointer

German Spaniel or **Wachtelhund** one of the most valued sporting dogs in Germany. To protect its working characteristics, the breed is rarely exhibited. It somewhat resembles the German Pointer; stands about 18 inches (46 cm) tall, and weighs about 45 pounds (20 kg). It has a fine nose and will retrieve from the water as well as on land. It has a long wavy coat and is smaller than a Springer Spaniel. Its color is black, tan, gray, stag red, or yellow red, with lighter markings.

German Spaniel

German Spitz Klein descended from much larger sled-pulling varieties, this diminutive breed stands about 11 inches (28 cm) tall, weighs about 20 pounds and is seen in most solid and blended coat colors. It is a favored lapdog in Germany.

German Spitz Mittel standard form of the German Spitz varieties, bred in virtually every solid color. It stands about 14 inches (36 cm) tall, weighs about 25 pounds (11 kg), and slightly resembles the Pomeranian. It was bred originally for farm work, but is mostly a companion today. Another name for this dog is Deutscher Mittel Spitz.

German Wirehaired Pointer or **Drahthaar** AKC group: sporting. It stands about 25 inches (63.5 cm) tall and has a beard and whiskers of medium length. The wiry coat is sufficiently long, dense, and water-resistant to protect the dog, and it lies harsh and flat. It is liver, liver and white-ticked, and both roan and solid color; no other colors are allowed. This dog carries the traits of a Pointer, Foxhound, and Poodle.

German Wirehaired Pointer

German Wolf Spitz longhaired northern-type dog that stands about 17 inches (43 cm) tall, and weighs about 42 pounds (19 kg).

germinal cells specialized cells in the gonads that produce gametes, either ova or spermatozoa.

gestation period of pregnancy. The length of pregnancy averages 63 days in the dog.

get progeny of a stud dog; the "get" of the sire. Example: Major's get always had his temperament.

giant breeds not an official designation, the term usually refers to the Great Dane, Newfoundland, Saint Bernard, Great Pyrenees, Irish Wolfhound, Mastiff, and other dogs reaching a weight of more than 110 pounds (50 kg).

Giant Schnauzer AKC group; working; Bavarian breed that is distinctly different from the Miniature and Standard Schnauzers, with a different ancestry. It is related to the Great Dane, the Bouvier des Flandres, and some rough-haired sheepdogs. It stands about 26 inches (66 cm) tall and sports a beard, whiskers, and bushy eyebrows. Its tail is docked, and it is black or salt and pepper in color, with a hard wiry coat and soft undercoat. It is used as a cattle dog, guard dog, and police dog.

Giant Schnauzer

Giardia genus of mobile protozoan organisms that sometimes cause intestinal disorders in dogs.

giardiasis infection from *Giardia spp.*

gig in sledding, wheeled cart used for training puppies and keeping working sled dogs in condition during the summer. Some gigs are made of old cars that have been stripped down to the chassis and tires.

gig

Gildersleeve English Setter strain that is popular in the northeastern United States.

ginger root pungent, aromatic spicy rhizome used in many herbal dog therapeutics.

gingiva oral mucous membrane that covers the gums.

girth circumference of the chest; ribspring, or heart girth.

give tongue, give cry, give voice describing the action of hounds that sound off or bay as they pick up and follow a scent trail.

glaciering in sledding, repeated water flows that freeze into layers of ice. Glaciering occurs most commonly in areas of permafrost or on shallow streams.

gland organ that produces a secretion or product.

glans penis sensitive distal portion of the penis.

glass eye eye with a pale blue iris, or one that has a washed out color. It is usually caused by diluted pigmentation in the iris.

glassy-eyed describes an animal that is staring fixedly. A sign or evidence of shock or extreme pain.

glaucous blue-ticked, blue, or blue and white color, as seen in blue merle collies.

Glen of Imaal Terrier badger dog of the British Isles. It stands about 14 inches (36 cm) tall, weighs about 30 pounds (13.6 kg), is wheaten, blue-tan, or blue brindle in color, and has bowed forelegs and a high-set, docked tail.

globular eye prominent, round eye, or a bugeye.

glomerulonephritis kidney disease or degeneration that is sometimes inherited. It is manifested by excessive thirst, vomiting, dehydration, and depression.

glow red to auburn markings that are seen on dark, usually black dogs.

glucocorticoids class of corticosteroids that are used to treat inflammation and itching in dogs; also used to prevent or counteract circulatory shock.

glucose 1. short for d-glucose, or dextrose, the naturally occurring blood sugar. **2.** sterile solution of 5 percent dextrose that is often administered intravenously as a support to ill or injured dogs.

gluteal referring or pertaining to the region of the buttocks and the gluteus muscle mass.

gluteus maximus major muscles of the buttocks.

glycogen chief carbohydrate storage material in dogs.

goat's milk mammary secretion of a goat; occasionally used as a supplement to puppies' diets.

go-bye in coursing, the action of a Greyhound that starts a length behind its opponent, yet passes it in a straight run.

goggle eye globular eye.

goiter thyroid gland enlargement causing a large neck swelling.

Golden Labrador yellow-colored Labrador Retriever.

Golden Retriever

Golden Retriever AKC group: sporting. This breed has the Tweed Water Spaniel and Newfoundland in its ancestry, as well as Irish Setters and Bloodhounds. It stands about 24 inches (61 cm) tall, weighs about 80 pounds (36 kg), and has a dense water-repellent undercoat and a flat or wavy guard coat of various solid golden colors. A versatile dog that is used for water retrieving, obedience, upland bird work, and field trials, it often serves as a companion dog, agility dog, and guide dog for the blind. (See photo, page 13.)

Golden Retriever Club of America 9900 Broadway, Suite 102, Oklahoma City, Oklahoma 73114.

Golden Wolf *see* dog of Java or dog of Sumatra.

Goldi short for a Golden Retriever.

goma Japanese word that means "sesame" and is used for the contrasting peppering that appears in native breeds.

gone away in foxhunting, going away after fox has been found and dispatched.

gone to ground in foxhunting, fox has gone into a burrow or den, or other underground cover.

good doer easy keeper, or a dog that looks good with a minimum amount of care.

good luck hound in ancient Germany, people sick with a fever would share a bowl of milk with a dog, chanting: "Good luck, you hound! May you be sick and I be sound!"

good range (gundog) (field) the best distance in front of shooter that a field dog can work.

Goodenough islands native dog wild dog that appears to have evolved from the Papuan hill race. It was a Spitz type, colored black with white markings on its brisket. It was short coated, with a bullet-shaped head, small erect ears, and a bushy tail.

Goodman strain popular American Foxhound strain bred in Mississippi, North Carolina, and Kentucky.

goose neck awkward appearing neck, one that is long, skinny, and arched.

goose rump croup that slopes downward and backward at a great angle.

goose step stiff legged gait with minimal flexion of the elbow joints.

Gordon Setter

Gordon Setter AKC group: sporting; of Scottish origin; a true setter that is sturdily built, with a stylish appearance. It stands about 26 inches (66 cm) tall and weighs about 75 pounds (34 kg), but there is significant acceptable variation in its size. The coat is soft and shining, straight or wavy, colored black, with feathers on the tail, and long ear hair. The tan markings are particularly important in size and location and are specified in the standard.

Gos d'Atura (Cerdá) *see* Catalan Sheepdog (shorthaired).

go through in agility trials, a command that sends the dog through a tunnel or a tire jump.

go to ground 1. in foxhunting, action of quarry that goes into hiding in a burrow. **2.** action of a terrier that follows quarry into a burrow.

go to the dogs 1. to attend a dog race. **2.** to fall apart in the face of adversity; to head for ruination; to overspend one's income.

go up in agility trials, a command that sends the dog over an A-frame, onto the ramp of a dog walk, or onto the seesaw.

Graa Dyréhund *see* Norwegian Elkhound.

grabber dog that has the propensity to roughly grasp food or toys that are offered to it, behavioral problem.

grabbing in hunting, field dog handler's action of reaching for a dog's collar, doubting the dog's manners.

gracing in racing, spectator terminology for Greyhound racing.

grading in racing, placing dogs in classes according to their past performance.

grafting puppies placing orphan puppies on a surrogate dam to nurse. The procedure often takes time and persistence to overcome the new dam's objections.

Gráhund or **Gray Elk Dog** one of a group of spitz-type dogs that was developed in Scandinavia; basically Swedish, rather than Norwegian, and rarely seen outside its native country. It is smaller and less stocky than the Norwegian Elkhound, with a curly tail and prick ears.

grain mite harvest mite that is nonparasitic but sometimes bites dogs; opportunist parasite.

Gram's stain method of staining bacterial microscope smears in which bacteria are classed according to their acceptance or rejection of stains. Example: Bacteria are classed either Gram positive or Gram negative.

Grand Bleu de Gascogne cross between the Bloodhound and the Saint Hubert Hound; French hunting dog of large stature. It is about 31 inches (79 cm) tall, and its blue color is basically white that is finely flecked with black hairs. It has a loud voice.

Grand Bleu de Gascogne

Grand Danois *see* Great Dane.

Grand Griffon Nivernais

Grand Griffon Nivernais French hunting dog similar to the Otterhound in appearance; developed in the province of Nivernais where it was used for hunting wild boar. It ranges in color from black to fawn, with gray being the most common color seen, has a long, shaggy coat, and has not become popular elsewhere in Europe. It stands about 24 inches (62 cm) tall and weigh about 55 pounds (25 kg).

Grand Griffon Vendéen best-known French griffon. It is white or yellow in color, with a double coat, long, furry ears, and a large head. It stands about 26 inches (65 cm) tall, weighs about 75 pounds (35 kg), and is a descendent of the Saint Hubert Hound.

Grand Griffon Vendéen

granulation small, rounded, fleshy (granular) masses of healing tissue that form in an open wound.

grass eating activity long thought to be a dog's remedy for illness but really preventive therapy for digestive upsets. Grass may be either an emetic, causing the dog to vomit, or a laxative.

grave serious outlook; describing a prognosis of the worst kind.

gravid pregnant; said of a uterus containing fetuses.

Graydog another name for the Weimaraner.

graze in herding, allowing stock time to quiet down or settle and feed in a designated area.

Great Dane

Great Dane AKC group: working; contrary to its name, its origin was Germany; probably descended from Tibetan Mastiff stock, although some say it has Irish Wolfhound blood. The minimum height for a male is 30 inches (76 cm), but larger dogs are preferred. Its weight ranges from 100 to 120 pounds (45–55 kg). Short-coated, it is found in many colors, including brindle, fawn, blue, black, and harlequin. (See photo, page 23.)

Great Pyrenees AKC group: working; of French origin. Its height of up to 32 inches (81 cm), and weight well over 100 pounds (45 kg), combined with its bearlike conformation, make it a formidable protector and companion. Its white, double, weather-resistant coat is sometimes shaded with markings of gray, badger, or reddish brown. This dog was used for sentry duty, guarding, herding sheep, packing, draught, and was a pet of the nobility. (See photo, page 24.)

Great Pyrenees

Greater Swiss Mountain Dog or **Grosser Schweizer Sennenhund** AKC group: working; largest of the four types of Swiss Mountain Dogs. Used as a drover in its native Switzerland, the Swissy is smooth-coated and colored black, tan, and white, stands about 28 inches (71 cm) tall, and weighs about 90 pounds (41 kg).

Greater Swiss Mountain Dog Club of America 91 Schoffers Road, Reading, Pennsylvania 19606.

greater trochanter bony prominence on the upper femur that is easily palpable.

Greater Swiss
Mountain Dog

Greek Greyhound coursing dog that works well on either hare or deer and resembles the Saluki. The most common coloring on its hard, short coat is black and tan.

Greek Sheepdog all-white shepherd that is related to the Kuvasz and Polish Sheepdog; found in Epirus, Macedonia, and southern Greece. It stands about 26 inches (66 cm) tall and has a short coat that is slightly wavy and erect ears.

Greek Greyhound

Greenland Dog or **Gronlandshund** breed that is closely related to the Eskimo Dog, but slightly lighter and shorter in the back. It stands about 25 inches (64 cm) tall, weighs about 70 pounds (32 kg), and may have descended from the Arctic Wolf. It can be used to track the breathing holes of seals in the ice, and is also a powerful sled dog. It is seen in virtually every color and combination of colors.

Greenland working dogs versatile dogs of no particular breed that pull sleds when there is sufficient snow. In the summer, they become pack dogs that can carry one-third of their weight on their backs for extended periods. They are very strong and are often kept in their native country as guard dogs as well.

Greek Sheepdog

greenstick fracture broken bone in which the bone ends are not totally separated, and the covering of the bone (periosteum) is intact.

Green vaccine early live-virus distemper vaccine of ferret origin. Temporary symptoms of distemper were often seen in young puppies that were immunized with this vaccine.

Greyhound AKC group: hound; one of the most ancient breeds; common in the Nile valley dating from 2900 B.C. According to the paintings and sculpture, the dog has changed very little. It stands about 30 inches

Greyhound

201

(76 cm) and weighs about 65 pounds (29 kg), is seen in many colors and patterns, and is short-coated. It is a gazehound that was used to hunt all kinds of game, but the hare is its natural quarry. It is now primarily a racing dog. It is the universal symbol of speed. "Greyhound" is a word that is derived from the Celtic word "grech," meaning "dog." The breed name may or may not have been connected with the common gray color of the breed. (See photo, page 19.)

grief very strong emotion that is commonly seen in dogs, especially when a loved one dies. A grieving dog often refuses food, and cries, whines, or howls.

Griffon á Poil Laineaux breed created from a Wirehaired Pointing Griffon and a Barbet. It is a keen gundog with a coat that is long and flattish, predominantly brown in color.

Griffon Belge variety of Brussels Griffon that is seen in black or black and tan, and black and red colors.

Griffon Bleu de Gascogne de Petite Taille French breed that has a rough coat, long ears, and an affectionate nature. It is smaller than the Grand Bleu, and rarely seen outside France.

Griffon Bruxellois *see* Brussels Griffon.

Griffon d'Arrêt á Poil Dur *see* Korthals Griffon.

Griffon Fauve de Bretagne breed originally used to hunt wild boar and foxes in Brittany, France. This breed is not known as a friendly breed and is rarely seen outside France. It stands about 22 inches (56 cm) tall and weighs about 44 pounds (20 kg). It has a coat that is rough to the touch and fawn in color.

Griffon Nivernais French pointer that resembles the Italian Spinone. It stands about 22 inches (56 cm) tall, and its bushy coat is gray blue, wolf gray, or grayish black, usually with red facial markings.

Grig-hound another name for the Greyhound.

grin dog's expression seen in many individuals of all breeds when the lips are drawn back in a smile; especially notable in the Samoyed.

gripping in herding, lightly biting or grasping the heels of one of the animals being herded. Gripping livestock without purpose is disallowed; acceptable gripping must be used only to control difficult stock, must be done quickly, and must not break skin.

Griffon Nivernais

grizzle banded hair with lighter bands on base with darker tips, giving coat color an overall blue-gray color.

Groenendael black, long-haired Belgian sheepdog named for a small city near Brussels. *See* Belgian Sheepdog.

groin inguinal area; posterior ventral abdomen adjacent to the thigh.

groom to comb, brush, bathe, trim nails, and make a dog neat and clean.

groomer person whose job it is to comb, brush, and bathe dogs.

grooming glove mitten with a soft plastic palm that has many tiny projections that effectively remove the dead hair from a dog.

grooming glove

grooming table a special table equipped with a slip-collar that is suspended from an elevated arm. This restraint is used to maintain the dog in a standing position on the table for combing or clipping.

groove shallow linear depression, either natural or surgically made.

Grosser Schweizer Sennenhund *see* Greater Swiss Mountain Dog.

ground foxhunting term for earth that harbors dens of the quarry.

ground glass poisoning often-suspected cause of dog illness that is rarely a reality. In truth, ground glass that is mixed with food usually causes very little damage to the intestine.

grooming table

ground itch type of pruritis caused by a canine hookworm infestation. *See* hookworms.

group one of the seven main subdivisions into which dogs are classified by the AKC. For dogs listed in each group, see sporting dogs, hounds, working dogs, terriers, toys, non-sporting dogs, and herding.

growl voice of an irritated dog; deep throaty warning that all is not well; rumbling complaint of a dog.

growth hormone pituitary gland secretion that is responsible for canine growth.

growth rate measure of the maturation of a puppy.

guard dog dog that is trained for protecting people or their possessions. *See* war dog, herding dog, junk yard dog, or schutzhund.

guard dog tests developed in Germany, training tests in which a dog must learn to protect its owner when attacked by another person, keeping him at bay without physically assaulting him or her. *See* schutzhund competition.

guard hair outer coat of double-coated dogs. Usually coarser than the undercoat.

guide dog dog specifically trained to lead a blind person.

guiding gently by the collar in obedience training, controlling the dog by holding any part of the collar, applying minimal pressure on the dog's neck.

gullet esophagus; tube or passage beginning at the pharynx, leading from the mouth to the stomach.

gum gingiva or mucous membrane surrounding the base of the teeth.

gun barrel front forelegs that are ramrod straight and parallel.

gundog dog of the sporting, hound, spaniel, or retriever breeds, which are used in hunting small game with a gun.

gun shy describing a dog that is afraid of guns and gunfire. An undesirable quality in a hunting dog, often seen when gun is fired too close to the dog and unexpectedly, before the handler has the confidence of the dog. It is not a natural phenomenon and it is not believed to be hereditary, but rather the fault of human action.

gut intestine or bowel.

gutter dog stray, homeless dog; feral dog that lives by scavenging.

gyp female Greyhound.

H

habit fixed or constant acquired behavior of a dog that is established by repetition.

habitat natural abode or home of an animal.

habituation gradual adaptation to the environment.

hackles hair on a dog's back that stands up stiffly and represents a dog's involuntary response to fear. Raised hackles make the dog look larger than it is.

hackles

hackney action trotting with the characteristic gait of a hackney pony; exaggerated, high-stepping gait.

hair of the dog that bit you expression that refers to the fable that you can desensitize yourself to future encounters by wearing some skin or hair of the dog that attacked you. More recently it is the belief that a person can relieve the effects of a hangover by consuming some alcohol again.

hair filamentous growth from follicles in a dog's skin; dog's coat.

hair wrapping method of tying up a Yorkshire Terrier's hair that involves oiling it, separating it into strands, rolling and wrapping it in paper; prevents shedding and loss of hair from chewing.

hair wrapping

hairball trichobezoar or a wad of hair that has collected in a dog's stomach or upper small intestine; typically matted together and sometimes vomited.

hairless dog one of various types of dogs that have very little or no hair covering; seen in Mexico, the West Indies, Africa, China, Egypt, and Turkey. These dogs are usually about 11 inches (28 cm) tall and weigh about 10 pounds (4.5 kg), with black, white, pink, or a mottled pattern to their skin.

hairlip congenital cleft at the midline of the upper lips that usually accompanies a cleft palate.

Halden Hound smooth-coated scenthound that comes from Norway that stands about 22 inches (56 cm) tall and weighs about 58 pounds (26 kg).

hairlip

Haldenstövare largest of the four stövare-type hounds that were developed near Halden, Norway. It is mostly white with black and brown markings, stands about 25 inches (64 cm) tall, weighs about 64 pounds (29 kg), and is kept primarily to hunt alone and works well in the snow.

Half-and-Half Dog progeny of a cross between the Bulldog and a terrier; originally called the Bull-and-Terrier dog, Half-and-Half, Pit Dog, Yankee Terrier, or Pit Bull Terrier; later took the name of Staffordshire Bull Terrier, and still later Staffordshire Terrier. Today the dog is known as the American Staffordshire Terrier.

half-prick ear same as a semiprick ear; one that bends forward at one-third the distance from the tip.

halitosis offensive, bad breath.

hallmark phenotypic characteristics that are specific to certain breeds or strains within a breed; characteristics by which a bloodline is recognized.

Hall's Heeler an Australian cross between the Collie and dingo that produced headstrong, rough biters. *See* Bagust Dogs.

hallucination perception not based on reality, such as seeing nonexistent butterflies. Puppies have been seen behaving as though they are having hallucinations.

halo circle or ring seen in a glaucomatous eye.

ham quadriceps femoris muscles that, together with other muscles, make up the bulk of the upper leg.

hamburger hound racing dog of the lowest grade or quality.

hames in sledding, curved support that leads from the harness or collar, to which the traces are fastened.

Hamiltonstövare or **Hamilton Hound** smooth-coated Swedish breed. It stands about 22 inches (56 cm) tall, weighs about 60 pounds (27 kg), has pendulant ears, a high-set tail, a black body, tawny limbs, and a white chest. It is a utility hound that has become popular in show rings; sometimes called the Swedish Foxhound.

Hampton-Watts-Bennet Hound early strain of American Foxhound.

hamstring tendon of the biceps femoris muscle of the hind leg.

handlebow upright handle at the back of a sled that the driver grips; also called the driving bow.

handlebow

handler 1. in sledding, assistant who helps harness the dogs at the beginning of a race. **2.** in showing, a person whose occupation is exhibiting dogs for themselves or others. AKC-licensed handlers exhibit dogs for a fee.

handler's post in herding, the point at which the handler and the dog begin the run.

handpluck to pluck an undercoat with the fingertips, using neither scissors or stripper.

hand signals commands that have been reduced to a nonverbal level. In obedience, these include stop, come, down, and sit.

handstrip to remove the dead or excess coat with the blade of a scissors or a knife. To pluck the coat.

handy in hunting, describing a dog that is useful and performs well in the field under various circumstances. Example: A gundog that works out of a boat or blind, and does well on quail and turkeys is handy.

hangdog look sad, woebegon, forlorn, dejected appearance, like a dog that has been hanged.

hanging ear pendulant ear; dropped ear; hound ear.

Hanoverian Schweisshund German-origin Bloodhound that was bred for its excellent nose. It is over 26 inches (66 kg) tall and weighs about 100 pounds (45 kg). It is colored gray-brown, red-brown, orange, or dark yellow, with no white markings.

Hanoverian Schweisshund

haploid having one-half the normal cellular number of chromosomes; seen in gametes, the sperm cells, or eggs.

Happa Dog dog that looked like a short-haired Pekingese or Pug, that was exhibited in England about the turn of the century; probably extinct today, or confined to China. It has a large head and a docked tail, and its color is black and tan, red, fawn, and cream.

harbour in hunting and foxhunting, resting place of game or quarry.

hard difficult to discourage, well-trained, and sound. Example: A good Chesapeake Bay Retriever is hard to the core.

hard-bitten describing a dog that endures punishment without complaint, such as a working or fighting dog that has the will to win.

hard-driving referring to hind leg power; term used to describe strong sled dogs, retrievers, and other working and sporting dogs.

hardened experienced in rough work or dedicated to working hard.

Harderian gland gland on the underside of the third eyelid or nicitating membrane. *See* cherry eye.

hard eyes particular gleam or frown on a dog's face that discourages confrontation.

hard-mouth characteristic of a retriever that mauls the retrieve by biting into the bird, thus spoiling it for human consumption.

hardpad aftereffect of canine distemper infection, and recovery, in which all the dog's pads are thickened, horny, cornified, often cracked, and unyielding. At one time, "hard-pad" was a synonym for canine distemper.

hard palate area of the roof of the mouth immediately behind the upper teeth, and in front of the soft palate.

hare any of the swift, short-tailed, long-eared, solitary lagomorph relatives of the rabbit that are common quarry for dogs.

hare finder dog that excels in finding rabbits aboveground.

harefoot dog's foot that has well-separated, long central toes; usually a long foot, like a rabbit's.

hare hound harrier; any dog that principally hunts hares.

Hare Indian Dog wild dog sometimes tamed by natives and used for hunting; found only with the tribes living along the Mackenzie River in the region of the Great Bear Lake of Canada. Looked somewhat like a coyote, with a small head and a slender muzzle. It is blackish gray colored and longhaired, with a white face, muzzle, belly, and legs.

hark in foxhunting, to pay attention to the voice of a hound.

hark forward in foxhunting, huntsman's encouragement to the hounds to work forward, or to press on.

hark in in foxhunting, to encourage the hounds to join another hound that is already on the scent trail.

harlequin coat color with odd-shaped splashes of blue or black on a lighter background color; seen in the Great Dane.

Harlequin Pinscher variety of Miniature Pinscher that were never popular with breeders. A white dog with variegated gray or tan patches, or brindle with white self markings.

harness **1.** yoke or series of straps fitted on a sled and cart dogs to hitch them to a sled or cart. **2.** straps fixed around the thorax of small dogs that take the place of a collar.

harness-banging in sledding, the jumping of an excited dog against his harness to attempt to start the team forward.

Harrier AKC group: hound; likely a smaller version of the English Foxhound. It is a scenthound that stands about 20 inches (51 cm) tall and weighs about 60 pounds (27 kg) with square proportions. It has a short dense coat that is virtually any color; black, tan, and white are predominant. Used to hunt hares and rabbits the world over, the Harrier has experienced great popularity because it can be followed on foot.

Harrier

harvest mite mite whose larvae is the chigger that causes skin irritation to dogs (and humans); also called red bug or sand flea. It lives in long grasses where it often bites dogs, and is an opportunist parasite of the dog.

hauling in herding, action by a sheepdog of bringing sheep in to the handler.

haunch hip and buttock region.

haunch bones two iliac crests or hip bones that are palpable or visible pelvic prominences.

Haute-Agooue Terrier *see* Niam Niam.

Haut Poitou smooth-coated scentdog from France that stands about 22 inches (56 cm) tall and weighs about 60 pounds (27 kg).

Havanese Bichon-type dog that is shown in the AKC Miscellaneous class. It stands about 10 inches (25 cm) tall, weighs about 10 pounds (4.5 kg), and is seen in virtually any color or combination of colors. It has a wavy, double coat that is sometimes parted down the middle of the back. (See photo, page 43.)

Havanese

haw 1. in sledding, a driver's command to the lead dog to make a left turn. **2.** third eyelid or nicitating membrane that appears at the inside corner of each eye but can be drawn up over the entire eye.

hawkeye golden-colored eye.

haw syndrome protrusion of the Hardarian gland and inversion or prolapse of the third eyelid.

hazel eye yellowish-brown eye.

HCh in herding trials, abbreviation for the title Herding Champion.

head **1.** in foxhunting, the hunting speed or ground covered by the pack. **2.** proximal extremity of the body, or the anatomical structure that contains the brain and organs of special senses. **3.** in herding, to go instinctively for the head or nose of livestock, a trait that usually confuses the stock and is rarely approved of by the handler.

head chopped off in racing, describing a dog that is beaten at the first turn.

headed in foxhunting, said of a fox that has been turned back, by the hounds or by natural barriers.

header **1.** in foxhunting, the leader of the pack, or frontrunner. **2.** dog that instinctively jumps at heads of cattle or sheep to turn them.

headgut foregut; first section of intestine; duodenum.

head planes profile contours of the skull.

heads up in foxhunting, describing the posture of hounds that are searching for a windborne scent by raising their noses from the ground.

headstrong in field trials, describing a dog that is strong-willed, doesn't pay attention to commands, and is difficult to train, control, or exhibit.

head tilt sign of an ear infection or foreign body in the external ear canal.

health certificate declaration made by a licensed veterinarian that the dog was examined and found free from signs of certain infectious diseases at the time examined.

health records detailed description of the illnesses and injuries suffered by a dog, medications that were given and recovery time, as well as the dog's vaccination and breeding history.

hearing sense that appreciates and processes sounds. The auditory ability of the dog is nearly twice as well-developed as that of the human. The dog hears pure tones of 35 kilohertz (KHz) (35,000 cycles per second); in humans, 20 KHz is tops.

Hearing Ear Dog dog that is specifically trained to aid the deaf.

Hearing Ear Dog Program c/o American Humane Association, 5351 South Roslyn Street, Englewood, Colorado 80110.

heart failure fatal stoppage of the heart's action.

heart room wide heart girth and a deep chest with good rib spring.

heartworm *Dirofilaria immitis*, a worm that lives in a dog's blood vessels and in the heart. Transmitted in larval form by mosquitoes, it is a fatal or grossly debilitating disease if not treated.

heartworm preventive oral medicine usually given in tablet form on a monthly schedule to a healthy dog to prevent heartworm infestation.

heartworm test any of several quick tests to discover immature heartworm larvae in the peripheral blood of dogs, or to detect mature heartworms within the heart.

heartworm treatment injections of a toxin, given over a period of several days to kill the adult heartworms and larvae.

heat 1. estrus, or standing heat; the time that a bitch will accept a male. **2.** obsolete system of operating field trials.

heatstroke or **heat prostration** common condition of dogs that are confined to cars in the summer with insufficient ventilation; characterized by rapid, shallow breathing, rapid heart beat, high body temperature (greater than 104°F [40°C]), weakness, nausea, dizziness, collapse, and coma. It is an emergency condition.

heavenly dog dog in ancient Chinese mythology, named Tien Ken, that was said to cause thunder when he traveled to earth from heaven.

heavy stock livestock that require a great deal of pressure from the dog in order to be driven.

he-dog intact male canine.

heel in obedience trials, command that causes the dog to walk at the handler's left side with its head even with the handler's left knee.

heel

heeler herd dog with the instinctive propensity to snap at the heels of cattle or sheep to control them.

heel free describing the action of a dog that heels while not on a leash.

heel work quick turns, about-faces, and other maneuvers while the dog is heeling free.

Heidi President Dwight Eisenhower's well-loved pet Weimaraner.

height measurement of a dog from the floor to the highest point of the withers (top of shoulder blade).

height

helix margin of the pinna (flap) of the ear.

helminth intestinal parasitic worm of the dog.

helminthicide vermicide; agent that is used to destroy helminths (worms).

hematinic substance that may be administered to a dog to increase its red blood cell production or activity. It is often composed of copper or iron supplements that are given to a dog to increase its production of hemoglobin or the blood's oxygen-carrying capacity.

hematoma blood-filled swelling caused by blood leaving the vessels and clotting outside them. *See* ear hematoma.

hematuria appearance of blood in the urine.

hemivertebra abnormality of vertebrae that can result in neonatal death; congenital pathogical anomaly sometimes seen in brachycephalic breeds.

hemobartonellosis infection with *Hemobartonella canis,* a red blood corpuscle parasite that destroys the blood cells and causes anemia in a dog.

hemoglobin red, oxygen-carrying pigment that is found within the red blood cells.

hemolysis pathological condition in which the cellular integrity of the red blood corpuscle is disrupted and hemoglobin is released from the red blood cells and appears in the serum.

hemolytic causing hemolysis. Certain bacteria are capable of causing hemolysis, notably *Streptococcus species.*

hemophiliac bleeder or an animal with a faulty blood-clotting mechanism that bleeds easily.

heparin substance that prevents or dissolves blood clots. It is derived from the liver of domestic animals used for food.

heparinize treatment with heparin to increase the clotting time.

hepato- pertaining to the liver.

heptatitis 1. any inflammation of the liver. 2. Infectious canine hepatitis is a specific liver disease of the dog presently called CAV-1.

herb leafy plant without a woody stem that is used as a household remedy or flavoring. Therapeutic herbs are often used in canine homeopathic medicines.

herder dog that has been bred to tend cattle or sheep.

herding handling, moving, or guarding of cattle, sheep, or other livestock; activities of a drover.

herding dog group AKC group that includes: Australian Cattle Dog, Australian Shepherd, Bearded Collie, Belgian Malinois, Belgian Sheepdog, Belgian Tervuren, Border Collie, Bouvier des Flandres, Briard, Collie, German Shepherd Dog, Old English Sheepdog, Puli, Shetland Sheepdog, Welsh Corgi, Cardigan, and Welsh Corgi, Pembroke.

herding instinct herding term for the inherited balance in a dog's temperament between its predatory drive and its submission to its master and willingness to obey his or her commands.

hereditability propensity or likelihood of a characteristic to be inherited.

hereditary genetically transmittable from the parents or ancestors.

heredity sum of characteristics, qualities, and potentialities that are derived from ancestors.

Herhound another name for the Greyhound.

heritable describing traits that are capable of being inherited.

hermaphrodite individual with gonads of both sexes.

hernia protrusion of a loop of intestine or part of an internal organ through an abnormal opening in the musculature.

herpes inflammatory disease characterized by small vesicles; caused by a virus.

herring gut describing the body of a dog that is thin, with little rib spring; one that is narrow, with little substance.

hetero- prefix meaning different, variant, or opposite.

heterochromia iridis two-colored eye, with parts of the iris pigmented differently from one another; seen most commonly in merle dogs, especially in Australian Shepherds.

heterosis increased vigor or stamina that occurs in the first generation of a hybrid; hybrid vigor.

HI abbreviation for the AKC title Herding Intermediate.

hiatus cleft or opening, such as esophageal hiatus, which is an opening in the diaphragm.

hide in racing, dog of only fair or ordinary class.

hidrosis secretion and excretion of sweat.

hie on in hunting, command from the handler to work in a different direction, usually accompanied by waving of the hand.

high describing a dog that is feeling its oats, one that is full of vim and vigor, and ready to tackle any challenge; eager to work.

high-backed *see* roach-backed.

high in hock describing a dog with a metatarsus of abnormal length.

high in withers describing a dog's topline that falls both to the neck and to the back, giving a swaybacked, ewe-neck appearance.

high jump 1. in the Open and Utility class in obedience trials, a 5-foot- (150-cm) wide jump bar that is adjustable from 12 to 36 inches (30–91 cm) at 2-inch (1-cm) intervals. The bar is situated above a base board that measures 8 inches (20 cm). **2.** in agility trials, bars or panels that are set at 12 and 18 inches (30 and 46 cm) high for small dogs, and 24 and 30 inches (60 cm and 76 cm) high for large dogs.

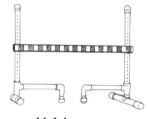

high jump

Highland Collie another name for the Bearded Collie.

Highland Deerhound another name for Scottish Deerhound.

high-mettled describing a dog in excellent physical and mental condition that is eager to perform and spirited.

high on leg describing a dog with too much leg for the amount of body it has that appears out of proportion or out of balance.

high scent in foxhunting, scenting, a fresh scent that is easily picked up above the ground; windborne scent.

high-set ears ears that are attached to the head near the occiput at the topline of its skull.

high-standing dog tall dog that is well balanced on long legs.

high-strung dog in field trials, one that is excessively exuberant and enthusiastic in performances.

high set ears

high swimmer dog that swims high in the water, a desirable characteristic of retrievers.

hike in sledding, the command of a driver to start the team moving, also used to urge the team to attain greater speed or to pull harder. (The well-known "mush" is rarely used.)

hill-worn dog in hunting, a worn-out, exhausted, over-worked dog.

hindhand perineal region of a dog; anatomical area posterior to the dog's croup.

hindquarters anatomical body region behind the flanks, including the pelvis, thighs, and hocks.

hindquarters angulation angle between the hip and femur; relative configuration of femur and pelvis.

hip anatomical region of the femoral articulation with the pelvis.

hip dysplasia serious disease of dogs that has a hereditary predisposition. It may include subluxation of the hip joint, a shallow hip socket, or a flattened femoral head; usually results in arthritis.

hip joint coxofemoral articulation; joint between the femur and the pelvis.

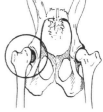

hip dysplasia

hippomane small, mysterious round tissue mass that is not connected to either the placenta or the puppies, that occasionally is found in the allantoic fluid at the time of whelping.

hip socket acetabulum, which is a cavity in the pelvis into which the head of the femur fits and with which it articulates.

histamine substance produced by the body upon exposure to an allergen; initiator of an allergic reaction.

histology study of microscopic tissue anatomy.

histoplasmosis systemic fungal disease of the lungs, causing pneumonia, chronic cough, and fever.

history collection of facts pertaining to an animal's health or illness that may be used to assist the diagnosis.

hit off in foxhunting, to recover the scent line at a check.

hobby breeders amateur dog breeders. *See* backyard breeders.

hock ring tuft of hair that encircles the hock in a formal Poodle show trim.

hock tarsal joint; joint between the stifle and pastern; calcaneal area.

hocking out bow-legged in the hind legs, with the hocks spread widely.

hocks well-let-down describing a shortened pastern; describing a short distance between the hock and the ground.

hocky having faulty hocks; noticeable deformity of the hocks.

hogback high, thin back; roach back.

hold at bay in foxhunting, to prevent the quarry from running while waiting for the remainder of the pack to arrive.

hold back in foxhunting, a slowing command to the pack that tells the dogs to stay between the whips and not to overrun the huntsmen.

holders dog's fangs; canine teeth; grasping teeth.

hold hard in foxhunting, warning to riders to slow up and not press the hounds.

holding the quality of hunting terrain. "Good holding" meaning good cover with lots of quarry.

holding area place where sled teams are organized and harnessed prior to the beginning of a race.

holding pen herding term for the pen on the outside of the course where the stock are kept before and after their use on the course.

holdout kennel *see* jinny pit.

hold over command in foxhunting to remain still, to not move ahead.

hold up 1. in foxhunting, a command to stop the hounds while hunting. **2.** in herding, a command to stop the sheep from moving away.

holloa in foxhunting, a cry of encouragement to the huntsmen or the pack.

hollow back depression of a dog's midback; swayback.

holt fox's den or an underground burrow.

homemade food dog's ration formulated in the family kitchen (usually a mistake).

hollow back

homeopathy system of therapeutics in which diseases are treated by drugs that are capable of producing symptoms like those of the disease. The drug that is used is given in minute doses.

home range general neighborhood in which a dog lives; neutral zone outside its marked territory in which most other dogs are allowed without challenge.

homing instinct innate ability of a dog to find its way home even when taken many miles away.

hond Dutch word for "dog."

honest foxhunting term to describe a hound with no hunting faults.

honorable scars former wounds that were gained while working and are working dogs' badges of distinction. Most AKC breed standards allow for these scars. Example: the scars of wounds that were incurred when a terrier tangled with a fox or badger.

honor a line in foxhunting, describing the action of a hound that gives tongue on the line of a quarry.

hooded ear standing or erect ear that curves forward at the tip and on the sides, forming a canopy.

hookup area in sledding, the area or enclosure where the sled dogs are harnessed and prepared for a race.

hookworm *Ancylostoma caninum,* an endoparasite with tiny hooklike appendages that fasten to the lining of the dog's intestine and can cause intestinal hemorrhage.

hookworm dermatitis inflammation of the skin that is associated with a hookworm infestation, hookworm larvae, and their tissue migration.

hoop jump *see* tire jump.

hormone endocrine secretion that has a specific effect on the activities of other organs.

horn 1. in foxhunting, musical instrument carried by huntsmen to call the hounds, control the hounds during a hunt, and let the hunt followers know where the dogs are at any given moment. **2.** material of which toenails are made.

horn

hospice dogs Saint Bernards that were so named for their work in rescuing travelers in the Saint Bernard Pass area of the Swiss Alps. They have worked in the company of monks from the Hospice since around 1700.

host animal that harbors and nourishes another organism to its detriment; animal that is parasitized.

hotbox feature race of the afternoon.

hotboxer outstanding prospect in the feature race of the day.

hot dog in racing, a fired-up Greyhound that is looking its best on the track.

hothouse dog dog of a hunting breed that was bred for bench showing without considering its hunting ability.

hot spot area of moist dermatitis; skin inflammation with exudation that is usually caused by flea bites or other skin parasites.

hot-wax in sledding, to treat the plastic strips on the sled runners with wax to decrease friction.

hound 1. any dog of the breeds forming the hound group. **2.** dogs of the sporting or terrier groups that hunt by sight or scent. **3.** mixed-breed dogs that are used for scenthunting or sighthunting. **4.** in sledding, any breed of dog other than a northern breed.

hound colors usually the black, tan, and white coat colors commonly seen in a foxhound hunting pack.

hound ears pendulant, dropped ears.

hound group AKC group that includes: Afghan Hound, Basenji, Basset Hound, Beagle, Black and Tan Coonhound, Bloodhound, Borzoi, Dachshund, American Foxhound, English Foxhound, Greyhound, Harrier, Ibizan Hound, Irish Wolfhound, Norwegian Elkhound, Otterhound, Petit Basset Griffon Vendéen, Pharaoh Hound, Rhodesian Ridgeback, Saluki, Scottish Deerhound, and Whippet.

hound-marked describing a dog that carries the markings of black, tan, and white that is common to scenthounds and certain terriers.

hound music baying, tongue, or voices of a pack of hounds on a trail.

hound pad rubber grooming tool with fine rubber studs that is made in the form of a glove or a brush and held in the palm of a hand.

hound trail artificial trail laid down for racing or trials.

hound work any scent-following exhibition.

housebreak to train a dog to defecate and urinate outside the house.

house dog any type of dog that lives in a domestic dwelling; usually refers to small dogs.

house dog disease *see* canine distemper.

household for the purpose of field trials, lure coursing, and other competition, the household includes those persons that comprise a unit living together in the same dwelling.

house-train *see* housebreak.

Hovawart black, black and tan, or gold-colored dog with a long, wavy coat that is primarily a companion dog and guard dog. Its original name "hofewart" meant "warden of the estate and farmyard." Currently recognized by the German Kennel Club, the breed became extinct about the turn of the century, but was recreated from local German breeds.

hover in foxhunting, a temporary refuge of the quarry; quarry's hiding place.

howl vocalization of certain dogs mimicking the call of a wolf or coyote; typical of arctic dogs.

howling dog superstition old English superstition that holds that a howling dog represents the Angel of Death passing by. It means that coffins will be brought from the direction of the howling dog. Two howls means a man's death; three howls means a woman's death.

HS abbreviation for the title "Herding Started."

HT abbreviation for the title "Herding Tested."

hucklebones protrusion of the two iliac crests of the pelvis.

huick in foxhunting, command to watch a particular dog's direction.

Humane Society of the United States, The 2100 L St., NW, Washington, DC 20037.

humerus upper arm bone, extending from the shoulder to the elbow.

hund German word for "dog."

Hungarian Cattle Dog *see* Pumi.

Hungarian Greyhound gazehound with a very short coat. It is about 27 inches (69 cm) tall, weighs about 65 pounds (29 kg), and is seen in all colors, including gray, black, dappled, white, and brindle. It has amazing speed and is used for racing or hunting foxes and hares.

Hungarian Hound scent dog that is seen in two sizes: the large Hungarian Hound that stands about 21 inches (53 cm) tall and weighs about 55 pounds (25 kg), or the small Hungarian Hound that stands about 16 inches (41 cm) tall and weighs about 24 pounds (11 kg).

Hungarian Pointer another name for the Vizsla.

Hungarian Sheepdog another name for the Komondor.

hunt 1. to participate in any sport in which dogs are used to pursue, retrieve, and sometimes kill their quarry. **2.** pack of hounds and horses used in foxhunting.

hunt counter in scenting, to take a scent in the reverse direction from which it was laid.

hunt followers in foxhunting, gallery, audience, or onlookers who do not actively participate in the hunt.

hunting any field sport, including shooting game.

hunting the clean boot pursuing the trail of a human runner.

hunt kennels kennels that belong to a foxhunting group or club.

huntsman person in charge of a pack of hunting hounds.

hup 1. in sledding, a driver's command to set the sled dogs in motion. **2.** in field trials, the command for a spaniel to sit and stay when used in the field. **3.** in hunting, command for bird dogs meaning *down*. **4.** obedience command to *jump*.

hurdles in obedience and agility trials, low barricades that are placed at intervals for the canine competitors to leap over.

hurricane warning nervousness often exhibited by some dogs when they sense a coming hurricane. Because of the high-pitched sounds of the wind whistling through cracks and window crevices, they often perceive a hurricane coming before humans do.

husbandry 1. responsibility of caring for a pet, including feeding, housing, grooming, and preventive health care. **2.** judicious use of resources, including the appropriate management of animals and their reproduction.

hush puppy southern U.S. recipe for deep-fried, highly seasoned cornmeal cake. It was formerly fed to dogs as a cheap food, but is now enjoyed by humans.

Husky inclusive term for Arctic sled dogs, including the Alaskan Malamute, Mackenzie River Dog, Toganee, Greenland Huskies, Baffinland Dog, Siberian Husky, Samoyed, some spitz types, and Eskimo Dogs.

HX abbreviation for the title "Herding Excellent."

hybrid offspring produced when two animals of different species are bred, such as wolf-dog crosses and coyote-dog. The term is currently extended to include the progeny of two dogs of different breeds, or the offspring of an outcross of the same breed.

hybrid vigor or **heterosis** improved stamina, vitality, and strength of the offspring of two different species.

hydatid cyst tapeworm life stage in which *echinococcus scolices* (reproductive elements) are found; often located in the abdomen of cattle or sheep.

hydrocephalus abnormal accumulation of fluid in a dog's cranial vault.

hydrophobia fear of water; early name for furious rabies in dogs.

hyena old-world scavenging carnivore that occurs wild on the African and Asian continents. It belongs to the Hyaenidae family and does not cross with dogs.

hyena dog *Lycaon pictus*, cape dog, South African hunting dog, or South African wild dog that has the general outward appearance of a hyena.

hyena

Hygenhound, Hygenstövare, or **Hygen Hound** smooth-coated scenthound from Norway that stands about 21 inches (53 cm) tall and weighs about 58 pounds (26 cm). It was developed by F. Hygen who used Holsteiner Hounds as the basic stock, and also included the Dunker. It is similar to other hounds in color and temperament, and is virtually unknown outside Norway.

hymen vestigial membrane occasionally found in the female dog; partially occludes the external orifice of the vagina.

Hygen Hound

hyperactive describing a dog that appears frenzied or frantic with increased activity.

hyperextension overextension. Example: Hyperextension of the knee involves the stretching of tendons, ligaments, and the joint capsule and results in a lameness of the hind leg.

hyperplastic nipple overgrowth of mammary nipple tissue that sometimes occludes the milk duct; often seen in aged bitches who have whelped numerous litters.

hypersialosis drooling, or oversecretion of saliva that is sometimes a hereditary condition in Newfoundlands or Saint Bernards.

hypertonic excessive tone or tension in a muscle.

hypertrophic osteodystrophy disease of young, large breeds that is manifested by swelling and pain of the ends of the long bones. Affected dogs may also exhibit fever and lethargy.

hypertrophy enlargement or overgrowth of an organ due to an increase in the size of its constituent cells.

hypotrichosis condition manifested by a reduced quantity of hair or the absence of coat.

Hyrcanus legendary King Lysimachus's dog that threw himself on the king's funeral pyre after the king died in one of Alexander the Great's battles.

hyup in sledding, a driver's command that sets the dogs into motion.

I

iatrogenic describing a disease or the symptoms of a disease that are inadvertently caused by a veterinarian or by therapy.

Ibizan Hound AKC group: hound; ancient breed that has been traced back to the Egyptian pharaohs. It stands about 25 inches (63.5 cm) tall and weighs about 50 pounds (23 kg). A gazehound, it is shown as one of two types: short-coated or wirehaired variety. It is colored white or red, solid, or in any combination of the two colors.

Ibizan Hound

ice hook in sledding, an anchor with sharp prongs that can be pounded into the ice. It lacks the fins and high handle of snow hooks.

Iceland Dog rare breed that stands about 16 inches (41 cm) tall and weighs about 30 pounds (14 kg). It has spitz characteristics, with erect ears and a curled tail and is seen in colors that range from white with fawn markings to golden red with black markings. It is primarily a house pet but is an instinctive herding dog.

Iceland Spitz longhaired northern dog with typical spitz characteristics. Found in Iceland, it stands about 14 inches (36 cm) tall and weighs about 35 pounds (16 kg).

Icelandic Sheepdog breed with the appearance of a Collie-Husky mix; spitz-type dog with prick ears and curled tail, somewhat similar to the Elkhound. Its height is about 20 inches (51 cm), it weighs about 50 pounds (23 kg), and has a black and white, long, bushy coat. It is a ferocious sheepdog and horse drover, and never made it as a show dog or companion.

Icelandic Sheepdog

ICH abbreviation for infectious canine hepatitis, a viral disease of dogs that primarily affects the liver; currently called CAV-1.

icterus yellow discoloration of tissues caused by hemoglobin seeping into the skin, mucous membranes, or other tissues; may be associated with vascular disease or the result of liver disease. *See* jaundice.

icthyosis type of hyperkeratosis; dry, rough, scaly skin.

ictus true seizure activity.

idiopathic epilepsy convulsive seizures that are seen without a known cause; usually thought to be hereditary in the canine.

Iditerod granddaddy of all dog sled races. The course now runs from Anchorage to Nome, a distance of more than 1,000 miles (1,609 km) of Alaskan wilderness. More than 50 sled teams compete in the annual race in temperatures as low as –50°F (–67°C). The record is held by Susan Bucher, who, in 1987, finished the race in 9 days, 5 hours, 43 minutes, and 13 seconds. The original Iditerod was an emergency run that carried life-saving diphtheria serum from Nenana to Nome in 1925, a distance of some 650 miles (1,046 km) that was covered in 5½ days.

I.D. Pet tattoo-based pet registry: 74 Hoyt Street, Darien, Connecticut 06820.

igloo commercially manufactured doghouse formed of fiberglass to resemble an igloo; available in various sizes.

Igloo Admiral Richard E. Byrd's Fox Terrier that traveled to the Arctic with him.

ileitis inflammation of the ileum.

ileocecal, ileocolic, or **iliocecocolic** refers to conditions of the lower small intestine, together with the upper large intestine. It involves the ileum, cecum, and colon.

ileum anatomical region of the third section of small intestine that extends from the jejunum to the cecum.

iliac crest prominent tips of the wings of the ilium (pelvic bones) that are visible in thin dogs.

ilio- related to the ilium, the pelvis, or the flank.

iliofemoral referring to the anatomical region of the pelvis and upper hind leg; hip region.

iliolumbar referring to the pelvis and the posterior back region.

ilium pelvic bone on which the acetabulum is located; also called the haunch bone. It connects to the sacral vertebrae at the sacroiliac junction.

Illyrian Hound wirehaired scenthound that originated in Yugoslavia. It stands about 20 inches (51 cm) tall and weighs about 39 pounds (18 kg).

Illyrian Sheepdog or **Sar Planina** Yugoslavian herding dog that resembles a Collie. It stands about 23 inches (51 cm) tall, weighs about 65 pounds (29 kg), and has a thick gray coat and a black mask.

Illyrian Sheepdog

image picture or graphic reproduction of bones or internal organs on X-rays, ultrasound film, or magnetic resonance films.

imbalance improper ratio or proportion of nutrients or electrolytes in the body.

immediate family for the purpose of various classes in dog shows and trials this includes the dog's registered owner, siblings, parents, grandparents, spouse, and children.

impacted anal sacs condition in which an obstruction occurs in the ducts of either of the two scent sacs situated immediately inside the anus. It often causes the affected dog to scoot on the floor, and, if it is not relieved, it may abscess.

impact fracture broken bone where the bone ends are driven together forcibly and override one another.

impaction something that is firmly lodged; usually refers to severe constipation.

impetigo disease of puppies that is manifested by blisters and brown crusts on the stomach.

implant graft that is taken from donor tissues and placed into the tissues of the recipient. Donor and recipient may be two separate animals or the same animal.

implantation site of embryonic attachment to the uterine wall.

implement to put into effect; to carry out.

impotence inability to perform sexually.

impregnation fertilization of an egg with a sperm cell to form a zygote; also known as fecundation or conception.

in and in inbreeding of dogs without regard to results.

inanimate 1. without life, or devoid of animation. **2.** describing a slow, sluggish, lazy dog.

inanition state of starvation; state of being deprived of life-supporting nutrition.

inappetence lack of appetite or desire to eat.

inbred descriptive of offspring of mated dogs that are closely related to each other.

inbreeding practice of mating siblings to each other: father to daughter, mother to son, or other animals closely related to each other.

incapacitate to disable; to deprive of natural mobility or strength.

incestuous breeding situation in which family members such as brother and sister, father and daughter, or mother and son are mated. In the wild it is a regular occurrence, but because of the natural survival of the fittest, it results in few problems.

incisor any one of the "biting off" or "cutting" teeth directly in the front of the mouth. There are six incisors in the upper jaw, six in the lower. They are named central, intermediate, and corner. *See* dentition.

incontinence loss of ability to control urinary elimination; self-soiling.

incoordination lack of synchronization of movement; staggering; failure of parts or organs of the body to work together in harmony.

incubate to promote a controlled and constant temperature to encourage the growth of a bacterial, fungal, or tissue culture.

incubation period time lapse between infection and the onset of signs of the disease.

incubator 1. environmentally regulated chamber that is used to incubate cultures. **2.** device that provides a controlled environment; used to raise orphaned puppies.

incus central of the three bones of the middle ear, sometimes called the anvil. It acts together with the other two bones to transmit sound waves to the inner ear. *See* stapes and malleus.

independent action in herding, the ability of a dog to act without human instructions; characteristic of a good herding dog.

Indian Dog in sledding, any husky-type dog that originated in a northern native village.

Indian Wild Dog or *Canis indicus* Dhole, Deccan Dog, or Kolsun; feral dog found in Tibet and the Gangetic plain of Indochina. It stands about 16 inches (41 cm) tall, weighs about 40 pounds (18 kg) and has a pointed muzzle, a large, flat head, and bushy tail. Its medium length coat is colored red, gray, tan, or light brindle with fawn and black markings. It preys on deer, wild pig, goats, sheep, and cattle.

indigenous occurring in that location or region; native; not foreign to a particular place.

individual merit selection method of choosing breeding stock based on the quality of the dogs chosen without regard to their pedigrees.

individual start in sledding, a starting order of a race where each team leaves at a specified interval. This method avoids tangles and confusion, and each team's progress is individually timed.

Indo China Wild Dog Indian Wild Dog.

induced estrus describing the state of a bitch that has been brought into season by the administration of hormones or by another bitch in season in the kennel.

inertia property of matter to remain at rest or in motion unless acted upon by a force. In whelping, uterine inertia is the tendency of a gravid uterus to remain at rest instead of contracting normally to produce puppies.

infant neonatal being; newborn puppy.

infectious canine hepatitis *see* CAV-1 virus infection.

infertile state of sterility, infecundity; state of being barren.

infestation invasion of the body with parasites such as arthropods or helminths, including fleas, ticks, mites, roundworms, tapeworms, and heartworms.

infield that part of a racing course enclosed by a fence, separating it from the track.

Info Pet Identification Systems microchip-based registry of dogs: 517 West Travelers Trail, Minneapolis, Minnesota 55337.

inguinal hernia hernia of the groin area that may be congenital.

inhalant medicine that is drawn in by breathing, as in some of the canine upper respiratory vaccines.

inherent describing a trait or quality that is innate, natural, or instinctive.

inherited describing characteristics, qualities, or traits that are genetically passed from parents to progeny.

inhibited prevented from happening; restrained process.

injected congested or reddened mucous membrane. Example: Conjunctivitis is manifested by injection of the sclera.

injection act of placing a substance into body tissues, or the product that is injected.

injury any act that harms, damages, or wounds.

innate congenital, hereditary trait; inborn quality or instinct.

inpatent closed, obstructed, or having a normal opening that has become closed.

inpatient patient kept in a hospital for therapy or diagnostic tests.

in pup or with pup bitch that is pregnant or has a gravid uterus.

in season said of an intact bitch that is demonstrating typical estrus activity.

Insecta class of arthropods that includes the fly.

insect growth regulator chemical agent that prevents the development and maturation of insect larvae into adults; a contemporary flea control. *See* Lufenuron®.

insecticide substance used to kill insects.

insemination deposit of semen, together with secretions of accessory sex glands, into the vagina of a receptive female.

inside hare

inside hare or **inside rabbit** in racing, the lure that travels on a track inside the racing strip.

instinct propensity of dogs to perform certain acts without training or conditioning. Instinctively they resemble and mimic their wild relatives, the wolves. Example: turning around and around before they lie down as wolves do to trample leaves and prepare a resting place.

intelligence ability of a dog to comprehend and perform commands and exercises.

intelligent disobedience learned behavior of a guide dog of disobeying its sightless master's command when obeying that command would lead them into a dangerous situation.

intensive of increased frequency or force.

interbreeding outcrossing or breeding of two different but similar breeds to one another.

intercondylar fracture broken bone that includes that portion of a bone that is involved in a joint.

interdigital dermatitis inflammation of the web of a dog's foot. It is often allergic in nature.

interdigital web membrane that extends between a water-retrieving dog's toes that aids in its swimming ability.

interestrous period time between the cessation of one estrous cycle and the onset of the next.

interference in herding, action of a person other than the handler in an attempt to control the competing dog from outside the exhibition ring.

interfering describing a gait in which the path of the forefeet cross over one another and one foot brushes the opposite leg each time it passes; faulty gait.

intermittent fever elevated body temperature that runs in cycles, with a normal temperature seen between the periods of fever.

International Veterinary Acupuncture Society 2140 Conestoga Road, Chester Springs, Pennsylvania 19425.

interseasonal period anestrus phase of a dog's estrous cycle.

intervertebral disk fibrocartilage cushioning structure located between the bodies of adjacent vertebrae, giving them mobility.

intervertebral disk protrusion slipped disk; herniated disk; displacement of a disk as a result of injury or heredity.

intervertebral disk

intestine hollow structure that leads from the stomach to the anus in which digestion takes place. The parts of the intestine are: duodenum, jejunum, ileum, cecum, colon, and rectum.

intimidate in field trials, the activity of a handler who flushes pointed birds by using a quirt, whip, crop, or leash in such a manner as to threaten the dog.

intimidation display facial expressions and body language that establishes rank and order in a pack of dogs or wolves without the pack actually fighting.

intrauterine contraceptive device object placed within the uterus to prevent fertilization, but does nothing to prevent estrus or a male dog's attention.

intravaginal contraceptive device proprietary device that was popular in the past. It was placed into a dog's vagina to prevent breeding and proved to be easily lost or pushed aside by a male dog.

intravenous within the vein; solution that is to be injected into a vein.

intravenous fluid therapy administration of corrective or supportive liquids directly into the bloodstream by means of a drip system.

intravenous pyelogram X-ray, sonogram, or MRI study of the kidney that includes its size, shape, and function.

intromission insertion of the penis into the vagina during normal copulation. Intromission in a dog is made possible by the os penis.

introvert anthropomorphic term that is applied to a shy dog.

intussusception telescoping or slipping of one section of intestine into the next.

inu Japanese for "dog."

intussusception

Inu Nus'to medium-sized, short-coated dog of Japan; similar to a Bull Terrier in appearance. The breed is a common companion to Japanese beggars.

in utero occurring within the uterus.

invasion onset of disease; harmless entry of bacteria into a body without causing disease.

invasiveness capacity and ability of a microorganism to invade the body.

inveterate describing a chronic or long-established malady, one that is difficult to cure.

invitation to play body language expression that usually takes the form of the dog stretching out its forelegs flat on the ground, with the hindquarters elevated, and typically accompanied by a wagging tail.

invitation to play

in vitro occurring within a test tube or beaker, an event that takes place in a laboratory.

in vivo occurring within a living body.

involuntary culling self-elimination of inefficient breeding stock in a kennel through natural attrition due to age and infirmity.

involution turning inward; shrinking or returning to a normal size. Example: Involution of the uterus following whelping requires several weeks.

in whelp pregnant or carrying puppies.

iris pigmented membrane situated immediately in front of the lens of the eye that has a central opening (pupil) through which light traverses.

Irish Blue Terrier another name for Kerry Blue Terrier.

Irish Elkhound or **Irish Greyhound** other names for Irish Wolfhound.

Irish Kennel Club principal dog registry of Ireland: 41 Harcourt Street, Dublin 2, Ireland.

Irish Red and White Setter breed that has been known in Ireland since the eighteenth century. It stands about 24 inches (61 cm) tall, weighs about 50 pounds (23 kg), has a well-feathered tail, and a bushy coat that is long, shiny, and parti-colored with a ground color of white with red patches. It is an agile gundog and a fine companion.

Irish Setter

Irish Setter AKC group: sporting; hunting dog for which there is no disqualification for size, but that usually stands about 27 inches (69 cm) tall and has a weight of about 70 pounds (32 kg). It has a moderate length coat that lies flat, and long, straight, silky feathering on its belly, ears, and brisket. The only acceptable color is red.

Irish Terrier AKC group: terrier; natural hunter of small vermin and game; one of the oldest terrier breeds. Its height is about 18 inches (46 cm), its weight is about 27 pounds (12 kg), and it is bright red, golden red, red wheaten or wheaten in color. It is an animated dog with a docked tail and a dense, wiry coat.

Irish Terrier

Irish Water Spaniel AKC group: sporting; water retriever that stands about 24 inches (61 cm) tall and weighs about 60 pounds (27 kg). It is the tallest of the spaniels, with a smooth or rat tail, and a double, oily coat that is dense, curled, and solid liver-colored.

Irish Wheaten Terrier another name for the Soft Coated Wheaten Terrier.

Irish Wolf Dog another name for the Scottish Deer-hound.

-Irish Water Spaniel

Irish Wolfhound AKC group: hound; also known as the Greyhound of Ireland. Of great size, the minimum height of the dog should be 32 inches (81 cm) and it should have a minimum weight of 120 pounds (54 kg). Its rough, hard, wiry coat is gray, brindle, red, black, pure fawn, or any other color that appears in the deerhound. This dog was used to pursue the gigantic Irish elk, as well as wolves. Its temperament is neither suspicious or aggressive.

irregular bite malaligned teeth with uneven spaces.

Irish Wolfhound

irrigate to flush with water, or to lavage or wash.

irritability abnormal or negative response to a stimulus.

Isabella fawn or light bay color that is rare in the Doberman Pinscher.

ischium lower part of the pelvis. Together with the ilium and pubis, it makes up the pelvic girdle.

isoflurane type of gas anesthesia commonly used in older pets because of its favorable safety margin.

isolate to separate an individual from others of the same species; to quarantine a dog in order to control the spread of a communicable disease.

isolation syndrome set of habits or traits of dogs that are raised with no human contact and without a period of socialization.

Isospora genus of coccidia, a protozoan parasite of the gut that causes diarrhea and general poor health in dogs.

Istrian Sheepdog

Istrian Pointer dog from Yugoslavia and Hungary that is seen in either rough-haired or smooth-coated varieties. Its height is about 20 inches (51 cm), its weight is about 45 pounds (20 kg), and its color is white with tan, red, or black markings.

Istrian Sheepdog Hungarian herding dog from the peninsula of Istria on the Adriatic Sea; similar in appearance to the Komondor and Kuvasz breeds.

Italian Bergama sheepdog; another name for the Bergamaschi.

Italian Greyhound

Italian Greyhound AKC group: toy; appears to be a miniature Greyhound. It stands about 13 inches (33 cm) tall, weighs as little as 5 pounds (2.3 kg) or as much as 15 pounds (33 cm), and has a short, slick, satinlike coat that comes in any color with or without markings. It is a high-stepping, animated little pet.

Italian Hound or **Segugio** pack hunter with an excellent sense of smell. It stands about 21 inches (53 cm) tall, and is seen in either a short-haired or a wire-haired variety. It is red, fawn, chestnut, hazelnut, with white patches, or tricolor. It is used on virtually all furred quarry.

Italian Hound

Italian Kennel Club Ente Nazionale della Cinofilia Italiana, 21 Viale Premuda, Milan.

Italian Spinone *see* Spinone Italiano.

Italian Volpino or **Italian Spitz** similar to the Pomeranian in appearance. They are long-coated, stand about 11 inches (28 cm) tall, weigh about 11 pounds (5 kg), are seen in solid white or red. and have tails that curl over their backs.

Italian Volpino

itis suffix to a word that denotes "inflammation."

ivermectin antiparasitic drug that is useful in preventing canine heartworm disease.

ivy leaf herb that is boiled in water for two hours, given to whelping dogs, and said to prevent afterbirth retention.

Ixodes genus of ticks that can transmit many dog diseases.

J

jabot throat hair fringe on Schipperkes and others.

Jack Russell Terrier named for Reverend John Russell, of Devon, who began the breed in England in 1870, currently being shown in the AKC Miscellaneous class. There are two Jack Russell varieties that are being bred: the smaller, shorter-legged variety which is frequently referred to as the Parson Jack Russell, stands about 11 inches (28 cm) tall and weighs about 13 pounds (5.9 kg); the larger is about 14 inches (36 cm) tall and weighs about 14 pounds (6.3 kg). It resembles the Fox Terrier, has a deep chest, V-shaped drop ears that are folded forward, and a coat that is smooth, broken, or rough. Its color is predominantly white with lemon, tan, or black markings on the muzzle and loins. It was developed to hunt foxes and raccoons, has an uncertain temperament, and is a spirited working dog. (See photo, page 44.)

Jack Russell Terrier

jackal *Canis aureus*, a wild canid that sometimes crosses with the domestic dog.

jacket dog's coat or the pattern of the coat color. Example: He had a short jacket of black over his tan body.

Jacob novelist Hugh Walpole's dog that inspired him to write: "I tremble to think of the many different breeds of dogs that have gone to his making—but he had character, he had heart, he had an unconquerable zest for life."

Jamthund *see* Swedish Elkhound.

Japanese Bear Hound another name for the Shishi.

Japanese Chin AKC group: toy; originally bred as a lap dog for the Japanese aristocracy. A short-muzzled dog of less than 7 pounds (3.2 kg), it stands about 9 inches (23 cm) tall. It is black and white, lemon and white, red and white, or brindle colored. Its coat is long, straight, and silky, and its heavily feathered tail is carried over its back.

Japanese Chin

Japanese Deerhound previous name for the Akita.

Japanese Fighting Dog or **Japanese Mastiff** *see* Tosa.

Japanese Kennel Club Japan Dog Federation, Chiyoda-ku, Kanda, Asahi-cho no 8, Tokyo.

Japanese Pug, Japanese Spaniel, or **Japanese Chin Chin** other names for the Japanese Chin.

234

Japanese Spitz name commonly applied to an entire group of related breeds; also used in connection with one specific breed. It is white in color, and was possibly developed from the German Spitz.

Japanese Terrier or **Mikado Terrier** cross between a small dog of Japan and the smooth Fox Terrier or Amertoy. It is a prick-eared, compact, cuddly lapdog. It stands about 12 inches (30 cm) tall, weighs about 10 pounds (4.5 kg), has a very short, smooth, and shiny coat, and is seen in white with black and tan markings.

Japanese Turf Dog *see* Shiba.

jaundice bile pigment that appears in the skin and mucous membranes, giving the dog a yellow coloration; often associated with liver disease.

Java Dog in Chinese mythology, ancestor of modern dog.

jaw either the maxilla (upper jaw) or mandible (lower jaw); bones bearing the teeth.

jaw panosteitis inflammation of the jaw bone that appears as an inherited predisposition in the Scottish Terrier.

jealousy hostility toward a rival, an emotion commonly associated with dogs and often brought on by the appearance of a new child or another pet in the family. Jealousy may elicit a loss of housetraining or a destructive tendency.

Jênterah one of the Malayan wild dogs. It has a red coat and a bushy tail and commonly preys on domestic poultry.

jerk and release training technique that employs a quick tightening and immediate release of the leash that is attached to the dog's choke collar.

jerk line 20-foot-long (51 cm) leash sometimes used as a training aid.

jewelled describing an eye with an iris that has a red tinge.

jingler in sledding, **1.** noisemaker, such as a string of bells, used instead of a whip to get a team's attention. **2.** dog that has bells tied to its harness.

jinked describing an injured back or loin.

jinny pit in racing, kennels used to house racing Greyhounds immediately prior to post time.

Japanese Spitz

Japanese Terrier

joint articulation or union of bones that is held together by ligaments, surrounded by a joint capsule, and allows movement of the bones in one or more planes.

Jones Terrier another name for Fox Terrier.

jowl pendulous lower lips of hounds.

Juan Fernandez Sheepdog feral breed or race found only on Juan Fernandez Island, Chile, a wild and voiceless dog that probably descended from the Patagonian Sheepdog.

judge 1. in showing, a person who is licensed by the AKC to compare each dog to a breed standard or perfect performance and rate it accordingly; may be licensed for a single or multiple breeds. **2.** in field trials, coursing, or herding, person who is licensed by the AKC to rate the performance of a dog in events that display its ability to engage in the work for which it was bred.

judging the wrong end of a lead considering the merits of the handler instead of the dog being exhibited.

jugal zygomatic arch that lies under the orbit; cheekbone.

jugular veins paired vessels located on either side of the neck that are responsible for the blood circulation from the head.

juice fluid produced by an animal and its organs, such as gastric juice and intestinal juice.

July Hound early popular strain of the American Foxhound.

jump in obedience trials, obstacle that is never less than one and one-half times the height of dog, but never more than 3 feet (91 cm), except for giant breeds for which the jump is set at the dog's withers' height.

jump demand in obedience trials, command to a dog to take the jump.

jumped in foxhunting, said of a fox that has been discovered and is suddenly forced to run away at full speed.

jump shooting duck-hunting sport in which the hunter and dog do not use a blind and shots are taken when waterfowl leave the water.

junior dog between the age of six months and eighteen months.

junior handling or **junior showmanship** showing or obedience competition among young people to compare their handling expertise and skill, not the quality of their dogs.

junkyard dog guard dog; one trained to protect an automobile junkyard; slang for a really vicious guard dog.

Jura Laufhund, Bruno from the Jura region of Switzerland, near the French border, descendent of the heavier French breeds of hunting dogs. It stands about 23 inches (58 cm) tall, weighs about 45 pounds (20 kg), and has a smooth, black and tan coat with saddle markings.

Jura Laufhund, Saint Hubert from the Jura region of Switzerland, of a heavier build than the Bruno variety, and has more wrinkles and a pronounced dewlap. It is probably quite similar to the now-extinct Saint Hubert Hound. It stands about 23 inches (58 cm) tall, weighs about about 44 pounds (20 kg), and has the same black and tan coloring as the Bruno except that the black markings often extend beyond the saddle.

Jura Laufhund

K

K symbol for the electrolyte "potassium" (kalium).

K9 Corps World War II organized group of U.S. servicemen from all the various branches who trained war dogs for use in the armed forces. They trained thousands of German Shepherds Dogs, Dobermans, Dalmatians, and other large dogs for ambulance duty, guarding prisoners, as sentry dogs, for mine detection, sledding, packing, and scouting.

Kabyle or **Kabil Dog** sheepdog native to the Kabyle Mountains, Ouled Naïles, and Shawias, and common throughout Tunisia and Algeria. Its height is about 21 inches (53 cm) and it weighs about 40 pounds (18 kg), and it has a long, soft coat that is colored fawn or white. It is primarily a shepherd dog but is also seen as a feral, nomadic scavenger.

Kabyle Dog

Kai or **Kai-tora** breed that originated in Japan. It stands about 20 inches (51 cm) tall, and weighs about 40 pounds (18 kg), is a well-muscled dog with erect ears, and a curled or sickle shaped tail that is set high. Its double coat is black or red brindle with white markings. It is an all-weather hunting breed.

Kaikadi scenthound from India that is shorthaired, stands about 17 inches (43 cm), and weighs about 38 pounds (17 kg).

Kalagh variety of Afghan Hound that is shorthaired with long hair found only on its head and ears.

Kanawar sheepdog of India that has a long coat, stands about 24 inches (61 cm) tall, and weighs up to 70 pounds (32 kg).

Kangaroo Dog or **Kangaroo Greyhound** largest of the Australian breeds. Its height is about 28 inches (71 cm), its weight about 80 pounds (36 kg). It is black and tan, tan and white, brindle, or pied, and its coat is short and harsh. Used for kangaroo hunting, it is probably of Irish Wolfhound and Greyhound lineage.

Kangaroo Dog

Kaninchenteckel another name for the Miniature Dachshund.

Karelian Bear Dog Scandinavian dog named for the Karelia province of Finland, also known as the Russian Bear Dog, Björnhund, and Karjalankarhukoira. It originated in Finland where it was used to hunt bear, moose, elk, and wolves. It stands about 23 inches (58 cm) tall and weighs about 50 pounds (23 kg). It is a longhaired black dog with white markings and a fully arched tail. It is being shown in Finland, where an attempt is being made to breed out the dog's quarrelsome tendencies without compromising its hunting skills.

Karst herding dog raised in the Yugoslavian mountains. It has a rough gray coat similar to that of a wolf and pendulant ears.

KCS abbreviation for keratoconjunctivits sicca, a dry-eye syndrome that is due to insufficient lacrimal secretion.

keel region of the underside of the brisket.

keel bone breastbone; sternum.

keeper dog that an owner likes and intends to keep. Example: That puppy is a nuisance, but he's a keeper.

keeper's dog guard dog belonging to a gamekeeper.

Keeshond (plural Keeshonden) AKC group: non-sporting; national dog of Holland; sometimes called the Dutch barge dog. Medium-sized, lovable, and affectionate, it stands about 18 inches (46 cm) tall, weighs about 66 pounds (30 kg), has erect ears, and holds its tail curled over its back. A Keeshond's double coat is long and straight, with a thick downy undercoat. It is gray in color, with black-tipped hair, and cream markings. It has never been used for hunting or other forms of work, except, perhaps, guarding.

Keeshond

Kelpie *see* Australian Kelpie.

kennel 1. backyard doghouse where family pets or breeding stock are kept. **2.** commercial establishment used to maintain a group of dogs, such as a boarding kennel. **3.** in foxhunting, fox's lair. **4.** foxhunting term for the hound pack's lodging place.

kennel-blind possessing a near-sighted view in which there is no fault found in one's own dogs, but all others fall short of glory.

kennel boy or kennel man person hired to clean kennels and exercise dogs.

Kennel Club, The British dog registry: 1-4 Clargis Street, Piccadilly, London W7Y8AB, England.

kennel cough contagious disease complex involving *pertussis* and *Bordetella* bacteria and possibly some viruses; spread by the coughing of kennel inmates.

kennel huntsman in foxhunting, person in charge of a pack of hounds and responsible for their care, exercise, and feeding.

kennelitis affliction of a shy dog that has spent most of its life in a kennel and has not been handled and socialized with human companionship.

kennel lameness nonspecific lameness, usually due to lack of exercise. It usually includes soft, tender pads and a lack of condition, and is seen in dogs that are perpetually kenneled.

kennel maid female counterpart of a kennel boy or kennel man.

kennel name official, recognized (sometimes copyrighted) name of a breeding kennel that is sometimes attached as a suffix to puppies' names on their registration.

kennel sickness disease complex that includes diarrhea, vomiting, coughing, inappetence, and general malaise; sometimes caused by overcrowding and lack of hygiene in a kennel.

kennel tick *see* brown dog tick.

kennel type bloodline or strain of dogs that has been developed by an individual breeder in a specific kennel.

keratosis wart or callus or any horny growth, especially on the skin.

Kerry Beagle

Kerry Beagle or **Pocodan** taller and heavier than the ordinary Beagle, very likely the result of outcrossing a Beagle with a Foxhound. Its height is about 23 inches (58 cm), weight about 60 pounds (27 kg), its color is black and tan, blue mottled, or blue with white markings, and it has a short coat and long pendulant ears.

Kerry Blue Terrier

Kerry Blue Terrier AKC group: terrier; native of Ireland. It stands about 18 inches (46 cm) tall, and weighs about 40 pounds (18 kg), and is short-backed, with a gaily erect, docked tail. Its color is any shade of blue gray from slate to a much lighter color, and the coat is soft, dense and wavy. In Ireland it is a gundog, used to hunt small game and birds, and is often employed in water retrieving. It is also sometimes used for herding sheep and cattle.

keyed up describing a dog that becomes overly excited or frightened in field trials held before an audience or gallery.

Khampas Hound gazehound of India that is short-coated and stands about 22 inches (56 cm) tall.

kibble dry dog food that is formulated wet and extruded into small, bite-sized forms before drying.

kicked-up toe also known as knocked-up toe. It involves a digital flexor tendon of a toe and is common to track and coursing dogs.

kicking in sledding, driver's action to help the sled along by standing with one foot on the sled, and pushing with the other; same as pedaling.

kid fox immature fox or fox cub.

kidney one of two glandular organs necessary for life; principal function is to filter urinary waste from the blood.

kidney stone hard mineral formation abnormally formed in the kidney.

kill dead quarry.

kinesiology study of motion or the movement of animals.

kinetic referring or pertaining to motion or movement.

kinetic balance continuation of balance while moving; smoothness of gait.

king dog in sledding, the dominant or alpha dog in a sled team, usually the lead dog.

kingdom one of the three major divisions of taxonomy: animal kingdom or plant kingdom.

King Tut President Hoover's pet German Shepherd Dog.

kink sharp bend in the tail; an undesirable deformity or disqualification in most dog breeds.

kink tail sharply bent or broken tail; normally twisted tail, as seen in the Boston Terrier.

kinky coat curly coat that stands rather than lies.

kinky disposition describing a dog that acts weird and behaves abnormally, or unpredictably.

Kishu Japanese breed that was originally a deer and boar hunter. It stands about 20 inches (51 cm) tall and weighs about 40 pounds (18 kg), has erect ears, a curved tail and a double coat. It is solid white, or red sesame-colored.

kissing spots tan or light-colored contrasting spots on each cheek of a dog.

kitchen dog *see* turnspit dog.

kit fox, *Vulpes macrotis,* or *Vulpes velox* red fox.

kissing spots

241

Klebsiella genus of bacteria often involved with canine respiratory infections.

knee stifle joint; articulation of the femur with the tibia and fibula.

kneecap patella, a sesamoid bone that lies in the tendon on the anterior surface of the stifle joint.

kneecap luxation hereditary condition in which stifle collateral ligaments are weak, bones are angled, and the kneecap slips easily off to one side.

knee cutting decree from King Canute of England, in 1016, that all commoners' dogs that were kept within ten miles of the king's forests must have their knees cut to prevent them from chasing the king's game. Lapdogs were excepted. *See* dog gauge; toe cutting.

knitting 1. weaving gait. **2.** specific obstacle course event in an agility trial in which the competing dog must travel in and out of a series of "weaving" poles that are set in a line. **3.** healing process of a fractured bone.

knitting and purling weaving motion of forefeet whose paths cross over one another.

knocked-down hip fractured pelvis, especially the ilium, that occurs as a track injury.

knocked-up toe *see* kicked-up toe.

knocking cry of hare hounds.

knuckle metacarpal or metatarsal joint; pastern, or dorsal surface of any foot joint.

knuckle over describing a carpus or wrist that is situated anterior to the dog's metacarpals. It gives the dog a clumsy appearance.

Kolsun *see* Indian wild dog.

Kombai gazehound of India that is smooth-coated, stands about 20 inches (51 cm) tall, and weighs about 29 pounds (13 kg).

Komondor (plural Komondrok) AKC group: working; Hungarian breed that stands about 32 inches (81 cm) tall and weighs about 135 pounds (61 kg). Its copious white, double coat falls into cords of coarse, curly hair; its long tail reaches the hocks and is carried below the topline. Characterized by imposing strength and courage, it accompanies sheep flocks, protecting rather than herding them.

Kooikerhondje working duck dog of the Netherlands that is also popular as a companion. It was named for a

knuckle

Komondor

hunting technique that requires the dog to chase ducks into a net along canals. It is a spaniel-like dog with drop ears and a wavy, long, red and white coat. It stands about 15 inches tall and weighs about 24 pounds.

Korthals Griffon name used in France for the Wirehaired Pointing Griffon. It is steel gray with chestnut markings and a short coat.

Kramforhländer product of a mating between a Wirehaired Fox Terrier bitch and possibly a Griffon Fauve de Bretagne. This breed originated with a Frau Schlienfenbaum, in Siegen, West Germany, after World War II. She fixed the characteristics of the litter by inbreeding, and it resulted in the Kramfohrländer; recognized by the German Kennel Club. It is a small dog that stands about 16 inches (41 cm) tall, weighs about 25 pounds (11 kg). Its coat is long or wirehaired (short) and wirehaired (long), and it is basically white with chestnut markings and a dark saddle.

Kuchi spitz-type dog from India with long hair that stands about 10 inches (25 cm) tall and weighs about 16 pounds (7 kg).

Kuochi mastiff-type dog of India that has a short coat, stands about 24 inches (61 cm) tall and weighs about 73 pounds (33 kg).

Kuri new Zealand breed, now extinct, that was kept mainly for its hair and meat. The long tail hairs were used for decorating spearheads, and its flesh tasted like lamb.

kuro Japanese word for "black"; refers to the black coat sprinkled with light fawn hairs that is found in some Japanese breeds.

kuro-goma refers to a black-sesame coat color with black peppering on a lighter black ground color, giving the coat a darker overall appearance.

kuro-tora term meaning black tiger in Japanese; referring to a black-striped brindle pattern on a dark ground color.

Kuvasz (plural Kuvaszok) AKC group: working; originated in Tibet as a guard dog. It measures about 29 inches (74 cm) tall, under 26 inches (66 cm) is a disqualification for males. Its weight is about 110 pounds (50 kg). It is big-boned, with a double coat of fine undercoat and coarse guard hair. Its color is always white, with heavily pigmented skin.

Kuvasz

Kwik-Stop® proprietary styptic powder that is used for stopping minor hemorrhages, such as a toenail that is cut too short.

Kyi-leo Lhasa Apso-Maltese mixture that stands about 11 inches (28 cm) tall, weighs about 15 pounds (7 kg), and resembles the Tibetan Terrier and the Shih Tzu. It originated in the San Jose area of California.

Kyle Terrier extinct relative of the Scottish, West Highland White, and Cairn Terriers.

L

Lab shortened name for the Labrador Retriever.

labium lip or lip-shaped organ.

labor whelping work of the bitch; voluntary and involuntary muscular contractions that produce a litter of puppies.

Labrador Retriever AKC group: sporting; originated in Newfoundland, not Labrador; a strongly built, tough, short-coupled gundog with a short, dense coat. It stands about 24 inches (61 cm) tall, weighs about 70 pounds (32 kg), and is seen in black, yellow, and chocolate colors, all without markings. It is a mild tempered dog that has proven to be an excellent companion dog and is the most popular dog in the United States at present. (See photo, page 15.)

Labrador Retriever

Labri *see* Pyrenean Sheepdog.

lacrimal ducts tear ducts that have their origin in the upper and lower conjunctival areas near the inside angle of the eyes. They drain into the nose.

lacrimation tears or the secretion of the lacrimal glands of the eyes.

lactation a bitch's natural milk production and secretion.

Laddie Boy Airedale Terrier that belonged to President Warren Harding.

Ladoga dog prehistoric dog of Anutchin; spitz-type dog.

lady pack in foxhunting, hound pack made up of females only.

Laekenois rare, rough-haired or wirehaired herding dog of Belgium. A pale red dog that stands about 23 inches (58 cm) tall and weighs about 50 pounds (23 kg), it was named for Laeken Castle in Holland and is also known as a Belgian Laekenois.

Laekenois

laid-back describing the angle produced by the scapula or shoulder blade, and the humerus. Example: He had excellent laid-back angulation.

Laika 1. group of spitz-like dogs found from Finland and Karelia to Tongoose and Voguls. They are very much alike, about 23 inches (58 cm) tall and weighing about 50 pounds (23 cm) with coats all medium to long. They are wolf-gray with a darker saddle and curled tails.

Laika

Lakeland Terrier

lamb clip

2. world's first space traveler, a dog from the Soviet Union that circled the earth in a satellite in 1957.

lair locality where a fox stays aboveground in daylight.

Lakeland Terrier AKC group: terrier; originally a fox-hunter that was used to follow foxes underground into their lairs. Its height is about 14 inches (35.6 cm), its weight is about 17 pounds (7.7 kg), it has a double coat with hard and wiry guard hair over a soft undercoat, and its color is solid blue, black, liver, red, and wheaten. Many are saddle-marked with blue, black, or liver.

lamb clip type of trim used on Poodles.

lame 1. favoring or limping on one or more legs due to injury or congenital deformity. **2.** in obedience trials, displaying an irregularity or impairment of the function of locomotion, regardless of its severity or cause.

lamping hunting with dogs after dark, using hand-held flashlights or an automobile spotlight.

Lancashire Heeler or **Ormskirk Terrier** working dog that is the result of Welsh Corgi crossed with Manchester Terrier. It stands about 12 inches (31 cm) tall, weighs about 13 pounds (6 kg), and is black with tan markings. It has a long tail, erect ears, and has the Corgi's herding instincts and the Manchester's vermin-catching skills.

land mine dogs during World War II dogs that were trained to sniff out spots of freshly turned soil, thereby detecting buried land mines, thus saving thousands of lives.

land spaniel dog used originally for falconry that was trained to find and flush upland game birds from the ground so the falcons could attack them.

Landseer a black and white strain of Newfoundland, named for Sir Edwin Landseer, a painter whose portraits popularized the breed. *See* Newfoundland.

Langerhans islets insulin-producing cells of the pancreas.

Languedoc sheepdog from France with long hair that stands about 17 inches (43 cm) tall and weighs about 46 pounds (21 kg).

lanky long in the back, long-legged, and usually thin.

lanolin purified form of hydrous wool fat used in many skin emollients; often prescribed to soften dogs' elbow calluses.

Lap Beagle pocket Beagle; small variety of Beagle.

lapdog dog that is able to comfortably sit on a person's lap; toy breed or companion dog, or any of the Oriental toy breeds; also known as sleeve dog.

Lapinporokoira or **Lapland Reindeer Dog** originated as a working dog in Finland; it stands about 22 inches (56 cm) tall, weighs about 66 pounds (30 kg), and is used to herd livestock and as a guard dog. It is a tough breed that resembles the spitz, with a dense undercoat, an uncurled tail, and a coat of black with brown or fawn markings.

Lapland Spitz Swedish breed with a long coat that stands about 18 inches (46 cm) tall and weighs about 42 pounds (19 kg).

Lapphund Lainkoira, Finnish Lapphund, or **Swedish Lapp Spitz** developed as a Far North herding dog, it stands about 20 inches (50 cm) tall and weighs about 47 pounds (21 kg). Used primarily on reindeer, it is a fearless dog that was used extensively in the Swiss army.

Lappland Sheepdog breed that originated in Finland and is used for herding. It stands about 18 inches (46 cm) tall, weighs about 45 pounds (20 kg), and has a long coat.

Large Münsterläander or **Grosser Munsterländer Vorstehhund** gundog bred in Westphalia from smaller varieties of German hunting breeds, mostly the German Longhaired Pointer. It stands about 24 inches (61 cm) tall, weighs about 65 pounds (29 kg), and is a striking combination of black and white with heavily ticked long hair.

larva immature stage of a parasite, the next stage after the egg; pleural: larvae.

larval migrans larvae of the dog roundworm, *Toxocara canis*, which sometimes inadvertently infests children, and migrates around deep in their organs and tissues. This condition is also known as visceral larval migrans.

laryngitis inflammation of the larynx; sore throat.

larynx mucous membrane-covered folds that give dogs the ability to make sounds; located between the top of the trachea and the root of the tongue.

Lassie Come Home story by Erick Knight of a faithful dog that returned to its young master over 1,000 miles (1,609 km) of rough country. *See* come-home dogs.

Lassie Rud Weatherwax's Collie that was actually named Pal. The dog chased motorcycles, barked constantly, and was given to Mr. Weatherwax as payment on a $10 boarding bill. He recognized its trainability and the dog later starred in many movies and had several namesakes who carried the Lassie tradition through later movies and a popular TV show.

lateral position toward one side or another, away from the median plane.

laudanum opium tincture, previously used for pain relief in animals and human beings.

lave-eared having pendulant ears, as in a hound.

Laverack strain English Setter strain of the eastern United States; predecessor of the Llewellin Setter.

layback 1. profile of a brachycephalic breed with its nose positioned on a plane that is caudal or posterior to the lower jaw. **2.** angle formed by the scapula and the humerus. For maximum mobility and agility of movement, this angle must be rather acute.

layback

lay on in scenting, to cast the hounds on a scent; to begin the hunt.

layon angle of the shoulder blade, compared to a vertical line.

Lazarus' dog leper's dog in the Bible that licked his master's sores and made him more comfortable.

lead 1. leash or strap that is fastened to a dog's collar and used to control the dog. **2.** one of the electrocardiogram wires or connections to the body that carries the electrical current from the heart to the instrument.

lead coupler in sledding, another name for a double neckline.

lead dog front dog in a sled team; trailbreaker. Example: A lead dog that is able to feel a solid trail under his feet through several inches of new snow is a valuable asset to the team.

leader alpha dog; strongest dog in a pack.

leading leg in sledding, the foreleg that extends the farthest forward and hits the ground last at a lope. The entire weight of the dog breaks over this one leg.

leadout racing term for the track groom that leads competitors from jinny pit to the starting barrier or box.

lead poisoning often fatal to dogs, if untreated; causes colicky signs of vomiting and diarrhea in most cases, but may cause convulsions. It occurs only if the dog eats lead in some form, and is not the result of gunshot.

leaky roof unlicensed race track that is operated by amateurs; also known as a flapping track.

leam *see* liam.

lean cheek describing chiseled or refined, or unwrinkled lines of the face; no jowls or excess flews.

lean head describing a dog's head that has an unwrinkled countenance with clean lines, one that lacks loose skin.

leash 1. any chain, rope, or strap that is fastened to a dog's collar, and is used to control the dog. **2.** in obedience trial, by definition, the leash must be leather, and long enough so that it can hang loosely when the dog is at heel.

leash law ordinance established by a state, county, or municipality that requires all dogs to be kept on leash when not confined. Such laws often include rabies vaccination requirements.

leather pinna of the ear, especially in pendulant eared dogs.

leather ends ears on short-coated hounds, especially pendulant ears that have been cropped.

Leauvenaar black German sheepdog thought to be the ancestor to the Schipperke and the Groenendael.

leaving checks when a dog refuses to come back to the place where it lost the scent of the quarry.

lecithin phospholipids found in animal and vegetable tissues; often useful in treating some skin ailments.

Le Diable famous black dog that belonged to a smuggler who occasionally dyed the dog brown, white, or gray. He carried contraband concealed beneath a false skin and operated along the French borders until he was shot by a customs official.

left in box in racing, describing a late starter in the race.

Legg-Calvé-Perthes disease or **osteochondritis deformans juvenilis** hereditary degenerative disease of the femoral head that is seen in young dogs.

leggy having unusually long legs; gangly; lanky in build.

legs well under body describing the acceptable angulation of all legs, set squarely under the dog.

Lelaps dog in ancient Greek mythology that was always sure of its prey, able to outrun any quarry, and overtake all that he hunted.

lemon belton color pattern consisting of yellow hair sprinkled intermittently with white hairs; English Setter color.

Lena Foxhound that in 1945 whelped 23 puppies, the largest litter ever recorded.

length body measurement of a dog taken from its withers to the croup; occasionally measured from the front of the forearms to the rear of the buttocks.

lens transparent, crystalline, elliptical structure behind the iris that is light refractory. It acts to bend the light rays and concentrate them on the retina.

lens luxation dislocation of the optic lens; occurs in old dogs following the formation of cataracts; occasionally an inherited condition.

lenticular sclerosis cloudiness of the lens of the eye that occurs as a normal aging change in older dogs; type of senile cataract.

Leonberg dog or **Leonberger** gigantic German dog that was originally a Saint Bernard-Newfoundland cross, but is now a distinct breed. The minimum height is 30 inches (76 cm) tall, its coat is long, rough, and waterproof, and it is seen in black, black and tan, tan and red, occasionally with white self markings. It is used as a draft dog in Flanders.

leonine lionlike, a term that is used to describe the Chow Chow.

leopard cur derogatory term that refers to the Catahoula Leopard Dog.

Leopard Dog *see* Catahoula Leopard Dog.

leopard spotting merle coat patterns.

lepidosis scaly eruption on the surface of the skin.

leporarius *see* Greyhound.

Leptospira canicola genus and species of an organism belonging to the *Schizomycetes* order; spirochete, or spiral microorganism that is pathogenic to dogs and other animals, particularly rodents.

leptospiriosis disease caused by the spirochete *Leptospira canicola*; spread by the urine of affected animals, causes kidney impairment, and sometimes death.

let down 1. describing hocks of great angulation, leaving them close to the ground. **2.** recess and rest period for hunting dogs, usually during the hot summer months.

lethal edema *see* anasarca.

lethargy drowsiness; lack of ambition; sometimes a sign of illness in a dog.

let sleeping dogs lie old proverb, which suggests that if you wake a guard dog, you may be bitten. The saying means to leave well enough alone.

leu in in foxhunting, command to dogs to move in and penetrate the quarry's cover.

leuth in coursing, the fenced holding area at the beginning of a gazehound course from which the dogs are slipped (released).

level or **level back** straight back that does not slope; describes a dog with its withers and haunch equally high and a straight topline between.

level

level bite even-fitting teeth in which the incisors are matched edge to edge with no overlapping.

level gait appearance of gliding over the ground with no significant rise and fall of the withers or rump.

level jaw or **level mouth** *see* level bite.

Levesque scenthound breed that originated in France from the interbreeding of English Foxhounds and French dogs. It stands about 22 inches (56 cm) tall, weighs about 58 pounds (26 kg). It is a large breed with a smooth coat that is primarily black and white in color, with small areas of brownish fur near the hocks.

Levesque

LH abbreviation for lutenizing hormone.

Lhasa Apso AKC group: non-sporting; native of Tibet that originated around the city of Lhasa. It stands about 11 inches (28 cm) tall, weighs about 15 pounds (7 kg), is seen in a wide variety of colors, with or without dark markings, and the coat is heavy and straight, but not woolly or silky. (See photo, page 37.)

Lhasa Apso

liam in scenting, collar and lead or leash, especially used on hounds, bloodhounds; dogs that are kept on a leash. Also spelled leam or lyam.

libido measure of sexual desire or reproductive urge.

license 1. permit to perform or practice acts that would otherwise be illegal (e.g., kennel license). **2.** a permit to own a dog (dog license).

licensed agility trial judged contest sponsored by an AKC licensed club in which qualifying scores toward agility titles are awarded.

licensed herding test test sponsored by an AKC licensed club at which qualifying scores toward herding titles are awarded.

licensed herding trial trial sponsored by an AKC licensed club at which qualifying scores and championship points toward herding titles are awarded.

licensed show show sponsored by an AKC licensed club and held under AKC rules that awards championship points.

lick granuloma or **lick dermatitis** area of proliferation of scar tissue that is caused by chronic licking. It often occurs on the lip, forefoot, or another easily accessible area of forearm; thought to be of psychogenic or psychological origin.

lick granuloma

lid smasher in racing, fast starting dog, one that seems to force the doors of the starting box to open.

lifesaving trials competition that began in 1929 in England to test Newfoundland dogs' skill in rescuing objects and humans from the water.

lift 1. in foxhunting, to remove the hounds from the scent or trail due to some problem that has arisen in the field. **2.** in herding, the moment the dog reaches the opposite side of the stock and moves them directly toward the handler, or the time between the outrun and the fetch.

ligaments 1. tough, fibrous bands that extend from bone to bone and hold the joints together. **2.** fibrous tissues that extend from the organs to the body walls, holding the organs in their places.

ligate to tie or bind with a ligature.

ligature thread, wire, or other filamentous material used to tie vessels off or to strangulate a part.

light-eyed describing a dog with scarcely enough pigment or color in its iris to meet the breed standard.

light in hindquarters describing skinny buttocks or a dog that lacks substance in the muscles of the hindquarters.

Lightning Rag Hound another name for the Whippet.

light sedge dog's coat color that is slightly darker than tan, less dark than chocolate.

light stock in herding, livestock moved with the slightest pressure from the dog; those that have a flight zone that extends a substantial distance from them.

like produces like theory of dog breeding that presupposes that all characteristics are genetic.

like to like breeding of dogs of similar appearance or phenotype.

limb any of the extremities; one of the four legs and its appendages.

limbus 1. fine black or brown line at the junction of the cornea and sclera of the eye. **2.** border or free edge of an organ.

limited race in sledding, race that limits the number of dogs in a team, such as a five-dog class.

limited registration AKC registration of a puppy that specifies that it cannot be shown or bred.

limosis abnormal hunger.

line 1. family of related dogs, usually bred by a single kennel. **2.** in foxhunting, the track of a quarry that is indicated by scent. **3.** a stripe, streak, or lineal mark on a dog's coat.

linebreeding mating two dogs that have the same bloodline but are not closely related; a technique used to concentrate and fix genetic features in a dog.

line hunter in foxhunting, a dog that sticks close to the scent or trail.

line out sledding, a driver's command to tighten the towline.

lineage genealogical decent from a common ancestor; dog's pedigree or family tree.

lineup in showing, the class finalists from which the winners are selected.

linked describing genetic traits that tend to be inherited together.

linty describing a coat of soft, dense, cottony consistency.

lion clip dog's trim pattern that resembles a lion's natural coat, usually with a heavy collar ruff and a tail tuft.

lion clip

lion color tawny tan coat color with darker shading, as seen in the Ibizan Hound.

Lion Dog of Pekin old name for the Pekingese.

lip either of the fleshy flaps that form the mouth orifice; labia.

lip-fold dermatitis area of skin infection found in breeds with wrinkled, folded, or heavy flews; often the result of continual dampness in the deep folds of the lips.

lippy full in flews; having heavy folded lips.

lip ulcer raw, irritated, and eroded lesion usually seen on the upper lip where the skin and mucous membrane have been licked away. *See* lick dermatitis.

lip ulcer

liquid nitrogen liquid form of the gaseous element that is used to freeze certain tumors and other unwanted structures. It is approximately –350°F (–l76°C); also used to identify dogs by "freeze branding."

listed dog dog that is entered in an AKC show without AKC registration.

Listeria genus of bacteria that is pathogenic for domestic animals.

listing fee dog show fee that is charged for the entry of a dog that is not registered with the AKC.

litter 1. all of the canine offspring from a single pregnancy. **2.** gurney or stretcher used for moving a wounded or ill animal.

litter kit set of papers and instructions prepared by the AKC and mailed to the breeder when a litter is registered.

littering act of whelping or giving birth.

littermates siblings; puppies born at the same time from the same pregnancy.

liver largest gland of the body. It is dark red in color and located in the anterior abdomen, immediately posterior to the diaphragm. Its principal function is to filter toxins and wastes from the blood.

liver belton coat color pattern made up of the intermingling of dark brown hairs with white hairs.

liver-colored dark red; reddish brown.

Llewellin Setter originally a strain of Welsh Setter or English Setter, and not a distinct breed. Its height is about 23 inches (58 cm), its weight is about 55 pounds (25 kg), it is black, black and white, tan, orange, liver, and all varieties of flecks and beltons, and it has a flat coat that is straight and of medium length. It is outstanding in field trials, and was a popular gundog in the past.

Llewellin Setter

loaded shoulders heavy, thick shoulder blades with excessive muscle over the shoulders; bulky forequarters.

lobe-shaped ear slightly folded, bamboo leaflike ear set at the back of the head.

lobular describing pendulous ears that have been surgically trimmed or rounded.

lochia vaginal discharge of a bitch that occurs for a week or two following whelping.

Lo-chiang Dog short-faced breed of the pug type well known in the Szechwan province of China in the eighth century; probable ancestor of the Pug.

lock natural tie that is seen in dogs when mating occurs; caused by the swelling of a structure known as the bulbus glandis on the penis after it has penetrated the vagina.

loin anatomical region located on the back between the last rib and the pelvis; dorsal or dorsaolateral area in front of the hind legs and behind the ribs.

long-cast long-bodied, as in the Dachshund.

long-coupled describing a dog that has a longer loin area than is usual or normal for the breed.

Long Dog or **Long Hound** Greyhound, any sighthound, or the Lurcher; probably a term originally related to the ability to pursue quarry at top speed for a long time.

long down in obedience trials, maneuver in which the dog lies down for three or five minutes while the handler moves to the opposite end of the ring or out of sight; part of both Novice and Open classes.

longhaired having a coat that is curly or wavy, with or without feathers.

Long-Haired Skye Terrier one of the Scottish Terrier breeds related to the Cairn, Scottish, West Highland White, and Kyle, all of which originated on the Isle of Skye.

long jump in agility trials, also known as broad jump; obstacle that is set no taller than 10 inches (25 cm) above the ground, and spans a distance of 20 or 36 inches (50 or 91 cm) for small dogs, 48 or 60 inches (121 or 152 cm) for large dogs.

long jump

long line 25- to 50-foot (7.5- to 15-m) -length of rope or strong nylon cord used as a leash for dog training.

long net net placed in the path of the quarry and used to snare it as it is driven down the path by a dog.

long sit in obedience trials, maneuver in which the dog must sit and stay while the handler moves away for three minutes.

longtail said of any of the long-tailed breeds, especially the Greyhound.

Loong Chua extinct variety of the longhaired, feathered Pug.

loose in foxhunting, to unleash the hounds and begin the hunt.

loose-coupled describing a dog that displays a weak, uncommonly long loin.

loose elbows ill-fitting elbow joint that allows abnormal movement and results in throwing both elbows laterally with each step.

loose-gaited having a swinging gait; flopping the elbows and hocks out.

loosely strung with every joint of the body floppy; results in a dog that has a loose gait.

loose-slung having sagging shoulders where the muscular attachment of shoulders is not tight and appears sloppy.

loose teeth teeth that have become movable in their sockets in the jawbones. They cause pain and are often infected.

lope canter; gait between the trot and gallop, an easy gait for a dog to maintain for long distances.

lop-eared having ears that hang down; having pendulant ears.

lordosis ventral curvature of the spinal column; swayback.

Los Chihuahuas periodical devoted to the Chihuahua: 12860 Thonotosassa Road, Dover, Florida 33527.

loss in foxhunting, referring to hounds that can no longer follow the scent line.

lost back in coursing, describing a dog's back muscles that have been torn loose from exertion.

Lo-sze *see* Pug.

loupe convex magnifying lens used to examine the external structures of the eye and other superficial body parts.

louse plural of lice; general name for one of several types of parasitic insects that either suck blood or bite; *Anoplura* suborder.

louse comb *see* flea comb.

Lowchen sometimes called the Little Lion Dog, this breed is shown in the AKC Miscellaneous class. It stands about 14 inches (35 cm) tall, and its soft, dense coat is rather wavy. It is an ancient breed thought to be related to the

256

Barbet and Bichon and might have originated in Germany. Any color and combination of colors are acceptable with no preference. It is usually shown in a lion clip. (See photo, page 43.)

lower thigh external anatomical region of the tibia and fibula.

low-set ears ears that are placed low on the head.

low-set hocks excessive angulation of the hock joints, resulting in hocks that are close to the ground.

low-set tail tail that is attached low on the croup.

lubb-dupp representation of the heart sounds that are heard with a stethoscope.

Lufenuron® insect growth or development inhibitor; one of the latest weapons to help control fleas in backyards.

lumbar concerning or referring to the upper loin region.

lumbar disk syndrome slipped or protruding intervertebral disk in the lumbar region of the spine, with accompanying paresis or paralysis; Dachshund disease.

lumbar vertebrae that portion of the spine that lies between the thorax and the sacrum. There are seven lumbar vertebrae.

lumber 1. to move in a cloddy, ungainly fashion. **2.** excessive musculature. **3.** fat or a preponderance of fat. Example: The dog is carrying too much lumber in the hindquarters.

lumbosacral anatomical region of the loins and pelvis.

Lundehund smooth-coated spitz-type dog that stands about 10 inches (25 cm) tall and weighs about 17 pounds (43 kg) that was originally bred on the island of Vaerog, near Norway. Its ability to catch puffins endeared it to the local people. To catch this gourmet delicacy, the dog had to climb up the rocky outcroppings to reach their nests. Currently Scandinavian working dogs, they are well muscled in spite of their small size.

Lundehund

lung either of the pair of respiratory organs that oxygenate the blood; located on either side of the heart in the thoracic cavity.

lungworm parasitic worm that lives in the respiratory tree of dogs; causes coughing and respiratory distress; *Filaroides, Oslerus, Angiostrongylus* genera.

lupoid having the gross or general characteristics or appearance of a wolf.

lupus autoimmune disease that affects the skin, mucous membranes, and various organs of the body.

Lurcher not a purebred; seen in Gypsy caravans; all-purpose utility dog with a body conformation similar to the Greyhound. Its height is about 24 inches (61 cm), its weight is about 50 pounds (23 kg), it has a long tapering head, small ears and a long, thin tail. Its color is black, black and tan, or tricolor, and its coat is short and harsh. It is considered an outcast that is not recognized by any registry.

Lurcher

lure in racing, stuffed rabbit skin used for Greyhounds to chase in a race. Now electrically propelled, it was first used in 1877 in England as a reel-operated lure that was dragged over a 400-yard (366 m) racecourse.

lure coursing training for sighthounds using an artificial lure.

lutein yellow pigment produced by the corpus luteum.

luteinizing hormone abbreviated LH; hormone secreted by the pituitary gland that acts primarily on the ovaries. It occurs in high concentrations in a bitch's blood during the estrus phase of her heat cycle. LH levels in the bloodstream are important to predict ovulation.

luxated patella dislocated kneecap; rupture, stretching, or congenital absence of a collateral ligament of the stifle that allows the kneecap to slip out of its groove in the femur, either medially or laterally. The condition has a hereditary predisposition.

luxation dislocation.

Luzerner Laufhund or **Lucernese Hound** Swiss breed characterized by a distinctive tri-color coat with pronounced black ticking, resulting in an over-all blue coloration. It stands about 23 inches (58 cm) tall, weighs about 44 pounds (20 kg) and is an active, friendly dog used for large game hunting.

Luzerner Neiderlaufhund short-legged variety of the Luzerner Laufhund that stands no taller than 16.5 inches (42 cm) tall. Probably resulted from crossing the larger dog with a Dachshund.

lyam *see* liam.

Lycaon pictus Cape Hunting Dog, African Hunting Dog, or so-called Hyena Dog. Assyrians and Egyptians used this dog for hunting from the fifth to the twelfth dynasty, but its domestic breeding was later abandoned.

Lycaon pictus

A big-eared dog that now ranges wild over the African savannah from Oubangui to Kilimanjaro, it is speckled, black, white, and yellow in a camouflage pattern, and hunts in large packs.

Lycaon tricolor somalicus *see* Somali Wild Dog.

Lycaon tricolor venaticus *see* South African Wild Dog.

lying hound describing a dog that gives tongue or voice when it is not on a trail.

Lyme disease tick-borne disease causing joint inflammation, arthritis, and general malaise. First seen on the northeast coast of the United States, it is now becoming widespread.

lymphatic system various lymph vessels of the body and the lymph glands that are associated with them.

lymph node gland in the lymph system that is actively associated with immunity and disease resistance.

lyssa cartilage under a dog's tongue, formerly thought to be associated with rabies. *See* tongue worm.

M

Macellaio Herding Dog Sicilian shorthaired breed that resembles the Rottweiler. Its ears are cropped, and it is black with brown markings.

Mackenzie Husky breed of sled dogs of Arctic ancestry; large freighting dog found along the Mackenzie River. It weighs 145 to 165 pounds (65.8–75 kg) and it is typically harnessed in a single-file tandem hitch.

macrosmatic having a well-developed sense of smell.

Macy dogs Macy's department stores kept Doberman Pinschers in the store to control thieves who hid in the store overnight, stole merchandise, then left soon after the store opened. The dogs also discovered runaway children, smoldering fires, and machines that were left running.

MAD abbreviation for Master Agility Dog.

Madame de Pompadour Dog *see* Phalene.

mad dog dog that is suffering from rabies, with a tendency to attack and bite anything in its path, whether animate or inanimate.

mad dogs and Englishmen in a Noel Coward poem: "Mad dogs and Englishmen go out in the mid-day sun; The Japanese don't care to, the Chinese wouldn't dare to; Hindus and Argentines sleep firmly from twelve to one, but Englishmen detest a siesta."

made up describing a dog that has reached maturity and is in the prime of life.

Magellan fox *see* Colpeo.

maggot soft-bodied larva of dog fleas, flies, and other insects.

maggot-infested dog one that has fly larvae (maggots) living in the feces, hair, and dead tissues of the anal area. *See* myasis.

magpie name given to flashy-colored black and white dogs, after the bird of that name.

Magyar Agár smooth-coated, coursing breed of Hungary that stands about 24 inches (61 cm) tall, weighs about 50 pounds (23 kg), closely resembles the Greyhound, and is a fleet-footed gazehound. It is not exhibited and is virtually unknown outside Hungary.

mahogany coat color of a deep chestnut red, almost reddish fawn; seen in some Irish Setters.

mahogany brindle black brindle on a mahogany ground color.

mahogany tan coat color of a reddish fawn that is sprinkled with yellow.

Maida Sir Walter Scott's Scottish Deerhound that was laid to rest in a marble mausoleum constructed for her interment.

maiden **1.** unmated female dog or a virgin bitch. **2.** in racing, dog of either sex that has never won a race.

maiden class in racing, race that is made up of dogs that have never won a race.

main earth in foxhunting, most likely place for a fox's den.

major win placing first (winners bitch or winners dog) in an AKC competition with enough dogs entered to merit the award of three, four, or five points.

making a wheel action of a dog's tail that is carried over its back in a full circle.

making game describing the attitude of a dog that is scenting game in the area but hasn't picked up a specific scent trail.

making the cut in field trials, remaining in competition after a number of other dogs have been eliminated.

maladjustment dog's defective or lack of adaptation to its environment.

Malamute *See* Alaskan Malamute.

male fern extraction from the root of a common fern, aspidium; used in the past as an effective canine vermifuge.

Malinois one of four varieties of Belgian Sheepdog. It stands about 23 inches (24 kg) tall, weighs about 53 pounds (24 kg), and is solid black. It is presently bred for shows, obedience, and guard work, in addition to herding.

malleability having the capability of being changed; having the capacity for adaptive change.

malleolus rounded processes on the lower end of the tibia and fibula at the hock joint.

Malinois

Mallorquin rough-coated or wirehaired Eivissenc. *See* Eivissenc.

malocclusion poor bite; improper relationship of teeth to one another. The bite is part of the standards of virtually every breed and is of critical importance.

malt grain that has been softened with water, and allowed to germinate. The odor of malt is appealing to a dog, and it is often used to flavor food or medicine.

Maltese

Maltese AKC group: toy; named for the island of Malta and having Bichon heritage. It stands about 10 inches (25 cm) tall, weighs 4 to 6 pounds (2–3 kg), and has long, white, silky hair that is parted down its back and touches the floor on either side; its tail is a longhaired plume that is carried over its back. Once called the Maltese Terrier, it was a renowned rat catcher, but is presently a companion dog. (See photo, page 33.)

Maltese cross in herding, two lanes that intersect at right angles, making a path that is wide enough to allow sheep to pass single file, first in one direction, then the other.

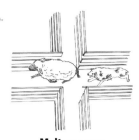

Maltese cross

malunion faulty, delayed, or improper healing of a fracture.

mammal order of vertebrates to which dogs belong; derives its name from the fact that all female members feed their young on milk that is produced by their mammae, or milk glands.

mammary gland or **mammae** milk-forming organ. The dog typically has 12 mammary glands.

mamma towel old blanket or towel that is used to help acclimate a puppy to its new home. It is first rubbed over the dam's face, head, and mammae to absorb her scent, then it is placed with the new puppy in its new environment.

Manboutou ancient Egyptian breed similar to the Niam Niam and Basenji.

Manchester Terrier AKC groups: terrier (Standard Manchester) and toy (Toy Manchester). The Toy Manchester Terrier weighs under 12 pounds (5.4 kg); the Standard Manchester Terrier weighs 12 to 22 pounds (10 kg). Both varieties have a coat that is smooth, tight, and glossy black, with mahogany tan markings that are distinct and don't fade into the black. They have erect ears and a tapered tail.

Manchester Terrier

Manchurian Snow Dog sometimes called the Mongolian Dog; looks like a large Poodle. It is built square, with heavy, white fleece.

mandible horseshoe-shaped lower jawbone into which the lower teeth are rooted.

mandibular prognathism hereditary protrusion of the lower jaw; undershot jaw in which the lower teeth extend anterior to the upper teeth.

mane growth of long hair that encircles the neck of some breeds; also called the ruff.

maned dog or **maned wolf** *Chrysocyol brachyurus. See* Aguara-Guaza.

mange infestation with ectoparasites, specifically mites; skin disorder manifested by redness and scaly, itchy lesions. *See* demodectic mange, psoroptic mange, and sarcoptic mange.

mangy slang term applied to any poor-quality or poorly conditioned dog or a dog infested with one of the mange mites.

manteau cloak; saddle markings of a dog.

mantle cape; saddle markings of dogs; dark markings found on the shoulders, back, and flank.

man trailer another name for a Bloodhound.

manual referring to or pertaining to the hand; hand signals given to a dog by the handler.

manubrium anterior bone of the sternum; forepart of the breastbone.

Maori Dog *see* Kuri.

marbled variegated, as veins in a rock; ticked with an intermixture of colors, with darker shades on a lighter ground color.

marbled Collie merle or harlequin-colored Collie.

marcel effect descriptive of a type of coat that lies in regular, continuous waves.

Maremaner, Maremma Sheepdog, or **Maremma-Abruzzi Sheepdog** native to the Tuscany and Apulia areas of Italy. It weighs about 80 pounds (36 kg), stands about 26 inches (66 cm) tall, and is a handsome white herding dog similar to the Kuvasz.

Maremaner

Marie Antoinette's Dog *see* Phalene.

mark 1. in retrieving, skill or ability of a dog to visually locate the spot where a bird fell when it was shot, and hold that place in its memory until given the command to retrieve. **2.** handler's command to the retriever before a shot is fired. **3.** spot or blemish, such as a kiss mark or thumb mark.

marking male dog's innate habit of distributing his urinary scent throughout his territory to tell others that he is in the area; usually on trees, posts, or other vertical surfaces.

marking hound in foxhunting, dog that is first to mark to ground.

markings shading or coloring on a coat that differs from the ground color.

mark to ground in foxhunting and beagling, **1.** to indicate the place at which the quarry has gone to ground and disappeared from view. **2.** referring to the actions and voice of a dog that has spotted a quarry's den.

marled *see* merle color pattern.

Marmaduke good-natured Great Dane that is the star of the comic strip by that name, drawn by Brad Patterson.

marshall in racing, person in charge or the primary official of a race event.

masculinize to produce male characteristics in a bitch by the use of male hormones.

mask 1. in foxhunting, fox's head. **2.** markings on a dog's face, such as the typical facial markings of a Siberian Husky or Alaskan Malamute. **3.** dark upper skull or muzzle, or the shadings of the foreface, as in the Mastiff, Boxer, and others. **4.** to cover or hide the symptoms of a disease by the administration of an ineffective drug.

masseters muscles of mastication located in the cheeks.

massive large; bulky; describing a dog that is heavy or gigantic.

mass start in sledding, race that is started with all of the teams lined up at the starting line; the first to cross the finish line wins.

master male owner or trainer of a dog; person to whom the dog responds. *See* mistress.

Master Agility Dog abbreviated MAD; a title awarded in agility trials.

Master of Foxhounds person in charge of a hunt; one who has responsibility for the pack; leader of the hunt.

mastication process of chewing food; the mashing and grinding of food with the teeth; a task that the dog does very poorly. As with other carnivores, dog's teeth are anatomically constructed for tearing and slicing its natural food, reducing it to a size that can be swallowed.

Mastiff AKC group: working; formerly called the Old English Mastiff. It stands a minimum of 30 inches (76 cm) tall, weighs about 190 pounds (86 kg), and has massive, heavy-boned, powerful musculature with a great heart girth. Its coat is fawn, apricot, or brindle, with a straight, coarse outer coat that lies flat. It has been bred in England for over 2,000 years. (See photo, page 26.)

Mastiff

mastiff dog corruption of "master of thief," signifying a dog's property-guarding duties; generic term for a large, powerful dog, a guard dog, or a mongrel.

match meeting of dogs to fight.

match or **match show** conformation competition held under AKC rules but without points being awarded; a practice or training show.

mate to copulate; to breed together.

maternal antibodies dam's circulating protective proteins that defend her from a specific disease, a portion of which will be passed to her puppies in the colostral milk. These protein antibodies create a passive or temporary immunity in the puppies.

maternal behavior instinct of a bitch to nurse and protect her pups; innate propensity to be a "good mother."

maternal impression effect that a bitch's treatment or experience during pregnancy has on her litter after they are born.

matin French term meaning a mastiff or cur dog; commonly used to designate a dog of great size, one that is very strong, one that can do as much work as a donkey, and is easier and cheaper to keep.

Matin Belge herding dog of Belgium that stands about 29 inches (74 cm) tall and weighs about 100 pounds (45 kg).

mating purposeful pairing, coupling, or breeding of animals.

mating behavior sexual behavior and courting rituals; in dogs, a bitch's estrus activities and attitudes and a stud's courting habits.

matrilineal said of inherited characteristics that follow the females of the bloodline.

matrix ground color of a coat; groundwork.

matron bitch that has had one or more litters. *See* brood bitch.

maturity usually connotes a dog's sexual maturity that is from eight months of age in small breeds to two years of age in large breeds.

Maupin Hound a breed or strain of foxhound that was similar to the Walker Hound, bred by George Washington Maupin in Kentucky. It has common ancestry with the Walker Hound.

MAX abbreviation for the Agility trial title Master Agility Excellent.

maxilla upper jawbone into which the upper teeth are rooted.

maze method of evaluating an animal's learning ability. that uses a series of blind alleys with one possible route to the food at the end.

mcg abbreviation for the metric weight-measure microgram that is equivalent to one one-thousandth of a gram.

meal 1. dry dog food that has been formed as, or ground into, fine granules, as opposed to biscuits or kibble. **2.** portion of food offered at a single feeding.

mealy describing a coat of a dull tan color.

measles vaccine human measles virus that is attenuated and administered to a dog to provide temporary immunity to canine distemper.

measurable breeds those dogs that have an upper or lower limit on their size in the AKC standard and are therefore subject to being measured by judges.

mechanical vector incidental, inanimate object that transmits a disease from one dog to another, such as a poorly washed dog bowl that has been contaminated by the germs that cause kennel cough.

meconium dark greenish, mucilaginous fecal material that accumulates in the bowel of a fetus and passes from the bowel shortly after a puppy is born. It is a mixture of secretions of the puppy's intestinal glands and amniotic fluid.

medial toward the median plane; opposite to lateral.

median furrow midline of the face from the stop to the occiput.

median plane imaginary plane through the longitudinal axis of a dog from its nostrils to its tail.

mediastinum space in the chest between the lungs where the heart is located.

medulla 1. marrow cavity of the bones. **2.** central portion of an organ.

meet gathering place of a hunt.

mega-esophagus greatly distended or enlarged gullet; inherited ballooning of the esophagus.

melon pips tan spots above each eye; also known as "four eyes."

member agility trial trial sponsored by an AKC member club, at which qualifying scores toward agility titles are awarded.

member herding test herding test sponsored and managed by an AKC member club, at which qualifying scores toward herding titles are awarded.

member herding trial herding trial sponsored and managed by an AKC member club, at which qualifying scores and Championship points toward herding titles are awarded.

member show bench show that is sponsored, produced, and managed by an all-breed club or specialty club that is a member of the AKC.

memory 1. faculty that recalls sensations and impressions. Dogs never seem to forget the voice of a person with whom they were closely associated, or a house where they have lived. **2.** anamnesis, or the biological phenomenon whereby certain white blood cells of the body recall past invasion of harmful protein substances and react to destroy them.

Mendel's Law of Alternate Inheritance law of dominant and recessive characteristics. It is applicable to dog breeding if sufficient offspring are produced, and if one-gene traits are being studied.

meniscus concentric intraarticular cartilage; "shock absorber" that is found in the knee and other joints.

mental image tests reasoning exercises that test the ability of dogs to perform tasks based on learned experiences.

mentum external anatomical region of the chin.

Meorman ancient breed of dog sometimes thought to be the ancestor of the Bouvier des Flandres and Old English Sheepdog.

merit of kill in coursing, evaluation of a gazehound that depends upon whether the dog overpowers its quarry by superior dash and skill, picks up the hare through accidental circumstances, or catches a hare that is turned into its mouth by another hound.

merle mottled or variegated blue or gray color (gray-blue ground color with black flecks) seen in Collies, Shetland Sheepdogs, and others, determined by a single or multiple dominated gene.

merle eye gray-blue eye seen in some blue dogs and is due to pigment dilution.

merry tail gay tail; any enthusiastic tail action.

mesaticephalic or **mesocephalic** skull shape of intermediate proportions; one that is intermediate between the brachycephalic and the dolichocephalic types.

messenger dogs army dogs that were trained to carry messages from command posts behind the lines to the front, and vice versa. *See* K9 Corps.

metacarpal pad footpad located behind the four toepads of the forefoot on which much of a dog's weight is borne.

metacarpus referring to bones leading from the carpus (wrist) to the toes; anatomical region of the forepastern.

metaldehyde snail and slug poison that is highly toxic to dogs.

metatarsal pad footpad located behind the four toepads of the hind foot on which much of the dog's weight is borne.

metatarsus referring to the bones leading from the tarsus (hock) to the toes; anatomical region of the hindpastern.

metestrus former name for the third phase of a bitch's estrous cycle; currently called diestrus.

Metzgerhunds literally; butchers' dogs. They were draft dogs that pulled butchers' carts and protected them from thieves.

Mexican Dwarf Dog another name for Chihuahau.

Mexican Hairless or **Xoloitzcuintl** small dog the size of a Fox Terrier, with a smooth, soft, unwrinkled skin. It stands about 12 inches (30 cm) tall, weighs about 18 pounds (8 kg), and is seen in any color. The skin is warm to the touch and hairless except for the tip of the tail and top of head.

Mexican Kennel Club Asociación Canofila Mexicana, Malaga Sur 44, Mexico City 19 DV.

Mha Si Savat shortcoated scenthound from Thailand that stands about 22 inches (56 cm) tall and weighs about 37 pounds (17 kg).

Miacidea carnivores or **Miacis** prehistoric "dog"; small carnivore with a long body and short legs that lived in the Oligocene period 40 million years ago. The descendants were of two types: *Daphaneus,* a heavy, long-tailed dog, and *Cynodictus,* a smaller, slender animal. It is the family from which evolved today's dogs and cats according to one theory. *See Canis palustris,* the Peat Dog.

Mick the Miller famous racing Greyhound that never lost a race in a three-year career on the English circuit.

microchip identification system of inserting microchips under the skin of dogs to permanently identify them. It requires reading by a scanner.

microfilaria larval stage of the heartworm; found in peripheral vessels of an infested dog. The larvae are transmitted from dog to dog by a mosquito that serves as a biological vector.

microphthalmia abnormally small eyes, an undesirable inherited characteristic of some breeds.

Microsporum canis common ringworm-causing fungus of the dog.

micturition urination.

micturition behavior urinary marking; propensity of male dogs at sexual maturity to lift one hind leg and direct its urine against a vertical surface; tendency to urinate more frequently than necessary and only expel part of the bladder contents, thus distributing it over a wider area.

Middle Asiatic Owtscharka Russian sheepdog seen in either long- or shorthaired varieties. It stands about 25 inches (63.5 cm) tall and weighs about 80 pounds (36 kg).

middle ear space behind the tympanic membrane (eardrum) containing the ossicles (bones) responsible for transmitting sound waves from the external ear canal through to the auditory nerves of the inner ear; cavity from which the eustachian tube leads. *See* ear ossicles.

middle piece that portion or anatomical region of the body between the shoulders and hind legs.

milbemycin one drug that is used to prevent heartworm disease.

military honors honors conferred during World War II when, at least one dog was awarded the Silver Star and the Purple Heart. These honors were later revoked; thereafter, Citation Certificates were awarded. *See* K9 Corps.

milk liquid mammary secretion that affords nutrition to puppies. A bitch may produce up to five quarts a day, with a butterfat content that is three times as rich as the cow's.

milk duct atresia lack of a normal opening in the nipple of a mammary gland.

milk fever postparturient tetany. *See* eclampsia.

milk of magnesia suspension of magnesium hydroxide that, when administered orally, acts as a mild, harmless cathartic or laxative.

milk rash allergic reaction to some components of cow's milk, manifested by a skin rash.

milk teeth deciduous teeth; temporary teeth of a puppy that are replaced by a permanent set.

mincing describing small prancing steps that produce little forward motion.

Miniature
Bull Terrier

mine detection dogs K9 Corps dogs that were trained in World War II to sniff out freshly turned earth that indicated the placement of land mines; a program that proved impractical and was discontinued.

Miniature Bull Terrier AKC group: terrier; small breed that is about 10 to 14 inches (25–35.6 cm) tall. It has sunken eyes, and small, thin ears, a flat coat that is short and harsh to touch, and is seen in white or colored.

Miniature Dachshund

Miniature Dachshund smallest variety of Dachshund. It competes in a class of 11 pounds (5 kg) or less at 12 months of age or older, has the same breed standard as other Dachshunds, and is not a separate breed.

Miniature Pekingese Sleeve Pekingese; small strain that is not accepted for showing.

Miniature Pinscher

Miniature Pinscher AKC group: toy; breed of German origin that appears similar to the Doberman Pinscher but is totally unrelated. It stands about 12 inches (30 cm) tall, weighs about 10 pounds (5 kg), and is a smooth-coated dog, colored red, black with rusty markings, or chocolate with rusty red markings. (See photo, page 33.)

Miniature Poodle middle-sized Poodle variety, not shown as a separate breed. *See* Poodle.

Miniature Schnauzer AKC group: terrier; breed of German origin; originally used as a ratter. It stands up to 14 inches (36 cm) tall, weighs about 15 pounds (7 kg), with a hard outer coat and close undercoat. It is shown with its hair plucked, a mustache, beard, and eyebrows, and is salt and pepper, black and silver, or solid black-colored, with no white patches. In the United States it is mostly a family companion. (See photo, page 27.)

Miniature Schnauzer

minimum smallest size allowable in a breed according to the standard.

minor penalty penalty of two and one-half points or less.

minor puppy young dog between the age of six months and one year.

Min Pin shortened version of Miniature Pinscher.

Miscellaneous class in showing, a transitory class offered by a club for rare breeds that are not fully recognized by the AKC; considered to be purebreds but of insufficient numbers to be registered. The Miscellaneous class represents dogs that are usually attempting to advance to complete AKC recognition. Presently, the AKC Miscellaneous class is made up of: Löwchen, Havanese, Jack Russell Terrier, Anatolian Shepherd Dog, and Spinone Italiano.

mismarked having coloring or markings that are not allowed by the breed standard.

mismate referring to inadvertent breeding; accidental or undesirable breeding.

mismate shot "morning after" injection of an estrogen product that is administered to a bitch that was mismated; usually prevents conception but can have many and varied complications.

mistress female owner or handler of a dog; person to whom the dog responds. *See* master.

mite member of the order *Acarina;* small parasitic organism that causes mange, such as *Demodex, Sarcoptes, Psoroptes, Notroedres, Chorioptes, Otodectes, Cnemidocoptes.*

mob in foxhunting, to surround the fox and kill it without giving it a chance to run.

mobility ability to move; having good movement.

Modder Rhu *see* Irish Setter.

modeled correct proportions; chiseled features.

modesty referring to a dog's emotion that becomes obvious to those who have clipped all the hair from a shaggy dog, only to find the dog hiding under the bed.

modified live virus vaccine made of living viruses that have been attenuated or modified so that they can no longer cause disease; they are still able to produce a protective immunity from disease when properly administered to a dog.

modifier gene one that influences other genes.

Moerman Bouvier Pikhaar breed related to Bouvier des Flandres. It is a large black dog with a longer head than the Bouvier des Flandres.

Mohammed's dog legendary dog named Kitmer that guarded the sleeping seven noble youths of Ephesus for 309 years.

moist food canned dog food.

molar one of the hindmost teeth of a dog that have relatively large grinding surfaces.

molera open fontanelle; soft spot in the center of a newborn puppy's skull.

Molossian dog Greek sculpture of a mastiff that belonged to Olympias, the daughter of King Pyrrhus. It is supposed to be a direct ancestor of the modern mastiff.

molt periodic normal loss of a dog's coat; seasonal shedding.

monestrus having or experiencing one estrus (heat) per season.

Mongolian Mastiff largest of the mastiff breeds; appears similar to the Tibetan Mastiff and a fierce guard dog.

Mongolian Sheepdog Tibetan herding dog that is perhaps the ancestor of many herding dogs.

mongrel cur; mutt; mixed breed; dog of unknown ancestry and questionable parentage.

Monilia or *Candida* genus of fungus that may be pathogenic to dogs.

Monkey Dog, Monkey Pincher, or **Monkey Terrier** *see* Affenpinscher.

monogenic relating to or controlled by a single gene.

monophyletic 1. having a common ancestor; belief that all dogs descended from one wild species and that the wolf is the progenitor of all breeds of dogs. **2.** referring to a breed that descended from a single outstanding dog.

monorchid animal with only one testicle that has descended into the scrotum.

monorchidism hereditary condition in which one testicle is normally descended into the scrotum.

monstrum fetal monster; puppy with a physical anomaly that interferes with its normal life and development; plural is monstra.

mops 1. profuse hair on the paws. **2.** German name for the Pug.

Mopshond or **Mope** European names for the Pug. Derived from *mopsen* meaning to grumble; possible reference to the dog's snoring habit or its facial expression.

Morford strain orange and white English Setter variety that originated in New Jersey.

mort in foxhunting, the trumpet sounding the death knell for the fox.

mortality death rate; ratio of those that die from a disease to those that survive.

morula traveling stage of an embryo as it divides and grows in the dam's oviduct. The morula occurs after the formation of the zygote and before implantation has taken place in the uterus.

Moscow Mastiff smooth-coated large dog from Russia that stands about 27 inches (68.6 cm) tall and weighs about 117 pounds (53 kg).

Moscow Watchdog longhaired, compact Russian bandog breed that stands about 25 inches (63.5 cm) tall and weighs about 120 pounds (54 kg).

mother female parent or dam.

motion sickness illness caused by the motion of automobile, boat, or airplane; manifested in the dog by nausea, salivation, and vomiting.

motor nerve nerve that, when stimulated, causes a muscle to produce an action.

motor skills relative ability to move easily and perform activities or tasks with a minimal of wasted motion.

mottled spots or splashes of dark colors that are randomly distributed over a lighter background coat.

moucher poacher; stray dog that scavenges for food; a feral dog.

Mountain Collie *see* Bearded Collie.

mountain lion dog hunting dog of various breeds that is especially trained to trail cougars or mountain lions. The Plott Hound in particular is used in this sport.

Mountain Music hound periodical: Sapulpa, Oklahoma 74066.

mousy 1. describing a small, shy dog. **2.** in racing, describing a smaller than normal Greyhound.

mouth 1. anterior opening of the alimentary canal, made up of the lips, tongue, and cheeks. **2.** type tooth closure seen in a dog, such as crooked, level, parrot, shark, wry, or others. **3.** hard or soft mouth of a retriever.

mouthing 1. in hunting, repeatedly gripping retrieved game, rolling it in the mouth. *See* hard mouth. **2.** in obedience trials, the action of a dog chewing or rolling the dumbbell in its mouth.

mouth-to-nose resuscitation technique of artificial respiration in which the human mouth is closed over the nostrils of a dog and air is forced into the dog's lungs.

mouthy in foxhunting, describing a hound as noisy and that gives voice when not on a scent trail.

move in showing, the judge's direction to the handler to lead the dog around the ring in order to judge its action and gait at a trot.

move close to brush or move with the hind legs nearly touching.

moves straight describing the action of a dog that has each of the four legs moving in a vertical line with no lateral deviation.

moving close describing the conformation exhibited by a dog that has hocks turned in and straight pasterns, making hind legs move close to each other.

Moyen Poodle midway in size between a Standard and a Miniature. *See* caniche.

Mudhol Hound smooth-coated gazehound from India that stands about 23 inches (58 cm) tall and weighs about 28 pounds (13 kg).

Mudi Hungarian Sheepdog breed that is also a versatile guarding dog as well. It has a black, longhaired, wavy coat, weighs about 25 pounds (11 kg), is about 16 inches (41 cm) tall, and has erect ears and a docked tail. It is a powerful dog rarely seen outside its native country.

Muggs Airedale hero of James Thurber's funny dog story *The Dog That Bit People*, a true account of a truly unique dog.

multiparous 1. producing more than one offspring from the same pregnancy. **2.** having experienced previous pregnancies.

mumbling in hunting, playing with a game bird while retrieving it; mouthing.

mummified fetuses dead fetuses that have lost all attachment to the uterus but are retained within the uterus for extended periods.

Munchener Dog former name of the Giant Schnauzer; named for Munich, Germany.

Münsterländer *see* Large Münsterländer and Small Münsterländer.

muscle tissue that has the ability to contract when stimulated by nerves. There are two types: the smooth muscle that is responsible for gut activity, and the striated muscle or skeletal muscle that causes the movement of an organism.

Münsterländer

muscle-bound 1. having heavy, excessive muscle development and being unable to move freely due to overdeveloped muscles. **2.** in sledding, describing a dog that has been worked very hard on heavy loads, has developed a broad chest and heavy shoulders, and a less fluid movement.

muscle tone measure of the firmness of a muscle mass; an evaluation of the condition of a dog.

muscular having well-developed muscles; athletic.

mush 1. in sledding, to drive or run a dog sled team. **2.** command of a driver to the lead sled dog and team to move forward (rarely used in this way).

musher sled dog team driver.

music in scenting, sound of hounds' voices on the trail.

mustache growth of long hair on a dog's upper lip.

Mustard and Pepper Terrier *see* Dandie Dinmont Terrier.

mutant product of a permanent genetic change.

mutation change in form, quality, or other characteristic that is a permanent transmissible variation and will breed true.

mute in foxhunting, describing a hound that gives no tongue or voice when on a scent trail.

mute trailers hereditary characteristic; dogs that remain mute while on a scent trail. The most common mute trailers are the Airdale, English Setter, Cocker Spaniel, Fox Terrier, and Collie.

mutilate to surgically and radically alter; to render imperfect or to cripple by surgical amputation of limbs or other techniques. *See* knee cutting and toe cutting.

mutt *see* mongrel.

mutton shoulders overly heavy shoulders.

muzzle

muzzle **1.** device that, when placed on a dog, prevents it from biting. **2.** in racing, special covering for the face that allows easy breathing but curtails fighting. **3.** front of the head, including the nose and lips, or the area of the face extending from the stop forward.

muzzle band white markings on the face of a Boston Terrier.

myasis fly strike; infestation of a living body by fly larvae; condition most often seen in old dogs' anal areas when common houseflies lay eggs that hatch into larvae, or maggots. Those maggots live in and feed on feces and degenerating tissues surrounding the anus.

N

NA abbreviation for Novice Agility dog.

nagging continually finding fault with a dog; scolding it frequently.

nail 1. hornlike, terminal appendage of the toes that is made up of modified epithelial cells. **2.** to take hold of a quarry in a firm, steadfast manner.

nailer dog that always grips its prey in a definitive manner.

naked dog any of the hairless breeds of dogs such as the Mexican Hairless and African Hairless.

nanism dwarfism; condition of stunted growth.

nape skin on top of the back of the neck; scruff behind the occiput and in front of the withers.

naris (plural: nares) nostril; opening into the nasal cavity.

nasal bone small bone that forms the top of the nasal cavity.

nasal cartilage structure deep to the visible nostrils that gives shape to the anterior muzzle.

nasal dermatitis skin inflammation and loss of pigmentation on the top surface of the foremuzzle.

nasal septum cartilage that separates or divides the two nares.

nasolabial line crease that runs from the side of a dog's nose to the corner of its mouth on the same side.

natal referring to or pertaining to birth.

National American Eskimo Dog Association 3863 McElhaney Road SE, Sublimity, Oregon 97385.

National American Pit Bull Terrier Association 24 Sunnybrook Lane, Clinton, Connecticut 06415.

National Beagle Club 8 Baldwin Place, Westport, Connecticut 06880.

National Dog Registry tattoo-based registry: P.O. Box 118, Woodstock, New York 12498-0116.

natural 1. not artificial; nonpathologic and normal for the species and breed. **2.** in obedience trials, free of affectation; behavior that is expected in the home or in public places.

natural dock stubby tail, no tail, or a shorter than normal tail with which a dog is born.

natural selection survival of the fittest; process by which wild animals' breeding stock is chosen without human intervention.

Navy dog the German Shepherd Dog was selected as the official Navy and Coast Guard dog during World War II. *See* K9 Corps.

Neapolitan Mastiff perhaps the oldest European breed; said to be a descendant of the Roman Molussus. It stands about 28 inches (71 cm) tall, sometimes reaches a weight of 150 pounds (68 kg), its ears are cropped very short, and its tail is docked long. It has great folds of skin around the neck and it is colored black, blue, tawny, or brindle.

neck 1. anatomical region located between the head and the thorax. **2.** constriction near the end of an organ or bone. **3.** section of a tooth between the crown and the root.

neckline in sledding, line that runs from the towline to the dog's collar to keep it from turning around or swinging out of line.

necklining in sledding, action of a dog that pulls back and drags against the neckline.

neck upside down ewe-necked; having a saddle neck; having a concave appearance to the dorsal cervical surface.

neck well-set-on describing a nice blending of the neck into the body, giving the dog a pleasing appearance.

necklining

Nederlandsche Herdershonden *see* Dutch Herder.

Nejdi one of the four varieties of Saluki. It has a smooth coat with no feathering. *See* Saluki.

nemato- referring to or concerning a nematode or parasitic worm.

nematocide agent that kills nematodes in a dog; worm treatment.

nematode endoparasite or worm that belongs to the class *Nematoda*.

Nembutal® proprietary name for pentobarbital sodium, a compound that was previously used as a canine anesthetic.

Nemural® proprietary vermifuge similar to arecolene.

neo- prefix that refers to or pertains to "new."

neomycin antibiotic frequently used to combat canine intestinal bacterial infections.

neonatal maladjustment syndrome in which a puppy or puppies do not nurse normally and do not seek their mother's warmth. The condition is most commonly seen following a difficult and prolonged birth.

Nepal Herder Dog longhaired herding dog from India that stands about 25 inches (63.5 cm) tall and weighs about 64 pounds (29 kg).

nervous describing an excitable or irritable dog that is easily upset.

nesting box *see* whelping box.

neurotic descriptive of the behavior of a dog that experiences anxiety and overreaction to stimuli.

neuter to render incapable of reproduction; to surgically alter or sterilize; to spay or castrate.

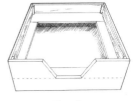

nesting box

neutered altered; rendered sterile.

New England Native Hound *see* American Foxhound.

New England Sled Dog Club oldest sledding club in the United States.

New Guinea Native Dog also called Papuan Native Dog, native to New Guinea and seen in two types: coastal and hill. The coastal type, colored red and white with a short coat, is used principally for fishing work; the larger, hill type, found inland, is colored black with self markings of white, has erect ears and a gay tail, and is used for guard and hunting duties.

New Guinea Singing Dog wild or semi-wild dog similar to the dingo that stands about 15 inches (38 cm), weighs about 22 pounds (10 kg), and is colored red with white or lighter shading. It has short, erect, rounded ears and has a distinctive musical voice. Members of this race are common in zoos and have been successfully domesticated.

New Guinea
Singing Dog

New Zealand Kennel Club P.O Box 523, Wellington 1, New Zealand.

New Zealand wild dogs longhaired dogs that resemble sheepdogs. Some are spotted; others are seen in solid colors of black or white. These dogs are often used as food by the natives. *See* Kuri.

Newfie short for Newfoundland.

Newfoundland

Newfoundland AKC group: working. Giant breed that stands about 28 inches (71 cm) tall, weighs about 110 pounds (50 kg), and has a coat that is flat, water-resistant, and double. Black is the predominant color, although brown and gray, with or without white markings are allowed. The Landseer variety has a white base coat with black markings. An excellent swimmer and used on boats for rescue work, this breed is now used as companion animal, draft dog, and pack dog. (See photo, page 24.)

Newfoundland Club of America 4908 Rolling Green Parkway, Edina, Minnesota 55436.

Newf Tide magazine of the Newfoundland Club of America: 195 Dollywood Drive, P.O. Box 160, Toney, Alabama 35773.

Niam Niam or **Nyam Nyam** mute relative of the Manboutou and Basenji, bred by the Niam Niam tribe of the Sudan on the Nile River. Of similar conformation to the Basenji, this dog is both edible and trainable for hunting.

nick beneficial mating; a breeding that produces excellent puppies.

nicotine poisoning poisoning seen when a dog develops a taste for cigarette or cigar butts and only occurs when the dog eats a great many of them. The symptoms are lethargy and coma.

nictitating membrane haw; third eyelid; located at the central angle of each eye where it is normally barely visible. It is capable of extending over the entire eyeball, but is rarely seen except when it is inflamed and swollen. It contains the Harderian gland.

nidicolous literal meaning: "sharing the nest of another animal"; used to describe the surrogate rearing of pups by a lactating bitch that is not the puppies' dam.

nidus small nest, especially a place in an animal where bacteria may lodge and multiply.

Nihon-ken smooth-coated spitz-type northern dog that originated in Japan. It stands about 18 inches (46 cm) and weighs about 42 pounds (19 kg).

Nihon Terrier smooth-coated Japanese terrier that stands about 14 inches (36 cm) tall and weighs about 17 pounds (7.7 kg).

Nipper at one time, perhaps the best known dog in the world. He is the black and white mongrel whose portrait brought him fame as the RCA Victor trademark.

nipple teat that contains the milk duct; outlet for milk from a mammary gland.

Nippon Inu another name for Akita.

nit louse egg usually seen as a minute, white structure attached to a hair on the dog's back.

Noah's dog folktale that tells of a hole in the bottom of the Ark that was plugged by a dog's nose. The act saved the Ark, but chilled the dog's nose forever, thus a dog's perpetually cold nose.

nobble in racing and coursing, act of cheating to win a competition by drugging a dog or otherwise interfering.

no course closed or void gazehound course.

nocturnal pertaining to the night; describing a dog that is most active during the hours of darkness.

no go gazehound course that is voided because the dogs lose sight of the quarry.

no-man's-land in sledding, stretch of trail near the finish of a race that is not governed by the usual trail rules; for example, the leader is not required to give up the trail to an overtaking team. Also known as the free zone.

nonslip retriever duck dog that works at heel or slightly behind the handler and retrieves game when it is shot, but doesn't point or flush birds.

non-sporting group AKC group consisting of American Eskimo Dog, Bichon Frise, Boston Terrier, Bulldog, Chinese Shar-Pei, Chow Chow, Dalmatian, Finnish Spitz, French Bulldog, Keeshond, Lhasa Apso, Poodle, Schipperke, Shiba Inu, Tibetan Spaniel, and Tibetan Terrier.

Nootka Dog sheepdog bred and kept by Nootka tribe of Vancouver, British Columbia.

Norbottenspets spitz-type dog developed in northern Sweden; possibly related to the Lunderhund, the German Spitz, or the Arctic Spitz. It stands about 17 inches (43 cm) tall, weighs about 33 pounds (15 kg), is white in color, with cream, red, or black markings and is kept mostly as a household pet and guard dog.

Norfolk Spaniel now-extinct variety of the English Springer.

Norfolk Terrier AKC group: terrier. It stands about 10 inches (25 cm) tall and weighs about 12 pounds (5.4 kg). A drop-eared, red dog, it is one of the smallest of the

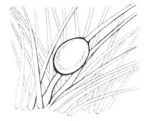

nit

Norfolk Terrier

working terriers. Its outer coat is hard, wiry, and straight, and it comes in all shades of red, wheaten, black and tan, or grizzle. Except for its drop ears, it is similar to the Norwich Terrier.

norm fixed standard for the ideal.

normal conforming to a type, standard, or regular pattern.

normal butyl chloride old and outdated vermifuge that is quite toxic to puppies and was a frequent cause of vomiting.

normal phenotype dog that exhibits the physical characteristics of the breed standard.

Norrbotten Laika

Norrbotten Laika longhaired northern dog from Norway that stands about 16 inches (41 cm) and weighs about 40 pounds (18 kg).

North African Gazelle Hound *see* Slughi.

North African Kabyle *see* Kabyle Dog.

North American wild dog *see* coyote.

North America Working Dog Association, Inc. 1677 North Alisar Avenue, Monterey Park, California 91754.

North American Working Dog Association Schutzhund club: 1677 North Alisar Avenue, Monterey Park, California 91754.

North Counties Terrier *see* Bedlington Terrier.

Northeastern Sleigh Dog longhaired northern dog from Siberia and Manchuria, China, that stands about 22 inches (56 cm) tall and weighs about 75 pounds (34 kg). It is similar to the Eskimo Dog but smaller in size. Often black and white in color, it is a very powerful sled dog.

North Russian Samoyed *see* Laika.

Northwest Indian Greyhound *see* Rampur Hound.

Norwegian Buhund

Norwegian Buhund Scandinavian working spitz breed, probably with Elkhound ancestors. It is self-colored, ranging from red to wheaten. It stands about 18 inches (46 cm) tall, weighs about 58 pounds (26 kg), and is a fast, agile dog that is remarkably strong for its size. It is used for both guarding and herding, and is rarely seen outside Scandinavia.

Norwegian Elkhound

Norwegian Elkhound AKC group: hound. It stands about 20 inches (51 cm) tall, weighs about 55 pounds (25 kg). Its coat is weather-resistant and heavy, and it is seen in varying shades of gray, with black markings. A herding and hunting dog in Norway, it is a close-coupled hound with prick ears.

Norwich Terrier AKC group: terrier. It is about 10 inches (25 cm) tall, weighs about 12 pounds (5.4 kg), has a double coat, the outer of which is hard, wiry, and straight, and it is seen in all shades of red, wheaten, black and tan, or grizzle. Except for the prick ears, it is similar to the Norfolk Terrier.

Norwich Terrier

nose 1. hunting dog's ability to scent game. **2.** special organ of the sense of smell, including the nares or nostrils, the nasal cavity, and the olfactory nerves. **3.** dog's muzzle or foreface.

noseband contrasting color over nose, as seen in the Papillon.

nose bump affectionate greeting instinct exhibited by all puppies. It involves touching or bumping with its nose and simultaneously licking a hand, face, or any exposed skin.

nose band

nose contact initial greeting between two adult dogs when they touch and sniff noses, then investigate and sniff anal areas.

nose leather fleshy tip of a dog's nose; nose pad.

nose out to follow a scent trail.

nose pad rubberlike external tissue that surrounds the nares.

nose work in scenting, tracking and successfully scenting and following a trail.

nose pad

noseworm rare parasite of the nasal cavity of dogs that causes sneezing and sometimes a nosebleed.

no-show dog that has been entered in a show or competition and does not make an appearance on time.

nostril external naris; opening into the nasal cavity.

Notroedres cati cat mange mite occasionally seen in dogs with skin problems.

Nova Scotia Duck Tolling Retriever dog of unknown or questionable ancestry, resembles the Golden Retriever and is a powerful swimmer. It stands about 21 inches (53 cm) tall, weighs about 50 pounds (22 kg), and is about the color of a red fox. This Canadian retriever has a unique manner of decoying its quarry: it lures ducks into the shooter's range by dashing up and down the bank of a lake enticing the ducks or geese to swim closer

Nova Scotia Duck Tolling Retriever

to the concealed hunter. In France and England, similar dogs were used to take ducks by means of a net into which the waterfowl were lured by the antics of the dog. (See photo, page 44.)

Novice A in obedience trials, the class for purebred dogs of either sex and breed that have not won the CD title. Handled by the owner or member of the immediate family, with no professional handlers allowed and a separate handler required for each dog entered.

Novice B in obedience trials, the same as Novice A, except a professional handler may compete, and more than one dog may be shown by a handler.

Novice class AKC class for inexperienced dogs; males and females are shown in separate classes.

nucha nape; scruff of the neck; skin at the nape of the neck.

nudging repeated pushing against a human's leg or arm with its nose, usually while wagging its tail, a greeting or sign of affection of a dog. This action may indicate recognition or a desire for food.

nuisance dogs pets that are allowed to run at large, bark, dig, scavenge, and create problems in their environment.

nulliparous never having given birth to a litter; describing a maiden, or virgin bitch.

nurse to allow puppies to suckle, or to feed puppies naturally from the mammary glands of their dam.

nursery special place in which neonatal puppies are confined for their protection.

nursing bitch female dog that is raising her puppies with normal lactation.

nux short for nux vomica or strychnine, a powerful, deadly poison for dogs. *See* strychnine poisoning.

Nyam Nyam Terrier *see* Niam Niam.

Nyctercutes procyonoides raccoonlike dog of Asia and Europe.

Nylabone® proprietary name for a bone-shaped dog chew made from nylon.

nymph stage of the life cycle of some arthropods following the larval stage and before the adult stage.

O

OA abbreviation for the Open Agility title.

obedience dog any dog that competes or is entered in an obedience trial.

obedience exercise any of the various parts of an obedience trial that may include *sit, stay, heel, recall, down, drop on recall, retrieve,* and *broad jump.*

obedience titles titles awarded for various classes; title awarded for successful completion of the Novice class is Companion Dog (CD). For successful completion of the Open class the title is Companion Dog Excellent (CDX); for the Utility class, the title is Utility Dog (UD).

obedience trial organized, judged competition for dogs and their handlers that stresses dog training and the responsiveness of a dog to its handler and that uses a standard set of requirements. The three levels of obedience are: Novice, Open, and Utility.

Obedience Trial Champion abbreviated OTC; designation that is used as a prefix to the name of a dog that has been recorded as having won that degree by the AKC. This is a highly coveted title that is extremely difficult to obtain.

obesity condition in which the body weight is greater than ideal or necessary, and the excess weight exerts stress on the skeleton or organs.

oblique eye eye that is set slantwise in a dog's face, with the medial corners lower than the outer corners; seen in the Alaskan Malamute, Bull Terrier, and others.

oblique shoulder shoulderblade that is well-laid-back or angled.

obstacle course series of ramps, jumps, hurdles, tunnels, and the like, used in agility trials.

obstacles in herding, objects placed in strategic locations to make up a trial course.

obtuse a dull or stupid dog. One that is difficult to train.

occipital crest peak; highest point of the head.

occipital tuberosity bony protrusion on the posterior aspect of the skull; so-called knowledge bump.

occiput prominent bone at the top rear of the skull.

occiputal protuberance prominent occiput, a characteristic of some hunting breeds, especially scenthounds.

occlusion dog's bite; manner in which the upper and lower teeth mesh with, or oppose, one another.

occult heartworm infection presence of adult heartworms in a dog's heart in the absence of circulating larvae in its bloodstream; a basis for false-negative heartworm tests.

OCD abbreviation for osteochondritis dissecans.

Odie Garfield's canine straight man in the comic strip by Jim Davis.

OES abbreviation for Old English Sheepdog.

oestrus another spelling for estrus.

off contact in herding, said of a dog that has lost control of the stock, either by being too far away or by losing concentration.

Old Danish Pointer or **Gammel Dansk Househund** breed that was developed from the Spanish Pointer. A useful gundog that is rarely seen outside Scandinavia. It stands about 23 inches (58 cm) tall, weighs about 53 pounds (24 kg), and is black and white.

Old English Bulldog former name for the Bulldog.

Olde English Bulldogge the result of American's attempts to breed a traditional Bulldog without the hereditary problems of the modern version of the breed. It stands about 25 inches (64 cm) tall, weighs about 105 pounds (48 kg) and is seen in colors that range from cream to mahogany with white markings.

Old English Sheepdog AKC group: herding. It is a large, profusely coated dog that stands at least 22 inches (56 cm) tall, weighs about 66 pounds (30 kg), has its tail docked closely, and has an outer coat that is hard and wavy, in colors of gray, grizzle, blue, or blue merle with white markings. Its dense undercoat is soft. (See photo, page 42.)

Old English Sheepdog

Old English Terrier *see* Welsh Terrier.

Old Family Red Nose Line red-colored, red-eyed, red-nosed Bull and Terrier-type dog that was imported from Ireland as a pit fighter.

oleander evergreen bush or tree of the southern United States, the sap of which is poisonous to the heart of dogs (cardiotoxic).

olecranon process upper tip of the ulna; point of the elbow.

olfaction sense of smell, or the act of smelling, that is well established in all canines.

olfactory bulb organ of scent located in the forepart of the brain.

olfactory nerve nerve that transmits the sensation of smell from the nares to the brain.

ololygmancy legendary telling of the future by the sounds of dogs that howl in the night.

Olpe *see* German Hound.

omega-3 fatty acids derivatives of coldwater fish oil that are used to treat various inflammatory skin diseases of dogs.

Omisto ancient mythological Japanese god of suicide; depicted as the body of a man with the head of a dog. He rode a charger with seven heads.

omnivore creature that eats both vegetables and meat. The dog is zoologically classed as an omnivore since it eats the partially digested vegetable matter in the intestine of its prey.

omnivorous capable of eating and digesting foods derived from animal and vegetable sources.

on in foxhunting, describes hounds that are following a live scent or quarry that has gone to ground and is trapped.

on by in sledding, the driver's command to a team to ignore an obstacle or another team.

on heat describing a bitch in estrus or showing signs of estrus.

onion head smooth head; one that lacks wrinkles.

on the flags actively competing in a show or exhibition.

open in scenting, said of hounds that have picked up the scent and are on trail and giving voice.

Open A in obedience trials, a class for dogs that have won a CD degree, but not CDX.

open bitch female dog that is not pregnant; breedable female dog.

Open class AKC class for adult dogs with experience that have not yet won an AKC Championship. The male and female classes are separated.

open coat

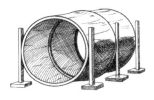

open tunnel

open coat dog's coat that is loose and parted; opposite of a tight coat.

open couplings anatomical term indicating a long-bodied and loosely built dog.

open foot splayed foot with the toes wide apart.

open-marked having a white ground color with black or tan spots.

open trailer in scenting, dog that opens, gives tongue, or bays when on a scent trail.

open tunnel or **pipe tunnel** in agility trials, obstacle that is about 24 inches (61 cm) in diameter and about 10 to 20 feet (3–6 in) long, made of semirigid nylon, cloth, or other materials. Suitably flexible conduit may be obtained from Peabody ABC Corp. P.O. Box 2928, Grand Junction Colorado 81502.

opisthotonos generalized muscle spasm that causes the dog's head and feet to bend backward and its abdomen to bow forward.

opossum small marsupial animal; quarry of hunting dogs in the southeastern United States.

opossum hunting dogs various scentdogs such as the Black and Tan Coonhound or Redbone Hound. They will instinctively trail opossums unless trained to the contrary.

orange belton coat color that consists of a blend of dark yellow or orange hairs mingled with white hairs, as seen in English Setters.

orb eyeball.

orbit bony sockets of the skull that contains the eye and accessory ocular structures.

orbital muscles bundle of muscle fibers that make up the elevation on which the eyebrow is located.

orchiectomy surgical removal of one or both testicles; castration.

order 1. in obedience trials, direction given by the judge to the handler, either verbal or by hand signal. **2.** taxonomic category subordinate to a class and superior to a family.

organic phosphate poisoning serious toxemia caused by common household insecticides. The signs are excessive watery salivation, diarrhea, twitching of the facial muscles, and ataxia.

organized competition shows or exhibitions governed by the rules of a club or organization.

organophosphate class of potent insecticides. *See* organic phosphate poisoning.

Oriental expression describing eyes that are set obliquely; Eastern eyes.

Oriental Spit old name for the Chow Chow.

origin 1. source, or where a particular breed or type of dog began or became popular. **2.** fixed end of a muscle to a bone.

Orion's dog in Greek mythology, Sirius, Orion's dog, was transformed into the brightest star in heaven.

Ornament Dog former name for the Chihuahua.

Orthopedic Foundation for Animals organization that reads and evaluates X-rays submitted to them and certifies dogs relative to hip dysplasia: 2300 Nifong Boulevard, Columbia, Missouri 65201.

os calcis calcaneus; tarsal bone; point of the hock.

os penis bone in a dog's penis that directs the penis into vagina of a female during copulation.

osteochondritis inflammation of bone and cartilage within a joint.

osteochondritis dessicans pathological condition caused by the development of abnormally thick joint cartilage that is highly vulnerable to damage. Occurs most commonly in the shoulders of puppies of breeds such as the Saint Bernard, Doberman, etc.

osteogenesis imperfecta hereditary condition in which the bones are subject to spontaneous fracture due to excessive brittleness.

osteosarcoma bone cancer; especially prevalent at the ends of the long bones of giant breeds.

Ostiak spitz-type dog of Siberia. Its color is fawn and gray-colored, with black markings. It is less a sled dog than a hunting and herding dog and is popular as a draft dog.

Ostiak

other end of the lead in showing and obedience, describing a handler who is being judged instead of the dog or a judge, who is watching the handler instead of the dog. ·

Otocyon megalotis bat-eared fox of Africa.

Otodectes cynotis common canine ear mite that is easily seen with an otoscope or magnifying glass; parasite that lives deep in the ear canal of dogs where it causes a heavy wax formation and extreme irritation.

otter small water-dwelling mammal, the quarry of many hunting dogs. It lives in rivers, streams, lakes, and oceans.

Otterhound AKC group: hound. It stands about 26 inches (66 cm) tall and weighs about 110 pounds (50 kg). Its outer coat is dense, rough, and coarse, 2 to 4 inches (5.1–10 cm) long, with a short, woolly undercoat. Any color or combination of colors are allowed. It is sad-looking, longhaired hound, said to be a Bloodhound wearing the wrong coat, with a rather musical voice and an excellent nose.

otter tail thick tail with slight taper.

Otto Sarge's uniform-wearing Bulldog buddy in the comic strip *Beetle Baily* by Mort Walker.

ouija board in sledding, a short toboggan or board that is fastened to the towline between the team and the sled, where a driver stands when using a gee pole.

Ouiji President Herbert Hoover's Norwegian Elkhound pet.

Ouled Naïl Dog another name for the Kabyle Dog.

out at elbow describing a dog with bowed forelegs and elbows turned out.

out at shoulder having a loose scapula, with the shoulderblades tipped outward instead of lying flat.

outbred outcross; product of outcrossing unrelated or distantly related parent dogs.

outcross 1. to mate dogs of a different strain within a breed. **2.** to mate dogs of different breeds.

out of term that refers to the dam of the litter. Example: He was out of Clementine, my best bitch.

out of coat describing a dog that is experiencing seasonal shedding or has a naturally poor coat; a lack of condition.

output yield or total produced. Example: In old dogs, the urinary output is increased due to the kidney's inability to concentrate urine.

outrun or **cast** in herding, maneuver in which the dog begins the contest by running in an arc to move from the handler to the balance point on the far side of the stock in order to move the stock back to the handler.

outside rabbit lure that runs outside the racing strip.

oval chest thorax that is deeper than it is wide.

oval eyes describing elongated eye openings that are usually seen with Oriental eyes.

ovarian fragments pieces of an ovary that are sometimes left in the abdomen when an ovariohysterectomy is done; may cause the dog to come in heat regularly.

outside rabbit

ovariohysterectomy surgical removal of the ovaries and uterus.

ovary one of the paired abdominal organs that produce ova (eggs) and reproductive hormones in an intact bitch.

overangulated describing excessive bending, of the shoulder or rear leg for example.

overbirdiness in field trials, the dallying over an old game scent or searching over the ground time and time again.

overbite dentition in which the upper incisors protrude over the lower incisors.

overbreeding 1. breeding of every bitch, regardless of her quality or condition; a natural phenomena that occurs when a breed becomes popular and people get greedy. **2.** situation in which a breeder tries too hard to achieve certain goals and places too much emphasis on size, color, coat quality, or another characteristic in the breeding stock. The result may be a physical defect or mental degeneration and can lead to abnormal behavior.

overbuilt 1. describing a back that slopes from the rear to the front. **2.** describing a generalized heavy musculature.

overfill absence of any visible bony prominences on the skull or excessive muscle mass on a dog's head.

overflow in sledding, water that floods the snow, usually on riverbeds, lakes, or swamps.

overhang 1. upper portion of the face that protrudes further forward than necessary. **2.** pronounced brow. **3.** fringe of hair that extends over the eyes.

overland in racing, said of a Greyhound taking a wide swing around the track.

overlay outer hair of the coat that is darker than majority of coat.

overmark in racing, especially Whippet racing, mark that is located 10 yards (9 m) past the finish line where a runner-up handler is located to catch each dog.

overreach to throw the hind feet forward excessively at the trot, causing them to land beside the forefeet. The condition is caused by an angulation fault.

overrun 1. action of hounds that do not check (stop) when they no longer have a scent. **2.** failure of the lure operator to maintain the lure at least 10 to 30 yards (9–27 m) in front of the lead hound, resulting in the lead hound passing or overtaking the lure. **3.** action of hounds that go past the place where the quarry has gone to ground.

overshot having front upper incisors that protrude over the lower incisors.

overtipped describing collie ears that break too close to the head, or any semiprick ears that break too low.

Owczarek Podhalañski or **Owczarek Tatrzañski** *see* Polish Sheepdog.

own in foxhunting, describing a hound that declares with its voice that it is on the scent of the quarry.

own the scent in foxhunting, said of hounds that recognize the trail and follow it.

owner handler person who owns and handles a dog in competition.

Owner Handler Association of America, Inc. Mrs. Mildred Mesh, 6 Michaels Lane, Old Brookville, New York 11545.

Owtscharka four related breeds of Russian origin. They stand about 30 inches (76 cm) tall, with a dense fawn or tawny coat that is tangled, and difficult to groom. Herding dogs, they are particularly adept at guarding against wolves and bears.

oxer *see* spread jump.

P

pace **1.** dog's gait in which the legs of one side move forward together simultaneously, then the legs of the other side move in unison, giving a two-beat rhythm and an easy rolling movement of the body. **2.** in field trials, speed at which a course is worked. **3.** in sledding, to regulate speed of a team to save the dogs' energy or strength.

Pachon de Vitoria smooth-coated Spanish pointing breed that stands about 21 inches (53 cm) tall and weighs about 60 pounds (27 kg).

pack **1.** in foxhunting, all of the hounds of a kennel that are hunted together. **2.** group of two or more dogs that run in a group (nuisance dogs or feral dogs).

pack action propensity of domestic dogs, when running together, to behave in a manner that is different from their usual, individual behaviors. In a pack, house dogs often display viciousness or destructiveness, and the attitude is infectious, feeding upon itself. There is a saying: "One dog is a pet; two dogs are a pack."

pack dog dog trained to carry a burden in pouches fitted to its back. In World War II pack dogs carried messages, carrier pigeons, food, and ammunition to and from the front lines. *See* K9 Corps.

pack hound hunting dog that is a member of an organized hunting pack.

pack leader **1.** alpha dog; dominant dog of the pack. **2.** human handler or master of the hounds.

pack mentality innate wolflike instinct of a dog to be loyal to the pack leader and demonstrate fidelity to its pack. This characteristic is supported by early experiences in a puppy's life and is one explanation of a dog's dependency on its human master.

pack sense in foxhunting, when the hounds run and hunt together and normally honor one another's voice.

pad one of the soft, tough, highly vascular, weight-bearing, cushioned appendages that are located on the volar or plantar surface of each toe, and a single larger one on each foot.

paddle abnormal movement of a dog's front feet to the side in the pattern of an arc.

paddler dog that walks with its forefeet wide apart.

paddock exercise area or confinement in which dogs are let loose to exercise.

paddock judge in racing, the official in charge of the Greyhounds before the start of a race.

Pa-erh *see* Pekingese.

pain sensation of discomfort, distress, or agony that is transmitted by the stimulation of sensory nerves.

pain tolerance relative capacity to endure discomfort.

Paisley Terrier Scottish terrier that appears in the ancestry of the Yorkshire Terrier. *See* Clydesdale Terrier.

palace dogs ancient China's symbols of the great protectors of their faith. Also called Buddha's lions, they were represented by the Pekingese.

palatable having an agreeable taste, a pleasing flavor; generally good to eat.

palate roof of the mouth that extends from the uvula at the rear to the upper incisors at the front.

pancreas abdominal organ that secretes digestive enzymes as well as insulin.

pancreatic atrophy shrinking of the pancreas; an inherited condition in some breeds of dogs.

panel jump in agility trials, a high jump that forms a solid wall over which a dog must jump.

Pan Hu five-colored dog in ancient Chinese mythology owned by the emperor of China, Kaohsin (2435 B.C.). The dog brought in the head of Kaohsin's enemy, General Wu, and, as a reward, the dog was married to the emperor's daughter.

panmixia random mating of dogs in an unmanaged breeding population.

pannus abnormal vascularization of the cornea in which pigment is carried into the cornea and deposited there by the aberrant vessels. It produces a dense corneal opacity, leaving the dog functionally blind; seen principally in German Shepherd Dogs.

panosteitis inflammation of various parts of a bone; a hereditary canine condition.

pant to breathe rapidly with the mouth open and the tongue distended. It is typical of a dog when tired or in hot weather. The action promotes cooling through the evaporation of saliva.

pap **1.** soft food such as bread soaked with milk. **2.** nipple of a mammary gland.

paper foot flat foot with a thin pad.

papers usually, documents that show the dog's pedigree, registration, health records, certification of healthy hips and eyes, and freedom from other hereditary diseases.

paper training teaching a puppy to defecate and urinate on newspapers that are spread on the floor of the home.

Papillon AKC group: toy. A little dog with fine bones and dainty features, it stands about 10 inches (25 cm) tall, weighs about 10 pounds (4.4 kg), and has long, straight silky hair and no undercoat. It is always particolored with patches of any colors allowed. A white blaze and noseband are preferred.

Papillon

Papuan Native Dog *see* New Guinea Native Dog.

parainfluenza canine cough complex caused by viral agents.

paraphimosis breeding problem manifested by a stricture of the prepuce, rendering the erect penis unable to return to its normal flaccid state.

parasite organism that lives on or in a host at the expense of the host. Ectoparasites such as fleas, lice, and mites live on the surface of the host, while endoparasites such as roundworms, tapeworms, and coccidia live within the host.

parathyroid glands paired small endocrine glands situated behind the thyroid gland. Their principal function is serum calcium regulation.

parent club national breed club that sets the official AKC standards of an individual breed.

pariah dogs variety of dogs of Asia, Africa, the Far East, and elsewhere. The name is taken from a low caste of southern India and means "outcasts" or "dogs with no master." They are thought to not be truly wild dogs, but domesticated dogs that have become feral scavengers and live in a semi-wild state on the fringes of human society. They vary in type from locale to locale but are of a common appearance regionally.

parity number of pregnancies a bitch has experienced.

paronychia inflammation of a toenail and nail bed.

parotid gland salivary gland located just below the ear.

parrot mouth pinched mouth with deformed upper and lower jaws and teeth resembling a parrot's beak; gross overbite.

pars another name for the anterior pituitary gland.

Parson Jack Russell Terrier another name for the Jack Russell Terrier.

parti-colored describing a coat of two colors, approximately equal in quantity and in random distribution. Neither color is dominant and neither is considered the ground color.

Partridge Dog *see* Drentsche Partrijshond.

parturition whelping; act of giving birth to a litter.

parvoviral endocarditis inflammation of the heart in conjunction with a parvovirus infection.

parvoviral gastroenteritis stomach and intestinal inflammation and infection caused by one of the parvoviruses.

pass in foxhunting, to overrun the scent drag.

passive immunity temporary protection or transient resistance to disease that is passed from a dam to her litter by way of antibodies in the colostral milk.

pass over in foxhunting, fail to mark or find the scent.

pastern region of the metatarsus that extends from the hock to the foot in the hind leg, and the metacarpal area of the foreleg.

pastoral dog sheep or cattle dog that is trained to stay with the herd as a guard dog rather than a herding dog.

PAT abbreviation for Puppy Aptitude Test.

patch area of the coat that differs in color from the ground color.

patella kneecap; sesamoid bone on the front of the stifle joint.

patellar luxation dislocation of the kneecap due to injury or hereditarily weak ligaments and/or anatomical abnormalities of the tibia.

patellar subluxation incomplete kneecap dislocation.

patent ductus arteriosus congenital, sometimes hereditary condition in which the normal fetal shunt between the aorta and pulmonary artery, just outside the heart, fails to close after birth.

paternity tests various methods used to determine the sire of a litter.

patrilineal tracing decent through the paternal side of the bloodline.

patrol dogs specially trained dogs that were used in both world wars to accompany advance patrols and give early warning of the enemy. *See* K9 Corps.

Patterdale Terrier or **Black Fell Terrier** small working terrier developed in northern England and named for the village of Patterdale. It stands about 12 inches (30 cm) tall and weighs about 13 pounds (6 kg); its short, coarse coat is colored black or mahogany, and is sometimes marked with lighter brown.

pattern appearance, arrangement, or design of the markings of a dog's coat.

Patti Sheepdog shorthaired herding dog of India that stands about 22 inches (56 cm) tall and weighs about 60 pounds (27 kg).

paunchy having a pendulant abdomen or one that is flabby and lacking firm muscle tone; describing a dog that is in poor working condition.

pause box

pause box in agility trials, a 4-feet (122-cm) square area that is outlined on the ground or floor with a ribbon or a flat frame. The dog must enter the area, lie down, and pause there for a specified time.

pause table in agility trials, a carpet-covered table 3 feet (91 cm) square and 12 inches (30 cm) tall for small dogs, or 21 to 30 inches (53–76 cm) tall for large dogs. They must jump to the table, lie down with no part of their body overhanging the table, and remain down for five seconds.

pause table

Pavlovian conditioning response to a given stimulus that becomes predictable after repeated pairing of the stimulus with a reward.

paw any of a dog's four feet.

pawing instinctive begging act that is manifested by the dog placing a paw on the owner's knee to attract attention or receive food.

PDA abbreviation for patent ductus arteriosus, a hereditary condition.

peach fawn pale tan coat color.

peak occiput or pointed top of the skull that is especially prevalent in hound breeds.

peak out in sledding, to bring a team to its maximum potential.

pearl eye pigmentary dilution of iris color that gives the appearance of a silvery or white eye. *See* walleye.

pear-shaped wide at the topline and narrow in the loin.

peat dog *Canis palustrus*, the skeleton of a prehistoric "dog" that was located in Switzerland. There is also skeletal evidence of its existence along the Rhine and in the ancient ruins of an old Roman military hospital.

pectineus muscle of the inner hind leg that contributes to the signs of hereditary canine hip dysplasia.

pectinotomy severing or cutting of the tendon of the pectineus muscle in an effort to relieve the signs of canine hip dysplasia.

pectoral concerning or pertaining to the breast or chest area.

pectus chest, thorax, or breast.

pedal concerning or pertaining to the feet.

pedaling in sledding, the action of a driver who stands on the sled runner with one foot and pushes the sled with the other in order to relieve the weight on the sled, assist in turning the sled, and help the team.

pedaling movement forming circle patterns with the hind feet, a wasted action that results in a lack of drive.

pediculosis lice infestation.

Pediculus genus of sucking lice.

pedicure nail trim; care of the feet and nails.

pedigree genealogical chart of a dog that shows two or more generations of ancestors.

pedigreed dog dog whose ancestry is known. It generally refers to a purebred dog.

Peerie Dog *see* Shetland Sheepdog.

peg tie stake that is driven into the ground and used to tether a dog outside.

Peke or **Peking Palace Dog** *see* Pekingese.

Peking Pug *see* Happa Dog.

Pekingese AKC group: toy; Oriental origin. It stands about 9 inches (23 cm) tall, weighs about 12 pounds (5.4 kg), has a broad flat skull, a flat nose, and a wrinkled, short muzzle. Its double coat is long and thick with an undercoat, it has a profuse mane and well-feathered

Pekingese

limbs. All colors are allowed: red, fawn, black, black and tan, brindle, white, and parti-color. The dog has had a host of other names such as Pen-Lo or Pa-erh. (See photo, page 34.)

pelage dense, feltlike undercoat of a Briard that serves as a protection against the cold.

pelt tanned animal skin with the hair left on; also the coat of various breeds of dogs.

pelvic relating to the region of the pelvis or croup.

pelvic limb either hind leg.

pelvis bony girdle made up of the ilium, ischium, and pubis, which are joined to the sacrum of the spinal column.

Pembroke Welsh Corgi *see* Welsh Corgi, Pembroke.

pemphigus disease of the skin characterized by blister-like lesions. It has an inherited cause in some dogs.

pen or **re-pen** in herding, to put stock into a specified holding area.

penciling dark thin lines or streaks of black or other dark contrasting color on the dorsum of the toes.

pendulant hanging down. Example: The Bloodhound has long, pendulant ears.

penis male organ of copulation; complex structure consisting of the glans penis, os penis, bulbus glandis, root, urethra, and shaft.

penitentiary hound Bloodhound kept by many prisons to track escapees.

Pen-Lo Pa-erh *see* Pekingese.

PENNHIP University of Pennsylvania technique for X-raying dogs at six months of age to detect signs of canine hip dysplasia, and predict its occurrence.

penning putting sheep in a pen made of a set of four connected panels or hurdles that have an open space just large enough for a sheep to pass through; final obstacle of the course.

penning

pennyroyal herb sometimes used to stimulate whelping. It is brewed into a strong tea and mixed with honey.

pentobarbital long-acting general anesthetic agent rarely used today except for euthanasia.

pepper and salt color combination of black and white hairs, giving a grayish cast to the dog's coat; seen in the Schnauzer and others.

Perdigueiro Portuguese

Perdiguero de Burgos

peppering black or dark hair interspersed with lighter hair.

Perdigueiro Portuguese Portuguese dog that originated in Spain. It stands about 22 inches (56 cm) tall, weighs about 60 pounds (27 kg), and its colors are red to cream with darker shadings and white markings, and the coat is rough. The Portuguese word *perdig* means "partridge," and the dog has developed as a functional bird dog.

Perdiguero Burgales Spanish smooth-coated pointer that stands about 21 inches (23 cm) tall and weighs about 60 pounds (27 kg).

Perdiguero de Burgos or **Spanish Partridge Dog** dog with an unmistakable dewlap beneath its neck, and thick flews. It stands about 29 inches (13 cm) tall, weighs about 66 pounds (30 kg), and is colored white, with dark brown spots or liver with white spots.

Perigord truffle edible fungus that grows under the ground and is a great delicacy in Europe. Dogs, notably Poodles, have been trained to sniff them out.

perinatal occurring immediately prior to or subsequent to whelping.

perineal hernia breakdown of muscles and ligaments on either side of the anus that allow the urinary bladder or rectum to fold forward into the hernial sac; often causes a bowel blockage and occurs only in males.

perineum anatomical region surrounding the anus from the scrotum or vulva to the tail.

perro Spanish word for dog.

Perro de Pastor Catalán (de Pelo Corto) *see* Catalan Sheepdog (shorthaired).

Perro de Pastor Mallorquin breed native to the Balearic Islands off the Spanish coast. It stands about 22 inches (56 cm) tall, weighs about 60 pounds (27 kg), and was bred to withstand the Mediterranean heat. It is seen in solid black and mahogany colors.

Perro de Presa, Perro de Pressa Mallorquin, or **Caode Bou** descendent of Spanish and Portuguese stock that was developed in the Azores. This dog is of the mastiff type, resembling the Alano. It is a heavy, large dog that stands about 24 inches (61 cm) tall, weighs about 140 pounds (63 kg), and is predominantly yellow in color.

Perros de Sangre literally translated "Dogs of Blood." They were trained mastiff-type war dogs that were used by the Conquistadores in Mexico.

Perro de Presa

Persian Greyhound *see* Saluki.

persistent estrus continual state of heat in which the bitch is always ready to be bred and has a continual vaginal discharge; sometimes caused by an ovarian cyst.

persistent frenulum of the penis cordlike strand of tissue extending from the glans penis to the prepuce that inhibits intromission and copulation.

persistent right aortic arch hereditary vascular defect that occurs immediately outside the heart and causes a discernible murmur.

personality dog's disposition; its quality of being socially adapted to a human environment.

perspiration sweat; excretion of waste water from the body. Dogs have few sweat glands and perspire primarily through the nose pad and footpads; relying on evaporation from their tongue for most of the body's cooling.

Peruvian Hairless rare breed that dates back to the Inca Empire in Peru. It stands about 16 inches (41 cm) tall, weighs about 20 pounds (9 kg) and is seen in three sizes: large, medium, and miniature. It is totally hairless except for a bit of fuzz on top of the head and the top of the feet. It has a dark skin and nose, and long, erect ears, and, frequently lacking teeth, its tongue is often sticking out.

pet dog any canine companion; purebred of less than show quality.

Peter Pan President Coolidge's first White House dog, a wirehaired Fox Terrier that frequently nipped the heels of visitors.

pet-facilitated therapy use of dogs to help people with special needs and for giving aid to the handicapped.

Petfinders dog registry requiring neither microchip nor tattoo: 368 High Street, Athol, New York 12810.

Petit Basset Griffon Vendéen AKC group: hound; bred originally for small game hunting; named for Vendée, the area of France in which it originated. It is a small version of the Grand Basset Griffon, and differs only in size. It is small *(petit)* and stands less than 15 inches (38 cm) tall; its rough coat *(griffon)* is white with any combination of lemon, orange, black, tricolor or grizzle markings.

Petit Basset Griffon Vendéen

Petit Bleu de Gascogne French breed similar to the Grand Bleu de Gascogne, but shorter in stature, being about 21 inches (53 cm) tall and weighing about 46 pounds (21 kg).

Its coat is black speckled on a white background with black markings. It is used mostly to hunt hare.

Petite Brabançon *see* Brabançon.

Petit Gascogne-Saintongeois smooth-coated scenthound of France that stands about 19 inches (48 cm) tall and weighs about 55 pounds (25 kg).

pet quality describing a purebred dog that does not meet the breed standard and should not be part of the breeding pool, but, even though it misses the mark as a breeding or showing prospect, it has all the characteristics of the breed. Many pet-quality dogs are great hunters, obedience dogs, agility dogs, and fine companions.

pet-sitters people who offer bonded service, staying with dogs while their owners are away from home.

Pet Transports pet travel agent: 68-77 Selfirdge Street, Forest Hills, New York 11375.

Phalene

Phalene French breed that was owned by Madame de Pompadour and Marie Antoinette. Except for its droopy ears, this breed is similar in virtually every description to the Papillon. It stands about 10 inches (25 cm) tall, and weighs under 9 pounds (4.1 kg), and has a thick, wavy coat of brown, red, yellow, and tricolor.

phalynx (plural phalanges) digit; toe.

phantom pregnancy *see* pseudocyesis.

Pharaoh Hound

Pharaoh Hound AKC group: hound; of Egyptian origin and one of the oldest domesticated dogs. It stands about 24 inches (61 cm) tall, weighs about 55 pounds (25 kg), and is lean and muscular, with a short coat and no feathering, and its color ranges from tan to chestnut with white markings.

Pharaonenhund smooth-coated scenthound from Spain that stands about 25 inches (63.5 cm) tall and weighs about 60 pounds (27 kg).

pharynx mucous membrane sac that is located between the mouth and the esophagus. It is continuous with esophagus, and is a part of the digestive system.

phenocopy dog unrelated to another but with a similar visible appearance.

phenothiazine old agent that was used to kill worms; anthelmintic or vermifuge.

phenotype inherited visible appearance.

Phentoin® proprietary name for diphenylhydantoin sodium, a common drug used to treat canine epilepsy.

pheromone chemical produced by organisms that stimulates a behavioral response in another of the same species, or sometimes a different species.

Philippine Islands Dog, Philippine Native Dog, or **Philippine Edible Dog** Its height is about 21 inches (56 cm), weighs about 45 pounds (20 kg), is tan, pied, fawn, white, or brindle colored, with a short smooth coat. The ears are erect, and the tail is docked. About Bull Terrier size, and said to be a good guard dog, it is raised for food, served roasted and stuffed with rice and spices, and considered a delicacy.

phimosis abnormal tightness of the anterior prepuce or foreskin that prevents the penis from leaving its sheath and makes mating impossible.

phooey command used by many dog trainers to tell the dog to stop whatever it is doing.

photophobia painful sensitivity to light (common problem of albino dogs).

Phu Quoc ancient Asiatic breed thought to be an ancestor to the dingo and Rhodesian Ridgeback. It is the only other breed known to have ridge of hair along its back. *See* Siamese Greyhound.

piblokto particularly virulent strain of canine distemper virus that wiped out thousands of Arctic dogs.

pica craving for unnatural food or a depraved appetite; propensity to consume nonnutritious, odd substances.

Picardy Shepherd or **Berger de Picard** French dog of the Picardy area that resembles the Griffon. It stands about 26 inches (66 cm) tall, weighs about 70 pounds (32 kg), has a beard and mustache and a rough coat in shades of gray and blue gray, or in various shades of tan.

Picardy Shepherd

Picardy Spaniel or **Epagneul Picard** It stands about 24 inches (61 cm) tall, weighs about 44 pounds (20 kg), and differs mostly in color, being gray speckled with large chestnut spots, and is a duck-retrieving specialist. It resembles a setter but it is actually a variety of the French Spaniel.

picker-up in racing, person hired to catch the Greyhounds after each race.

picket stake to which a dog is tied.

Picardy Spaniel

picket line in sledding, a long cable or chain with snaps or short lines along its length to secure the dogs temporarily.

pick it up in sledding, the driver's command to the team to go faster.

pick of the litter best pup in the litter.

pick up finish or end of a dog fight. When a handler believes his dog has lost, he can pick the dog up.

pi dog *see* pariah dog.

piebald or **pied** color pattern in which black and white colors appear in blotches; parti-color with equal amount and distribution of two colors; pinto.

pigeon-breasted pinched or prominent sternum.

pigeon-toed having toes that turn inward.

pigeon training using a live pigeon that is enclosed in a netlike sack and thrown for the gundog to retrieve.

pig eye tiny, sunken, squinty eye.

pig jaw overshot jaw; overbite in which upper incisors extend over the lower.

pigmentation deposition of coloring in the skin, mucous membranes, coat, eyes, nose, and eyelids.

pikhaar Flemish term meaning "hair that pricks," the nickname for the Bouvier des Flandres' rough coat.

Pila Dog hairless dog of Argentina.

pile undercoat that is dense and soft.

piley describing a double coat of soft and hard texture as seen in the Dandie Dinmont Terrier.

Pillow Dog *see* Chihuahua.

pilo-erection reflex activity of tiny muscles in the skin that cause the hair on a dog's back to stand when stimulated. The stimulus is emotional, usually fear or anger. *See* hackles.

pin brush grooming tool with tiny wire pins (like a carding tool) that is used to remove a shedding undercoat.

pincer bite level mouth that has neither underbite nor overbite.

pinched front having a narrow or close front with the forelegs too close together.

pinna that part of the ear that is outside the head; flap or leather.

pin brush

Pinscher 1. breed somewhat smaller than the Doberman that has existed in Germany since the nineteenth century. Also known as the German or Standard Pinscher, it stands about 18 inches (46 cm) tall, weighs about 20 pounds (9.1 kg), has drop ears that are usually cropped, and its tail is docked. It is seen in colors similar to those of the Doberman. **2.** German word for terrier.

Pinscher

pin the bull action at the finale of bullbaiting contests, when the dog is able to bring the bull to its knees by gripping it by the nose and applying intense pressure.

pinto *see* pied.

pin-toeing moving with a pigeon-toed gait.

piperazine vermifuge or anthelmintic that was commonly used in the past for ridding dogs of roundworms.

pipestopper tail thin tail, carried straight and usually cropped long.

pipe tunnel *see* open tunnel.

pips spots of contrasting color on the brows.

piroplasma red blood cell parasite of dogs that is transmitted by ticks.

pit walled-in enclosure or ring used to confine dogs while they are engaged in dog fights, bullbaiting, or bearbaiting.

Pit Bull Terrier progeny of the Bulldog and a Terrier, originally known as Bull-and-Terrier or Half-and Half-Dog. It later became the Staffordshire Bull Terrier.

pit dog dog bred and kept for fighting other dogs in a ring or pit.

pitted teeth or **mottled teeth** aftermath of canine distemper in which areas of the permanent teeth are void of enamel.

pituitary endocrine gland attached to the base of the brain that secretes many hormones that have dynamic effects on the body.

place finishing a race second, behind the winner.

placenta saclike organ that envelopes a fetus, attaches to the lining of the uterus, and provides nutrition to the unborn puppies.

placenta eating normal instinctive eating by the bitch of one or all of the placentas as they follow each puppy from the birth canal at the time of whelping.

placings judge's selection of winner, second, and third in a dog show or competition.

plaiting movement of the forefeet in which the paths of the feet cross each other.

planes bony plates or flat surfaces of the skull that are used to describe the head.

plantar concerning or pertaining to the bottom of the hind foot.

plaque deposit of tartar on the surface of a tooth. It is a forerunner to gingivitis.

plasticity quality of being conformable or malleable; ability to change.

platelet tiny blood component that is active in the formation of a blood clot. *See* thrombocyte.

plates hair mats; feltlike mats of uncombed hair on a dog.

Plato's dog Plato personified and characterized the dog as a philosopher.

plodding slow, deliberate gait of a dog, in which its feet land heavily on the ground.

Plott Hound

Plott Hound hunting breed that stands about 24 inches (61 cm) tall, weighs about 55 pounds (25 kg), is colored brownish brindle with a black saddle, and has shorter ears than other hounds. A free-opening hound with a bawling cry and an exceptional nose, it was developed in the Smoky Mountains of Tennessee and North Carolina to hunt bear. It is now used on raccoons, mountain lions, wild cats, and virtually all larger game.

pluck to remove a dog's dead coat by hand and thin its coat a few hairs at a time.

plucky exhibiting a willingness to work; displaying readiness or exuberance.

plume long hair on the underside of the tail, as seen in the Longhaired Dachshund.

plumed well-feathered tail.

Plum Pudding Dog early name for the Dalmatian.

Pluto famous dog created by Walt Disney that belongs to Mickey Mouse.

poach to shoot game illegally, out of season, or on protected lands; to trespass. *See* flapper shooting.

Poacher's Dog *see* Lurcher.

Pocket Beagle small variety of the Beagle; stands 9 to 12 inches (23–30 cm) tall.

Podenco d'Ibiza *see* Ibizan Hound

Podenco Ibicenco *see* Evissenc.

Podenco Mallorquín (de Pelo Duro) *see* Eivissenc (wirehaired).

Podengo Portugueso Medio sighthound descended from the Podengo Portugueso Grande; it stands about 22 inches (56 cm) tall, weighs about 44 pounds (20 kg), and is seen in both a wirehaired and shorthaired variety. Its colors are fawn, yellow, red, and white. One of the most popular breeds of Portugal.

Podengo Portugueso Pequeño small game hunting dog that is largely confined to Portugal. It stands about 12 inches (31 cm) tall and weighs about 13 pounds (6 kg). It is actually a miniature sighthound but has the general appearance of a Chihuahua. It is seen in both smoothhaired and wirehaired varieties and in various shades of red and fawn.

Poe Dog or **Canis pacificus** domesticated wild dog of Tahiti and the Sandwich Islands. A smoothhaired, rust-yellow dog with crooked legs, it is fed breadfruit, fattened, cooked, and eaten by natives who consider it a delicacy.

point 1. in field trials and hunting, to indicate where game birds are hiding by striking a pose with the dog's nose pointing at the birds. **2.** soft spot on an abscess that is ready to open.

point dogs in sledding, pair of dogs in a sled team that are positioned immediately behind the lead dog.

point dogs

pointed said of a coat's ground color that is accented by darker shades on the ears, muzzle, tail tip, and sometimes feet.

Pointer AKC group: sporting; English origin. It stands about 27 inches (69 cm) tall, weighs about 70 pounds (32 kg), and has a long tail that tapers to a point. It has a short, dense coat that is colored lemon, liver, or orange, in combination with black. "A good Pointer can't be a bad color," appears in the standard.

pointer any of the gundogs that indicate where game is hiding by pointing at it with their nose. Examples: German Shorthaired Retriever, German Wirehaired Pointer, Weimaraner.

Pointer

point of elbow olecranon process of the ulna bone.

point of hock tuber calcis of the tarsal bone.

point of shoulder projection on the anterior border of the scapula or shoulder blade; humeroscapular joint, or the junction of the humerus and shoulder blade.

point rating schedule fixed by the AKC for awarding points toward a Championship, based on the number of dogs or bitches that compete in the class and other factors. The maximum number of points that can be awarded in a single show is five.

points 1. color of the hair on the legs, face, ears, and tail. **2.** in showing, awards earned by winning dogs that accumulate to earn a title. It takes 15 points, including two major wins of three points or more to become an AKC Champion.

point-to-point in foxhunting, a straight run after a fox.

Poitevin

Poitevin French foxhound. It stands about 25 inches (63.5 cm) tall and is tricolor with black patches. It has a strong voice, an excellent nose, and a dedication to hunting in the brush.

poke carriage of the neck at an abnormally low angle.

police dog 1. dog that has been specially trained for investigative (scenting) work or to assist in apprehending criminals. **2.** old nickname for the German Shepherd Dog.

Poligar hunting dog similar to the Rampur Hound.

Polish Hound

Polish Hound or **Ogar Polski** old Polish scenthound with a short, hard coat that is black with tan markings. It stands about 26 inches (66 cm) tall, weighs about 71 pounds (32 kg), and is used primarily for hunting wild boar; has a keen nose and bays loudly when on a trail.

Polish Lowland Sheepdog found throughout Europe; belongs to the Bergamasco Sheepdog group. It stands about 20 inches (51 cm) tall, weighs about 35 pounds (16 kg), and has a thick, wavy coat that is not curly. It slightly resembles the Old English Sheepdog and is perhaps the most common herding dog of Poland.

Polish Lowland
Sheepdog

Polish Nizinny Sheepdog longhaired herding dog of Poland that stands about 16 inches (41 cm) tall and weighs about 43 pounds (19.5 kg).

Polish Sheepdog native herding dog of Poland. It stands about 30 inches (76 cm) tall, weighs about 90 pounds (41 kg), and has a long soft, wavy coat and a docked tail.

Larger than the Russian Owtscharka, it is also used for draft work.

Polish Tatra Herd Dog This is a large breed that stands about 25 inches (63.5 cm) tall, weighs about 78 pounds (35 kg), is longhaired, and resembles the Kuvasz. The female is taller than the male. This breed is kept along the border areas of Poland to herd sheep and guard against wolves.

Poltalloch Terrier *see* West Highland White Terrier.

polydactyl having more than four toes and one dewclaw on a foot.

polydipsia excessive consumption of water.

polymyxin generic name for antibiotics that are derived from *Bacillus polymyxa.*

polyphagia increased consumption of food or gluttony; excessive eating; having a voracious appetite.

polyvalent vaccine vaccine that contains immunizing agents for more than one disease in a single vial.

Pom short for Pomeranian.

Pomeranian AKC group: toy; descended from spitz-type dogs of Iceland. It stands about 10 inches (25 cm), tall, weighs 3 to 7 pounds (1.4–3.2 kg), and has a cobby appearance. Its profuse coat is double with a long, coarse outer coat that is well feathered. It is seen in red, orange, cream, sable, black, brown, and blue. (See photo, page 32.)

Pomeranian

Pomeranian Sheepdog or **Pommerscher Huethund** herding dog; stands about 24 inches (61 cm) tall, weighs about 60 pounds (27 kg), and has an all-white, medium-length coat.

pompom tuft of carefully trimmed hair on a Poodle's tail or legs.

Pont-Audemer Spaniel French origin. It stands about 22 inches (56 cm) tall, weighs about 45 pounds (20 kg), its abundant, disheveled coat is grayish chestnut in color, and it has a profuse mane. Its ears are pendulant and its tail is docked. The dog has a characteristic tuft of long hair on its head that hangs over its ears. It is a hunting breed that specializes in swamp hunting, although it is an excellent all-around gundog and retriever on waterfowl and upland birds.

Ponto Victor Hugo's dog that followed him into exile.

Poodle

pooch fond name for a pet dog of any breed or mixture.

Poodle AKC group: non-sporting or toy. Poodles are shown in three size categories: The Standard Poodle is over 15 inches (38 cm) tall, the Miniature Poodle stands between 10 and 15 inches (25–38 cm), and the Toy Poodle is 10 inches (25 cm) tall or less. Standard and Miniature Poodles are shown in the AKC non-sporting group, while Toy Poodles are shown in the toy group. Each variety has a dense, curly coat and is seen in solid colors of black, blue, gray, silver, brown, café-au-lait, apricot, and cream. (See photo, page 35.)

Poodle clip any of the various styles of hair sculpturing that people have designed for Poodles. Examples: puppy, English saddle, continental, lamb, lion, Dutch, or working.

Poodle parlor establishment specializing in trimming Poodles and other dogs that require clipping.

Poodle-Pointer a crossbred dog that results from breeding a Standard Poodle and a Pointer. It stands about 26 inches (66 cm) tall and is dark brown to black in color.

Pooper Scoop® patented shovel designed to pick up, bag, and discard dog feces.

popped the box in racing, the action of a dog that came away from the starting barrier very quickly.

Porcelain smooth-coated French scenthound of elegant appearance. It stands about 21 (53 cm) inches tall, weighs about 57 pounds (26 kg), has long, pendulous ears, and is white with orange markings that are often circular in shape. It is lighter than other hounds and has relatively thin legs.

Porcelain

porcupine quills sharp, detachable appendages on the back and tail of a porcupine that imbed themselves in a dog's skin when the porcupine is harassed or attacked by the dog. The quills have the capacity to migrate deep into the dog's tissues, and, if not removed promptly, can cause the loss of an eye or even death.

Porcupine River Husky *see* Mackenzie River Husky.

Portuguese Cattle Dog herding dog that is somewhat little smaller than the Portuguese Sheepdog. It stands about 24 inches (61 cm) tall, weighs about 75 pounds (34 kg), is seen in all shades of brindle and gray, and it has a short, harsh coat and a long, thick tail.

Portuguese Cattle Dog

Portuguese Diving Dog or **Portuguese Fishing Dog** previous names for the Portuguese Water Dog.

Portuguese Podengo or **Portuguese Rabbit Dog** is seen in three sizes: 12 to 16 inches (30–41 cm), 16 to 20 inches (41–51 cm) and 22 to 27 inches (56–69 cm) tall, and in all colors from black to white, usually fawn or gray, with red or tan head markings. It is the most popular breed in Portugal and used is exclusively for hunting rabbits.

Portuguese
Podengo

Portuguese Pointer stands about 25 inches (63.5 cm) tall, weighs about 60 pounds (27 kg), and has a short, smooth coat, large pendulous ears, and a docked tail. It is seen in colors of fawn or sedge, with red or tan ears and head markings, and is a robust, energetic hunter.

Portuguese Sheepdog stands about 22 inches (56 cm), weighs about 40 pounds (18 kg), and is colored black and tan, red and tan, and tan, with long or short hair. Massively built and ferocious, this dog is used as a guard for the flocks of sheep that are kept in the high mountains.

Portuguese
Sheepdog

Portuguese Shepherd originated in the Alentejo province, south of Lisbon and is of mastiff ancestry. Its short, thick coat is a combination of dark brown or black, with white patches. An aggressive dog that is not shown at this time, it is a guard dog as well as a herding dog.

Portuguese Water Dog AKC group: working; originally bred to help fishermen by herding fish into nets, retrieving lost objects, and carrying messages from boat to boat. It stands about 22 inches (56 cm) tall, weighs about 55 pounds (25 kg), and has a profuse, thick, single-layer coat that is either curly or wavy, and is shown clipped. The colors are black, white, or various shades of brown, and may be a combination of black, brown and white.

Portuguese
Shepherd

Posavac Hound Yugoslavian scenthound breed. It stands about 22 inches (56 cm), weighs about 45 pounds (20 kg), and has a thick coat, tail feathering, and colors of reddish, yellow, and vivid tawny. It is used to hunt hare and roebuck.

post-distemper tooth mottling *see* pitted teeth.

posterior situated behind or toward the rear of the dog's body.

Portuguese
Water Dog

posterior birth type of birth that occurs when puppies are positioned backwards in the birth canal and present the tail and hind legs. *See* presentation.

posterior pituitary hormone oxytocin, a natural endocrine secretion of the pituitary gland. It is sometimes administered to stimulate uterine contractions at the time of or following whelping.

postnatal referring to the first days of a newborn's life.

postpartum following parturition; describing any condition or disease that follows immediately after the birth of a litter.

postpartum metritis inflammation of the dam's uterus following whelping.

posture attitude of a dog's body; the way it stands.

potage mixture of blood, bread, and meat that is fed to foxhounds.

pot-casse bell-tone bark, said to be characteristic of an Old English Sheepdog.

potential in racing, describing a dog that is ready to go but not yet actively racing.

pot gut grossly distended abdomen.

pothook tail tail that is carried over the dog's back with a small curve at the tip.

pot hunt to hunt cripples or winged birds that are easy to shoot.

potlicker derogatory term for a Greyhound of poor quality.

Potsdam Greyhound breed that was developed in Prussia; small Greyhound that was bred purely for companionship.

potterer in foxhunting, hound that dwells on a scent for a long time.

pouch excess skin on the point of the hock that hangs in folds.

poultry dog dog that has been specially trained to herd poultry such as turkeys and geese; commonly a Border Collie.

pounding gait gait in which the forefoot stride is shorter than the hind, causing a clumsy movement with the forefeet hitting the ground heavily.

power potent energy; ability to exert force, especially with the hind legs. Example: My hound has the power to finish well.

PRA abbreviation for progressive retinal atrophy, an inherited disease of the eye that often appears before one year of age, but sometimes later; eventually leads to blindness.

Prairie wolf *Canis latrans: see* coyote.

prancing bouncing gait in which the forefeet are raised high; inefficient gait that produces little forward motion.

prefix identifying term that precedes a dog's name, usually a title or kennel name.

pregnant with pups; in whelp.

Prelabri *see* Pyrenean Sheepdog.

premium dog food dog food that meets the highest standards for palatability, nutrition, and balance, as shown by feeding trial results.

premium list printed catalog that shows all entries, classes, prizes, and ribbons to be awarded at an AKC show.

premolar tooth situated posterior to the incisors and anterior to the molars. *See* dentition.

prenatal immediately before birth.

prepotency ability of a dog to pass certain characteristics on to its offspring.

prepubic period of about six to ten months of a puppy's life before sexual maturity is reached.

prepuce sheath covering the penis.

presence charisma or charm of a dog in the show ring that attracts attention.

presentation body attitude of puppies as they enter the birth canal. *See* anterior, posterior, and breech presentations.

pre-slip in foxhunting, action of a hound that slips before the tallyho is sounded by the master of the hunt.

press in foxhunting, to encourage hounds to speed up their work beyond their capacity to do so.

pressure bandage dressing applied directly over a wound with sufficient pressure to stop bleeding. A means to control hemorrhage that is preferred to a tourniquet in most cases.

pressure or **power** in herding, the influence that a dog's presence has on the livestock.

pressure point in herding, the exact position and distance from the sheep that the dog needs to assume in order to move the livestock quietly in the desired direction.

prey quarry; animals that serve as food for predators.

prick ears pointed ears that stand erect without cropping.

pricking casting hounds on a visible trail.

primary hair dog's guard coat hair.

primary teeth puppy's milk teeth; its deciduous teeth.

primiparous first or initial pregnancy.

Prince Charles Spaniel English name for the English Toy Spaniel.

proestrus first stage of the estrous cycle of a bitch that is manifested by vaginal bleeding.

professional handler person who is licensed by the AKC to show dogs for the dogs' owners and charge a fee for the service.

Professional Handlers' Association organization of licensed handlers.

progathism having an undershot jaw or an underbite.

progenitor ancestor; parent.

progeny offspring; descendants.

proglottid tapeworm segment or joint; reproductive part of the body of the tapeworm that passes in the stool and often sticks to the anal hair.

proglottid

progressive retinal atrophy complex of inherited, degenerative diseases of the eye that lead to blindness.

prolactin hormone from the pituitary gland that stimulates milk secretion by a bitch's mammary glands.

prolapse slipping of a body part in which it falls from its usual position, as in a prolapsed uterus or a prolapsed eyeball.

prolapsed eyeball condition that exists when the globe of the eye is extruded from its normal position and lies on the cheek, suspended by muscles, the optic nerve, and blood vessels. It is seen most often in the Pekingese.

prominent eye round, protruding, bulging eye.

prompt response in obedience trials, obeying without hesitation, immediately, quickly.

propagation production of offspring; continued increase in numbers of a species.

propeller ear earflap held in a lateral direction from the head.

propped in racing, checked; describing a dog that stops or hesitates during a race.

propped stance standing with the legs spread out, the hind feet abnormally placed behind the dog, and the forefeet likewise in front.

proppy too straight in the stifle.

prostate gland accessory sex gland that surrounds the urethra at the neck of the urinary bladder and produces some of the fluid portion of the semen.

prostatitis inflammation of the prostate gland.

protective instinct innate, specific trait of dogs to defend their owners or other dogs of their acquaintance, often risking their own lives in the process.

protein complex nitrogen-containing molecule that is made up of amino acids, and is found in many plant and animal tissues. Proteins are essential elements of a dog's nutrition.

Proteus genus of bacteria that is pathogenic to dogs and is often involved in skin infections.

Protozoa microscopic organisms that may be pathogenic to dogs.

proud bitch female dog that is in season or in heat.

proud tail gay tail.

proven stud male dog that has sired one or more litters.

proximal nearest to a point of reference; opposite of distal.

pruritis itching sensation.

pseudocoprostasis mat of perineal hair mixed with feces that prevents normal defecation.

pseudocyesis false pregnancy; condition in which a bitch goes through the motions of pregnancy without carrying puppies; phantom pregnancy.

Pseudomonas genus of pathogenic bacteria that is associated with a greenish exudate and a pungent odor.

Psoroptic mange pruritic skin disease caused by the *Psoroptes* mange mite.

PT in herding trials, an abbreviation for Pre-Trial Tested, a herding dog title.

P-Tex® in sledding, a type of plastic that is manufactured to be glued to the bottom of sled runners to reduce friction.

ptosis drooping of the upper eyelid due to paralysis of a nerve.

ptyalism excessive secretion of saliva; oversalivation.

puberty sexual maturity or onset of the capability of mating and reproducing.

pubescent having reached or arrived at puberty.

pubis bone of the pelvic girdle.

puce dark reddish brown as seen on the coat of the Irish Water Spaniel.

Pudel *see* Poodle.

puerperal tetany calcium deficiency usually seen at or shortly after parturition. *See* eclampsia.

puff decorative tuft of hair.

Pug

Pug AKC group: toy; of Oriental origin, originally bred in the Buddhist monasteries in China, and very popular in Holland as well. It stands about 11 inches (28 cm) tall, weighs about 15 pounds (6.8 kg) and is squarely built, with a fine, smooth, soft coat. Its colors are silver, apricot-fawn, or black, it is frequently seen with a mask, or dark muzzle and ears, and it has moles on the cheeks and thumb marks of black. (See photo, page 34.)

Pug (Bastard) probably a Pug-Italian Greyhound mixture of the Middle Ages. The dog was black or dark brindle with a white face and brisket. It had a small head, a roach back, and a deep chest.

pug-nosed describing a brachycephalic face; a short, pushed-up muzzle.

Puli

Puli (plural: Pulik) AKC group: herding; Hungarian origin. It stands about 17 inches (43 cm) tall, weighs about 40 pounds (18 kg), and has a dense, weather-resistant coat. The outer coat is wavy or curly and the undercoat is woolly. It is seen in solid colors of black or rusty black, and all shades of gray and white.

pull out in showing, judicial process of taking potential winners from the remainder of the class in order to select the finalists.

pulp center of a tooth that houses the nerves and vessels.

pulse expansion and contraction of an artery. The pulse rate of a dog is 80 to 120 per minute, depending on its size. Smaller dogs have a more rapid pulse than larger dogs. It is easily taken on the inside of the hind leg, halfway between the stifle and the hip. The pulse rate is equivalent to the heart rate.

Pumi Hungarian outcross of the Puli and other droving dogs from Germany and France. Smaller than the Komondor and the Kuvasz, it stands about 18 inches (46 cm) tall, weighs about 29 pounds (13 kg), has a long, corded coat, and is quite fearless. It is a noisy dog with some hunting skills, and occurs in self-colored shades, with gray most common.

Pumi

pump-handle tail tail that falls down from its attachment, then takes a horizontal turn at the end.

pumping *see* pedaling.

punch sledding term for the action of the sled teams' feet breaking through the frozen, icy crust on the surface of the snow trail.

punchy describing a surface snow that has partially melted, then frozen with an icy crust that is not strong enough to support the team and sled.

puncture wound piercing, penetrating wound.

pupil aperture or opening of the iris that allows light to enter.

pup or **puppy** immature canine, generally less than one year old.

puppy aptitude test imperfect temperament test administered by a qualified trainer; intended to predict adult behavior.

Puppy class AKC show class that is made up of puppies that are six to nine months or nine to twelve months of age; male and female classes are separated.

puppy clip *see* Poodle clip.

puppy crazies *see* zooms.

puppy factory, puppy farm, or **puppy mill** dog-breeding establishment that places quantity above quality and produces many questionable puppies. *See also* overbreeding.

puppy food special diet formulated to meet or exceed the nutritional requirements of growing puppies.

puppy pen portable, collapsible pen that is used for puppy confinement in the house, usually made of hinged panels.

puppy-proofing arranging the household in such a way as to minimize hazards available to a new pup and protect the family's valuables from the puppy's destructive teeth.

puppy pyoderma *see* impetigo.

puppy show judged competition that awards no Championship points and that is designed for immature dogs to afford them experience.

puppy stakes class for dogs under 18 months of age.

puppy strangles disease usually caused by staphylococcus that is manifested by multiple lymph gland enlargements.

purebred progeny of parents of the same registered breed.

puscha hybrid cross between a Poodle and a side-striped jackal.

pushed accelerated a dog's training to the maximum.

put down in showing: **1.** groomed and ready for the show ring. **2.** said of dogs in a class that have not been placed. **3.** put to death, put away, or euthanize.

put to sleep euthanize; give a humane and painless death.

putrifaction decomposition of organic matter.

putting on the dog affecting stylishness or dignity, an expression applied to a special occasion.

putty nose *see* Dudley nose.

Puwo hybrid cross between a Poodle and a wolf.

puzzling seeking the scent; searching with the nose to the ground in an effort to pick up a trail.

pyloristenosis narrowing of the opening between the stomach and the duodenum that is occasionally congenital in dogs.

Pyrenean Herder long-coated herding dog from Spain that stands about 29 inches (74 cm) tall, and weighs about 100 pounds (45 kg).

Pyrenean Hound, Pyrenean Mastiff, or **Pyrenean Mountain Dog** other names for the Great Pyrenees.

Pyrenean Sheepdog mountain herding breed of southwest Italy that is about 20 inches (51 cm) tall, and weighs about 40 pounds (18 kg), is seen in grays and brindles, and has a fairly long, harsh coat.

pyrethrin agent that has the insecticide properties of the flowers of the pyrethrum plant, a variety of chrysanthemum; synthetic chemical used primarily to control ticks.

Pythagoras' dog theory theory from the Greek philosopher who, upon returning from a stay in Egypt, taught his followers to hold a dog to the mouth of a dying person so that the dog would then receive the human's departing spirit.

Q

QCR® in sledding, abbreviation for Quick Change Runner® system, an invention that allows a driver to change the plastic on the sled runners quickly and easily.

quadrant quarter of a circle; one of the four quarters of a region of a dog's anatomy.

quadriceps having four heads. Example: the quadriceps femoris, the large muscle mass of the anterior hind leg that is composed of four muscles that has a single tendon of insertion on the tibia.

quadriplegia paralysis or paresis of all four legs; inability to walk.

quadruped any four-footed animal; an animal that normally moves on four feet.

quail upland game bird that is commonly hunted with dogs.

quake to tremble, shake, or quiver. Example: You can tell when my German Shorthaired is on top of a covey by her quaking tail.

qualify in obedience trials, to achieve a sufficiently high score to progress to the next level of competition.

qualifying heat timed preliminary field trial to cull out dogs of less than notable quality.

qualifying score 1. in obedience, test score of 170 points or more. **2.** in lure field trials, 50 percent of the total possible combined points from the preliminary and final courses.

quality individual merit of a puppy that includes its value as a show dog as well as its personality. *See* show quality, breeding quality, and pet quality.

qualm 1. sudden attack of nausea and vomiting. **2.** sudden emotion, such as doubt or fear.

quarantine literally, a period of 40 days; isolation period of several days or a week from others of the same species, in an effort to limit the spread of disease. Australia enforces a total canine quarantine and allows no dog importation. Great Britain enforces a six-month quarantine in an official kennel. Sweden, Norway, Finland, and Hawaii impose a four-month quarantine at the owner's expense. Denmark has a six-week quarantine and requires a permit as well. Most European countries such as France, Spain, Italy, Belgium, Holland, and Germany welcome canine tourists providing they have a current rabies vaccination (more than one month old, less than one year). The same is true of Canada, Mexico, Puerto Rico, Cuba and most South and Central American countries. Temporary show permits may be valid in some countries.

quarrelling in sledding, grumbling among the team as they are harnessed.

quarry game, prey, or object of a hunt. The original meaning of "quarry" was "entrails of game," given to the dogs after the chase.

quarter 1. in hunting and field trials, to range back and forth in front of the handler in a quarter circle or in a systematic manner. **2.** designation of the region of the front or hind limbs.

quarternary ammonium compounds common household disinfectants that are strong bases with bacteriocidal or bacteriostatic properties, and can be quite toxic to dogs.

Queen Anne front bowed legs, with the elbows out and the toes pointing inward.

queer acting strangely, or performing out of character. Example: My Pointer was queer this morning from a tick in his ear.

quest 1. in agility trials, the search for objects. **2.** in hunting, the search for game.

quick soft fleshy part of a toenail that contains vessels and nerves.

quick champions superior dogs that win their 15 Championship points in three consecutive shows on a single circuit, under three different judges.

quick

quiff prominent forelock or eyebrows.

quilled or **quill** *see* porcupine quills.

quitter in racing, dog that gives up the chase when it is behind.

R

Rabbit Beagle small Beagle. *See* Pocket Beagle.

Rabbit Dachshund toy or small Dachshund.

rabbit dog any dog that specializes in rabbit pursuit, notably the Terrier, Beagle, and Basset.

rabbit earth in foxhunting, burrow used by a fox for shelter.

rabid infected with rabies virus.

rabies fatal viral disease of all warm-blooded animals, including dog and human, which is spread by the saliva of an affected animal. Rabies, although widespread throughout the world, does not occur in Hawaii.

rabies certificate veterinary document that identifies the dog and verifies that it has received a rabies vaccination.

rabies tag metal or plastic tag worn on a dog's collar that has a number that corresponds to the rabies certificate.

raccoon dog any of the hound breeds that are bred to hunt raccoons, such as the Black and Tan, Bluetick, and Redbone.

Raccoonlike Dog short-legged wild dog with a thick, fleecy coat and brownish gray coloring with black markings on the shoulders, stomach, and above the eyes. A nocturnal and burrow-dwelling dog that feeds on fish and small mammals, it is found in Russia, Sweden, Finland, China, and Japan where its pelts are marketed under the name of Japanese fox.

race type or breed of dogs; group of dogs having common conformation and characteristics that share a common genetic makeup.

race marshall official of a Greyhound race; person in charge of the actual race.

rachis spinal column.

rachitic affected with rickets.

racing in beagling, describes a Beagle or other hound that depends on speed rather than nose to keep in front of the pack.

racing Greyhound special strain of Greyhounds that are bred for speed instead of conformation.

racing sled in sledding, lightweight, maneuverable, and well balanced snow vehicle constructed on runners that is equipped for a team of racing Huskies and competition in dogsled races.

racy Greyhoundlike, describing a long-legged dog with tucked-up flanks, muscular, and slightly built.

radial paralysis frequently encountered extensor paralysis of a dog's foreleg, with or without fracture. It is often the result of a car accident.

radius one of the two bones of the forearm; the ulna is the other.

Rafeiro do Alentejo Portuguese dog that exceeds 28 inches (71 cm) tall and 110 pounds (50 kg). It has a short, thick coat of black, tan, or yellow, or a combination thereof, and a bearlike head.

Rafeiro do Alentejo

rage syndrome genetic predisposition in Springers, Cockers, and other breeds, in which the dog has a sudden violent tantrum. A condition that causes mild-mannered pets to inexplicably attack the furniture, their owners, or their families.

ragged rough-appearing muscular construction; long and loose.

railbird or railrunner Greyhound that stays close to the inside of the track.

Rajapalagam Mastiff shorthaired dog from India that stands about 29 inches (74 cm) tall and weighs about 140 pounds (63.5 kg).

rake grooming tool with long teeth that is used to remove the dead coat from longhaired breeds.

rale abnormal respiratory sound heard with a stethoscope that is indicative of pneumonia.

Ram-Kutta another name for the Indian Wild Dog.

Rampur Hound or **Rampur Greyhound** northwest India breed that was kept for pursuing jackals and wild dogs and colored black, black and tan, and gray, with yellow eyes and a Roman nose. It is an intelligent dog of questionable temperament.

ram's nose dog's convex facial profile that is similar to a Roman nose; typical of the Bull Terrier.

rancid having the musty smell of decomposing organic material.

random mating nonselective mating practice often used in puppy mills, where quantity rather than quality is the standard.

range 1. distance at which a bird dog searches for game in front of its handler or shooter. **2.** limitations of motion of a part. Example: The injury shortened the range of his right foreleg.

rangy tall, lean, long-bodied, light-framed, and high on the leg.

ranking order level of dominance of each member of a dog society established by smelling of the anal area, displaying, and, if necessary, by fighting.

rare breed breed of dogs not commonly seen. *See* miscellaneous breeds.

raspberry leaf herb that is commonly used by dog breeders on their preparturient bitches to ease whelping. Because the tea that is brewed from raspberry leaves is quite bitter, it is often mixed with molasses.

Rastreador Brasileiro dog capable of hunting jaguars and the other big wild cats of South America. It was bred from German Shepherd Dogs, Foxhounds, and others.

rat rodent that is the vector of diseases such as leptospirosis. It is commonly found around granaries and is hunted with small dogs called ratters or rat terriers.

rate in foxhunting, to punish a hound by whipping or scolding it.

ration dog food; amount of food allowed at each meal.

rat pit enclosure in which ratting competitions are held for Schnauzers and Terriers.

rattail thick root; long, pointed tail with smooth or curly hair and a naked tip; seen in the Irish Water Spaniel.

rat terrier no longer a specific breed; small dog used to catch and kill rats and other vermin.

ratting trials contests designed for Schnauzer competition that are still held in some areas of England.

rattle in foxhunting, horn's sound when the fox is killed.

rattle-headed describing a silly or untrainable dog of questionable intelligence.

rawhide bone dog chew made of untanned leather that is twisted or tied in knots when wet, then allowed to dry.

reach measure of each step of forward motion.

reach of front measure of forward stride taken by the forefeet.

reachy describing a long, striding, economical movement, a gait that is typical of the Greyhound in which the hind feet and forefeet are far apart.

reachy neck goose neck; long, slender neck.

reaction 1. dog's response to a stimulus or command. **2.** adverse shock response to a vaccine. **3.** allergic phenomenon that involves an invading protein allergen and the response of the body's immune mechanism.

reading in herding, referring to the ability of the handler to understand and anticipate the thoughts of the stock and the dog in order to maintain control over both.

rear pastern metarsus; anatomical region between the hock and the foot.

reasoning tests battery of tests designed to illustrate the ability of dogs to form mental images and to reason. One such test uses four doors with food behind them; one is left unlocked and can be pushed open. The rule is that on each trial a different door is left unlatched. Dogs often avoid the one that was unlocked on the preceding test, which shows recognition, memory, intelligence and reasoning.

recall in obedience trials, a phase of the *come on command* training. The dog is in a *sit* or *down-stay* position and is "recalled" to the handler to go to *heel* and *sit*.

receive action of a bitch to allow a male to breed her.

receptive describing a bitch in heat that allows a male to breed her.

reckless in racing, refers to a dog that is rough and does not heed other dogs in the race.

recover to pick up a lost scent; to find a scent after a check.

recovery time in sledding, the time required for dogs to recover from a run and to be ready to continue; time required for the sled dog's pulse and respiration to return to normal.

rectal prolapse situation in which the terminal bowel slips outward through the anus, and turns inside out. It is usually result of intense straining.

rectal temperature body temperature that is taken by inserting a thermometer into the anus. It is typically 101 to 102.5°F (38.5–39.5°C) in healthy adult dogs.

rectum short, hindmost section of the large bowel that follows the colon and ends at the anus.

red coat color that is reddish orange ranging from a light or yellow red to a stag red.

Red and White Setter early English breed thought to be one of the progenitors of the Brittany and Irish Setter.

Red and White Spaniel another name for the Welsh Springer Spaniel.

Redbone Hound southern U.S. breed that was originally called a Saddleback and was later bred to a uniform solid red color. It stands about 26 inches (66 cm) tall, weighs about 70 pounds (32 kg), with a typical houndlike conformation and voice. It is a coonhound that is also used to hunt bear, cougar and wildcats, and has a well-developed treeing instinct.

Redbone Hound

red bug larvae of a tiny mite that lives on grass and weeds and may bite dogs and cause itching; opportunistic parasite of the dog. *See* chigger, sand flea.

red fawn Japanese designation for a coat of dark reddish gold color.

red fox or ***Canis vulpes*** common fox that is seen in North America.

red mange *see* demodectic mange.

red sable or **red sesame** rich red color with an overlay of black hairs that blend in with the red.

Red Setter or **Red Spaniel** other names for the Irish Setter.

red speckle roan color made up of red ticks on a white ground color; seen in the Australian Cattle Dog.

reduce 1. to replace a luxated joint and immobilize it. **2.** to line up the broken ends of a fractured bone and immobilize them. **3.** to replace a hernia. **4.** to lose weight.

reducing diet special formulation of dog food used to provide adequate nutrition while supplying fewer calories than regular dog food, thereby causing the dog to lose weight.

red water infection with *Leptospira canicola*; a transmissible kidney infection of the dog that causes bleeding in the urine (hematuria).

red water fever infection with *Babesia cani* (babesiosis), a parasite of the red blood cells of dogs that causes anemia.

red wolf or ***Canis rufus*** *see* Aguar-Guaza.

Reedwater Terrier *see* Border Terrier.

reel leash long nylon line wound on a reel that retracts by means of a spring when a button is pushed.

referee dog show official who resolves conflicts between judges.

reflex automatic, involuntary muscular or glandular response to a stimulus, such as jerking the head up in response to a loud noise or salivating in response to the sound of a can opener.

refused in racing, describing the action of a dog that won't leave the starting gate or won't run.

regenerative anemia anemic condition in which the body is actively replacing lost or destroyed red blood cells (erythrocytes).

region particular anatomical area of the body, such as the facial region, withers region, or croup region.

register to file the appropriate documents in order to list a dog with a canine registry such as the AKC.

registered litter puppies from parents that have been registered with the AKC or another registry and for whom a litter kit has been received.

registration certificate document that contains a description of a dog and states that it has been registered.

Reh Pincher German dog that has been suggested as the ancestor of the Miniature Pinscher; named for the reh deer.

reinforcement technique used in training. *Positive reinforcement,* the most widely accepted form of obedience training, employs rewards to teach a dog new behaviors. For example, as soon as a dog responds properly to a command, it is given praise or a treat. *Negative reinforcement* employs aversive stimuli, most often to change undesirable behaviors. For example, the sofa leg on which a dog has been urinating is sprayed daily with a commercial dog repellent; the dog is repeatedly repelled by the smell and eventually avoids the sofa leg altogether. Negative reinforcement is often confused with *punishment.* In negative reinforcement, the stimulus (spraying the dog repellent on the sofa) *precedes* the dog's behavior in the attempt to prevent it from occurring. In punishment, the stimulus *follows* the dog's behavior (e.g., hitting or yelling at the dog after it urinates on the sofa), in the attempt to prevent later repetitions of the behavior. Dog-training experts concur that punishment is the least effective approach to dog training.

rejudging in herding, requiring a dog to repeat its performance if that performance is prejudiced by peculiar and unusual conditions.

release word vocal signal from the handler that the training exercise is finished.

relief dog in coursing, fresh dog that is sent into make the kill when the original dog is not able to finish within the time allotted.

remove from the ring in herding, to end the run because the dog is lame, sick, or unproductive.

repeat mating breeding a bitch to a male that sired that female's previous litter.

repellent spray preparation sold to keep dogs off furniture and other objects, or to prevent chewing.

reproductive cycle *see* estrous cycle.

reproductive tract those organs and structures associated with producing a litter: female's ovaries, fallopian tubes, uterus, and vagina; male's testicles, epididymus, vas deferens, urethrea, and penis.

rescued dogs dogs that have been taken from pounds or other undesirable quarters and placed in good homes.

rescue dogs canines specifically trained to search for and help people in trouble. *See* avalanche dogs, ambulance dogs.

rescue societies organized groups that seek out and claim certain breeds of dogs from dog pounds or shelters and place them in selected homes.

research dogs dogs kept in canine laboratory colonies maintained specifically for research such as feeding trials.

resentment in obedience trials, showing of resistance on the part of the dog, or unwillingness to be trained.

Reserve Winners Bitch or **Reserve Winners Dog** substitute for Winners Bitch, or Winners Dog in case that dog is disqualified after the judging; sometimes called "Best of Losers."

response reaction to a stimulus **1.** in obedience, reaction to a command. **2.** in medicine, reaction to therapy that can be positive or negative; quick or delayed.

restraint in field trials, excessive cautioning by the handler while a dog is on point.

retained placenta afterbirth kept within the uterus following birth.

retained testicle one or both testicles that have not normally descended into the scrotum by an appropriate time and remain hidden in the abdomen or inguinal canal. *See* monorchid and cryptorchid.

retina sensitive lining tissue of the inside of the eye that receives images and converts them to chemical and nervous signals to the brain.

retinal atrophy hereditary disease that kills the pigment cells located in the middle of the retina, impairing the dog's ability to see fixed objects. Doesn't interfere with seeing moving objects, since the outer rim of the retina perceives motion.

retinitis inflammation of the retina.

retire in herding, to end a run at the request of the handler.

retrieve in hunting, to locate birds that are shot by the handler, pick them up, and return them to the handler.

retriever dog that picks up game for a hunter; certain breeds of dogs that instinctively retrieve. *See* Golden Retriever, Labrador Retriever, Chesapeake Bay Retriever.

Retriever Field Trial News, The Grange Building, 435 East Lincoln Avenue, Milwaukee, Wisconsin 53207.

revaccination second vaccination; booster vaccination.

reverse scissors bite undershot bite in which the lower incisor teeth close in front of and touch the upper incisors.

reverse sneeze forceful effort to inhale repeatedly, usually accompanied by a honking noise similar to a cough; often associated with respiratory allergies.

Rhabditis strongyloides small worm that normally lives in the soil but occasionally lives in dog's hair follicles.

Rhipcephalus sanguineus Latin name for the brown dog tick or kennel tick; single-host parasite in which all of the life forms feed on the dog.

Rhodesian Ridgeback AKC group: hound; often called the Rhodesian Lion Dog. It was bred by the Dutch, Germans, and Huguenots in South Africa, and was influenced by the Hottentots' wild dogs. A hardy hunting

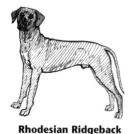

Rhodesian Ridgeback

dog that stands about 27 inches (69 cm) tall, weighs about 75 pounds (34 kg), it has a short coat of a wheaten color, and a long tail. An outstanding characteristic of the breed is the ridge of forward-growing hair that runs along the dog's spine. (See photo, page 17.)

rib one of the 26 bones extending from the vertebrae to the sternum, forming the thoracic cage. (Note: The last rib is a floating rib and does not connect with the sternum)

ribbed up having a long rib cage or ribs that angle back from the vertebrae; showing the desirable roundness in the rib cage.

ribbon award for placement in a dog show. It is lettered to indicate the type of show and the placement, and the registry's logo is imprinted on it.

rib cage ribs, spine, and sternum that form the bony thoracic vault containing the heart, lungs, and associated structures.

rib spring lateral curvature of the ribs; heart girth.

rickets bone disease of puppies that is caused by a mineral imbalance or improper nutrition.

rickettsiae microscopic organism, smaller than a bacterium, which can enter the body cells and cause disease.

rickettsiosis dog disease caused by a rickettsiae organism, transmitted by liver flukes, and obtained by eating raw salmon or trout; salmon poisoning in dogs.

ridge projecting bony structure.

ridgeback line of hair growing and lying in the opposite direction from the rest of the coat along the spine. *See* Rhodesian Ridgeback.

ridgling, rig, or **riggot** dog that has only one normally descended testicle; monorchid dog.

Riesenschnauzer another name for the Giant Schnauzer.

rig in sledding, a wheeled cart built specifically for training sled dogs during the summer.

right in field trials, describing a dog that is tuned to the competition and performing to the best of its ability.

right-of-way in sledding, right of a team that comes within 20 feet (6 m) of the team ahead to have the leading team yield to the overtaking team by coming to a full stop, off the trail.

ring enclosure or roped off area where dogs are judged.

ring craft in showing, attribute of a handler who shows a dog to its best advantage.

ringed eyes spectacles; dark markings surrounding the eyes.

ringer in coursing, a fraudulent substitute.

ring runner ring steward's assistant in a conformation show.

ring sense in showing, the ability of a dog to grasp or comprehend what is needed to win, and to provide it.

ring stern curled tail that makes a full loop.

ring steward chief assistant to the judge in a dog show.

ring tail tail that forms a circle and is carried to one side, as seen in the Appenzeller Sennenhund.

ringworm disease of the skin caused by a fungus such as *Microsporum spp.* and *Trichophyton spp.*

Rin-tin-tin German Shepherd Dog belonging to Lt. Lee Duncan, who found the dog as a puppy in a German trench in World War II. The dog was brought to the United States and became the highest paid dog actor of all time.

riot in foxhunting, activities of hounds that run anything but the hunted quarry, such as chasing rabbits or squirrels.

Rip famous narcotics-sniffing canine in the Miami International Airport. Rip once detected marijuana inside steel-reinforced concrete pedestals that were contained in sealed, galvanized steel boxes.

ripple said of a coat that is wavy, not curly.

riverside strain popular strain of flat-coated retrievers developed in England by Reginald Cook.

roach back or **roached** arched back of a dog; convex curvature of the thoracic and lumbar regions.

roading in scenting and hunting, locating quarry by following the ground scent.

roach back

road trials Dalmatian competition that was begun to perpetuate the dog's ability to work with horses.

roadwork jogging, running, or other exercise of a working dog as a part of its conditioning.

roaming free describing the activity of a stray dog or one that is not confined.

roan equal mixture of white hairs blended with darker-colored hairs.

Robertson Hound early strain of American Foxhound, similar to the Walker, July, and Trigg types.

rocking horse gait one that is characterized by an excessive rise and fall to the back.

rocking horse stance standing with all legs extended away from the body, like a sawhorse or hobbyhorse.

rolling action or **rolling gait** dog's forward progress that is characterized by swaying alternately to the right and left.

Romanian Herder longhaired Romanian herding breed that stands about 28 inches (71 cm) tall and weighs about 58 pounds (26 kg).

Romanian Sheepdog national dog of Romania. It stands about 25 inches (63.5 cm) tall, weighs about 110 pounds (50 kg), is long-coated, and is colored white with red or tan patches, sable, or grizzle and tan. It is both a shepherd and a guard dog.

Romanian Sheepdog

Roman nose facial profile that forms a convex line from the nostrils to the forehead. Seen in the Bull Terrier.

root of muzzle stop or the beginning of the foreface.

root of tail junction between the tail and the body.

rope walking leaving a single track with all four feet; also known as single tracking.

Roquet another name for the Pug (Bastard).

Roman nose

rose ear small, drop, folded ear that shows the burr, as seen in the Bulldog or Greyhound.

Roseneath Potlalloch Terrier *see* West Highland White Terrier.

rosette 1. award for placement in an AKC show; imprinted, and similar to a ribbon, only more ornate. **2.** chest marking of a small tan patch on black and tan dogs.

rostral forward; toward the oral or nasal region.

rotenone organic insecticide that is sometimes used as a mitacide for mange on the dog.

Rothbury Terrier early name for the Bedlington Terrier.

Rottweil Dog, Rott, or **Rottie** other names for the Rottweiler.

Rottweiler

Rottweiler AKC group: working; mastiff-type dog that stands about 27 inches (69 cm) tall, weighs about 110 pounds (50 kg), has a double coat, with an outer coat that is straight and lies flat. The color is always black with rust or mahogany markings, and it has a docked tail and pendulant ears. (See photo, page 21.)

Rottweiler Metzgerhund butcher's dog; Rottweiler.

rough-and-tumble shooting another name for jump shooting.

Rough-Coated Bohemian Pointer Czechoslovakian hunting dog that stands about 26 inches (66 cm) tall and has a coarse-haired coat that is water repellent. It works well in any terrain and is extremely responsive to its handler.

Rough-Coated Collie another name for the Collie.

Rough Greyhound another name for Scottish Deerhound.

Rough-Haired Terrier *see* Wirehaired Fox Terrier.

Rough-Haired Vizsla bred from the usual fine-coated Vizslas and the rough-coated German Pointers. This breed has all the attributes of the Vizsla as well as a coat that protects it in cold weather. It is not a recognized breed or variety of the AKC-registered Vizsla breed.

roundbone femur; thighbone.

round eye eye with a symmetrical, circular opening.

Round-Headed Terrier Boston Terrier.

rounding cutting, shortening, or trimming the leathers of a Foxhound.

roundworms ascarids, an endoparasite that lives in the small intestine of dogs; *Toxocara canis.*

router in racing, a stamina dog, or one that can maintain a fast pace for a long distance.

Rowett strain Beagle strain that was the first brought to the United States by General Richard Rowett of Ohio. He greatly influenced American Beagles, and some modern Beagles can trace their ancestry to the Rowett bloodline.

Royal Dog of Scotland Scottish Deerhound.

royal Dutch clip Poodle clip pattern.

rubber nose pad; soft, moist, hairless tissue that surrounds the nostrils openings.

rubber band disease common condition of house dogs that occurs when a dog manages to get a rubber band around a foot, jaw, scrotum, or other appendage. The rubber band contracts, the tissue swells, and the resultant pressure may cut through tissues and cause infection and pain.

rubber hocks twisting hocks.

rubbing rag in showing, a dog that continues to be shown without any wins; poor-quality show dog.

ruby 1. rich dark red color. **2.** Japanese term for the dark red chestnut coat color found in King Charles Spaniels.

Ruby Spaniel *see* English Toy Spaniel, one of the four varieties seen in England.

rudder tail or stern of a dog.

ruff frill or apron of long hair around a dog's neck.

Ruff nondescript mutt that is seen in the *Dennis the Menace* comic strip, drawn by Hank Ketcham.

rufus coloration basic red color.

rump upper region of the hindquarters; gluteal area.

run 1. in foxhunting, the fox chase in its entirety, from the find to the kill. **2.** in herding, each individual dog's trial performance.

run heel in scenting, to backtrack and pick up the scent.

runner assistant at a judging ring who aids the ring steward in getting the dogs into the ring to be judged.

runner-up in racing, handler who waits to catch the dog beyond the finish line of the race.

running fits paddling with all four feet while lying on side; seizure behavior seen in strychnine poisoning, epilepsy, and eclampsia.

running line wire or cable, stretched between two trees or posts above 6 feet (1.8 m) in height, with a 10-foot (3 m) chain that slides along the line on a ring; used to tether dogs for exercise.

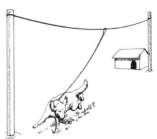

running line

runny eyes *see* epiphora or conjunctivitis.

runoff in field trials, competition to determine the final placement.

run out in herding, to go in and out after sheep.

run over in foxhunting, to overrun the ground scent, giving the quarry time to escape.

runt small, weak, but anatomically normal puppy without any visible congenital deformities. The runt of the litter is often an aggressive eater that is indistinguishable from its siblings at full growth.

runup in coursing, dash that is made from the slips to the hare.

rupture 1. hernia. **2.** tearing of muscles or tendons.

russet gold color of the Vizsla, a reddish brown.

Russian-Finnish Laika northern-type dog from Russia that stands about 17 inches (43 cm), weighs about 42 pounds (19 kg), and is longhaired.

Russian Greyhound *see* Borzoi.

Russian Hound resembles the Estonian Hound, but is larger and red or brown with white markings. It is used to hunt alone, and pursues foxes, hares, and badgers.

Russian Hunting Courser longhaired gazehound from Russia that stands about 28 inches (71 cm) and weighs about 90 pounds (41 kg).

Russian Owtchar *see* Owtcharka.

Russian Steppe Courser shorthaired gazehound from Russia that stands about 25 inches (63.5 cm) and weighs about 52 pounds (24 kg).

Russian Tracker ancient breed of Russian circus dog, having its origin as a guardian of sheep. Some say it is an ancestor of the Golden Retriever. It stood about 30 inches (76 cm) tall, and weighed about 100 pounds (45 kg). The Golden Retriever was supposedly produced by a cross of Russian Tracker with the Bloodhound.

Russian Wolfhound *see* Borzoi.

rut heightened sexual activity of a male when in the presence of a female in estrus.

Russian Tracker

S

Saarloos Wolfhond breed that was developed in the Netherlands by crossing a wolf with a German Shepherd Dog. It is about 28 inches (71 cm) tall, weighs about 80 pounds (36 kg), and its color is gray to red, with wolflike markings. It is wary and aggressive toward other dogs and has strong pack instincts.

Sabe *see* Egyptian Sheepdog.

saber-legged having a hock bent at a more acute angle than normal, so that the hind feet are well under the body.

saber tail tail that is carried in a semicircle, as in the Basset Hound.

sable inherited coat color of black-tipped hairs on a silver, gray, gold, fawn, or brown ground color.

Sabueso Español de Monte scent hunting dog of the Iberian Peninsula of Spain, traceable to the old Celtic Hound. It stands about 20 inches (51 cm) tall, weighs about 52 pounds (24 kg), is smooth-haired with no feathering, and is black, red, orange, and white in color. This dog is hunted in packs and used for tracking.

**Sabueso Español
de Monte**

Sacred dog of Greece according to Greek legend, this was a dog that was kept in the sanctuary of Asclepius, the god of medicine at Epidaurus. Its function was to lick the sick and heal them.

sacrum triangular bone formed of three fused vertebrae, that articulates with the lumbar vertebrae and the coccygeal vertebrae and is connected to the pelvis at the sacroiliac junction.

saddle black coat marking over the back and sides in the form of a saddle.

saddle back excessively long back with a dip behind the withers.

Saddleback name for the first Redbone Hounds that were characterized by a black saddle. That marking was later bred out, and the result is today's solid red dog.

saddlebag one of a pair of carrying sacks that are dropped across a dog's back. It has the shape of an equine saddlebag and is made to fit a special harness.

sagittal crest hind part of the occiput.

Saint Bernard

Saint Hubert Hound

Saluki

Saint Bernard AKC group: working; very large and powerful dog developed in the Swiss Alps. It stands a minimum of 27 inches (68.6 cm) and weighs over 100 pounds (45 kg). A massive dog with a dense, shorthaired, wavy coat, it is seen in red and white, red, brown, and white, and usually has a white blaze and markings. (See photo, page 23.)

Saint Germain Pointer or **Braque Saint Germain** gundog of France that originated in Saint Germain en Laye. A short-coated dog with orange and white coloring, it is an industrious, quiet hunting dog.

Saint Hubert patron saint of hunting.

Saint Hubert Day feast holiday in France and Belgium that is celebrated on November 3, when the hounds are blessed in a colorful ceremony.

Saint Hubert Hound large-bodied, heavy-boned hound with an excellent nose. It was named after the patron saint of hunting who founded a monastery in the Ardennes where the hound is bred. It is colored black with red markings.

Saint Vitus' dance convulsive disorder; another name for the chorea that is seen with canine distemper.

saline solution preparation containing sodium chloride in a dilute concentration that is often used for washing fresh wounds.

saliva clear, viscid secretion that originates in the salivary glands. It contains ptyalin, a digestive enzyme, and its purpose is to moisten and soften food and to start digestion.

salivary gland one of several saliva-secreting glands such as the sublingual and parotid glands.

salivary mucoceles collection of saliva under the skin caused by trauma to a salivary gland or its duct.

Salmonella genus of bacteria that causes numerous intestinal infections in dogs and other mammals.

salmonellosis an infection by *Salmonella species*.

salt and pepper black hairs and white hairs that are mixed to give an overall grayish appearance to some breeds, notably Schnauzers.

Saluki AKC group: hound; smooth-coated, long-tailed sighthound; said to be the oldest purebred dog in the world. It is usually seen in fawn, golden, and red colors with black and tan markings, and has feathers on the legs, thighs, and shoulders. It stands about 28 inches (71 cm) tall, weighs about 66 pounds (30 kg). Also known as the Persian Greyhound, it was used to hunt gazelle, hence the name Gazelle Hound.

Samojedskaja another name for Samoyed.

Samoyed AKC group: working; bred originally to be shepherds, sledge dogs, and companions. It stands about 22 inches (56 cm) tall, weighs about 65 pounds (29 kg), is solidly built, with a double coat of white. Its undercoat is soft and woolly, with an outer coat of harsh, straight hair. The tail is carried forward over the back or side. (See photo, page 25.)

Samoyed

Samoyed smile typical facial expression seen on Samoyeds; the mouth is slightly curved up at the corners.

sanctioned agility trials informal events that do not award AKC points or titles but are produced with the sanction of the AKC, using that organization's rules and standards.

sanctioned herding tests and trials informal herding events at which participating dogs do not compete for Championship points or qualifying scores.

sanctioned match informal match at which no Championship points are awarded. Champions may not compete, and Winners class is not offered.

sand flea biting mite found in long grass and on beaches. It is an opportunistic parasite of the dog that may cause dermatitis.

sand toe lameness seen in racing Greyhounds and caused by the impact of the foot on the ground.

Sandy large, nondescript dog made famous in the *Little Orphan Annie* comic strip drawn by Leonard Starr.

San Joaquin valley fever fungal infection. *See* coccidioidomycosis.

Sanshu-ken northern Japanese longhaired breed that stands about 19 inches (48 cm) and weighs about 42 pounds (19 kg).

Santa Catharina Dog species of bush dog found in Brazil.

sapling in coursing, untried pup of racing age.

saprophyte organism that lives on dead or decaying matter.

sarcoma malignant neoplasm of connective tissue origin.

sarcoptic mange skin disease caused by an infestation of *Sarcoptes scabiei var. canis,* a mite of dogs that is often first seen on the tips of the ears and later spreads to the remainder of the body. It is manifested by intense itching, redness, and scaliness, and is diagnosed by a microscopic examination of a skin scraping.

Sarplaninac breed native to Sar Planina Bosnia; a shepherd of Bosnia and Albania. It is a heavy dog that stands about 27 inches (68.6 cm) and weighs about 120 pounds (54 kg). Its long double coat is colored gray; white or yellow is a disqualification.

sashi-o Japanese term that means sickle tail; however, it refers specifically to one that is carried slightly forward and lower than normal.

Savoy Sheepdog longhaired French herding dog that stands about 19 inches (48 cm) tall and weighs about 50 pounds (23 kg).

sawhorse stance stance in which all four legs are spread away from the body.

scab crusty covering of a healing wound.

scabies *see* sarcoptic mange.

scale 1. thin, platelike structure that is shed from the skin or epithelium. **2.** in agility trials, another name for the A-frame or A-ramp.

scale clerk person who weighs the dogs immediately before a race.

scaling process of cleaning the teeth to remove tartar and plaque.

scalp skin that covers the skull.

Scamp President Theodore Roosevelt's companion, a small rat terrier.

scapula shoulder blade; flat, thin, triangular bone.

scarify to cause a scar; to make a series of small, superficial skin incisions.

scent 1. one of the two most keenly developed senses of the dog; for example, a female in season can be detected by a male dog a mile away. **2.** body odor of the quarry. **3.** one of various odors that dogs use to mark their territory that are produced by oil glands around the footpads, cheeks, anal glands, anal sacs, and urine.

scent cone in hunting terminology, a triangular scent pattern to which gundogs respond. For a scent cone to form, three things are required. First, there must be a strong source of gaseous particles of scent; second, the scent particles must be as light as air; and third, there must be a fairly strong breeze. The scent cone emenates from a bird in the grass in a downwind direction. Upon entering the cone, the birddog moves to the highest concentration of scent, regardless of the direction he was facing when he entered the cone.

scenthound dog that hunts by following the scent of the quarry rather than by seeing the quarry.

scent hurdles agility competition in which the dog must jump a hurdle, then choose an article by scent that belongs to its handler.

scenting highly specialized, instinctive ability of the dog. Its ability to scent fatty acids is a million times greater than the human's ability.

scent marking urinating or defecating on objects to establish and maintain a territory.

Schäferhund another name for the German Shepherd Dog.

Schapendoes Dutch dogs about the size of Pulis. They are used for sheepherding are also fine companions.

schedule advance notice of classes and judging times of a show.

Schillerstövare or **Schiller Hound** Swedish hound breed. A shorthaired breed that stands about 22 inches (56 cm) tall and weighs about 52 pounds (24 kg). It is a relatively fast breed that closely resembles the other scenthounds. It is kept mostly for hunting and is rarely seen outside Scandinavia.

Schillerstövare

Schipperke AKC group: toy. Although occasionally called the Dutch Dog, it originated in the Flemish provinces of Belgium and its name is Flemish for "little captain." It is sometimes known as the Belgian Barge Dog. It is about 12 inches (30 cm) tall, weighs about 16 pounds (7.5 kg), prick-eared, with a short coat on the face, medium on the body, and long in the ruff, cape, jabot, and culottes. It is solid black in color.

Schipperke

Schnauzer *see* Miniature Schnauzer, Standard Schnauzer, and Giant Schnauzer.

schutzhund dog that is specially trained and conditioned for guard and attack work.

schutzhund competition tests of a guard dog's training in attacking a well-padded "enemy."

Schweizer Laufhund Swiss hunting hound that is lighter in body and smaller in size than the traditional French breeds. It stands about 20 inches (51 cm) tall and weighs about 40 pounds (18 kg), has pendant ears, and a chiseled head with no flews. It is a scenthound that is seen in colors of white with orange or yellow markings, or a solid red.

sciatica pain associated with the sciatic nerve, extending into the thigh and leg.

scimitar tail tail held behind the body, curved upward, with more bend in it than a saber tail; seen in the Dandie Dinmont Terrier and Bedlington.

scissors bite bite characterized by the upper incisors extending over the lower incisors, but touching the lowers, like the blades of scissors.

scissura splitting; midline between the halves of the skull.

Sclater's Dog wild South American dog originally named *Canis microtis*. It stands about 14 inches (36 cm) tall, and weighs about 20 pounds (9 kg), and is black with a red mask and a pale belly. It is short-coated, its ears are small, round, and held erect, and it has a very long tail.

sclera glistening white fibrous membrane that covers the eyeball. It surrounds and joins with the transparent cornea in front of the eye.

scleritis inflammation of the sclera.

scolex "head" of a tapeworm; intestinal attachment end of the worm from which the segments are produced.

scoliosis lateral curvature of the spine.

scooting common sign of an anal sac impaction in which the dog sits down and drags its bottom along the floor.

scoring in foxhunting, the opening of the entire pack that gives voice or gives tongue, indicating they are on scent.

Scotch Colley Dog or **Scotch Sheepdog** *see* Collie.

Scottie another name for the Scottish Terrier.

Scottie jaw *see* craniomandibular osteopathy.

Scottish Deerhound AKC group: hound; known in the past as the Irish Wolf Dog, Rough Greyhound, and Highland Deerhound. It stands about 31 inches (69 cm) tall, weighs about 100 pounds (45 kg), its color is usually

Scottish Deerhound

brindle and gray, and its coat is harsh and wiry, and 3 or 4 inches (7.6–10 cm) long.

Scottish Kennel Club 3 Bruinswich Place, Edinburgh, EH75HP, Scotland.

Scottish Spaniel extinct relative of the Irish Setter.

Scottish Terrier AKC group: terrier; typical terrier, well-muscled and compact. This prick-eared dog stands about 10 inches (25 cm) tall, weighs about 20 pounds (9 kg), and has a dense undercoat with an intensely hard, wiry outer coat of iron gray, brindle, grizzled black, sandy, or wheaten color with no white markings. (See photo, page 28.)

Scottish Terrier

scours diarrhea; infectious enteritis accompanied by diarrhea.

scout in field trials, a handler's assistant.

scout dog canine that has been trained to watch the perimeter of an army encampment and warn of intruders. *See* K9 Corps.

scratch to remove a dog from competition.

scratch pack in foxhunting, pack of hounds that have been collected from various sources and put together for a hunt.

screaming fear behavioral syndrome in which a dog leaves the room where children are at play because its sensitive hearing is irritated or injured by the shrill shouting of high-pitched voices.

screen panel of diagnostic tests that are used to differentiate between diseases with similar signs.

screw tail naturally bobbed tail that is short and twisted.

screw tail dermatitis inflammation sometimes accompanied by a skin infection that is related to the wrinkles and folds in front of a screw tail.

scrotum pouch or bag of skin that contains the testicles.

Sealydale or Sealydale Terrier small South African terrier that is a descendant of crosses between the Sealyham and the Airedale. It stands about 13 inches (33 cm) tall and is white with black and tan markings.

Sealyham Terrier

Sealyham Terrier AKC group: terrier. It stands about 10 inches (25 cm) tall, weighs about 20 pounds (9 kg), has an undercoat that is soft, with a hard, wiry top coat, and is seen in white, with lemon, tan or badger markings on the head and ears. This drop-eared dog was developed to hunt badger, otter, and foxes, but it has evolved as a companion dog.

search-and-rescue trials competitive tests made popular in Europe that simulate tracking and rescue of lost or injured humans.

season heat, or estrus period in which bitch can be bred.

seasonality time from the beginning of one estrus until the beginning of the next.

seat rabbit's nest or resting place.

sebaceous cyst pocket of thick, greasy sebum in or under the skin.

sebaceous gland secretory structure of the skin that connects with a hair follicle, and produces sebum.

seborrhea abnormal production of sebum that causes a crusty, scaly skin.

sebum waxy or fatty lubricating secretion that is produced by sebaceous skin glands and discharged into hair follicles. It coats the hair shafts as they grow.

second mouth permanent teeth that are found in a dog of at least six months of age.

second series in field trials, some dogs that are selected by judges, after dogs have been run as drawn, to compete again in order to choose a winner.

second string in sledding, a team of younger or lower-quality dogs that is kept in training in addition to the main racing team.

second thigh anotomical region from the stifle to the hock; region of the tibia and fibula.

sectorial teeth carnassial teeth or sheering teeth.

sedative agent that produces a calming effect and is sometimes used for chemical restraint.

sedentary dog one that is inactive; couch potato.

sedge dead grass color; dark tan.

seed sperm cell; ovum.

Seeing Eye dog *see* guide dog.

Seeing Eye, The training center for guide dogs: P.O. Box 375, Morristown, New Jersey 07963.

seek back in obedience trials, to send a dog back in its path to find an article the handler has dropped that is heavily impregnated with the handler's scent. It is a scent discrimination tracking exercise.

seen retrieve in retriever trials, game that has been visually "marked" and is retrieved by sight. A bird that falls in the dog's field of vision, making it unnecessary for the dog to use its nose.

seesaw or **teeter-totter** in agility trials, 12-foot (30 cm) plank that is set on a fulcrum about 2 feet (61 cm) high. The dog must climb up one side and down the other, balancing in the center over the fulcrum, and exiting in a straight line.

segment reproductive portion of a tapeworm that breaks off the worm, passes out the gut, and is seen stuck to the anal hair or on the feces.

Segugio shorthaired Italian scenthound that stands about 21 inches (53 cm) tall and weighs about 57 pounds (26 kg).

seizure sudden attack of epilepsy or other convulsive disorder; manifested by regidity, muscle spasms, or uncontrollable paddling of the legs, with the back arched and the head thrown back. Its causes include viral, bacterial, and fungal infections of the brain, brain tumors, intoxication, head trauma, or low blood sugar. Seizures may be familial in nature (idiopathic epilepsy) and usually the animal returns to normal between episodes.

selective mating scientific breeding to produce specific characteristics.

self color one whole color with or without shadings.

self-colored nose nose color that matches the dog's coat color.

self-hunter dog that hunts alone without benefit of a handler, and often eats the game.

self-marked dog one that is a single solid color with faint shading on the chest, feet, and tail.

self-tail natural bobtail; very short tail a dog is born with.

self-tie premature swelling of a dog's bulbus glandis outside the prepuce.

self-whelper brood bitch that has no trouble with parturition.

semen composite ejaculate of a male that contains sperm and fluid produced by the accessory sex glands.

semidrop ear ear that falls over or breaks at the tip.

semierect ears or **semiprick ears** aural appendages that are carried erect with the tips breaking forward.

seesaw

semimoist dog food *see* soft-moist dog food.

seminal vesicle accessory sex gland that produces most of the fluid portion of a dog's semen.

send out *see* cast.

Sennenhunde *see* Appenzeller.

sense faculty by which properties of things are perceived.

sense organs specialized tissues, such as the eyes, ears, nose, palate, skin, that perceive outside stimuli.

sensible dog one that is comfortable in its environment and takes training easily; one that does not panic in strange situations.

sensitive dog one that is able to perceive sensations easily and responds quickly to training.

sensory concerning or pertaining to the senses, such as sight, touch, smell, taste, hearing.

sensory nerve nerve or nerve trunk that transfers pain and other sensations from the skin and organs to the brain.

sentry dog one specially trained for sentry duty in the army. *See* K9 Corps.

separation anxiety feeling of apprehension and state of agitation experienced by some dogs when the owner leaves for more than a few minutes.

septum wall that divides two portions. Example: The nasal septum is the partition between the nostrils.

sequella complications and results of a disease. Example: Pneumonia is a common sequella of distemper.

Sêrigala Malayan wild dog.

Serra da Estrela Portuguese herding dog that stands about 25 inches (63.5 cm) tall, weighs about 80 pounds (36 kg), and is seen in both shorthaired and longhaired varieties.

Serra de Aires longhaired herding dog from Portugal that stands about 17 inches (43 cm) tall and weighs about 32 pounds (14.5 kg).

service mating; single breeding by a stud dog.

service pup pick of the litter given in payment for the use of a stud dog.

servility submissiveness; state of being lower in the pecking order of the pack.

sesamoid bone small, flat bone or cartilaginous mass that is encompassed in a tendon and moves over a bony surface. Example: the patella or kneecap.

set to point or to indicate location of game. *See* setter.

set and crawl in herding, the action or attitude of a dog that freezes sheep in their tracks by crouching and creeping toward them causing them to move slowly.

set on indicating the place where the tail is attached to the rump and its position relative to the back.

seton drain made of a strip of linen or silk that is drawn through a wound to keep it open and establish drainage.

sett badger's burrow.

setter dog that was originally used to find birds, then made to lie flat on the ground while a net was thrown over both the dog and the birds. The contemporary meaning is a bird dog that instinctively locates game and points it.

setting dog setter of no particular breed.

settle 1. in foxhunting, the action of a pack that has gathered and is joining an individual hound's find. **2.** in herding, to allow the stock time to calm and adjust to the situation.

set up in showing, posed or stacked in a stance that presents the dog's best appearance to the judge.

set-up dog that is exhibited or displayed in the show ring.

sex gender differentiation of those individuals that produce sperm from those that produce ova.

sex determination genetic process that controls gender at the time of conception.

sex-limited describing a characteristic that occurs in only one sex.

sex-linked describing genetic traits that are carried on the sex chromosome.

sex ratio number of males compared to the number of females in a litter.

sexual maturity ability to breed; puberty.

sexual receptivity normal attitude of a bitch in estrus when she will stand and receive a breeding male.

shade gradated hair color; color of hairs that are generally white at the base and colored toward the tip.

shaft long, slender part of a bone or organ.

shaggy-dog story humorous, sometimes overlong and pointless tale.

Shaky-i longhaired Tibetan herding dog that stands about 21 inches (53 cm) and weighs about 60 pounds (27 kg).

shallow brisket lack of heart girth or depth of rib cage; shallow chest.

shallow-flewed referring to the depth of the upper lip, as in early Beagles that were classified as shallow-flewed or deep-flewed. The shallow-flewed were said to be the fastest; the deep-flewed were more musical.

shambling slow-footed or uncoordinated; not alert.

Shami one of four varieties of Saluki; smooth-coated with feathered ears and tail and a slight feathering of legs and toes.

Shan Dog *see* Chow Chow (smooth-coated).

shank lower foreleg or hind leg; tibia or radius.

Shantung Greyhound Chinese variety of Whippet with a wiry coat.

shark mouth extremely overshot jaw.

sharp describing a dog with tendency to bite without warning.

Shar-Pei *see* Chinese Shar-Pei, the Americanized version of a Chinese Fighting Dog.

sharp-tipped describing pointed and erect ears.

shaved rail in racing, railrunner; the path of a dog that races close to the inside of track.

Shawia Dog *see* Kabyle Dog.

shearing bite another name for a scissors bite.

sheath skin surrounding an organ or structure; prepuce, or foreskin of the penis.

shed to molt; to lose coat; normal renewing of a dog's coat that occurs about twice a year.

shedding herding maneuver in which the dog separates or divides the livestock and holds an individual or a group for a specific length of time; separating lambs from ewes.

she-dog bitch; female canine.

sheepdog herding dog that specializes in handling sheep

sheepdog trial judged competitive herding event that utilizes one or two dogs. Under the direction of their handler, the dogs control and drive three or five sheep through a predetermined course.

shelly descriptive of a dog that is light in bone; one that has a shallow, narrow, or weedy body.

Sheltie *see* Shetland Sheepdog.

Sheng Trou another name for the Lhasa Apso.

shepherd dog that is bred or trained to herd sheep.

Shetland Sheepdog AKC group: herding; a working dog of the Shetland Islands. This dog is nicknamed Sheltie, and is often called miniature Collie. It stands about 15 inches (38 cm) and has a double coat that is black, blue merle, or sable, with white or tan markings. Its legs are well feathered, and it has an abundant mane and frill. (See photo, page 39.)

Shetland Sheepdog

Shiba Inu AKC group: non-sporting; smallest of the Japanese native dog breeds developed for hunting by sight and scent. It stands about 16 inches (10 cm) tall, weighs about 22 pounds (10 kg), and is seen in three colors: bright orange-red, black with tan points, and sesame. All colors are marked or shaded with Urajiro (cream color); pinto or other colors and markings are serious faults.

Shiba Inu

Shih Tzu AKC group: toy; name means "lion" in Chinese, but it bears little resemblance to the king of beasts. It stands about 9 inches (23 cm) tall, weighs about 15 pounds (6.8 kg), and has a domed head, short muzzle, and undershot jaw. Its long, double, luxurious coat comes in all colors. (See photo, page 31.)

Shih Tzu

Shikoku ancient breed of Japan that was developed as a hunter. It stands about 20 inches (51 cm) tall and weighs about 50 pounds (23 kg), has erect triangular ears and a well curled tail, and is seen in colors of sesame, black sesame, red sesame, black brindle or red brindle. It has a double coat that lies flat.

Shilluk Dog African dog similar to the Basenji, bred by the Shilluk and Dinka Nilotic tribes.

shin forward edge of the tibia; region of the anterior aspect of the hind leg below the stifle.

Shishi largest of the Japanese inu or spitz types. It is used mostly in bear and boar hunting, and sometimes as a fighting dog. Its colors are about the same as those of the Akita.

Shikoku

shivering quaking or trembling that is often a sign that the dog is suffering from an obscure pain, but also is associated with cold temperatures and excitement.

shock condition of acute peripheral circulatory failure and a progressive body response to an insult. It includes a multitude of recognizable signs: pale or cyanotic membranes, decreased cardiac output, dyspnea, fixed eyes, and unconsciousness.

shock collar battery-powered, remote-controlled collar that subjects the dog that wears it to a minor electrical shock administered at the discretion of the handler.

Shock Dog fashionable toy dog in the eighteenth century in England that was white with black or red markings.

shock-headed dog one with copious, unruly hair on the head.

shoes in sledding, plastic or metal products that are used on the sled's runners to increase speed by reducing friction.

shoot organized hunt for game birds using dogs as pointers and retrievers.

shooting dog in field trials, dog that does not perform as well in front of a field trial gallery, audience, and judges as it does in a private shoot.

short back *see* close-coupled.

short-eared dog *see* Schlater's Dog.

Shorthaired Skye Terrier *see* Cairn Terrier.

shot-breaker in retriever trials, dog that jumps from the boat or duck blind immediately after a bird is shot without waiting for the handler's command; indicates a loss of control of the gundog.

shot-breaking describing the behavior of a dog that is standing steady for a bird to be flushed and immediately chases the bird when a shot is fired without waiting for the retrieve command, or without waiting to see if the bird is shot.

shotgunning in racing, action of a dog running wide nearing a turn, then cutting sharply to save ground.

shoulder anatomical region of the withers; top of the shoulder blades; joint between the humerus and scapula.

shouldering action of a dog pushing a competing dog with its body to gain an advantage.

shoulder slope angle of the scapula. *See* layback.

show in racing, position of the dog that finishes in third place.

show-bred describing a bitch that has been mated with the intention of producing show dogs.

show color to have a vaginal discharge; seen when a bitch is in season.

show dog successful competitor in dog shows or field trials.

showing haw said of a dog that has its third eyelid pulled up across the eye due to eye irritation or illness.

showing teeth describing a bulldog mouth or the brachycephalic characteristic that exposes a dog's lower teeth when its mouth is closed.

showmanship handler's ability to exhibit a dog to its best advantage.

show quality characteristics of the choicest puppies of a litter or those that approximate the breed standard; describing puppies judged most likely to win in dog shows.

show slip lead-collar combination used to exhibit a dog in the show ring.

shuffled back in racing, said of a Greyhound that is forced to withdraw from a bunched field due to crowding.

shy timid; afraid of people; describing a dog that pulls away or hides from humans.

shy breeder dog with an inconsistent, unreliable breeding capacity.

shy feeder reluctant eater; dog that requires encouragement to eat.

sialosis heavier than normal flow of saliva; excess production of saliva.

Siamese Greyhound or **Phu Quoc** shorthaired gazehound from Thailand that stands about 21 inches (53 cm) tall and weighs about 40 pounds (18 kg).

Siberian Husky AKC group: working; originally bred by the Chuckchi people in Asia as an endurance sled dog. A medium-sized Arctic dog of the spitz type, it stands about 22 inches (56 cm) tall, weighs about 50 pounds (23 kg), and is seen in any color, especially wolf gray and white, or sable and white, with dark facial markings. It often has a mask. (See photo, page 22.)

Siberian Husky

Siberian Sheepdog *see* Tooroochan Sheepdog.

Siberian Wild Dog undomesticated dog ranging across Asia. It is colored red in the summer and white in the winter.

siblings puppies that were born in the same litter.

sib-mating or **sibbing** breeding brother to sister, or mating siblings or littermates.

Sicilian Branchiero nearly extinct Italian herding dog that stands about 22 inches (56 cm) tall, weighs about 60 pounds (27 kg), and is colored black, black and tan, tan and fawn, and brindle. The coat is short and harsh, the ears cropped, and its tail is docked.

sickle-hocked describing metatarsal bones that are not vertical and form an acute angle with the tibia, causing a sloping rear pastern that often is manifested by a stilted gait.

sickle tail tail that is carried out and curved upward above the level of the back in a semicircle.

side-gaiting or **side-winding** trotting at an angle to forward progress, in a crablike fashion.

side-lay in foxhunting, the reserve hounds that are kept for replacement.

side-wheel another name for pace.

sighthound hound that hunts by sight, as opposed to one that hunts by scent; also known as gazehound. Sighthound breeds include Greyhound, Saluki, Borzoi, Whippet, and many others.

sign objective, physical evidence of a disease. It differs from a symptom in that a symptom is subjective and is the patient's interpretation of how he or she feels.

signal nonverbal, manual direction from the handler to the dog.

silent dog whistle instrument that produces a sound of such a high frequency that it is not heard by human ears, but is audible by a dog. *See* Galton Whistle®.

silent heat estrus period with no visible discharge, vulvar swelling, or other outward signs.

Silky Terrier AKC group: toy; developed in Australia as a cross between Australian and Yorkshire Terriers. It stands about 9 inches (23 cm) tall, weighs about 11 pounds (5 kg), is covered with a single, silky coat, and is seen in colors of blue and tan.

Silky Terrier

silver eye *see* walleye.

simocyon late Miocene-epoch mammal with a broad high skull. It was originally thought to be an ancestor of the dog but is probably not directly related to the canine species.

Sindh Mastiff shorthaired breed from India that stands about 29 inches (74 cm) and weighs about 141 pounds (64 kg).

sinew tendon of a muscle; tough fibrous tissue.

single bar jumps in agility trials, a bar, supported by uprights, over which the dogs must jump.

single-breed shows specialty shows; dog shows at which only one breed is shown. They may award AKC Championship points if held by a licensed or member club.

single bar jumps

single coat coat that is one layer thick, lacking an undercoat.

single lead in sledding, said of a team with only one dog used as a leader.

single track or **fox track** gait in which all four feet follow the same line and the footprints form one track; also known as ropewalking.

singletree in sledding, the rigid part of the freight harness that fits behind the dog and prevents the side straps from rubbing on the dog's hind legs.

singletree

sinking in foxhunting, said of an exhausted fox near the end of a hunt.

sinus cavity or a hollow space, especially in a bone.

sire father; male parent of a litter.

sit in obedience trials, a command from the handler that causes the dog to sit at his or her side. In a Novice class, all dogs must sit and remain stationary for one minute while their handlers are at the other end of the ring. In the Open class, they must sit for three minutes with their handlers out of sight.

sit

sit square to take a sitting position at right angles to the direction in which the handler is facing.

sit to flush in hunting, to remain in a sitting position until the birds are flushed.

sit to shoot in hunting, to remain in a sitting position until a shot is taken and the command is given to retrieve.

skeletal muscles striated muscles that are attached to bones of the skeleton by tendons and are responsible for the motor functions of the body.

skeleton sum of the bones of the body; bony framework of the body. There are 310 bones in the skeleton of a female dog; 311 in the male.

skewbald coat color with brown swatches on a white ground color.

skewfoot deviation of the toes toward the midline; pigeon-toed.

ski dogs *see* avalanche dogs.

skijoring sport in which a team of one, two, or three dogs pulls the handler who is standing on skis.

skijoring

skim milk cow's milk from which all fat has been removed.

skin integument of a dog; its body's outer covering; pelt of a dog.

skin scraping thin sample of the surface of the skin taken with a scalpel to be examined under a microscope; usual manner of diagnosing a mite infestation on a dog.

skirter in foxhunting, jealous hound that runs wide of the pack and does not contribute to the hunt.

skirting in beagling, action of a dog that runs alongside those that are on scent in an effort to try to get ahead of them by catching the scent at a turn.

skulk number of foxes collectively; used in the same context as a herd or a flock.

skull bony framework of the head that encloses the brain and other vital organs.

skully having a coarse, thick skull.

Skye Terrier AKC group: terrier; may have predated the other terriers from Scotland and hails from the Island of Skye. It stands about 10 inches (25 cm) tall, weighs about 23 pounds (10 kg), has a profuse, straight coat, and is seen with either drop or prick ears. Its coat is hard and flat, and the color ranges from black, blue, gray, silver, platinum, fawn, or cream, in solid colors.

Skye Terrier

slab-sided having little rib spring; flat-ribbed.

slack in foxhunting, having an absence of enthusiasm or a lack of spirit; describing a dog without purpose.

slack back *see* swayback.

slack loins poor muscle structure in the abdomen and loins; out of condition.

slate blue dark, grayish blue coat color.

sled bag sack that fits inside a sled basket and functions to protect the load. It is filled with the essential equipment for dog sledding.

sled basket area of a dog sled that holds the load.

sled dog dog that specializes in pulling a snow vehicle on runners; Husky. *See* Siberian Husky, Alaskan Malamute, Eskimo Dog, Samoyed, and others.

sledge snow vehicle that is mounted on runners for weight-pulling contests. *See* racing sled.

sled harness *see* bridle.

Sleeve Pekingese miniature version of the Pekingese, so small that it can be carried in the Chinese coat sleeves.

sleuth hounds scent dogs used to trail escaped felons for great distances. *See* Bloodhound.

slew-footed feet or toes that turn out; opposite of pigeon-toed.

slicker brush rubber or soft plastic brush with tiny projections that grip and remove a dog's dead coat.

slicker brush

slide clear glass plate used to hold samples to be examined under a microscope.

sling type of bandage or soft splint that is used to hold bone fragments and joints together or to limit a limb's movement, as in the Ehmer sling.

slip lead or **slip collar** lightweight collar-lead combination used on show dogs during exhibition.

slipped kneecap or **slipped stifle** *see* patellar luxation.

slipper person who holds the Greyhounds on leash while the hares are released and given a head start.

slip lead

slipper foot long, oval-shaped foot.

sloping tipping toward the ground; declining.

sloping back topline that declines from the withers to the rump.

sloping pastern metacarpus or metatarsus that deviates from vertical.

Slot Hound another name for the Bloodhound.

slough dogs scent dogs used to trail criminals through bogs and marshy sloughs. *See* Bloodhound.

slough or **sluff** mass of dead tissue that is cast out from the living tissue.

Slovakian Hound or **Slavensky Kopov** hound that is the national breed of Czechoslovakia; related to the Polish Hound, but smaller in size. It is a scenthound that stands about 18 inches (46 cm) tall, weighs about 36 pounds (16 kg), has a short coat, and is always black and tan in color.

Slughi

Slughi or **Sloughi** dog of North Africa; similar to, but smaller than, the Saluki. It stands about 24 inches (61 cm) tall, weighs about 54 pounds (24 kg), has a short, smooth coat that is not feathered, and is colored sandy yellow with tan or fawn ears and darker mask. It is used for hunting gazelles, hares, and foxes.

Smalandsstövare or **Smaland Hound** Swedish scenthound that was originally used for hunting in the dense forests of southern Sweden. It stands about 20 inches (50 cm) tall and weighs about 40 pounds (18 kg). A predominantly black dog with white and tan markings, it has a short tail and is a popular show dog.

Small Münsterländer, Kleiner Münsterländer Vorstehhund, Heidewachtel, or **Spion** birddog developed in Westphalia, Germany from the Dutch Partridge Dog. It stands about 22 inches (56 cm) tall, weighs about 33 pounds (15 kg), and its moderately long coat is always liver and white.

smartly in obedience trials, quickly, vigorously.

smeller scent-impregnated article used as a drag in Bloodhound trials.

smellers tactile hairs or whiskers that grow on a dog's muzzle. They were once thought to be part of the dog's olfactory system.

Smithfield large, black, square-headed, bobtailed English herding dog. It has a rough coat, a white frill around the neck, and long, floppy ears.

smoke coat color that is a hazy gray or sometimes a slightly bluish gray.

smooth coat type of coat with short hair that lies flat against the skin.

Smooth-Coated Collie *see* Collie.

Smooth Fox Terrier AKC group: terrier; of English origin. It stands about 15 inches (38 cm) tall, weighs about 18 pounds (8 kg), has a smooth, flat coat that is hard and dense, and is colored white with black and brown markings. It has V-shaped ears that break above the skull line

Smooth
Fox Terrier

and a docked tail. This dog was bred to work with hounds in foxhunting. As its name implies, it was bred to go to ground, and haul the fox from its lair.

Smooth-Haired Griffon *see* Brabançon.

Smooth-Haired Toy Pinscher *see* Miniature Pinscher.

smooth muscles nonstriated muscles involved with the involuntary muscle system. In the gastrointestinal tract, the smooth muscles cause peristaltic waves and push the food through the gut for digestion.

Smoushond nearly extinct breed of the Netherlands that stands about 17 inches (43 cm) tall, weighs about 30 pounds (13.6 kg), has a rough coat, and is colored all shades of wheaten and red to black. Its ears and tail are cropped and it has a rough, hard coat, eyebrows, a mustache, and a beard.

smudge dark brown or black somewhat circular marking on the head.

smutty describing a blend or overlay of markings instead of sharp outlines that are more desirable in most breeds. Example: Smutty markings are a fault in the Akita.

smutty nose brown or tan nose pad or rubber.

snail poison *see* metaldehyde poisoning.

snap dog's sudden biting action that seems to be a near miss. It may be caused by fear and it could be aggressive but often is only a warning.

Snap Dog *see* Whippet.

snarl dog's low-pitched growl, accompanied by lips pulled back from the teeth; serious warning to stand back.

snatch in racing, to make an unsuccessful attempt to grab the lure.

snatching hocks seen in a trot; hocks that turn outward quickly as they pass the supporting leg, twisting the pastern far under the body.

snatch of hocks power or drive obtained from the hocks in a moving dog.

sniffer narcotics dog; dog trained to sniff out contraband, explosives or drugs; airport dog.

sniffles *see* coryza.

snip narrow white head marking over the muzzle that surrounds the nose.

snipey describing a pointed muzzle; usually evidence of a weak head.

snippy face weak, pointed muzzle that lacks depth and breadth.

Snoopy Charlie Brown's famous Beagle in the comic strip *Peanuts,* by Charles Schultz.

snow anchor in sledding, another name for a snow hook.

snow hook anchor attached to the sled that is used to temporarily hold a dog sled and team.

snow nose nose pad or nose rubber that turns pink in the winter.

snowshoe foot sled dog's wide foot with thick fur between the toes that protects the pads and gives the dog greater traction.

snowshoe foot

snub rope or **snub line** rope used to tie the sled to a tree or post and keep the dogs stopped during the hookup; also refers to the long rope that is trailed behind a sled for a novice driver to grab in case he or she falls from the sled or the team gets away.

sociability dog's propensity to get along with and communicate with humans.

socialization process of adapting to a human environment.

socket hollow or depression, such as the hip socket (acetabulum) or eye socket.

socks white coloration on a dog's feet and lower legs.

Socrates' dogs referring to the Greek philosopher who, in his teachings, swore "by the dog."

soft back back that sags downward or a slight swayback.

Soft Coated Wheaten Terrier AKC group: terrier; its ancestry seems to be in Ireland. Its height is about 18 inches (46 cm), and its weight is about 35 pounds (16 kg), it has a single coat that is soft and silky, slightly wavy, and its color is any shade of wheaten. (See photo, page 29.)

Soft Coated Wheaten Terrier

soft-mouthed describing a retriever that doesn't maul retrieved game, one that handles retrieved birds carefully.

soft-moist describing a type of dog food that appears to have the consistency of hamburger. It sometimes contains preservatives and sugar to maintain its consistency and has a shorter shelf life than dry dog food.

soft palate rear of the roof of the mouth.

soft-tempered in herding, describing a dog that shows little aggressiveness when pressed by wild or stubborn sheep.

solar dermatitis pathological sunburn and tissue erosion that begins on the dorsum of the muzzle and includes the nose pad. It is the result of lack of pigmentation in the tissues and an inherent sensitivity, and is often seen in Collies, Shelties, and Australian Shepherds. *See* collie nose.

sole bottom of a foot; area between the footpads and toepads.

solid color one uniform color in a dog's coat.

solid jumps in agility training, high jumps that are actually barriers rather than poles.

Solomon Islands Native Dog probably a variety of the New Guinea Native Dog that has gone feral in the southeast Solomons, Ulawa, and Mala islands where it feeds on wild pigs. It has a short, black coat with white markings.

Somali Wild Dog or **Somali Hunting Dog** variety of African wild dog that is confined to Somalia, in the southern Sudan. This wild dog hunts in groups of 15 to 20 animals and is a menace to livestock breeders. It is about 24 inches (61 cm) tall, weighs about 60 pounds (27 kg), and has a harsh dark coat and a tan saddle.

sonorous having a loud, resonant sound, such as the warning growl of a dog.

Sorter dog that was historically the hero and savior of the ancient city of Corinth and was the sole survivor of 50 dogs that were given the job of guarding Corinth. All the other dogs were slain, but Sorter managed to alert the troops. The grateful citizens of the city erected a marble statue to the dog.

sorty group of dogs of the same breed.

sound 1. in peak physical health or perfect condition. **2.** exhibiting flawless movement.

sour describing a Husky that is lacking desire to pull a sled; may be caused by an accident, poor training, or poor management.

South African Hunting Dog *see* Cape Hunting Dog.

South African Wild Dog or *Lycaon tricolor venaticus* often mistakenly classified with hyenas; well known for the damage it causes to domestic livestock. Its height is about 26 inches (66 cm), its weight is about 65 pounds

South African Wild Dog

(29 kg), it is colored tortoiseshell, a mixture of black, fawn, yellow, and white, and it has very large, erect ears.

South Russian Owtscharka longhaired shepherd dog of Russia that stands about 24 inches (61 cm) tall and weighs about 78 pounds (35 kg).

soy pellets form of soy flour used as a supplement for dogs to provide lecithin, protein, and roughage.

Spalding-Norris strain early strain of the American Foxhound.

Spaniel type of hunting dog used to locate and retrieve game; listed in the AKC sporting group.

Spaniell Gentle dog used in early England to treat stomachaches. It was held to the abdomen to "succour and strengthen quailing and quamming stomachs." During the treatment, the stomachache was supposed to pass from the human to the dog. *See* English Toy Spaniel and King Charles Spaniel.

Spanish Greyhound

Spanish Greyhound or **Galgo** bred from the Sloughi. It stands about 25 inches (63.5 cm) tall, weighs about 66 pounds (30 kg), has an arched back, and short coat of tawny white, brindle or a combination thereof. Used for hunting rabbit and hare in the regions of La Mancha and Alicante in Spain, it pursued, caught, killed, and retrieved its quarry. It is presently used as a track racer.

Spanish Kennel Club Real Sociedad Central de Fomento de las Raas Caninas en España, 20 los Madrazo, Madrid.

Spanish Mastiff large and powerful guard dog that will also hunt big game. Related to the ancient Molossus, this breed is larger and the head is more refined.

Spanish Pointer or **Perdiguero** native to southern Spain; heavily built dog that appears something like the Italian Bracco. It stands about 22 inches (56 cm) tall weighs about 70 pounds (32 kg), and its coat is tan, red, and white.

spay to perform an ovariohysterectomy; to surgically remove the uterus and ovaries, rendering a female dog sterile or incapable of reproduction.

spay-neuter clinic subsidized veterinary hospital that provides pet spaying and castration operations at lower costs than those of private veterinarians. It is often associated with a shelter and is established to help control the pet population explosion.

speak in foxhunting and scenting, to cry or give voice; to give tongue, bay, or bark when on scent.

Speathos riveti *see* Ecuador Bush Dog.

specialist show judge with particular interests in a single breed or a group.

specialization of cells after the initial cell division in embryonic growth, particular cells that perform different functions are referred to as specialized. They develop into liver cells, skin cells, tonsilar cells, and so forth.

Special or **Specials dog** dog that has already won its AKC Championship and is competing in a show for Best of Breed.

Specials Only Class class in which only Champions compete.

specialty club dog fancy organization that confines its interest to one breed.

specialty show AKC show offering Championship points for a single breed.

species taxonomic category subordinate to a genus and superior to a variety. Example: The scientific name of the domestic dog is *Canis familiaris*, and *familiaris* is the species name.

species hybrid offspring of a cross of two species, such as a jackal and a dog, a canary and a finch, or a jackass and a horse.

spectacles peculiar circular markings that surround the eyes of certain breeds, giving them the appearance of wearing eyeglasses.

spectacles

speedy dogs Greyhounds. They have been clocked at over 40 miles (64 kg) an hour.

Speothos panamensis Central American Bush Dog.

Speothos venaticus Bush Dog of South America.

sphincter circular muscular band that regulates the opening and closing of an organ orifice.

spiked in coursing, suffering a cut caused by the toenails of another contestant.

spike tail short, pointed tail.

spine backbone; sum of all of the vertebrae; made up of bones in the cervical, thoracic, lumbar, sacral, and coccygeal regions.

Spinone Italiano

spinous ear tick

spinner dog that turns in circles rapidly, usually one that has been confined in a small space for a long time.

Spinone Italiano Italian gundog that has become very popular in Britain. Shown in the AKC Miscellaneous class, it is about 24 inches (61 cm) tall, weighs about 70 pounds (32 kg), its color is white, or white with lemon or brown patches, blue or blue-roan, and its coat is short and wiry. (See photo, page 44.)

spinous ear tick or ***Ornithodoros megnini*** parasite that lives in the outer ear canal of dogs.

spiral fracture break of a long bone by torsion, with the production of curved, tapered, pointed fragments.

spirochete spiral-shaped microscopic organism that can cause canine diseases such as leptospirosis.

spit dog *see* turnspit.

Spitske or **Spits** *see* Schipperke.

spitz type of dog that possesses wolflike characteristics. They make up most of the northern or Nordic breeds and include the sled dogs such as the American Eskimo, Alaskan Malamute, Siberian Husky, and Samoyed, and are related to other northern dogs such as the Akita, Norwegian Elkhound, and Pomeranian. Spitz-type dogs have erect ears and double coats.

splashed having irregularly spaced patches of contrasting colors on the coat.

splay or **splayed foot** flat foot with spreading toes and weakened pasterns.

spleen abdominal lymphatic organ that weighs about 1 ounce (28.3 g) for every 25 pounds (11 kg) of the dog's body weight. It acts to purify the blood, destroy wornout red blood cells, and produce new blood cells.

split heat *see* false heat or wolf heat.

spontaneous ovulation natural tendency of bitches to ovulate at a specific time during estrus.

spooky hound timid hound, one that is easily upset or frightened by the crowd.

spoon ear *see* bat ear.

sporadic occurring occasionally; not epidemic in occurrence.

spore reproductive element of certain bacteria and fungi.

sport 1. different or unusually colored puppy. Examples: a single liver-spotted Dalmatian in a litter of black and white; a single yellow Labrador in a litter of black Labs. **2.** organized amusement or recreational activity that involves sporting dogs.

sporting group AKC group that includes: Brittany, Pointer, German Shorthaired Pointer, German Wirehaired Pointer, Chesapeake Bay Retriever, Curly-Coated Retriever, Flat-Coated Retriever, Golden Retriever, Labrador Retriever, English Setter, Gordon Setter, Irish Setter, American Water Spaniel, Clumber Spaniel, Cocker Spaniel, English Cocker Spaniel, English Springer Spaniel, Field Spaniel, Irish Water Spaniel, Sussex Spaniel, Welsh Springer Spaniel, Vizsla, Weimaraner, and Wirehaired Pointing Griffon.

spot dark mark on a dog's head.

spotted describing a coat color with many coin-sized patches of black or liver that are spread over a white ground, as in the Dalmatian.

Spotted Dick old name for the Dalmatian.

spotting present system of running field trials in braces with individual dogs judged on performance.

spread **1.** distance between a dog's forelegs. **2.** rib spring.

spreader bar *see* singletree.

spread foot *see* splayed foot.

spread hocks *see* bowed hocks.

spread jump in agility trials, obstacle constructed of two poles that are spaced slightly apart from one another with one slightly higher that the other, the lower pole first, and the higher pole a few inches farther away. The dog must jump both. Also known as "oxer."

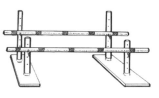

spread jump

spring in hunting, to flush game birds from their hiding place; to put birds to flight.

Springer Spaniel *see* English Springer Spaniel.

spring of ribs **1.** normal curvature of the thoracic cage. **2.** good heart girth.

springy action bouncing gait; pronounced leg action.

sprint race in sledding, organized race that is divided into four classes: unlimited, in which teams of 7 to 16 dogs race 12 to 30 miles (20–49 km); the seven-dog class, in which four to seven dogs race 7 to 12 miles (12–20 km); the five-dog class, with teams of three to five dogs that run from 5 to 8 miles (9–13 km), and the three-dog class, where two or three dogs run 3 to 5 miles (1.8–9 km).

sprinter dog that shows early speed but falls back in a long race.

spur *see* dewclaw.

spur collar

spur collar chain choke collar with blunt wire prongs that press against the dog's neck when the collar is tightened; sometimes used for training obstreperous dogs. It is outlawed from the grounds of an obedience trial.

square head broad skull with a deep muzzle.

squat bandy-legged; short; built close to the ground.

Squirrel Dog nickname for the Papillon.

squirrel tail short tail carried up and curving over the back, parallel to the topline.

stabilizing rudder in sledding, skatelike blade that is attached to the sled's runner. It is used by the driver to press against the ice to prevent a sideways skid.

stable in a fixed or unchanging position.

Stabyhoun

Stabyhoun or **Staby** small gundog of Spanish descent; developed around Friedland in the Netherlands. It is a longhaired pointer that stands about 19 inches (48 cm) tall and weighs about 62 pounds (28 kg). It is a good water dog and a fine retriever but has never gained much popularity outside its native country.

stacking teaching a dog to stand in a show stance that exhibits its characteristics favorably.

Staffordshire
Bull Terrier

Staffordshire Bull Terrier AKC group: terrier; borne out of an ancestry that was involved in dogfighting, bullbaiting, and bearbaiting. It was first called a Bulldog Terrier, then Bull and Terrier. It stands about 15 inches (38 cm) tall, weighs about 30 pounds (13.6 kg), and has a short, smooth coat in colors of red, fawn, white, black, or blue and any shade of brindle, with white markings.

Staffordshire Terrier former name of the American Staffordshire Terrier.

Staghound scenting breed of southwest England that was used to hunt foxes and stags; very few if any packs exist today. The dog stands about 24 inches (61 cm) tall, weighs about 75 pounds (34 kg), and is colored and marked much like the English Foxhound.

stag red reddish coat color that approximates the color of an adult male deer.

stained describing a ground that has mixed scents, usually from hunt followers who have crossed the original game scent.

stake 1. in lure field trials, separation of entries in a breed based on specific qualifications. **2.** in field trials, the designation of a class.

stake out to fasten dogs to a long chain with shorter chains attached at intervals. This confines the dogs temporarily or in camp and is used for periods of rest on a long trip.

stale line in foxhunting, fading scent trail.

stamina vigor, staying power, or endurance.

stance posture assumed by the dog in the show ring to exhibit its conformation to the best advantage.

stanchion vertical structural component of a dogsled.

stanchion sled *see* basket sled.

stand action or posture of a bitch in heat that shows her willingness to be bred.

standard or **breed standard** description of an ideal dog of a specific breed. Breed standards are written by individual breed clubs, agreed upon by the breeders, and maintained by the AKC.

Standard Poodle *see* Poodle.

Standard Schnauzer

Standard Schnauzer AKC group: working; middle size of the three distinct breeds called Schnauzers. It stands about 19 inches (48 cm) tall, weighs about 52 pounds (23 kg), and has a hard, wiry coat that is plucked for showing. The Standard Schnauzer is seen in pepper and salt or black colors, and has eyebrows and whiskers. The breed's principal historic vocation was as a guard dog and ratter, but it has been trained to retrieve game and to guard flocks of sheep.

stand for examination part of a conformation show in which each dog stands still while the judge palpates it.

standing heat period of estrus in which a bitch will stand for a male to breed her.

standoff coat long, heavy, double coat that stands away from the body as opposed to lying flat; seen in the Pomeranian and Chow Chow.

Staphylococcus genus of bacteria that causes numerous infections.

stand for examination

tar small white spot seen on the chest of many dogs.

staring coat hair covering in poor condition; unhealthy coat that is dry and harsh.

starter 1. official who signals for the race to begin. **2.** another name given to the Welsh Springer Spaniel.

starting box confinement for Greyhounds immediately before a race from which they begin to run.

station in showing: **1.** placement in position in a manner that will enhance the dog's appearance. **2.** comparative height from the ground, such as high stationed or low stationed.

staunch or **stanch 1.** in field trials, to remain on point, standing or dropped, until the birds are flushed. **2.** in foxhunting, describing a reliable dog, one that is trustworthy.

stay obedience command to remain in the *sit* or *down* position until another command is given.

stayer in racing, a dog with great stamina that runs well in long races.

steadiness ability of a second dog to hold and not retrieve the downed bird when its bracemate is commanded to *fetch*.

steady in hunting, said of a dog that remains in the original pointing position after the birds are flushed and a shot is fired.

steel blue silvery, dark grayish blue coat color.

steep having a vertical appearance; having poor angulation.

steep front upper arm and shoulder blade that are vertically aligned and situated.

Steinbracke one of a number of European hound breeds that are kept for hunting hares; restricted to Germany. It has a short coat that is tricolored; a good nose, and is an industrious tracker.

stenotic nares congenital defect of brachycephalic breeds in which the opening of the nostril is narrowed and sometimes collapses when the dog inhales.

stern 1. dog's tail. **2.** in foxhunting, tail of a fox.

sternal ribs first 12 ribs on each side that are attached to the breastbone by cartilage.

stern high having an elevated rump or a topline that gradually inclines from withers to croup.

sternum breastbone, an unpaired bony plate that attaches to the ribs, and is the ventral part of the thorax; keel bone.

steward **1.** ring assistant to the show judge, whose duties do not include judging. **2.** to manage, care for, or protect the animals and plants in our environment.

stifle knee joint; articulation between the tibia and fibula and the femur.

stifle band shaved area between the stifle ring and hock ring of a Poodle.

stifle ring bracelet of hair that is sculptured around the stifle of a Poodle.

stillborn prenatal death, or a puppy that has been delivered dead.

stilted **1.** said of the particular gait associated with a straight-hocked dog. **2.** having a short, choppy, restricted gait typical of a dog with straight hocks.

stilty **1.** high on leg. **2.** having poor angulation.

stimulus agent that influences or produces a functional reaction in an organism.

sting tail tail that is tapered to a sharp point. *See* bee sting tail.

stippling roan, ticked, or spotted appearance.

stock dog any herding breed; dog accustomed to working livestock.

Stockhaarig shorthaired, smooth-coated Saint Bernard.

stockings *see* socks.

stomach first digestive section of the gut; pouch that is situated below the esophagus, before the small intestine.

stomach juice combination of hydrochloric acid and a proteolytic enzyme called pepsin.

stool feces or waste from the bowel.

stoop describing the action of hounds that hunt or trail with their noses to the ground.

stop medial depression of the skull between the eyes at the junction of the nasal bones. Example: Collies have virtually no stop.

stop hound dog that hunts slowly and deliberately.

stopper pad carpal pad.

stove up become lame or to suffer from cramps or tired muscles related to work.

strabismus involuntary deviation of the eyes. Convergent strabismus is cross-eyed; divergent strabismus is the term used to describe eyes that focus away from the plane of the nose in opposite directions.

straight winning position at end of the race.

straight ahead agility command to finish the dog walk or other exercise in a straight line. The dog loses points for jumping sideways as it finishes.

straight-backed having a topline that does not dip or rise.

straight-hocked lacking normal angulation at the tarsal joint.

straight on in sledding, driver's command to go straight past a turn in the trail or past an obstacle or distraction.

straight pastern having less than normal angulation at the carpal joint.

straight running in Whippet racing, a short race on a flat, straight course.

straight shoulder having less than the normal angulation of the shoulder blade; opposite of well-laid-back.

straight stifle lacking normal angulation in the tibio-femoral joint.

strain group of related dogs having a common phenotype and genotype; bloodline.

strained overworked or overexercised.

straining ineffectively contracting abdominal muscles, a sign of constipation or an inability to urinate.

stray ownerless, homeless dog.

streaming in foxhunting, running at full pace and full cry across open ground.

street dog *see* stray, or feral dogs.

Streptococcus bacterial genus that causes numerous diseases, including pneumonia.

stress physical and psychological pressure brought on a dog during training or working.

striated muscles muscles of the heart and voluntary muscles that attach to the skeleton.

stride measure of the distance covered in a single step.

strike in foxhunting, to discover the scent of the quarry to find or start.

strike hounds in foxhunting, hounds that possess keen noses and are the first to find a trace of scent.

strip to thin a dog's coat using a knife or scissors blade.

stripper comb with sharpened areas between the teeth that is used to strip old hair from a dog's coat.

stripping knife tool used to pluck or strip a dog's coat.

strong-eyed describing a sheepdog that can hold the sheep by staring at them.

Strongyloides genus of nematodes or worms that are parasites of dogs.

strychnine poisoning poisioning caused by strychnine or *nux vomica*, a highly toxic alkaloid. It is occasionally used to control unwanted varmints such as coyotes, and is inadvertently eaten by dogs. It causes nervousness, anxiety, convulsions, and death within minutes, depending on the amount ingested. The signs are similar to 1080 poisoning.

stubby describing an abnormally short tail.

stud place of residence or the kennel in which a stud dog is kept.

stud book register AKC listing of dogs that have sired or produced a litter of puppies that have been registered by the AKC.

stud dog male dog of exceptional quality that has fathered proven progeny.

stud fee agreed-upon breeding fee paid to an owner of a stud dog for the use of the dog.

stump tail that remains after surgical docking; naturally short tail.

Stumpy-Tailed Cattle Dog breed of Australia that is only slightly different from the Australian Cattle Dog. It is square in conformation, but otherwise is very similar to its counterpart except for its naturally bobbed tail.

sty inflammation of a sebaceous gland of the eyelid.

style 1. qualities displayed by a dog in hunting; its class or flair. **2.** gracefulness or fluidity of movement of a show dog; its ring presence.

Styrian Mountain Hound or **Styrian Mountain Bracke** takes its name from the province of Styria, Austria and is similar to the Istrian Hound. It stands about 18 inches (46 cm) tall and weighs about 47 pounds (21 kg). It is a wire-haired scenthound, red to wheaten in color. Its loud baying call when in pursuit of quarry can be heard for miles.

Styrian Mountain Hound

subluxation partial or incomplete dislocation of the bones of a joint.

submission response attitude of a dog when it contacts a dog of superior size or strength. A dog shows submission to another by rolling on its back and exposing its belly. This response is seen most often in puppies.

submissive urination uncontrolled release of bladder contents that is seen in young puppies or submissive dogs when intimidated by humans or other pets.

substance possession of a desirable quantity of bone or development.

substantial penalty in obedience trials, three points penalty or more.

suckle to nourish a puppy or supply milk from the dam's mammary glands to her litter.

Suening or **Saur** dog that was made king over the conquered subjects of King Eystein, who reigned from 1001 to 1023 in Norway. This lucky dog had his own court, counselors, guard, and officers, and ruled for three years until he died in a fight with a wolf.

suffix 1. title attached to dog's name, such as Alphonse Merryweather CD. **2.** kennel name that is added to the dog's name, such as Alphonse Merryweather of Kingswood.

sugar worms slang for invalid assumption. Erroneous belief that candy that is eaten by a dog will give it worms.

sulfur nonmetallic element that occurs either free or combined in sulfides or sulfates and is used in medicine for treating certain skin diseases. Some people hold the erroneous belief that a block of sulfur in a dog's drinking water will purify the water. It won't because sulfur isn't water-soluable to any extent.

Sumatra Batak breed of guard dogs of the Batu, in Sumatra; also used for hunting and occasionally eaten.

Sun Dog another name for the Pekingese. The name was related to the dog's coat color.

sunken pastern *see* down in pastern.

Suomalainen Pystykorva *see* Finnish Spitz.

superciliary arches brow bones; supraorbital ridges.

supplemental transfer statement official document used to transfer the ownership of a registered dog.

Surinam Dog *see* Carrisissi.

surrogate one that serves as a substitute; dam that nurses and raises a litter or puppies that are not her own.

survival instinct inherited behavior of an animal that governs finding food, shelter, safety, and propagating the species.

suspension trot gait with the hind feet stepping in front of the forefeet, due to the speed of the gait. In this gait, all four feet are off the ground at the same time.

Sussex Spaniel AKC group: sporting; English breed. It stands about 15 inches (38 cm) tall, weighs about 40 pounds (18 kg), has a massive body and a rich golden liver color. Its coat is flat or wavy with moderate feathering.

Sussex Spaniel

Svensk Valhund stock or herding dog of Sweden that closely resembles the Welsh Corgi in looks, size, and working style.

Swabian Working Dog one of the probable ancestors of the German Shepherd Dog.

swamp back exaggerated swayback.

swan neck long curved neck. *See* gooseneck.

sweater Greyhound that worries and frets and loses weight while waiting to race.

sweat gland exocrine gland that excretes waste products and water from the skin, and helps to cool the body by evaporation. In the dog, these glands are mostly confined to the footpads, with a few scattered over the body.

Swedish Elkhound breed that is slightly larger than the Norwegian Elkhound. It measures about 23 inches (58 cm) tall, weighs about 66 pounds (30 kg), and has a gray or black coat.

Swedish Foxhound sometimes called the Swedish Beagle. There are several varieties seen in Sweden, with black, yellow, or bear-brown short coats.

Swedish Jämthund longhaired northland-type dog that stands about 23 inches (58 cm) and weighs about 51 pounds (23 kg).

Swedish Kennel Club Svenska Kennelklubben box 110 43, 161 11 Bromma.

Swedish Shepherd or **Västgötaspets** other names for a herding breed that looks similar to the Welsh Corgi in conformation. *See* Vallhund.

swimmer dog

swing dogs

Swiss Hound

Swedish Youth Dog Organization Sveriges Hundung-dom Box 111 21, 161 11 Bromma.

swimmer dog puppy born with minimal use of its legs and insufficient coordination and muscle development to walk. It exhibits extension of all four legs lateral to its body.

swing dogs pair of dogs that are harnessed just behind the point dogs.

swinging making wide loops by reaching too far at checks or when the scent is lost.

Swiss Beagle tricolored Beagle about 15 inches (38 cm) tall, with a short, smooth coat. It exists in several varieties.

Swiss Hound tireless dog used on deer, boar, or hare in Switzerland. The three varieties of this hound are 12 to 21 inches (30–53 cm) tall. The Jura variety is black and red, the Bernese is white, marked with black and red, and the Lucerne is white, flecked with gray and marked with red and yellow.

Swiss Hunting Dog another name for the Swiss Beagle.

Swiss Mountain Dogs a group of breeds that includes four varieties: Bernese Mountain Dog, Appenzeller Sennenhund, Entlebucher Sennenhund, and Greater Swiss Mountain Dog.

Swiss Niederlauf Hound shorthaired or wirehaired scenthound from Switzerland that stands about 14 inches (36 cm) tall and weighs about 28 pounds (13 kg).

Swissy nickname for the Greater Swiss Mountain Dog.

sword tail long, thick, pointed tail that is carried straight, as in the Labrador Retriever.

Sydney Silky or **Sydney Terrier** other names for the Silky Terrier.

sylvatic rabies reservoir for rabies in foxes, wolves, skunks, bats, and other wild mammals.

symmetry beauty of form that results from balanced proportions in a dog.

T

tab flap, pinna, or leather of the ear.

table back broad, flat, level back.

table scraps leftover human food sometimes used for dog treats and sometimes as a main course; usually a poor choice.

tactile hair one of the long stiff hairs or whiskers that grow on a dog's muzzle, each of which has a separate sensory nerve. They allow the dog to measure the size of an aperture before entering.

tactile hair

Taenia pisiformis tapeworm of dogs that uses rabbits as its intermediate host.

Taenia soleum, saginata, marginata, **and** *ovis* tapeworms of dogs that use pigs, cattle, and sheep as intermediate hosts.

Taenia taeniaformis tapeworm of dogs that uses rodents such as rats, mice, or squirrels as its intermediate host.

Tahl-Tan Bear Dog Canadian breed that stands about 15 inches (38 cm) tall and is seen in black and white or blue-gray patterns. Its coat is moderately short and it has a short, thick, bushy tail. This dog is used for bear hunting; it worries the bear by circling and yapping with a foxlike bark.

Tahl-Tan Bear Dog

tail coccygeal appendage; wagging end of a dog.

tail chasing behavior in which the dog pursues its own tail by turning in tight circles. Seen in bored dogs with too little to occupy them. In puppies it is simply a manner of inane play.

tail cropping practice of amputating a dog's tail at a particular length to comply with the breed standard.

tail feathers long hairs that occur on the posterior of a dog's tail.

tail hounds in foxhunting, hounds that are always following at the rear of the pack.

tail set relationship between the tail and the body; position of the attachment of the tail on the croup.

tail sucking puppy's habit of sucking its own tail; thought to be caused by weaning the pup too early.

take it easy in sledding, command to slow down and set a reasonable pace.

Talbot early name for the Dalmatian.

Talbot Hound hunting dog that is thought to be an ancestor of the Black and Tan Coonhound.

Talisman Dog another name for the Lhasa Apso.

tallyho in foxhunting, a cheer from horsemen announcing the first viewing of a fox.

tamed iodine one of a variety of organic iodine compounds that are used frequently in veterinary medicine as disinfectants, surgical preps, scrub soaps, and wound cleansers. *See* Betadine®.

tan light reddish brown or fawn coat color.

tan brindle coat color in which the underlying color is tan, with brindle or darker gray mottling.

tandem hitch in sledding, hitching of dogs to the sled in single file.

tandem hitch

tapering head head that narrows from the skull to the muzzle.

tapetum retinal covering at the rear of the eyeball; reflective layer of the retina.

tapeworm internal parasite of a dog that attaches to the lining of the dog's intestine by its scolex (head), and grows to enormous lengths. It is a two-host parasite that uses the dog as a definitive host, and various other animals or insects (such as fleas) as intermediate hosts.

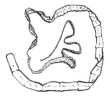

tapeworm

tapeworm segment section of the tapeworm's body that breaks off and passes from the dog's bowel. It is seen on the dog's feces or attached to its anal hair. When dried, a tapeworm segment appears like a grain of rice. Each segment contains hundreds of ova that are infective to the tapeworm's intermediate host, such as a flea.

Tarfgi *see* Welsh Springer Spaniel.

tarsal joint or **tarsus** hock joint; complexity of small bones that are positioned between the metatarsal bones and the tibia and fibula.

tar-sulfur old veterinary skin remedy that is still sometimes in use today; made of diluted pine tar, juniper tar (oil of cade), or coal tar, in combination with finely ground sulfur.

tartar encrustation that forms on the teeth; dental plaque.

Taruma Hunting Dog *see* Arecuna Hunting Dog.

Tasmanian Dog or **Tasmanian Tiger** native dog or wolf of Tasmania that is nearly extinct; not a true dog, having only four mammae, and only 46 teeth; sometimes confused with the Tasmanian devil. It stands about 20 inches (51 cm) tall, is tan or black with yellow stripes over the hindquarters, and has a wolflike head.

Tasmanian Dog

tassel feathering seen on the ends of the ear leathers in a Bedlington Terrier.

taste buds end organs lying chiefly in the tongue that transmit the sensation of taste. Dogs do not have a keen sense of taste, due to their underdeveloped taste buds, but rather, they eat what smells good to them; they taste with their noses.

Tasy or **Tazy** quick, powerful old coursing breed that is confined to Russia. It resembles the Greyhound but is coarser in build and is used to hunt a variety of quarry, from hares to wolves.

Tattoo-A-Pet tattoo-based registry: 1625 Emmons Avenue, Brooklyn, New York 11235.

Tasy

tattoo identification permanent record of a dog's ownership by impregnation of a dye into the skin of the dog with needles; usually takes the form of numbers or letters.

taut coat short, tight coat that lies flat against a tight skin.

tawny light tan, or lion-colored.

taxi dogs guard dogs carried in the past by New York taxi drivers on the seat beside them.

Tazi another name for Saluki; Persian word for Arab.

TD abbreviation for Tracking Dog, a title earned by scent dogs in AKC tracking tests.

TDD abbreviation for Team Draft Dog, a title given to all dogs of a team that compete successfully in team draft test competitions.

TDX abbreviation for Tracking Dog Excellent, an advanced title that is awarded to scent dogs that successfully complete the necessary tracking tests.

team group of more than two working dogs acting in concert and performing a useful function; sled team or draft team.

Team class in showing, special class for four dogs of the same breed that belong to the same owner.

team dogs in sledding, dogs between the swing dogs and the wheel dogs.

teapot tail tail that is carried in an upward curve, dropping at the tip.

tears normal lacrimal secretion that lubricate and bathe the eyeball.

tearstain rustlike stain often seen on the cheeks of brachycephalic breeds, Toy Poodles, and others; sometimes caused by tearing related to plugged nasolacrimal ducts or epiphora.

teaser bitch in season used to excite a male in order to collect semen for artificial insemination.

teat nipple of a mammary gland with an aperture through which milk is secreted.

Techichi Aztec sacred dog that may have been crossed with Asiatic hairless dogs to produce today's Chihuahua.

Teckel *see* Dachshund.

Teddy Bear Dog Akita or Chow Chow puppy.

teeter-totter *see* seesaw.

teething said of a puppy going through the process of dentition. Teething is painful for some puppies, which may be the reason some puppies are chewers.

telegony false belief that some of the characteristics of a litter of puppies can be derived from a male that the bitch was bred to in the past, before being bred to the sire of the litter.

Telomian rare breed of Malaysian origin, found near the Thailand border. The dog is about 18 inches (46 cm) tall, weighs about 20 pounds (9 kg), and has a short, sleek coat, erect ears, and wide-set eyes. It is sable and white in color, and is often seen climbing the ladders that lead to the aborigines' houses built on stilts.

Temnocyon one of two early Miocene canines, the progeny of which were theoretically the hunting dogs of Africa and India and include the African hunting dog, Lycaon, and Indian hunting dog, Dhole.

temperament mental attitude or character of a dog; its disposition or personality; mode of emotional response to stimuli.

temperature normal measurement of heat; body temperature for dogs is 101.5°F (38.5°C), with a range of plus or minus one degree.

tenacious holding fast; persistently adherent.

tender mouth in hunting, attribute of a dog that retrieves a game bird without damaging it.

tending in herding, supervising a flock of sheep while the flock is grazing.

tendon strong fibrous cord of connective tissue that attaches a muscle to a bone.

tendonitis inflammation of a tendon.

Tenerife Dog bichon-type dog from Tenerife, Canary Islands.

tenesmus ineffectual urge to urinate or defecate, commonly caused by a bladder or bowel infection.

teniacide vermicide; agent administered to a dog to kill tapeworms.

teniafuge vermifuge; agent administered to a dog that is designed to expel tapeworms from the intestine.

Tennessee Brindle smooth-coated scenthound from the United States that stands about 23 inches (58 cm) tall and weighs about 40 pounds (18 kg).

Terceira Island Watchdog *see* Fila da Terceira.

term normal end of a bitch's nine-week pregnancy.

terminal ring curl at the end of the tail in some breeds.

terminology nomenclature used to describe a condition.

terrier small courageous utility dog originally developed to enter the ground dens of its quarry and drive or draw them out. Terriers have been used to locate and isolate badgers, foxes, and vermin of all kinds.

terrier front having short, nearly vertical upper arms.

terrier group AKC group that includes: Airedale Terrier, American Staffordshire Terrier, Australian Terrier, Bedlington Terrier, Border Terrier, Bull Terrier, Cairn Terrier, Dandie Dinmont Terrier, Smooth Fox Terrier, Wire Fox Terrier, Irish Terrier, Kerry Blue Terrier, Lakeland Terrier, Manchester Terrier, Miniature Bull Terrier, Miniature Schnauzer, Norfolk Terrier, Norwich Terrier, Scottish Terrier, Sealyham Terrier, Skye Terrier, Soft Coated Wheaten Terrier, Staffordshire Bull Terrier, Welsh Terrier, and West Highland White Terrier.

terrier trials standardized and judged tests of terriers' ability to work in the burrows of their quarry or to catch and kill vermin.

territorial aggression propensity of a dog to defend its home territory from other dogs.

territoriality instinctive trait of dogs (especially males) to establish, mark, and sometimes to defend a district or region to which they are attached.

Tervuren Sheepdog *see* Belgian Tervuren.

Tesem hunting dog of ancient Egypt that may be extinct today. Descendants of the breed are the Basenji, Manboutou, Niam Niam, and Shilluk Dogs of Africa.

test breeding mating dogs for the specific purpose of discovering the possibility of a hereditary fault in the sire or dam.

testes testicles.

testicle male gonad; one of a pair of egg-shaped glands that are situated in the scrotal sac and produce sperm.

testicular tumors growths in the gonads that may be malignant or benign.

testosterone male hormone responsible for secondary male sex characteristics.

tetanus acute infectious disease caused by the toxin of a bacteria, *Clostridium tetani;* causes muscle spasms, lockjaw, and paralysis.

tetany muscle twitching, spasm, or convulsion.

tetracycline teeth yellow staining of the enamel of the permanent teeth of dogs that received large doses of tetracycline before their adult teeth erupted. The enamel is of normal strength and hardness.

texture tactile and visual characteristics of a dog's coat.

thallium poisoning toxic reaction caused by a fungicide and rodenticide that contains thallium. Thallium can cause acute convulsions or chronic loss of hair, depending on the amount ingested.

that will do in herding, a handler's command to release the dog from its work; release command.

theobromine component of chocolate that can stimulate the central nervous system and cause toxicity in dogs. It is a compound similar to caffeine.

therapy dog dog kept by a nursing home or an elder care facility to bring peace and happiness to its residents.

Therapy Dogs International organization that promotes the use of dogs for pet facilitated therapy: P.O. Box 2796, Cheyenne, Wyoming 82203.

theriogenologist specialist in the discipline that addresses the reproduction of animals.

thickset solidly muscled, broad; built low to the ground.

thigh region of the hind leg that lies above the stifle and below the hip.

thighbone femur; bone that articulates with the tibia and fibula on one end and the pelvic acetabulum on the other end.

Third Capitulary custom Roman Catholic custom of giving the blessing outside in front of the church door, a practice that stemmed from the insistence of early sportsmen that their dogs accompany them to Mass and the clergy's insistence that dogs be excluded from the church.

third eyelid haw; nicitating membrane located in the medial or nasal corner of the eye. This protective membrane is capable of covering and protecting the eye.

Thisbe Marie Antoinette's faithful little dog that was not allowed to enter prison with her but watched at the door for days.

thoracic concerning or pertaining to the chest or chest cavity.

thoracic limbs forelimbs or front legs.

thoracic vertebrae bones (13) that form the top of the rib cage, which articulate with the ribs.

thorax chest; body cavity situated in front of the diaphragm and behind the neck. It contains the lungs, heart, esophagus, thymus and trachea.

three-dog night expression for a very cold night, derived from the practice by ancient Australian aborigines of wearing no clothes and sleeping in shallow depressions in the earth, using their dogs as covers against the cold. A five-dog night is really cold!

three-headed dog in Greek mythology, Cerberus, the three-headed dog, guarded the gates of Hell and only Hercules was able to subdue him.

throat lower part or bottom of the neck; internal anatomical region that extends from the mouth to the beginning of the esophagus or trachea; external anatomical region of the pharynx and larynx.

throatiness loose skin under and around the neck that gives a dog a sloppy appearance.

throatlatch lower region of the neck immediately behind the mandible.

throw to produce, as in a bitch that throws four puppies in every litter.

throwback puppy that has a resemblance to a particular ancestor; one that does not resemble its littermates. *See* sport.

throwing coat losing the hair covering seasonally or after a pregnancy. *See* blown coat and shedding.

throwing tongue in scenting, giving voice, speaking, giving tongue.

thrown out in foxhunting, referring to either a hound or horseman losing position in the chase.

throw off in foxhunting and scenting, to cast the hounds or begin the hunt.

thrust propulsion with force. Example: The rear leg thrust of a malamute is the key to its pulling ability.

thrust of hock amount of drive displayed in a dog's rear leg action.

thumb marks 1. desirable black or dark spots in the region of the pastern in some dogs. **2.** white or rust spots on the front ankles that disqualify Miniature Pinschers from a show.

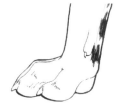
thumb marks

Thuringian Pinscher ancestor of the Doberman Pinscher.

Thuringian Sheepdog ancestor of the German Shepherd Dog.

Thylacimus cynocephalus *see* Tasmanian Dog.

thymus ductless gland composed of lymphoid tissue that is located in the thorax and is instrumental in the establishment of a dog's immune system. It is most active in newborn puppies, and atrophies in adults.

Tibetan Mastiff

thyroid 1. endocrine gland located in the throat. **2.** hormone secreted by the thyroid gland that has a dynamic effect on health and metabolism.

Tibetan Mastiff breed that stands about 27 inches (68.5 cm) tall, weighs about 130 pounds (59 kg), and is colored black and tan or black and red. Its ears are pendulant and the tail is plumed and carried over the back. It serves as a ferocious guard dog or tie dog.

Tibetan Spaniel

Tibetan Spaniel AKC group: non-sporting. It stands about 10 inches (25 cm) tall, weighs about 14 pounds (6.3 kg), and has a flat-lying double coat that is silky in texture and of moderate length. All colors and mixtures of colors are allowed and white markings on the feet are common.

Tibetan Terrier AKC group: non-sporting; profusely coated, medium-sized dog. It stands about 15 inches (38 cm) tall, weighs about 25 pounds (11 kg), has a double coat with a long wavy topcoat, and is seen in every color and combination of colors.

Tibetan Terrier

tibia shinbone; lower leg bone that extends from the stifle to the tarsus; paired with the fibula.

tic spasmodic movement; muscular twitching.

tick blood-sucking arachnid parasite of a dog. Ticks have complex life cycles that may include parasitic activity with other animals and birds. *See* brown dog tick, tick paralysis, tick-borne diseases.

tick-borne disease malady or disease transmitted or vectored by a tick. Example: Lyme disease is a tick-borne disease vectored by the deer tick.

tick

tick collar plastic dog collar impregnated with a chemical that either repels or kills ticks.

ticked said of a coat that contains areas of dark hairs blended with white ground color hairs.

tick paralysis reversible paralysis of dogs caused by a toxin in the saliva of female wood ticks *(Dermacenter sp.)* and usually seen in areas heavily infested by those ticks. The condition can be fatal and is treated by quick removal of the tick from the dog.

t.i.d. Latin abbreviation used in prescriptions for *ter in die* meaning three times a day (administer the designated dose three times daily).

tie natural phenomenon of dog breeding in which the bulbus glandis of a male's penis swells inside the bitch's vagina. The dogs are virtually locked together for 15 or 20 minutes, during which time ejaculation takes place.

tie breeding normal copulation of dogs in which the male has becomes tied or locked to the female.

tied at the elbows having close elbows and front legs that swing forward in an outward arc.

tie dog dog that is generally tied up and used as a watchdog or guard dog, historically a Mastiff.

tie-in stakes small wooden or metal posts that are driven into the ground to securely anchor a dog's leash, confining the dog while allowing it some freedom to run.

tie-in stakes

T'ien Ken *see* Heavenly Dog.

tiger brindle black-striped pattern on a gold ground color.

Tiger Dog or **Tiger Mastiff** *see* Great Dane.

tight-fitting jacket 1. dog's skin that is without wrinkles. **2.** dense, hard coat, as seen in the Welsh Terrier.

tight-lipped dog that has clean lips without flews, or upper lips that are not copious or folded.

timber 1. in showing, size of a dog's leg bones or the sturdiness of its legs. **2.** in foxhunting, a wooden fence, gate, stile, or rail. **3.** in racing, hurdle.

Timber Doodle Charles Dickens' small white terrier that he later renamed Snittle Timbery because he felt it suited the dog better.

Timber Wolf Dog said to be a fine sled dog, this breed is the largest and most ferocious of the Huskies. It is the progeny of the timber wolf *(Canis nubilus)* and a Husky. It stands about 29 inches (74 cm) tall, weighs over 100 pounds (45 kg), and is seen in colors of gray and black or gray and white.

timid or **shy** referring to a dog that won't race in a tightly bunched pack.

tinea fungus infection of the skin. *See* ringworm.

tip apex of the ear flap (leather).

Tipuri northern-type dog from India. It is a smooth-coated dog that stands about 14 inches (36 cm) tall and weighs about 40 pounds (18 kg).

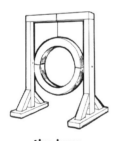

tire jump or **hoop jump** obstacle in agility trials, made from a motorcycle tire or auto tire that has an aperture of 15 to 24 inches (38–61 cm). The tire is suspended in a frame that is rigid so that the tire doesn't move. It is elevated from the floor slightly.

tire jump

Tiroler Brache or **Tyrolean Hound** natural instinctive hunter developed to use in the Austrian mountains in all seasons. It is a breed that slightly resembles the Dachshund, stands about 18 inches (46 cm) tall, and weighs about 45 pounds (20 kg), has large eyes, wide, thin ears, and a short, thick, hard coat that is red, black, or reddish yellow. It points and retrieves and is used as a tracking dog

titles awards for successful completion of dog competitions that are usually added to the dog's name in a prefix or suffix. Examples: Ch, CDX, TD, and so forth.

TNT Toys periodical devoted to toy breeds: 8848 Beverly Hills, Lakeland, Florida 33809-1604.

toboggan in sledding, flat-bottomed snow vehicle that has no stanchions or rails. It has a broad, solid floor that slides along the snow, is more durable, more stable, and carries larger loads than basket sleds, but is much heavier.

toboggan

toboggan sled modern sled that is elevated on runners and is equipped with a plastic bed.

Toby John Steinbeck's English Setter that saw things that weren't there. Steinbeck wrote that Toby would stand and bark at an oak tree for an hour at a time in the full moon.

toe digit; one of the four terminal appendages of the foot.

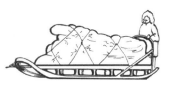

toboggan sled

toe cutting practice that William the Conqueror promoted in which three toes were amputated from the feet of all dogs that were foreign to his packs to slow their speed.

toeing in having pigeon toes or forefeet that rotate toward each other.

toeing out having forefeet that are rotated away from each other.

toenail hardened, protective covering of the tip of a toe.

toe sucking bad habit of puppies that have been weaned too early; similar vice or habit to tail sucking.

Toganee large Canadian Husky, similar to the Mackenzie Husky or timber wolf.

tolerance capacity to endure pain or hardship without physical effect.

tolling dog dog that is trained to run up and down a lakeshore to lure curious ducks into the range of the handler's shotgun; also used in Nova Scotia to lure waterfowl into a net.

Tomarctus animal evolved from *Cynodesmus* in the late Miocene epoch that was very doglike in appearance.

tone degree of vigor and tension of a muscle or body part.

tongue in foxhunting, voice of a hound; cry, speech, or bay of a hound that is sounded when it is on a scent trail. To "give tongue" is to announce to everyone in earshot that the dog is on the quarry's trail.

tongue worm lingual frenulum, a cordlike structure that lies in the lower portion of the tongue. In the eleventh century an English treatment for rabies was to take the "worm" from under an affected dog's tongue, cut it into sections, and bury it in a fig, a custom that persisted until the nineteenth century.

tonsil one of a pair of lymphatic organs located at the rear of the throat.

tonsillectomy surgical removal of the tonsils.

tonsillitis inflammation of the tonsils.

tonus slight and continual tension of muscles that produces normal posture.

Toonie Dog *see* Shetland Sheepdog.

Tooroochan Sheepdog Siberian sheepdog of the Laika type, with erect ears and a curled tail. Its black or black and white "wool" is collected and used by natives.

topcoat outer coat of a double-coated dog.

top dog best dog of the racing day.

topical 1. concerning or pertaining to a localized or regional spot on a dog's skin. **2.** describing a medicine that is prepared for use on the skin only.

topknot long hair on top of the head of heavy-coated breeds such as the Yorkshire Terrier.

topline dog's "skyline"; outline of the uppermost limits of a dog's dorsum from the withers to the tail set (sometimes includes the arch of the neck).

tora-ge Japanese term that means "tiger-haired" and is used to describe those dogs with a brindle pattern coat color.

torsion pathological twisting of an organ on its long axis. *See* volvulus.

torso body trunk including the abdomen and thorax.

torticollis contraction of cervical muscles that causes a twisting of the neck.

Tosa or **Tosa-Inu** Japanese Mastiff that was bred for fighting. It stands about 24 inches (61 cm) tall, weighs about 80 pounds (36 kg), and has a short, black, tan, or brindle coat, a broad head, and drop ears. It has copious loose skin folds around the neck, small eyes, and is quite aggressive.

tottering moving in an unsteady, clumsy gait that lacks forward thrust.

Tour Champion dog that earns all of its AKC Champi onship points on a single dog show circuit.

Touring with Touser directory of hotels and motels that accommodate guests who are traveling with dogs; published by Gaines TWT, P.O. Box 8172, Kankakee, Illinois, 60901.

tourniquet compression band, such as a cord or belt, that is placed between a wound and the heart to stop arterial bleeding until professional help can be obtained.

towline or tow rope in sledding, the hitch line that runs from the sled to the lead dog, and has rings placed at intervals to which the individual dogs in the team are fastened; also called the gangline.

towline

Toxascaris leonina roundworm of cats that is occasionally found in dogs.

Toxocara canis roundworm of dogs. *See* nematode.

Toy Boston Terrier Boston Terrier (miniature).

toy dog 1. dog of one of the breeds listed in the AKC toy group. **2.** any small companion dog or lapdog.

Toy Fox Terrier not recognized by the AKC as a separate breed; created from the Smooth Fox Terrier, Chihuahua and others. It originated in the United States in about 1930, and has been produced at various times in various numbers for many years. It stands about 10 inches (25 cm) in height and weighs about 5 pounds (2–3 kg). It is usually tricolored with white predominating. (See photo, page 44.)

Toy Fox Terrier

toy group AKC group that includes: Affenpinscher, Brussels Griffon, Cavalier King Charles Spaniel, Chihuahua, Chinese Crested, English Toy Spaniel, Italian Greyhound, Japanese Chin, Maltese, Miniature Pinscher, Papillon, Pekingese, Pomeranian, Toy Manchester Terrier, Toy Poodle, Pug, Shih Tzu, Silky Terrier, and Yorkshire Terrier.

Toy Manchester Terrier AKC group: toy; small variety of the Manchester Terrier with the same breed standard as the Manchester except as regards its weight and ears. Its upper size limit is 12 inches (30 cm) tall and 8 pounds (4 kg), and its ears are not cropped. It is not regarded as a breed apart from the Manchester Terrier.

Toy Poodle shown in the AKC toy group but not considered a separate breed. *See* Poodle.

Toy Terrier descendant of the Manchester Terrier, this erect-eared little dog must weigh over 5.5 pounds (2.5 kg) and is seen in black and white pinto colors.

Toy Manchester Terrier

trace dark stripe down the back of a Pug.

traces in sledding, rigging that includes the towline, necklines, and tuglines that lead from the dogs' harnesses to the point of pull on the sled (whiffle tree); lines that the dogs pull to move the sled.

trachea windpipe; hollow organ that extends from the larynx to the bronchi and is a part of the respiratory tree.

tracheitis inflammation of the trachea seen in most cases of kennel cough.

track **1.** course that is laid out for racing Greyhounds or Whippets. **2.** to follow a scent trail.

tracker scent dog.

tracking test of a dog's ability to follow a human scent over a trail of 440 to 500 yards (402–457 m). The scent trail must be 30 minutes to two hours old. Tracking dogs are worked on 30- to 60-foot (9–18 m) leashes.

Tracking Dog abbreviated TD, a title for a dog that has earned sufficient points in AKC tracking trials.

Tracking Dog Excellent abbreviated TDX, a title for a dog that has earned sufficient points in AKC tracking trials.

tracking leash extralong leash used to train tracking dogs.

trail **1.** marked route that keeps dogsled races on the proper course. **2.** command or signal from an overtaking driver to alert the sled team ahead that he or she wishes to pass. The team ahead must give trail and allow the overtaking team to pass, except in no-man's-land. **3.** trace, or scent mark that has been left by an animal, especially a quarry. **4.** to follow an established route or a scent trace.

trail barking hereditary tendency to give voice, bay, or bark when on a scent trail. Some of the open trail barkers are: Bloodhound, Plott Hound, Black and Tan Coonhound, Springer Spaniel, Beagle, Dachshund, and Foxhound.

Trailhound in scenting, **1.** breed that was developed in the Lake District of England and used as a draghound in competition. A course is laid with aniseed oil and the hounds race against each other over the rough terrain. The breed resembles foxhounds and is a valued family pet as well as a competitor. **2.** any dog used to compete in a contest that involves following an artificial scent trail.

trailing following a scent trail.

trail leader in sledding, a dog that will lead a team down a marked trail but won't necessarily take commands from a driver. This type of lead dog is sometimes used to judge trail hazards and to locate a hidden trail. A good trail leader will feel the solid trail through a foot of fresh, undisturbed snow and will lead the team over it.

trail markers in sledding, markers that indicate what direction to take. Examples: a red flag on the right means to take a right turn; a red flag on the left means to take a left turn; a blue marker means to go straight ahead.

trained off in racing, referring to a dog that is over-trained and burned out.

training collar choke collar; chain or nylon cord that has a ring on either end that can be formed into a noose. It is placed on the dog's neck in a way that does not choke but affords better control of the dog.

trait innate or inherited characteristic or behavioral pattern.

transfer of ownership AKC form that allows ownership of a registered dog to be transferred from one person to another.

transverse fracture bone that is broken perpendicular to its long axis in a more or less straight line in a single plane.

trap **1.** in agility trials, obstacles that are placed in close proximity to one another. **2.** in racing, starting gate or starting box of a Greyhound race.

trash cord or trash lead long leash attached to a dog's collar and allowed to trail behind the dog to facilitate training.

Travis strain early American variety of foxhound.

travois dogs dogs used by American Indians to pull a V-shaped vehicle made of two poles, called a travois. The point of the V was tied to the dog's harness and the other ends of the poles were dragged on the ground. Cargo was then strapped to the apparatus, and pulled along behind the dog. Those same dogs were used by American Indians to carry packs and some of their puppies provided meat for the Indians to eat.

travois dogs

treats goodies or attractive enticements used to get a dog's attention. They are used in training and showing to encourage desired behavior.

treeing causing the quarry to seek refuge in a tree.

Treeing Walker strain of Coonhound that appears similar to a Foxhound and specializes in treeing raccoons.

tremor involuntary quivering, quaking, or trembling.

triangular eye sharply defined eyelid angles in which the upper lid and two lower lid angles form a three-cornered shape.

triceps having three heads, such as a muscle with three heads.

trichobezoar wad, ball, or accumulation of hair in the stomach or intestine of dogs.

Trichophyton mentagrophytes nonfluorescing parasitic fungus of the dog.

Trichuris vulpis canine whipworm that inhabits the cecum, and sometimes causes chronic diarrhea.

tricolor black, tan, and white coat color typically seen in Hounds, Collies, and other dogs.

Trigg Hound early, popular strain of American Foxhounds.

trim to groom a dog for showing by clipping, plucking, or stripping its coat.

trip unsuccessful effort to kill a hare; action of a coursing hound that throws a hare off its legs but can't hold and kill it.

Triple Champion dog that has been awarded title of Champion in conformation shows, field trials, and obedience trials, or any other combination of Championships in three separate disciplines.

triple-marked retrieve in retriever trials, successful act of a dog to mark the landing place and retrieve three birds that are shot simultaneously.

trismus involuntary spasm of the masticatory muscles that makes it difficult or impossible to open the mouth.

trochanter palpable lateral bony projection situated just below the neck of each femur.

trophy prize won in competition.

trot dog's two-beat diagonal gait in which the left front and right hind foot hit the ground together, and the right front and left hind foot hit the ground together.

trousers long hair on the hind legs of certain dogs, such as the Afghan Hound.

trowel-shaped ear ear that is wider in the middle than at its attachment or its tip.

true action movement of the legs and feet in a forward line without deviation.

true front dog's forequarters that conform to the breed standard.

truffle hunter or **truffle dog** dog (notably the Poodle) that is trained to sniff out the subterranean, edible fungus. Truffles are a delicacy in England, and truffle hunting was once a large cottage industry. Once the truffles were found by the Poodle, Dachshunds were often used to dig them out. Some Poodles managed to find 1,650 to 2,200 pounds (150 to 200 kg) of truffles a week.

Trumbo strain early strain of American Foxhounds.

trumpet temple; depression on the skull just behind the eye socket.

Trumpington Terrier an ancestor to the Norwich Terrier; another name for Fox Terrier.

Trypanosoma genus of blood parasite that attacks a dog's red blood cells.

tube elongated hollow organ such as the fallopian tube.

tube-feed to use a stomach tube to give nutrition.

tuber calcis hock bone or the prominent portion of the tarsal bone that projects posteriorly; point of the hock.

tucked-up 1. naturally small-waisted at the loin, as in the Dalmatian or Greyhound. **2.** having the loin muscles contracted in a poorly conditioned dog.

tuck-up dog's underbelly or the ventral loin area.

tug or **tugline** in sledding, short leather strap, rope, or chain that attaches a dog's harness to the towline or gangline, and is used to pull the sled; also known as the backline.

tularemia rabbit fever; disease of rabbits, humans, and some domestic animals, including dogs, which is transmitted by insects such as fleas.

tulip ear ear that stands erect with a slight forward and inward curvature.

tumor abnormal swelling or enlargement of tissue that may be benign or malignant.

tunnel agility trial obstacle that is one of three types: a closed tunnel that is made of fabric; an open tunnel that is made of flexible material and is 24 inches (60 cm) in diameter and 10 to 20 feet (25 to 50 cm) long, and a crawl tunnel of variable height that is 24 inches (60 cm) wide.

turgid swollen and congested.

turkey herding activity of a dog that is specially trained to herd poultry, especially a Border Collie.

Turkey Hunting Dog another name for the Boykin Spaniel that was originally bred to find, flush, and retrieve turkeys.

Turkish Hairless Dog local name for a hairless dog that is similar to the Mexican Hairless.

turn in coursing, to overtake the hare and double it back, at not less than a right angle.

turn of stifle angle of the stifle joint; angle formed by the femur in its articulation with the tibia and fibula.

Turnspit long-bodied dog from Great Britain that was trained to walk inside a cage-type treadmill that turned a cooking spit over a fire.

Turnspit

turn-up brachycephalic chin or bulldog chin; forward-projecting chin.

tusk long tooth that projects outside the lips; canine tooth abnormality.

twisted stomach *see* gastric torsion and volvulus.

twisting hocks rubber hocks; hocks that twist both ways as they bear weight.

twist tail tightly curled tail, as in the Pug.

two-ply coat double coat.

type prevailing appearance of a particular breed of dog; characteristics that distinguish a breed.

typey having a superior body conformation; meeting the breed standard.

typical presenting the distinctive features of a type.

Tyrolean Sheepdog native to the Austrian Tyrol; similar to the Welsh Sheepdog or the British Working Collie.

Tyroler Bracke smooth-coated Austrian scenthound that is seen in two sizes: the larger stands about 17 inches (43 cm) tall and weighs about 46 pounds (21 kg), the smaller stands about 14 inches (36 cm) tall and weighs about 40 pounds (18 kg).

Tyrolese Hound resembles the Austrian Hound that originated in the Tyrol region. It is tricolored and has a rough coat with a brush tail.

Tyrolese Hound

U

UD abbreviation for Utility Dog.

UDT abbreviation for Utility Dog Tracker.

UDTX abbreviation for Utility Dog Tracker Excellent.

ugliest mutt contest judged competitive event in the Fredricksburg Virginia Dog Mart Day. *See* Dog Mart Day.

UKC abbreviation for the United Kennel Club that was originally founded to carry the registry for the American Pit Bull Terrier.

Ukrainian Sheepdog well known in Russia. It is similar to the Komondor and stands about 24 inches (61 cm) tall with a long, rough, thick, coat and a woolly undercoat. It has a long forelock, long ears, and a plumed, gay tail. It has been used as an army messenger as well as a common shepherd dog.

Ulmer Hound or Ulmer Mastiff *see* Great Dane.

ulna one of the two bones of the foreleg; the other is the radius. They extend from the elbow joint to the carpus.

ultraviolet beyond the violet end of the color spectrum; between the rays of violet and X-ray. An ultraviolet light source is used to diagnose certain fungi of dogs that fluoresce in ultraviolet light.

umbilical cord structure made up of vessels and membranes that extends from the unborn fetus to the placenta. It is the system by which an embryo or fetus receives sustenance and eliminates body wastes.

umbilical hernia congenital outpouching of abdominal tissues at the navel that results from a breakdown or lack of normal fusion of the abdominal muscles.

umbilical hernia

umbilicus location of the previous attachment of the umbilical cord; navel or belly button.

umbrella short veil in a Chinese Crested Dog.

unapparent estrus silent heat; lack of typical outward signs during a bitch's estrus.

unbroken 1. describing any dog that has not been trained and tried in the work it was bred for. **2.** describing a puppy that has not been housetrained.

uncinaria genus of hookworm; blood-sucking parasite that lives in the intestine of dogs.

uncoiling in scenting, starting from a check in a circular or spiral pattern, seeking the trail.

unconditioned response dog's instinctive reaction to a given stimulus.

unconscious receiving no sensory impressions and insensible to pain.

uncouple in foxhunting, to remove the coupling collars that hold two hounds together.

underbite condition in which the lower incisors protrude outside of the upper incisors; undershot jaw.

undercoat deep, insulating part of the hair of a double-coated dog. It is usually finer and shorter than the outer coat.

underdog term that was probably first used in dogfights to describe the dog that was on the bottom most of the time and was taking a beating; presently used for the long shot or improbable winner in a contest.

underground mutton meat from a rabbit.

underhung describing an undershot jaw or a bulldog jaw.

underline contours of the lowest point of the abdomen, chest, and brisket.

underscissors bite or **reverse scissors bite** dog's tooth structure in which the lower incisors fit outside and touch the uppers.

undershot jaw lower jaw that is longer than the upper, in which the lower incisors protrude well beyond the uppers; brachycephalic or bulldog jaw.

underslung jaw *see* undershot jaw.

unearth to cause a fox or other quarry to leave its burrow in the ground.

unentered dog dog that has not yet been trained or competed in its work.

unilateral cryptorchid misnomer used to describe a dog that has only one testicle descended into the scrotum. *See* monorchid.

uniparous describing a first pregnancy; primiparus.

United Kennel Club purebred dog registry that registers a greater number of breeds than the American Kennel Club. 100 East Kilgore Road, Kalamazoo, Michigan 49001-5598.

United Schutzhund Clubs of America registry of German Shepherd Dogs, guard and attack dogs. 3704 Lemay Ferry Road, St. Louis, Missouri 63125.

United States Dog Agility Association Box 850953, Richardson, Texas 75085.

unlimited race sledding race in which no limit is placed on the number of dogs that can be run on each team. It is usually a longer race than a sprint and often run by teams of 16 to 22 dogs.

unpigmented having no pigment or less than normal pigmentation in a dog's eyelid margins, eyes, nose pad, or other structures.

unseen retrieve in retriever trials and hunting, game bird that is retrieved by scent alone.

unsex to castrate or spay.

unsighted dog in coursing, one that has lost sight of the quarry.

unsound physically incapable of normal performance. It may refer to lameness or conformation faults that are temporary or permanent.

unspoiled dog in hunting, untrained gundog.

unsteady dog dog that is likely to cause problems; undertrained dog or a dog that has not been worked.

untraining practice of altering a dog's behavior to instill training of another type.

ununited anconeal process elbow dysplasia; developmental failure of the anconeus to fuse to the shaft of the ulna.

upfaced having a short, turned-up muzzle.

upland game birds any ground-nesting fowl, including pheasants, grouse, quail, and others.

upper arm anatomical region located between the elbow and the shoulder; anatomical region of the humerus.

upright shoulder scapula that has a lack of proper angulation; straight shoulder or a shoulder more vertical than desired.

upsweep curvature or upturned portion of the lower jaw or chin of some brachycephalic breeds such as the Bulldog.

urajiro means "white rear" in Japanese; refers to the almost pure white underside of a dog.

urinary marking propensity of male dogs to urinate on vertical surfaces in their territory.

Urocyon cinereoargentus eastern gray fox whose habitat includes most of North America, Central America, and South America.

Urocyon littoralis island gray fox of North America.

urticaria itchy, inflamed, elevated patch on the skin.

U.S.P. abbreviation for United States Pharmacopoeia.

uterine fatigue loss of uterine muscular contractions due to prolonged labor and the tiring of the uterine muscles.

uterine horns paired branches of the uterus that lead from the uterine body to the oviducts, the place of embryo implantation.

uterine inertia absence of uterine contractions at the time of parturition.

uterine prolapse slipping of the uterus into the vagina or outside the animal; inversion of the uterus; casting of the womb.

uterine torsion twisting of the uterus on its long axis.

uterus female's hollow reproductive organ that consists of a body and two horns in which the embryos are attached.

utility class competitive obedience class that is made up of dogs that are working toward the title of Utility Dog.

uvula pendulant portion of the posterior soft palate that hangs down in the back of the mouth.

uvulectomy surgical excision of the uvula. It is often a part of the complex of operations performed on a Bulldog to improve its ability to breathe.

V

vaccinate to inject an immunizing agent into an animal for the purpose of producing immunity to a disease.

vaccine manufactured antigenic product made up of a suspension of live or killed microorganisms and designed to elicit an immune response when introduced into the animal.

vaccine response propensity or ability to produce immunity to a disease after having been vaccinated.

vaccine virus replication in-vivo multiplication of a live virus from a vaccine that was administered to an animal.

vaccine virus shedding casting off of a replicating live virus from a vaccinated animal.

vacuole space or empty cavity formed inside a living cell.

Vaghari Hound smooth-coated gazehound from India that stands about 23 inches (28 cm) tall and weighs about 28 pounds (13 kg).

vagina hollow female reproductive organ situated between the vulva and the cervix; vaginal vault.

vaginitis inflammation of the vagina.

valley fever *see* coccidioidomycosis.

Vallhund Swedish herding dog that resembles a Welsh Corgi. It stands about 14 inches (35.5 cm) tall, weighs about 25 pounds (11 kg), and is gray with a dark mask, dark ears, and a saddle. Its coat is short and harsh, ears are erect and pointed, and tail is docked or naturally bobbed.

Vallhund

vanity emotion of a dog that is frequently associated with show or performing dogs, in which the show dog may enjoy the attention received in clipping, brushing, and handling. It is also seen in dogs that learn tricks; they are said to be more alert and responsive and better behaved than other dogs, and to enjoy the applause of the audience.

variety division of a breed for show purposes that is based on coat type, size, or color.

varmint rat, skunk, or other rodent quarry.

varminty describing an expression of intense, keen brightness.

vas deferens duct, canal, or tube that extends from the epididymus though the urethra. It is the means of passing semen from the testicle.

vasectomy operation performed to surgically cut or tie the male's vas deferens, rendering him sterile and incapable of siring puppies. This operation does not render him impotent, nor does it stop his sexual desire.

Vastgöta Spitz *see* Vallhund.

Veadeiro Catarinense smooth-coated scenthound from Brazil that stands about 24 inches (61 cm) tall and weighs about 61 pounds (28 kg).

vector biological or mechanical means of transferring a disease from one dog to another; carrier.

veil long hair that is seen on the head of a Chinese Crested dog.

veiled coat overlay of long, fine hair on a dog.

Vendéen Hound French ancestor of the Griffons that is probably extinct today. It was closely related to the Welsh Hound and Chien Fauve de Bretagne.

vent **1.** opening or outlet, such as the anus. **2.** describing the light-colored hair under the tail of some dark-colored breeds.

ventrad in the direction of the belly. It is the opposite of dorsad.

ventral concerning or pertaining to the belly or in the direction of the lowest part of the abdomen.

verbal command direction given to a dog by voice.

vermicide drug used to kill intestinal parasites.

vermifuge drug used to expel intestinal parasites.

vermin external parasites, such as fleas, ticks, mites, lice, and others.

vernepator *see* Turnspit dog.

verruca wart or wartlike skin elevation.

vertebra one of the bones of the spine.

vertebrae plural of vertebra. The spinal column or the sum of all bones of the spine of a dog consists of 7 cervical, 13 thoracic, 7 lumbar, 3 sacral, and 1 to 22 coccygeal vertebrae.

vertex top or summit; highest point or crown of the head.

vet shortened name for Doctor of Veterinary Medicine, or veterinarian.

vet check examination by a veterinarian prior to the sale or exhibition of a dog.

veterinarian graduate of a college of veterinary medicine who is licensed to practice veterinary medicine, surgery, and dentistry.

veterinary relating to the science and art of prevention, cure, or relief of diseases of animals.

veterinary assistant person trained to help veterinarians in the medical and surgical care of animals; veterinary technician or animal health technician. Some states require veterinary technicians to be licensed.

Veterinary Pet Insurance insurance agency for pets: 4175 LaPalma Avenue, Suite 100, Anaheim, California 92807.

Vetrap® proprietary elastic bandage material that clings to itself and is frequently used on dogs.

vetting subjecting a dog to a critical soundness evaluation or health appraisal by a veterinarian.

vice bite bite that occurs when incisors meet evenly, tip to tip, without any overlap; even bite or a pincer bite.

vicious unruly, fierce, malicious, or dangerously aggressive (a serious flaw in a dog's temperament).

view in foxhunting, to see the quarry; to have the quarry visible to the naked eye.

viewed away in foxhunting, said of the quarry that is seen going away from cover.

Vikha longhaired herding dog from India that stands about 18 inches (46 cm) tall and weighs about 40 pounds (18 kg).

Vilde Honden early Dutch settlers' name for *Lyacaon pictus*, the South African (or Cape) hunting dog; literally translated as "wild dog."

village dog in sledding, any of the crossbred working huskies that originate in Alaskan villages. *See* Indian dogs.

virgin bitch female dog that has not been bred.

virile describing a male dog that has a normal reproductive capacity and a normal sexual desire.

visceral larva migrans migration of the larvae of canine roundworms through the walls of intestines and sometimes other tissues of a human, especially a child, who is more likely than an adult to consume the incubated egg of the canine ascarid.

visual field expanse of space that can be perceived by an individual in an instant without moving the eyes. A dog's visual field is about 250 degrees, while a human's visual field is only about 180 degrees. Dogs, therefore, receive impressions from the side and to the rear more effectively than a human does. *See* binocular vision.

vitality physical and mental vigor of a dog; capacity of a dog to live and enjoy itself.

vivaparous producing live young; referring to parasites that give birth to live larva and do not lay eggs, such as the canine heartworm.

vivisection cutting or performing surgery on a living animal for the purpose of instruction.

vixen female fox.

VizsLa

Vizsla AKC group: sporting; solid-colored pointer from Hungary. It stands about 23 inches (58 cm) tall, weighs about 66 pounds (30 kg), has a short, smooth, dense single coat that is a solid golden rust color, eyes of the same color, and a brown nose pad.

vocabulary number of words or expressions that a dog recognizes and associates with an action. A 20-word vocabulary is easily attainable for most dogs.

vocal folds paired structures of the pharynx that correspond to a human's vocal cords and are the source of a dog's voice.

voice in foxhunting, the sound of hounds on a trail; tongue, speech, bay, bawl, or cry.

volar bottom or sole of the forefeet. *See* plantar.

Volpino spitz-type breed that originated in Italy; always white in color with a double coat. It stands about 11 inches (28 cm) tall, weighs about 10 pounds (5 kg), and makes an excellent watchdog.

voluntary at will or accomplished in accordance with the will or choice of the dog. Example: Dogs are easier to train if the tasks they are asked to accomplish are voluntary.

volvulus twisting of a portion of the gastrointestinal tract upon itself. *See* gastric torsion.

Von Willebrand's disease hereditary blood-clotting deficiency.

Vorstenhund see Small Münsterländer.

V-shaped ear drop ear that tapers to a point.

Vulpes genus of the family Canidae.

Vulpes cana Blansford fox of Europe and Asia.

Vulpes chama Cape fox of Africa.

Vulpes corsac Corsac fox of Europe and Asia.

Vulpes ferrilata Tibetan sand fox of Asia.

Vulpes fulva American red fox found over much of North America.

Vulpes leucopus Arctic fox of India, a rare cousin of the dog.

Vulpes macrotis kit or swift fox of North America; also known as *Vulpes velox*.

Vulpes ruppelli sand fox of Asia and Africa.

Vulpes velox American kit fox or swift fox that is spread over much of the temperate regions of North America.

Vulpes vulpes Old World red fox of Europe and Asia.

vulpine foxlike; having a foxy appearance.

vulva outermost female reproductive structure, consisting of two vertical lips and a small vestibule.

vulvitis inflammation of the vulva.

W

Wachtelhund or **German Spaniel** German hunting breed. It stands about 19 inches (48 cm) tall, weighs about 66 pounds (30 kg), its colors are brown, brindle, and red, and it has long, thick, wavy hair.

waddling walking in a clumsy, swaying fashion that is characteristic of an obese dog.

wag waving, shaking, or rapid motion of a dog's tail that accompanies pleasure or positive feelings. Example: A hundred dollars will buy a pretty good dog, but it won't buy the wag of his tail.

Wah wild dog of India that is heavily built and ferocious. It has a large head, a short dark-tipped tail, and is colored tan with a black muzzle.

waisted having narrow loins.

walk **1.** slowest gait of a dog in which three feet are on the ground at the same time. **2.** to take a dog out for exercise.

Walker Hound

Walker Hound popular strain of American Foxhound that is similar to that breed in size and general appearance. Although not recognized by the AKC, it is used in hunts everywhere. Pedigrees are kept by the hunts and breeding is carefully controlled.

walk on handler's command for the dog to walk toward the sheep.

walleye **1.** parti-colored blue and white eye with a pale bluish, whitish, or colorless iris; eye with a blue iris that is sprinkled with white; also called blue eye, glasseye, fisheye, or pearl eye. **2.** divergent strabismus or eyes that are pointed in opposite directions, away from the median plane.

walrus puppy *see* anasarca puppy.

wanderer discontented puppy that is suffering from neonatal maladjustment syndrome.

war dog dog trained in specific duties during times of war. *See* ambulance dog, guard dog, K9 Corps, land mine dog, messenger dog, and sentry dog.

ward room in an animal hospital that accommodates several patients.

warfarin powerful anticoagulant rodenticide that is occasionally the cause of dog poisoning. It can cause internal bleeding in dogs by interfering with vitamin K and its prothrombin activity.

Warfdale Terrier *see* Airedale Terrier.

warm tan coat color of dark mahogany.

warranty guarantee of the soundness of a dog provided by the breeder.

Warrigal *see Canis dingo.*

wart benign, localized swelling of the skin or mucous membranes that is often caused by a virus.

wash lotion, soap, or other liquid that is therapeutically applied to the skin for cleansing or soothing it.

waster weedy dog of sickly constitution.

watchdog tie dog or a dog that is used for the primary purpose of guarding personal property.

watch eye *see* walleye.

waterdog water retriever or a dog that likes water, regardless of its retrieving ability.

water drawer dog that was trained to walk on a treadmill to turn the wheel that lifted buckets of water from a well.

water fowl game birds that inhabit water, such as ducks, geese, and others.

waterlogged puppy *see* anasarca puppy.

water pie diet of water only that is sometimes used as a remedy for obesity in dogs.

water retriever dog that has been trained to enter the water and retrieve birds that have been shot.

water shy describing a dog that refuses to retrieve from the water.

Waterside Terrier ancestor of the Yorkshire Terrier; so named because it roamed the banks of rivers and canals killing rats and eating garbage from barges. *See* Airedale Terrier.

water test 1. competition for water retrievers in which dogs are worked singly out of a blind. **2.** Newfoundland rescue dog trials that are sponsored by the Newfoundland Club of America.

water-wise retriever 1. one that enters the water, no matter how cold or rough it is, and is able to navigate and work. **2.** one that enters fast-moving water downstream from where the quarry has fallen so as to avoid swimming against the current if possible.

Wavy-Coated Retriever *see* Flat-Coated Retriever.

wax cerumen found in a dog's outer ear canal.

way to me in herding, a command to move the dog counterclockwise around the livestock, to circle to the right.

weak dog in herding, a dog that refuses to take control of obstinate sheep.

weaning physically preventing puppies from nursing their dam and feeding them solid food.

wear to use the dog beyond its physical capacity, an overwork debility.

wearing 1. in herding, action of a dog that holds the flock up against the handler by running back and forth on the opposite side of them. **2.** in herding, action in which the dog turns the sheep back or keeps them from going in the wrong direction.

wear Sunday clothes in field trials, to perform well in the field under any circumstances.

weasley having a long pendant body with the general appearance of a weasel.

weave poles in agility trials, an obstacle in which 5 to 12 poles are set 18 to 24 inches (46–61 cm) apart. The dog must enter from the right, and weave in and out through the obstacle. A fast time is ten poles in less than three seconds.

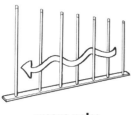

weave poles

weaving gait in which the dog throws its elbows outward and its pasterns inward. *See* knitting and purling.

webbed toes type of foot found in retrievers and other breeds associated with water in which toes are connected to one another by a thin web of skin. The webbing makes the foot a more effective water paddle for swimming.

wedgy having a lack of chiseling or a lack of refinement.

weedy having a lightly formed body that is delicate and rangy or stunted.

weepy having continual drainage of the eye from irritation, infection, or obstruction of a nasolacrimal duct.

weight-pulling competition judged competition in which a loaded sledge is pulled by a dog across a snow-packed level area for a designated distance, in an allotted amount of time. Dogs compete in classes that are designated according to the dog's weight.

Weimar Pointing Dog *see* Weimaraner.

2 inches (5.1 cm) long and the color is white; any other color is a fault. (See photo, page 27.)

Westminster Show one of the most prestigious dog shows in the United States, held annually in February by the Kennel Club of New York City in Madison Square Garden. It is one of the country's oldest and largest dog shows.

Westphalian Dachsbracke short-coated German scenthound that stands about 13 inches (33 cm) tall and weighs about 15 pounds (7 kg). It is a packing hound that was developed from crosses between Dachshunds and German Foxhounds.

Westphalian Dachsbracke

West Siberian Husky *see* Ostiak.

West Siberian Laika longhaired northland-type dog that hails from Siberia. It stands about 21 inches (53 cm) tall and weighs about 46 pounds (21 kg).

wet neck folded, loose skin on the ventral throat, with a heavy dewlap and superfluous flesh in the throat region.

Wetterhoun hunting dog that works well in the water; from Holland with a background in the Friesian Islands, but may also be related to Scandinavian dogs. It stands about 20 inches (51 cm) tall, weighs 35 pounds (16 kg), and has a thick, curly coat that repels water. It is seen in liver, black, liver and white, and black and white colors. An otter specialist that has been adapted into an all-around gundog and also kept as a guard dog, it is rarely seen outside Germany and the Netherlands.

Wetterhoun

wheal edematous, urticaria-type swelling of the skin that is accompanied by itching.

wheat cereal grain from the plant *Triticum vulgare*. It is used extensively in dog foods and contains many good nutritional elements.

wheaten yellow-tan coat color that ranges from pale yellow to pale gold, or ripe wheat color.

Wheaten Terrier *see* Soft Coated Wheaten Terrier.

wheel back having a severely arched topline.

wheel dog in sledding, usually among the heaviest and most powerful dogs of the team that are harnessed in the position immediately in front of the sled. They take the heaviest load when turning the sled.

wheel dog

wheeze whistling sound made when there is a partial obstruction in the dog's respiratory tract.

whelp 1. to give birth to a litter of puppies; bitch's parturition. **2.** puppies of a litter.

whelping box special box designed to accommodate the nesting bitch prior to and during whelping, and to contain the newborn puppies and their dam after whelping. It is constructed with a rail inside the box all the way around, offering protection for the puppies and preventing them from being stepped on or from being laid on by dam.

whelping date predicted time that the dam is due to whelp.

whelps unweaned litter of puppies.

whiffle tree in sledding, the pivoted, swinging bar to which the traces are fastened, allowing the sled to be pulled straight.

whiffle tree

whimper low, whining, broken sound; cry of complaint.

whine high-pitched, plaintive, or distressed cry that is typical of a puppy seeking attention.

whip in sledding, driving tool that is used for snapping only. A 3-foot (91 cm) length is the maximum allowed in competitive racing.

whipper-in in foxhunting, huntsman's assistant who controls hounds.

Whippet AKC group: hound; Greyhound in miniature. It stands about 20 inches (51 cm) tall, weighs about 28 pounds (13 kg), has a short, close, smooth coat, and is seen in all colors. In spite of its diminutive size, this dog is raced competitively and typically runs on a 200-yard (183 m) straight course. (See photo, page 19.)

Whippet

whip tail long, thin, tapering, pointed tail that is carried straight and resembles a whip; characteristic of Pointers.

whipworm *Trichuris vulpis* endoparasite that lives in the cecum of dogs and often causes diarrhea in its host.

whirlbone patella or kneecap.

whiskers long tactile or sensory hairs on each side of a dog's upper lip.

whistle shrill musical sound, or an instrument that makes the shrill sound. *See* Galton Whistle®.

white dog of Wales Welsh myth. In some parts of ancient Wales, it was believed that when a white dog came near to a dying person, the soul of that person would be saved. A black dog was a sign that the person's soul was lost.

whitelies white body color that is marked with red or brown.

white merle solid white Collie with small bluish eyes that is usually deaf and blind and sometimes sterile; also known as homozygous white or homozygous blue.

whoa in sledding, a command for the team to stop.

whole-colored of one color; self-colored.

whorl spiral turn or twist of a dog's coat that is usually seen on the chest.

wicket measuring device used to determine a breed height disqualification.

wide runner in racing, dog that chooses to run on the outside of the track.

wild dogs name for about 36 species that have been identified worldwide.

wild dogs of New Zealand race of longhaired dogs that resemble sheepdogs. They are eaten by the aborigines who also use their skins for clothing.

Wildehond *see* South African Wild Dog.

wildfowlers those who hunt wild game birds with a gun and a dog.

wind scent of the quarry off the ground.

Windhund Polish sighthound that has been around for centuries. It is a loving dog that was used originally for hawking. It has much the same appearance as a Greyhound, stands about 21 inches (53 cm), and is probably a cross between an Asian sighthound and the English Greyhound.

window jump in agility trials, obstacle that consists of a section of a wall with a window cut into it. It is suspended above the ground by a frame and the agility dog must jump through the window.

window jump

windpipe trachea; air channel that extends from the pharynx to the bronchi.

winging having a rotary pattern in the forward motion of the feet that is similar to dishing.

wing-tipped cripple bird downed by a shot that leaves it able to speed away on foot, giving the retriever a run for its money.

Winners Bitch in showing, bitch that takes home the points; best bitch of the breed or variety that is shown in the five regular classes.

Winners Class AKC class made up of the winners of the Puppy, Novice, Open, American-Bred, and Open classes. Male and female classes are separated.

Winners Dog male dog that takes home the points; best male dog of the breed or variety shown in the five regular classes.

Wire Fox Terrier AKC group: terrier; English dog closely related to the Smooth Fox Terrier; was developed as a fox hunter that pursued its quarry into its burrows. It stands about 15 inches (38 cm) tall, weighs about 18 pounds (8 kg), has a twisted coat of dense, wiry texture like coconut matting, with a short undercoat, and is predominately white with markings of darker colors. (See photo, page 30.)

Wire Fox Terrier

wirehair coat of hard, crisp, harsh, and wiry texture that is often twisted and is compared to coconut matting.

Wirehaired Beagle breed that is now extinct. It was a Rough-Coated Beagle.

Wirehaired Pinscher another name for the Standard Schnauzer.

Wirehaired Pointing Griffon AKC group: sporting; from Holland. It stands about 23 inches (58 cm) tall and has a double coat, with the outer coat medium, straight, and wiry. It is colored steel gray with markings of brown, chestnut brown, roan, or white and brown, and has a docked tail and a brown nose pad.

Wirehaired Pointing Griffon

Wirehaired Styrian Mountain Hound from the Stryian region of Austria; hunting dog that is about 19 inches (48 cm) tall and has a rough coat of red or yellowish colors. It is popular with hunters in Austria, Germany, and Yugoslavia.

Wirehaired Vizsla or **Drótszörü Magyar Vizsla** rare form of the Vizsla that was bred to better withstand retrieving in cold water. It stands about 24 inches (61 cm) tall, weighs about 66 pounds (30 kg), and is a coarse-coated cross between the German Wirehaired Pointer and the Vizsla.

witch's milk rarely seen milk secretion that comes from the mammae of a newborn puppy.

withers top of the shoulders that is usually the highest point of a dog's back.

wobbler syndrome cervical malformation-malarticulation; inflammation of the spine in the neck region. It is an inherited syndrome in some breeds.

wolf *see Canis lupis.*

wolf claw hind dewclaw.

wolf color refers to the fact that there are two basic pigments that all wolf coat colors exhibit: black and red, and the absence of pigment that is white. Various dilution and combinations of these two pigments account for all wolf colors and patterns. The wolf often displays an evenly distributed mixture of black, reddish brown, and gray in its coat.

wolf cub immature or young wolf.

wolf dog Borzoi and other breeds that have been used for hunting wolves.

wolf gray having a gray coat color that is similar to that of a wolf.

wolf heat *see* split heat.

womb uterus.

Woodcock Spaniel *see* Cocker Spaniel.

Wood's light ultraviolet light with a nickel oxide filter that is used to demonstrate the presence of fluorescing fungi, such as *Microsporum canis.*

woof low, muffled bark of an insecure or uncertain dog.

wooly having a coat similar to sheep's wool, with a thick undercoat.

Working Dogs of America 1164 Wall Road, Webster, New York 14580.

working group AKC group that includes: Akita, Alaskan Malamute, Bernese Mountain Dog, Boxer, Bullmastiff, Doberman Pinscher, Giant Schnauzer, Great Dane, Greater Swiss Mountain Dog, Great Pyrenees, Komondor, Kuvasz, Mastiff, Newfoundland, Portuguese Water Dog, Rottweiler, Saint Bernard, Samoyed, Siberian Husky, and Standard Schnauzer.

working terrier any terrier that is presently used for its original purpose, such as foxhunting, badger hunting, rabbit hunting, or varmint hunting.

worm 1. endoparasite or any of the varieties of intestinal parasites of dogs. (Note: Ringworm is a fungus that is found on the skin of dogs and is not a worm.) **2.** to administer a vermifuge or vermicide to a dog.

wormer vermifuge or vermicide that is administered to a dog to rid it of worms.

worming treating for internal parasites; administrating a vermifuge or vermicide.

wormseed oil highly irritating, toxic drug that was used in the past as a vermicide.

wormy infested with intestinal parasites.

worried in foxhunting, quarry that is torn to pieces by hounds.

wound injury to the body that involves disruption of the continuity of body structure or skin.

Woyawai Dog *see* Taruma Hunting Dog.

wrench in coursing, action of the hare to suddenly of its own volition deviate from the straight line in which it has been running away from the hounds.

wrinkle folded skin in areas over the forehead, sides of the face, above the tail, and around the eyes.

wrinkling having copious wrinkles in the skin of the face.

wrist carpus; front pastern; complex joint between the radius and ulna and the metacarpals.

wry mouth twisted jaw that results in malocclusion of the teeth; crossbite.

wry neck twisted neck; torticolis.

Wurttemburg Shepherd probable ancestor of the German Shepherd Dog.

XYZ

xenology study of the relationship of parasites to their hosts.

Xoloitzcuintli rare dog that has been in existence since pre-Columbian civilizations and has remained unchanged for thousands of years. It is a hairless breed that was the product of mutation many generations ago. It is seen in three sizes: less than 13 inches (33 cm), 13 to 18 inches (33–46 cm), and 18 to 23 inches (46–58 cm) in height. Colors range from blue to tan and brown, but all puppies are born white or spotted. The breed was a delicacy in the diet of the Incas as well as being considered a healing dog and prophet.

Xoloitzcuintli

xyphoid cartilage sword-shaped cartilage that is a caudal extension of the breastbone or sternum.

Yankee Terrier another name for the Staffordshire Terrier, American Bull Terrier, or Pit Bull Terrier.

yap shrill bark of toy dogs.

yappy describing some dogs that have a tendency to bark at everything or nothing.

yard dog dog kept to protect property.

yawing walking with a crablike gait.

Yellow Pointer Vizsla.

yelp dog's distress call; cry of pain or fear.

yip high-pitched bark of small dogs or puppies, or the sound of a fox.

Yorkshire Terrier AKC group: toy; origin is probably from the Waterside Terrier and the Black and Tan Terrier. It stands about 9 inches (23 cm) and must weigh less than 7 pounds (3.2 kg). Its tail is docked, and its long hair is silky and fine and grows until it touches the floor. It is seen in colors of blue and tan. (See photo, page 31.)

Yorkshire Terrier

yowl howl; plaintive cry.

Yugoslavian Herder descends from mastiff stock. It is over 25 inches (33 cm) tall and has a long gray and white coat. It is a herding dog and doubles as a guard dog.

Yugoslavian Hound traditional scenting breed that is kept for hunting foxes, hares, and similar quarry. It is medium-sized with a short, thick coat that is black and tan in color.

Yugoslavian Istrian Pointer *see* Istrian Pointer.

Yugoslavian Mountain Hound or **Jugoslavenski Planinski Gonic** scenthound that originated in the former country of Yugoslavia. It stands about 22 inches (56 cm) tall, weighs about 55 pounds (25 kg), and is black and tan colored. It has a smooth outer coat with a full undercoat.

Yugoslavian Tricolored Hound or **Jugoslavenski Tribarvni Gonic** breed distinguished from the Yugoslavian Mountain Hound by its markings. Its colors of black and tan are marked with a facial blaze of white and white front. Found only in a very localized region of southern Yugoslavia, it is both a sighthound and scenthound and also makes a fine companion.

zoology biological study of animals.

zooms or **frenzies** propensity of puppies to frantically run about with no purpose; type of self-entertainment.

zoonosis disease of animals that may be transmitted to humans; for example, rabies.

zoophile person who is attracted to animals; antivivisectionist.

Zwergschnauzer another name for Miniature Schnauzer.

zygomatic arch curving bony arch located under the eye that forms the cheekbone.

References

Alderton, David. *The Dog*. Secaucus, NJ: Quill Publishing Limited, Chartwell Books, Inc., 1984.

Alderton, David. *Dogs*. New York: DK Publishing, Inc., 1993.

American Kennel Club. *The Complete Dog Book, 18th Edition*. New York: Howell Book House, 1994.

American Kennel Club Publications (Raleigh, North Carolina):

Herding Regulations. 1995.

Lure Coursing Tests and Trials. 1996.

Obedience Regulations. 1995.

Regulations for Agility Trials. 1996.

Retriever Hunting Test Procedure Manual. 1992.

Baer, Ted. *Communicating with Your Dog*. Hauppauge, NY: Barron's Educational Series, Inc., 1989.

Baer, Ted. *How to Teach Your Old Dog New Tricks*. Hauppauge, NY: Barron's Educational Series, Inc., 1991.

Bairacli-Levy, Juliette. *Complete Herbal Book for the Dog*. New York: Arco Publishing Co., 1977.

Boorer, et. al. *The Treasury of Dogs*. London: Octopus Books, Ltd., 1972.

Bordwell, Sally et. al. *The American Animal Hospital Association Encyclopedia of Dog Health and Care*. New York: William Morrow and Company, 1994.

Clark, Timothy T. *The Dog Lover's Reader*. New York: Hart Publishing Co., 1974.

Collins, Miki and Julie. *Dog Driver*. Loveland, CO: Alpine Publications, 1991.

Daniels, Julie. *Enjoying Dog Agility*. Doral Wilsonville, OR: Publishing Co., 1991.

Davis, Henry P. *Modern Dog Encyclopedia*. Harrisburg, PA: Stackpole Company, 1958.

Dorland's Illustrated Medical Dictionary, 23rd Edition. Philadelphia: W.B. Saunders Co., 1951.

Encyclopedia Americana, 1994 Edition, Danbury, CT: Grolier, Inc., 1994.

Flamholtz, Cathy. *Celebration of Rare Breeds, Vol. II*. Ft. Payne, AL: OTR Publications, 1991.

Grosvenor, Melville B. *Man's Best Friend.* Washington, DC: National Geographic Society, 1974.

Hubbard, Clifford L.B. *The Observer's Book of Dogs.* London: Frederick Warne & Co., Ltd, 1962.

Jackson, Frank. *Dictionary of Canine Terms.* Ramsbury, Wiltshire, UK: The Crowood Press, 1995.

Johnson, Norma. *The Complete Puppy and Dog Book.* W. Hanover, MA: Halliday Lithograph Co., 1974.

Kay, William J. *Animal Medical Center of New York's Complete Book of Dog Health.* New York: Macmillan Publishing Co., 1985.

Kirk, et. al. *Current Veterinary Therapy, Small Animal Practice.* Philadelphia: W. B. Saunders Co., 1974.

Klever, Ulrich. *The Complete Book of Dog Care.* Hauppauge NY: Barron's Educational Series, Inc., 1988.

Kojima, Toyoharu. *Legacy of the Dog.* San Francisco: Chronicle Books, 1995.

Margolis & Swan. *The Dog in Your Life.* New York: Random House, 1979.

McGinnis, Terri. *The Well Dog Book.* New York: Random House, 1974.

Merriam-Webster's Collegiate Dictionary, 10th Edition. Springfield, MA: Merriam-Webster, Inc., 1993.

Mery, Fernand. *The Life, History, and Magic of the Dog.* New York: Madison Square Press, 1970.

The New Encyclopedia Britannica, 15th Edition. Chicago: 1982.

Pearsall, Milo. *Dog Obedience Training.* New York: Charles Scribner's Sons, 1958.

Pinney, Chris C. *Caring for Your Older Dog.* Hauppauge, NY: Barron's Educational Series, Inc., 1995.

Pitcairne, Richard H. *Natural Health for Dogs and Cats.* Emmaus, PA: Rodale Books, 1982.

Rice, Dan. *The Complete Book of Dog Breeding.* Hauppauge, NY: Barron's Educational Series, Inc., 1996.

Stoneridge, M.A. *A Dog of Your Own.* Garden City, NY: Doubleday & Company, Inc., 1970.

Unkelbach, Evie and Kurt. *The Pleasures of Dog Ownership.* Englewood Cliffs, NJ: Prentice-Hall, 1971.

World Book Encyclopedia, 1993 Edition. Chicago: World Book Inc., 1993.